THE LAST
OF HIS KIND

THE LAST
OF HIS KIND

CLAYTON KERSHAW
AND THE BURDEN OF GREATNESS

ANDY McCULLOUGH

hachette
BOOKS

New York

Hachette Books
Hachette Book Group
1290 Avenue of the Americas
New York, NY 10104
HachetteBooks.com
Twitter.com/HachetteBooks
Instagram.com/HachetteBooks

First Edition: May 2024

Published by Hachette Books, an imprint of Hachette Book Group, Inc.
The Hachette Books name and logo is a registered trademark of the Hachette Book Group.

The Hachette Speakers Bureau provides a wide range of authors for speaking events.
To find out more, go to hachettespeakersbureau.com or email
HachetteSpeakers@hbgusa.com.

Books by Hachette Books may be purchased in bulk for business, educational, or promotional use.
For information, please contact your local bookseller or Hachette Book Group Special Markets
Department at: special.markets@hbgusa.com.

The publisher is not responsible for websites (or their content) that are not owned by
the publisher.

Editorial production by Christine Marra, *Marra*thon Production Services.
www.marrathoneditorial.org

Set in 11.5 point Adobe Caslon Pro

Library of Congress Cataloging-in-Publication Data has been applied for.
ISBNs: 978-0-306-83259-8 (hardcover), 978-0-306-83261-1 (ebook)

Printed in the United States of America

LSC-C

Printing 1, 2024

To my Ganny,
who always let me read at the dinner table

CONTENTS

We all want to be great men
And there's nothing romantic about it.
I just want to know that I did all I could
With what I was given.

    —The Wonder Years,
       "I Just Want to Sell Out My Funeral"

PROLOGUE

Clayton Kershaw once tried to explain to his wife, Ellen, the longevity of his friend Zack Greinke. What made Greinke special, well into his second decade in baseball, was his capacity for reinvention. Greinke could transform himself—finding new pitches, new patterns, new ideas—to stay elite.

Ellen thought about that. Greinke had been pitching in the major leagues since 2004, four years before her husband debuted. Clayton Kershaw was one of the few men in modern baseball who could say he was better than Zack Greinke. He was one of an even smaller group who others would say was the best ever.

"What about you?" Ellen asked. "You don't reinvent yourself."

Kershaw considered his response. "I'm just trying to figure out," he explained, "how to make what I do keep on working."

Clayton Kershaw understood, through a forge of anguish and rigor, the paradox at the root of all greatness. He understood that he could never stay satisfied. But he could also never lose what made him special. He has walked that tightrope on one of baseball's grandest stages for more than fifteen years. He has shouldered the burden of greatness.

This is a book, as Kershaw's former general manager Ned Colletti put it, about "the blessing and the curse" of those who strive for greatness. It is a book about what greatness demands of those who achieve it.

And it is a book about why greatness resonates with those who come within its wake.

This is a book about Clayton Kershaw's life. He is still a young man, not yet forty. Within his journey, though, is a path to understanding athletic stardom in America's twenty-first century: the astonishing riches, the perilous stakes, the relentless requirements. Kershaw decided at a young age that he would strive for the highest summit he could climb. This book explains what happened next.

CHAPTER 1

THE FIFTH DAY

The five-day cycle would begin again soon, and so Clayton Kershaw tried to diagram how it had defined his existence for the past twenty years. He pressed his fingertips into his kitchen table. The rewards of the cycle surrounded him. The fireplace crackled in the living room. Above it hung a row of stockings, one for each of his four children. A pile of Amazon Prime packages lay by the front door. That night, Santa Claus would ride on the back of a fire truck and greet the families of Highland Park, the posh Dallas neighborhood Kershaw had called home for most of his life. Christmas was two weeks away.

In the winter of 2022, when he invited me to his home, Kershaw was only two months removed from standing at a crossroads. He had faced this juncture before, and he would face it again. He had chosen to keep playing, which meant he had chosen once again to divide his life into five-day schedules. This was the standard for pitchers in Major League Baseball. For four days, they prepare. On the fifth day, they perform. This cycle shaped Kershaw and enriched him and tormented him.

For more than fifteen years, the fate of the Los Angeles Dodgers— one of baseball's glitziest, most prestigious franchises, a financial behemoth worth approximately $4 billion, during that stretch the winners of eleven division titles, three National League pennants, and the 2020 World Series—had revolved around Clayton Kershaw's fifth day. He was the best left-handed pitcher of his generation, the spiritual heir to Sandy Koufax. On his way to becoming a ten-time All Star, three-time Cy Young Award winner, and the first pitcher to win the National League MVP award since Bob Gibson, Kershaw reveled in the four days of training, the camaraderie of teammates, the trappings of athletic stardom. As he approached his thirty-fifth birthday, there were times he thought he could stay in this cycle forever. But then he remembered how the last day, when he had to pitch, made him feel.

"It's just the fifth day that is—it's a lot," Kershaw said. "The stress. The preparation. The pain. All that stuff, it takes a toll."

For once, his body did not ache. During the summer of 2022, he dealt with persistent back trouble. Discomfort accompanied most pitches. A sense of apprehension greeted him most mornings: Is my back going to hurt today? With rest and rehabilitation, the pain faded. He felt better than the previous winter. After an elbow injury had sidelined him for the 2021 postseason, Kershaw worried he would need the first surgery of his life. He avoided going under the knife, but still felt persistent reminders of his sudden frailty. He could not shampoo his hair or write his name. When he picked up a baseball to throw again, his elbow barked for a month. "But I kept throwing," he said. "And finally it got better."

And so he did what he had done every spring since the final days of his boyhood. He reported to spring training with the Dodgers. He had eschewed an opportunity to sign with his hometown Texas Rangers, the favorite team of his youth, a franchise run by his Highland Park neighbor, longtime friend and former training partner Chris Young. When Kershaw told Young he was returning to Los Angeles, "It broke my heart," Young recalled. Young wondered if he would have another chance. The idea of Kershaw leaving the Dodgers felt preposterous.

Kershaw had debuted at Dodger Stadium two months after his twentieth birthday. He soon set the industry's standard. He starred like few others before him. He suffered for his achievements. "He's gotten some injuries over the years, where you're always like, 'This might be the one,'" former teammate Zack Greinke said. "And then it seems to never be the end of it." In recent years Kershaw had damaged the cartilage of his hip, torn a lat muscle, frayed tendons near his elbow, and herniated a disk in his back. He had recovered from each of these without surgery, but the toll was mounting. Some of his ailments represented the natural result of a profession built around the unnatural act of repeatedly throwing a spherical object overhand. Some of it resulted from his unconventional delivery, the heavy thudding of his six-foot-four, 225-pound frame into the earth, the violent trajectory of his left arm behind it. "It's like a car crash every time he throws," another former teammate said. And some of it stemmed from Kershaw's unique combination of precociousness and effectiveness. He was so good, so young, and depended upon so much, there was bound to be a bill.

By the end of 2015, when he was twenty-seven and had already won three Cy Youngs, he had accumulated more than 1,600 innings—a total surpassed by only two other pitchers at that age during the past thirty-five years. CC Sabathia never made an All-Star team after thirty-two. Félix Hernández never threw another pitch in the majors after thirty-three. In 2022, at thirty-four, Kershaw started the All-Star Game at Dodger Stadium. The honor served as a valediction as Kershaw approached the sunset, but it was not without merit. He finished the season with a 2.28 earned-run average, better than all but five other pitchers. Even in decline, few could touch him. His career 2.48 earned-run average was the lowest of any starting pitcher since the sport livened its baseball in 1920—better than Koufax, better than Pedro Martínez, better than Greg Maddux, better than all who came before or after.

The 2022 season had ended earlier than expected. The 111-win Dodgers had fallen to the upstart San Diego Padres. Kershaw lost his only postseason start. A few years earlier, his outing would have produced howls about his inability to perform in the postseason. But Kershaw had tempered that narrative when he won two games for the victorious Dodgers in the 2020 World Series. The championship ended a seven-year crucible of October agony and checked the final box of his

Baseball Hall of Fame résumé. It also made others wonder, as the injuries accumulated and his children grew older and the stress of the five-day cycle compounded, about the end. "At this point," said A. J. Ellis, Kershaw's former catcher and one of his closest friends, "it's like, what keeps driving him?"

Two months before another spring training, Kershaw was thinking less about why he kept going, and more about why he might stop. His kids. His back or his shoulder or his hip. Or, he admitted, he might retire for a more primal reason. The burden of greatness, the standard he alone set for himself, the strain it took to be Clayton Kershaw—all of it was growing tougher and tougher to tolerate. He could only give his all so many times.

"That's ultimately what will drive you to stop, when it becomes too much to get ready for that day, every day," Kershaw said. "I probably put more stress on it than most."

* * *

One day in the summer of 2013, a movie star visited the Dodgers clubhouse. This was not unique for Hollywood's home team, save for two things: The star showed up late. And the star showed up on a day when Clayton Kershaw was pitching.

When the man entered the room, the group erupted. The players hollered catchphrases immortalized on the silver screen. As the Dodgers shouted about motherfucking snakes on motherfucking planes, Kershaw stewed at his locker, in full uniform, his No. 22 spread across his back. He slipped into a jacket, which he wore before every start, with "that zipper that zips all the way to the top no matter if it's April or July in fucking Miami," one former teammate said.

Kershaw stood up. In his left hand, as he usually did, he held a baseball. His right hand carried his black Wilson 2000A CK22 glove, the same glove he had worn since his rookie season. He was a product of routine and a captive of routine. He believed his devotion to habit girded him through the 162-game season. Others believed it left him vulnerable to failure in the moments of the highest pressure. In his early years, before the game humbled him and sent him searching for answers, he would not deviate from his schedule, diagrammed down to the minute. The routine called for him to walk into the Dodgers dugout at 6:20 P.M. He did not have a second to spare, even for Hollywood royalty.

"Clayton!" the actor shouted, holding up a hand as Kershaw stomped past. "My man!"

Kershaw would not meet his eye. He saved his death stare for later, when he saw the team official who set up the visit. He stormed out. He left Samuel L. Jackson hanging.

*　*　*

It was worse before he became a father.

In the years before Cali Ann Kershaw was born, in January of 2015, her father had built a reputation for dominating opponents during games and spooking teammates before them. For the four days between starts, Kershaw was a dedicated worker and a delightful presence. On sunny days, he sported outdated flip-down sunglasses in the dugout. He played cards on the team plane and unleashed righteous flatulence. While sauntering through the cafeteria one afternoon, he swiped a chicken finger off a teammate's child's plate. He projected wholesome goofiness. "He's the only guy I ever played with," said former teammate Dan Haren, "who I would let date my wife."

The fifth day was different.

It started before he arrived at the ballpark. "You wake up in a mood where you don't want to talk," Kershaw said. He was silent but not still, his legs restless, his mind racing, his heart thumping. He considered vomiting. He was not exactly angry or nervous, although it sometimes looked that way. He just felt consumed by the task that awaited him, when he needed to climb atop the pitcher's mound, alone, and be Clayton Kershaw. He loathed interactions, even with Ellen. "It's like, I don't even want to waste the breath," Kershaw said. "I couldn't even get the words out."

Before his final season in high school, Kershaw received tutoring from local pitching guru Skip Johnson. Johnson barely charged Kershaw for the lessons. Kershaw never forgot that kindness. Years later, the University of Oklahoma hired Johnson as its baseball coach. When he got the job, Johnson texted Kershaw. It took two messages before Kershaw responded. Worried about an emergency, Kershaw sounded thrilled when Johnson shared the news. Johnson asked for a favor. The athletic department was putting together a press release. Could Kershaw say something nice about him? "Skip, I can't give you a quote," Kershaw said. "I'm pitching tonight."

To ease into those fifth days, after Ellen moved to Los Angeles following their wedding in December 2010, the couple watched television. Clayton consumed episodes of *CSI* before starts. Ellen learned not to bother him. The edict passed through his inner circle. He rarely returned calls. He ignored texts. His friends used separate group chats on the fifth day. After Cali was born—and followed by sons Charley, Cooper, and Chance—Kershaw stowed his morning misanthropy. Instead of watching Grissom and Willows solve crimes, he spent the hours with "the kiddos," as he called them. The children used him as a bearded jungle gym. "He, at all times, has one of the kids in his lap, wrestling him, hugging him," Ellen said.

After Kershaw became a parent, the transformation took place as he drove to work. Upon arrival, he slipped into his uniform, spikes and all. "That's not normal," former teammate Tony Watson said. Several hours before one game, one of A. J. Ellis's minor-league managers visited the clubhouse. The man made a request. "My son," the manager said, "is the biggest Clayton Kershaw fan. Is there any way he can sign a baseball for him?" Ellis knew the proposition was dicey. But he figured it worth the risk. Kershaw did not say a word. He scribbled his name, glaring at Ellis the entire time.

Kershaw conserved syllables but made noise. He paced the clubhouse, bouncing a baseball against the walls. He flipped curveballs, burning off energy, searching for the right feel. In his early years, veterans like catcher Brad Ausmus tried to snatch the ball and loosen Kershaw up. It never worked. As time passed and Kershaw's stature grew, the pranks ceased. "You felt like the season was on the line every time he pitched," former teammate Skip Schumaker said. The environment alternated between edgy and festive. Tension mingled with the excitement of teaming with the best pitcher in the world. Former Dodgers reliever J. P. Howell called Kershaw "Off Day," because no one else was necessary when he started. Another reliever refused to wear cleats to the bullpen when Kershaw pitched. Yet almost all dared not goof off around him. The players learned to peek around corners and keep their ears open. If they heard *pock-pock-pock*, they turned around. If they crossed his path, they averted their eyes. Some teammates cracked jokes about not wanting to purloin his oxygen. Everyone understood to whom the precious resource belonged. "When he walked in, his demeanor, his attitude—it was like, 'Shit, I can't mess around today,'" former Dodgers closer Kenley Jansen said.

Kershaw's schedule was hard-wired into him and did not permit distractions. He ate a turkey sandwich before every start, the same meal dating back to high school. In the majors, he prepared his own at the ballpark: mustard and cheese were necessities, lettuce and onions preferable, mayonnaise forbidden. When he settled into the clubhouse cafeteria, seats emptied and conversation cooled. "You have to sit there, and you're like, 'You just sucked all the energy out of the room because of your psychosis over having to pitch in a couple hours,'" Ellis said.

After Kershaw ate, he repaired to the training room. An unoccupied table awaited him. On his first day as a Dodger, Chase Utley hopped onto the table. Utley commanded respect around the sport. Even so, Dodgers massage therapist Yosuke Nakajima warned him that he needed to move. "He's going to be here in about three minutes," Nakajima explained. "I suggest you get up." Nakajima, who had spent more than twenty years with the Dodgers as a massage therapist and was known to all as "Possum," served as Kershaw's gatekeeper. Jansen often lounged on the table before Kershaw appeared. "That's Kershaw's table!" Nakajima would say. "Get up!" The staffers prepped the space for him. Kershaw required a Red Bull and a protein bar. Late during his time in Los Angeles, third baseman Justin Turner barged into the room, famished after a workout. He spotted the protein bar sitting on the table and wolfed it down. Nakajima cried out: "What are you doing?" Turner begged Nakajima to find a replacement.

The training room was Kershaw's sacrosanct space. Once he arrived, fully dressed, cleats on but unlaced, he controlled the real estate. The television always showed a baseball game. He demanded quiet. Kershaw once menaced utility player Kiké Hernández for blaring a Snapchat video.

A couple of years later, rookie Kyle Farmer sat beside Kershaw at his locker on his day.

"What's up, Kersh?" Farmer said. Kershaw grunted, stood up, and left. Hernández walked over.

"Don't talk to him," Hernández warned.

"What?" Farmer said.

"He will rip your fucking head off if you talk to him," Hernández said.

Hernández, an impish fellow, did not do as he said. Over the years, he enjoyed trying to make Kershaw giggle on the fifth day. He could identify Kershaw's defense mechanism. Kershaw would pull his mouth sideways to stifle a grin, and compulsively stretch his hamstrings, kicking his legs in the air. Laughter was not an option.

Few other Dodgers were so brazen, even those who knew him best. Ellis often checked the trainer's room to see if Kershaw was napping. A slumbering Kershaw foretold misery for the opponents. A sleepless Kershaw meant Ellis might need to calm his ace during the game. The duo often discussed the need to "play with no regrets," Ellis said. "Like, have you done everything you can mentally, spiritually, physically, emotionally to be ready to play this game?" On the four days before the fifth day, while Kershaw might have made for more pleasant company, he maintained a meticulous regimen of lifting, running, and scouting.

He fortified his body so he could pitch as long as possible on that fifth day, and he sharpened his mind so he could dissect opponents as efficiently as possible on that fifth day.

The pregame study became apparent two hours before every start, when Kershaw convened with Ellis and pitching coach Rick Honeycutt. Ellis and Honeycutt met before the meeting, to make sure they were in lockstep. Once the session began, the catcher and the coach listened as Kershaw diagrammed how he would attack each hitter, not just once or twice or three times but four times. Kershaw outlined how he would start the game and how he would finish it. He discouraged dissent, Ellis explained: "I might say, 'You know, I think backdoor slider—' 'No!' And I'd be like, 'I think backdoor slider—' 'No! Did you hear what I said? No backdoor sliders!'" Kershaw required evidence to change the plan he had formulated. And even if the suggestion had merit, he might not take it. "I was stubborn," Kershaw said. "I was stubborn."

He was slow to trust. He kept a small circle of friends, the same group since high school. He kept others at a distance. Dodgers manager Dave Roberts considered Kershaw "the hardest player I've ever had to manage, as well as the fiercest competitor," because he was so talented and so obstinate and so wary of change. Kershaw liked to do things the way he liked to do them. He was precise about everything. If Kershaw entered the dugout at 6:20 P.M., as he did the day he did not make Sam Jackson's acquaintance, that meant Nakajima had cocooned his left arm in heat packs and slathered his lower back with Cramergesic ointment at 5:58 P.M., he had chugged the Red Bull at 6:10 P.M., and he was due to stretch in the outfield at 6:23 P.M. A coach came to stretch him at 6:36 P.M. He threw the same sequence of pitches in the bullpen. He spoke the same prayer: "Lord, whatever happens, be with me." And then he treated the opposing hitters with the same disdain he treated conversation on the fifth day.

"He is as nice a guy as there is," former teammate Jamey Wright said. "But on that fifth day, he is an animal."

What almost all of his teammates did not understand, in part because Kershaw did not tell them, was the anxiety at the root of his relentlessness.

*　*　*

One day when he was a boy, a couple of years after his parents divorced, Clayton Kershaw asked his mother, Marianne, a question.

"Mom, we're rich," he told her. "But we're not Highland Park rich, are we?"

Kershaw was a perceptive child. He resided in a different economic stratosphere than his schoolmates. The Kershaws, not wealthy by most standards, were renters in a district that sold forever homes. Highland Park represented a cocoon of privilege, a land of endless opportunity both academic and athletic—his childhood friends would become bankers and real estate developers and, in the case of Matthew Stafford, a Super Bowl–winning quarterback. After the divorce he saw less and less of his father, a musician named Christopher Kershaw. Marianne worked long hours as a graphic designer but still borrowed money to stay in Highland Park.

For a while, Clayton split time between his parents. His father was often late picking him up. When his mom was in charge of transportation, he begged her to take him hours before games, so he wouldn't be tardy. The powerlessness affixed him with anxiety. He vowed that once he controlled his whereabouts, he would always be on time. Chris eventually remarried and faded from the picture. He resided on the periphery of his son's life, not exactly absent, but far from present. Most of Marianne's hours were consumed by work. Clayton often ate dinner at friends' homes. He learned to fend for himself. "I don't feel like Clayton has ever been able to feel a weightless joy, if that makes sense," Ellen said. "He has been responsible for so long."

In high school, Kershaw recalled, "money became an issue." He picked up hints. "I never was like, 'Oh, I don't have enough shirts to wear,'" he said. "It was never to that point. But it was like, 'Hey, don't fill up your tank all the way today.' I remember that. 'Hey, I have ten dollars. Go get as much gas as you can.'" Most of his peers could forecast their futures across unlimited horizons. Kershaw worried his own path was circumscribed. His mother could barely afford to keep him in a good public school. Paying for college felt impossible. "When I got old enough to figure that out, I had that anxiety built in," Kershaw said. "Just like, 'Man, how are we going to do this?'"

The answer came in the form of his left arm. He had loved baseball since boyhood. In his adolescence, he realized he could no longer treat it like a game. That was when the cycle started. He hated going to school on the days he pitched. He couldn't concentrate in class. He could not always control his pregame meal or enforce silence around him. But he still radiated intensity. "Just imagine a kid sitting on a bench, with a mean mug, staring off into a blank space," said childhood friend and former Dodgers teammate Shawn Tolleson. Added youth coach Tommy Hernandez, "He was not a lot of smiles."

To fortify himself, he looked inward and upward. He made the varsity baseball team as a chunky freshman with competitive zeal and a decent curveball. He underwent a growth spurt after his sophomore year. As college coaches and professional scouts flocked to his games, he connected his growing stature to a larger purpose.

A month before his fifteenth birthday, Kershaw visited a girl's locker. Ellen Melson was friendly and bubbly, enamored with the drill team and the Backstreet Boys. When he asked her out, she said yes. The Melsons became a surrogate family, offering the warmth he had longed for in his own home. Clayton and Marianne joined them for holidays. Kershaw tagged along to Sunday service at Highland Park Presbyterian Church. Through conversation with Ellen, he reshaped his faith. Kershaw had seen God as a distant presence. Ellen convinced him the Lord was near, that God's grace was all around him.

He came to see his own growing athletic talent as a gift from above. His left arm was not just an appendage. It was an instrument. The ability thrust upon him, he decided, meant he owed something. A verse from Colossians 3:23 became his favorite: "Whatever you do, work at it with all your heart, as working for the Lord, not for human masters."

In time, Kershaw saw his faith deepen. He evolved from a good high school pitcher into a great one. When the Dodgers selected him with the seventh overall pick in the 2006 draft, Kershaw felt his faith in the Lord had been rewarded. What the draft did not do was dismiss the responsibility he felt toward himself and his mother. One of the first things Kershaw did with the $2.3 million bonus was pay off Marianne's debts. He was less sure how to respond when his father called. "Once I got drafted, it was a lot of, like, 'Can I have money?'" Kershaw said.

Granted financial freedom for the first time, Kershaw did not relent. He learned the rhythms of the professional pitcher's five-day cycle. The cycle sustained him as he announced himself as one of the game's most promising young players. At every stage, there was a new motivation. Reaching the majors. Making millions in arbitration. Conquering opponents at the highest level. "There's always some new reason to climb the mountaintop," he said. By the time Kershaw had checked all those other boxes, by the time in 2014 he signed a record-setting $215 million extension that eased his financial worries for good, he was consumed by the one box he had not checked.

*   *   *

Few men are great enough to be defined by what they cannot do. For a long time, Clayton Kershaw was one of those.

Kershaw's excellence built an aura of invincibility. "To be that good every year, for that long, it's fucking impossible," former teammate Alex Wood said. Friend and foe used the same language to describe him. "To me, he's the greatest left-handed pitcher of all time," New York Yankees ace Gerrit Cole said. Madison Bumgarner, a longtime foil with San Francisco, was less equivocal. "I think he's the best pitcher to ever play," Bumgarner said. Brandon Belt, another former Giant, called Kershaw "the best pitcher that I faced, every single year in the big leagues." Greinke had pitched in twenty big-league seasons. "I think the highest of him of any pitcher I've played with," Greinke said. Paul Goldschmidt, a longtime National League West rival, called Kershaw "my favorite guy in baseball. My favorite player. I hate to say that about a pitcher."

Kershaw threw hard, but others threw harder. His curveball and his slider were sharp, but others were nastier. He was a big man, with an unconventional delivery, but others stood taller and moved in stranger ways. "You have to look at the man, how competitive he is," former Giants manager Bruce Bochy said. "It doesn't work unless you have that inside you." To Andrew Friedman, the architect of the Dodgers' late-aughts juggernaut, Kershaw was "the greatest competitor I've ever seen firsthand." Brandon McCarthy, a teammate for several seasons, wondered if Kershaw's ability veered into the supernatural. "Is this just a gift?" McCarthy said.

Which made what happened to Kershaw in October so confounding. The Dodgers reached the postseason every year from 2013 to 2019. In each of those seasons, the Dodgers failed to win the title. On five occasions, Kershaw cost his team the final game. After a while, Kershaw's postseason failures morphed from an odd coincidence into a nationwide fixation. He became the central figure of October baseball. Why couldn't he do it? Why couldn't he win it all? When would he hoist the World Series trophy that had eluded his franchise for so long? The Dodgers had not called themselves champions since 1988, when they won the title on the sturdy back of Orel Hershiser and the gimpy legs of Kirk Gibson. Kershaw was supposed to end the drought. Instead, he was blamed for extending it.

In 2017, Kershaw collapsed in the World Series against the Houston Astros, unaware of his opponents' illegal sign-stealing system. "I still have PTSD about that," he said. In 2019, he surrendered a pair of game-altering home runs against the Washington Nationals. In the dugout, he hung his head and gazed into the gloaming of Chavez Ravine. All around him, his teammates bristled with tears and stewed with rage on his behalf. They knew how many innings he had thrown in his twenties, before his body broke down. They saw him sacrifice a day from his precious schedule to pitch on short rest in October, which made him an anomaly among his peers in the 2010s. "Some pitchers flat-out refuse the ball, unless they're at full strength," former teammate Michael Young said. "Kersh has never done that." They witnessed all the hours he poured into his craft. They lived through his fifth day and they recognized how much it meant. "Every time he failed, I know how deeply that hurt him," said former teammate Josh Lindblom.

At times, teammates and friends worried about the weight on Kershaw's shoulders. The Dodgers had staked so much on him. He was a first-round pick, a No. 1 starter, the face of the franchise. From his earliest days as a Dodger, he drew comparisons to Koufax, the southpaw who starred as the team transitioned from Brooklyn's Boys of Summer to the kings of Southern California. "He's the savior for the Dodgers, and he's the next coming of Sandy Koufax for the Dodgers," former Dodger Justin Turner said. "That pressure on his back in following Sandy's footsteps is a real thing."

Despite a fifty-two-year gap in age, Kershaw and Koufax were friends. But Kershaw rejected the notion that he needed to follow in anyone's footsteps. "I was like, 'The next Sandy Koufax?' I have no interest in being Sandy Koufax," Kershaw said. "And I don't want to live up to that. I had no interest in being that. I had different reasons and different motivations."

The weight Kershaw hauled was his and his alone. After the loss to the Nationals, he stood shell-shocked inside his clubhouse. He wondered aloud if everything about his reputation as a choker was warranted. He stared into an abyss and only saw himself. He knew he needed to change. So he did, in ways that were subtle and profound, embracing new concepts without losing sight of himself. When the team finally won the World Series a year later, in a season upended and truncated by the Covid-19 pandemic, his overriding emotion was relief.

"You don't know the burden that you carry," he said. "Because at some point, you just get used to the weight on your shoulders."

After an injury-plagued 2021 and the disappointing end to 2022, Kershaw pondered the depth of his reasons and motivations. As he prepared to resume the five-day cycle, he had to take stock. He didn't need the money. His case for Cooperstown was complete. "I have no individual goals," he said. His body could use rest after two decades of pitching-inflicted trauma. But the possibility of another championship still beckoned. And so the cycle loomed.

*   *   *

The day after Santa Claus visited Highland Park, Kershaw stood inside the kitchenette of his charity's office, a three-minute drive from his home. He had finished a throwing session after he dressed and fed his children. He often told friends that his dream job after baseball would be crossing guard at their elementary school. But he knew there would be more hours to fill. Maybe the family would buy an RV and take a tour of America that wasn't built around ballparks. He had traveled so much in his career, but seen so little. He had never been to Hawaii, never been to continental Europe. He could not plan a trip that did not include time to throw. On his honeymoon, at a resort in Mexico, he brought baseballs to chuck into bedroom pillows.

"Does part of you," I said, "look forward to—"

"Yes," Kershaw said. "One hundred percent."

"Like, not being in this cycle," I said.

"It'll be great," Kershaw said. "I can't wait for that. There are so many great things about both. The hard part is not wanting the other thing."

He thought about something Ellen often told him: "Don't take your time for granted." He was the rare man who could still make his living playing a game designed for boys. Among his brethren, he was the rarest of the rare, one who would be remembered long after he threw his last pitch. He wanted to honor that gift. He needed to work at it with all his heart. "I'm never, like, trudging through another season," Kershaw said. "This was our choice. I didn't have to play. We decided we wanted to do it. I wanted to do it."

The RV trips, the gig as a crossing guard, and the decades of freedom could wait. For now, he had agreed to another year of fifth days. Because of that, he felt, he owed his franchise, his teammates, and himself nothing short of everything.

CHAPTER 2

HOME LIFE

The school day ended at 3 P.M., and boys and girls streamed into the streets of Highland Park. The Kershaw children did not travel far. Their front lawn overlooked the elementary school playground. Clayton and Ellen bought the property before Cali was born. A few years later, Ellen's sister moved into the house two doors down. Their father, Jim Melson, still lived a few blocks away, in the house where Ellen grew up. The neighborhood lawns were interwoven and endless, emerald patches threading each home into the same tapestry, with children spilling across the properties.

A collection of Kershaw kids, their cousins, and friends gathered outside the house. Some danced across the grass. Others bounced on a trampoline near the Kershaws' garage. The parents lined hot chocolate, marshmallows, and whipped cream along the stone steps before the front door. The modern-day Rockwell scene lasted a few minutes before rain sent everyone scampering into the Kershaws' living room.

"It's not quiet often around here," Kershaw said. "It's pretty fun. It's pretty fun."

The parents piled onto couches in the living room. The children flung themselves to the ground. Ellen wrote names on scraps of paper and placed them in a cup. Seven-year-old Cali announced the opening of the proceedings: "Secret Santa, everyone!"

Kershaw pulled up a chair at the kitchen table. He wore a stained white hoodie and gym shorts; his aversion to pants is significant enough that he once vowed to avoid them for an entire baseball season. Ellen wore a pink crewneck that read: "Merry & Bright." I had asked if they still bought each other presents. Ellen gawked at me while her husband laughed. "She's, like, a Christmas elf," Kershaw said. Ellen gave the children instructions: only spend $20 on the gift, and don't ruin the surprise.

"Don't tell anybody, Charley!" Kershaw cooed at his eldest boy, who had recently turned six.

With the names drawn, the kids spread across the house. Standing beside her father, Cali opened a container of beads and homemade, multicolored jewelry. Before Cali was born, Kershaw had never considered how he might parent a daughter. He realized he wanted "to be the dad who she can tell everything to." As she picked over the beads, he pondered a father-daughter bonding exercise.

"Would you ever want to try golf?" Kershaw said.

"Never," Cali said.

"What if Dada wants to play and you could hang out with him?" Kershaw said. "Would you want to?"

Cali shook her head, no. Kershaw was undeterred.

"Cool," he said.

He was beaming from ear to ear.

*   *   *

A day later, Jim Melson sat inside his office at Kershaw Management. He had a theory about the lives we are born into and the lives we fashion for ourselves.

"This is a little bit speculative," Melson said. "But if you and I grew up with a single mom, in a situation like Clayton and Marianne, and you didn't have the experience of a family, in the holistic sense, then I think you're a little bit starved and anxious for that."

Melson pointed to the four children, to a two-decade partnership with his daughter. A home filled with laughter and chaos and kids romping across lawns and living rooms.

"I mean, he really is just living what he didn't have early on."

*   *   *

Kershaw diagrammed his youth into separate epochs. "I had a great childhood, one through ten," he said. He meant this, he said. "I'll always be thankful for ages one through ten." He had developed this explanation over time. It elided the upheaval he experienced, and the gaps carved into his memory. As a boy, he sensed tension between his parents. The hunch became a reality one afternoon in the late 1990s, when Chris and Marianne Kershaw asked him to join them in the living room.

"I was probably nine or ten," Kershaw said. "I can't remember the exact age. They weren't sleeping in the same rooms. And so I was like, 'That's weird. Maybe Dad was just working late or whatever.' And then, finally, they both sat me down and said, 'We're getting a divorce. Dad's going to move out,' or whatever."

As Kershaw grew older, he realized his memory could be fickle. He rarely retained dialogue or dramatic sequences or inventories of his interior life. In their place resided an index of digits and figures and spatial configurations. He could memorize birthdays, phone numbers, song lengths. He could recall the price he paid for his first car ($37,000 for a Ford F-150 King Ranch truck) and his agent's first commission ($84,000). His sister-in-law, Ann Higginbottom, occasionally called from the DMV when she forgot her plate number. "I guarantee you," Shawn Tolleson said, "that if I texted him right now and I said, 'What's the license plate number on my Dodge Ram that I had when I was sixteen?' he would remember that."

After a game in Phoenix, Kershaw and a couple of others once visited Zack Greinke's home. Greinke unveiled a Diamondbacks-branded dune buggy. "We've got to drive this," Kershaw said. Greinke stayed back, mumbling the passcode to his gated community. Kershaw tooled around Scottsdale for half an hour with A. J. Ellis and video coordinator John Pratt. Back at the gate, without saying a word, he punched in the code.

But memories—the stories we tell ourselves, the stories we tell about ourselves—were elusive for Kershaw. Sometimes it exasperated his wife. "Ellen will say, 'Do you remember when the kids . . . ?' Or 'Remember when we did . . . ?'" he said. The slipperiness of his recollections extended from the inconsequential to the seismic. He could not say how his parents met. He could not explain why they split. The details disappeared into the void.

"I don't remember the exact conversation," Kershaw said. "But I remember sitting in the living room." He added, "It doesn't really bother me anymore. I think that's how my brain works. I remember the places. Like, I remember where the chairs were."

*   *   *

One night in 1985, the story goes, the legendary rhythm and blues guitarist Bo Diddley showed up to a gig at a Dallas club called Poor David's Pub, but his keyboard player didn't. The audience at every concert includes dreamers who imagine themselves sharing the stage with their heroes. Rare is the attendee talented enough to do it. Chris Kershaw had that kind of talent. That night at Poor David's, he pounded the keys as the man who wrote "Who Do You Love?" played the hits.

"Music," Chris Kershaw once said, "is my life. I've always been a musician, even though I would rather be a pro basketball player. But I was better at this."

Chris was speaking to Jonathan Wolfert, his boss at JAM Creative Productions, the radio-station jingle studio where Kershaw worked for about twenty years. In 1994, Wolfert conducted a series of interviews with his fellow musicians, including one with Kershaw, who unspooled the details of his early life. His father, George Clayton Kershaw, met his mother, Alice Irene Evans, known as Peggy, while stationed in Australia during World War II. The couple married in 1943. Christopher George Clayton Kershaw was born six years later in Manhattan, where his father worked as a chemical engineer. In his forties, George Kershaw changed careers. He became an Episcopal minister. The family eventually returned to Texas, where George had grown up. He spent the rest of his days preaching around Dallas.

George's profession proved pivotal for his only son. Chris sang in the church choir. He learned to read music and blend his voice with the group. At the St. Mark's School of Texas, a private all-boys school, Chris was more of a singer than a sportsman. The 1967 yearbook described him as the "best singer in the class," "the 'never was' of the basketball team," and a "two-year veteran of B-team baseball," though he did earn a varsity letter in baseball as a senior. His term running the school's closed-circuit radio-TV station was marred by budgetary issues. He sang in the glee club and the school choir while serving as president of the folk club his junior and senior years. "He was a very well-liked guy, a very easygoing guy," recalled Jerry Carlson, a fellow traveler among the St. Mark's folkies.

Through the Hockaday School, St. Mark's sister institution, Chris met local music impresario Tom Merriman. After Chris played the lead in Hockaday's production of *Bye Bye Birdie* as a junior, Merriman introduced Chris to the jingle business. Merriman specialized in producing tight, bright musical advertisements designed to catch the listener's ear. "I ended up working summers for him for two years," Chris told Wolfert. "Sang a few Beach Boy–kind of jingles for Tom, at age sixteen." His first jingle was for a Frisch's Big Boy in Omaha, Nebraska. After high school, Chris tried college in Tennessee before coming home to attend Southern Methodist University, where he graduated with a degree in musical theory and composition. He was looking for gigs as a keyboardist and bass player when he started working for another jingle company, PAMS.

The company stashed its younger staffers in a unit called Studio C. That was where Kershaw met Wolfert. "Studio C is where they did all the experimental stuff, the younger kind of stuff," Wolfert recalled. Wolfert operated on the other side of the glass, engineering, mixing, and editing the music Chris made. Chris possessed a deep array of skills: He could play different instruments. He had a knack for melody. He could hit the high notes as a tenor. He had accurate pitch and excellent tone. His diction was precise, which was crucial in the jingle game. "He did really good stuff, especially in the 1970s, when he was really focused on it and concentrating," Wolfert recalled. He was quick with a quip, a good hang. But Chris was better at making music than making it in the music business. He left PAMS in the mid-1970s and opened a few studios of his own. He wrote spots for Coors, Southwest Airlines, and Barq's root beer. He composed an anti-littering song for the Texas Highway Commission, "Don't Mess with Texas," and another for the Texas Tourist Development Agency, "Have a Good Time in Texas." Eventually he reunited with Wolfert, who had opened his own studio. Chris tried to make peace with the scope of his work. He told people he preferred the security of a steady paycheck over the romance of life on the road. "I think everybody among us has had a shot, or a try, or an aspiration to doing semi-famous stuff," Chris told Wolfert. "But a lot of us are married, [with] small kids, home mortgage, suburbs, life, real people."

One night in the 1980s, Wolfert was working late in his office off Interstate 75 when he heard people talking in a nearby studio. Chris was giving a woman a tour. "It seemed like they had just come from dinner, some kind of date, and he was going to impress her by showing her the studio," Wolfert recalled. That was the first time Wolfert remembered meeting Marianne Tombaugh.

Marianne Louise Tombaugh was born in Topeka, Kansas, in 1953. She was the adopted daughter of Robert Tombaugh, a chemist who taught at Kansas Wesleyan University, and Ethel Tombaugh, a kindergarten teacher. The family featured a link to astronomical history: Robert's brother, Clyde, discovered Pluto in 1930. While walking at night, Marianne sometimes searched the sky for her family's cherished dwarf planet.

Marianne grew up in Salina, in central Kansas. She played the piano as a child and fell in love with Motown. At Salina Central High School, she worked on the school newspaper. She graduated from the University of Kansas with a degree in graphic design, which brought her to Dallas. An exhibition at Texas Christian University once featured her work. She was the creative director at a local ad agency, part of the metroplex's bustling professional milieu that also encompassed the jingle business. When she started dating Chris, they made an attractive couple. "She was the greatest, most fun girlfriend ever," recalled Babs Mayeron, a friend of Marianne's dating back to the 1970s. Marianne and Mayeron were close like Lucy Ricardo and Ethel Mertz—except they both wanted to be the titular character, so they called each other Lucy and Lucy. "She was just a sweet soul," Mayeron recalled.

Marianne married Chris on September 24, 1987, according to Texas court records. An October 5 notice in *Adweek* congratulated them on their nuptials and New England honeymoon. A little less than six months later, on March 19, 1988, the couple's only child, Clayton Edward Kershaw, was born. He had his mother's smile and his father's sandy brown hair. His cheeks stayed chubby well into his youth. He loved pizza and chicken fingers. The young family settled in Dallas's Preston Hollow neighborhood, which happened to be near the Mayerons. After he grew up, Clayton connected his passion for baseball to his mother's friends: John Mayeron, Babs's husband, possessed a massive collection of cards, books, and memorabilia. Sometimes Clayton accompanied the Mayerons to Texas Rangers games: he started wearing the number 22 because of Rangers first baseman Will Clark. Clayton often threw backyard batting practice to their son, Kyle. As the older boy, Kyle dictated who hit and who pitched. "Clayton would say, 'Is it my turn to bat yet?' And Kyle would say, 'No, Clayton, just pitch me a few more,'" Mayeron recalled.

The memories Clayton shared of his father usually involved sports. "Just personality-wise, I don't remember a ton," he recalled. The length of Chris's shifts at the studio stuck with him: Chris worked 9 A.M. to 1 P.M. or 2 P.M. to 6 P.M. Clayton visited his dad's office but never connected with melody or rhythm or free-flowing expression. "I think we had a love of sports [that was] similar," Kershaw recalled. "But his brain was so much more creative." Clayton felt more comfortable attending Dallas Mavericks games at Reunion Arena, where his dad had season tickets. Chris brought his son to one of his fantasy football drafts, conducted on paper, at a bar. They played catch and hoisted jumpers together. "He did all that," Clayton recalled. "Like a dad should. I am thankful for that." Kershaw loved the dogs his dad brought home, a chocolate lab named Nestle and a mutt named Mikey.

One of Clayton's first organized baseball teams was called the Dodgers. They celebrated victories by headbanging to Survivor's "The Eye of the Tiger" on car rides home. In elementary school, he wrote a book report about Sandy Koufax. Like Koufax, he showed an early grasp of the curveball, which he learned as a preteen. "He just had good feel and good hands," recalled Tommy Hernandez, who coached Kershaw on the Dallas Tigers travel club. But he took part in other sports, too, in between episodes of *Saved by the Bell*. He helped the fourth-graders at Bradfield Elementary win a YMCA track meet at SMU. Marianne took him to ice-skating lessons and roller-hockey leagues. At the studio, Chris bragged about how many goals his boy had scored in soccer. The pride Chris showed toward his son was obvious. "Which is why it was really sad, later on," Wolfert recalled.

The house was often quiet. Clayton noticed Chris was home less often. He sensed his parents drifting apart, but he was too young to understand why. Clayton was reluctant to discuss his father's demons, but others who knew the Kershaws indicated Chris developed a drinking problem. The family's world started to wobble. Marianne tired of her husband's behavior. "Oh, I'm not telling you all the stories," Mayeron recalled. "There were times when Chris would do some real asinine things. I would just be there to be supportive. Listen to her cry, listen to her be mad."

"Right around nine or ten is when it started doing this," recalled Kershaw, using his hand to mimic the twists and turns of a roller coaster. "We had to move a lot. They were living in separate rooms." Eventually Marianne and Chris sat Clayton down in the living room and told him. "It was just kind of yuck," Kershaw recalled.

The couple officially divorced on October 17, 2000, according to Texas court records. Clayton was twelve.

* * *

After he grew up, when he decided to raise a family, Kershaw made a resolution. He would not be like his father. "I do think it's helped me as a dad," he said. "I really do. Because I just want to be there nonstop. I don't want to miss a thing." A few days before Santa Claus visited Highland Park, he ventured with the family to the high school basket-ball game. Charley watched from Kershaw's lap. The next morning, the schedule created a conflict: Charley and Cali each had an 8 A.M. bas-ketball game. Kershaw was the assistant coach of Cali's team—but he was the head coach of Charley's. His son won out.

"He probably knows what it's like to be the kid that doesn't have his dad at every single game," Ellen said. "And so he's going to do it."

His commitment to his children—his commitment to not be like Chris—was more challenging during the baseball season. His adher-ence to the five-day cycle provided for his children. But it also kept him away from them. There were times when Kershaw felt torn between his loneliness and his profession. He felt guilty asking the children to uproot their lives in Highland Park during the school year. Sometimes he set his alarm for 4:30 A.M. on the West Coast, so he could call before a big day at school. When the family visited Phoenix for spring training, he raided the local Target: Lego sets for Charley, arts and crafts supplies for Cali. Just before I visited Highland Park, Kershaw and Ellen celebrated their twelfth wedding anniversary. He ordered five towering sets of balloons, one for his wife, one for each child.

During the season, when Clayton was away from the children, Ellen kept him informed while not highlighting his absence. When three-year-old Cooper played soccer, Ellen texted a steady stream of videos. But she made sure to include how ridiculous the occasion had been: Cooper was young enough that he could not differentiate between the two goals, so he scored one in each. At times, Ellen felt overwhelmed by the logistics of it all, coordinating flights with young children, making sure they didn't miss school or sports or activities. "I'm constantly trying to manage the balance of how long Clayton can go without us," Ellen said. "Because this is the hardest on him to be alone."

He had spent enough time by himself as a boy. He had lived in a quiet household, his mother reeling, his father absent. He did not want that for himself. And he did not want his children to know the hurt he had experienced, the hurt he had buried, after his family dissolved.

"I think it starts with just being present," Kershaw said. "And so that's what's hard about baseball sometimes. And ultimately, that will drive me to stop, if my arm doesn't do it first. The second I hear, 'Dad, where were you?' Or 'I miss you,' it's like, okay. I don't need to do this anymore."

CHAPTER 3

THE BOY IN THE BUBBLE

Five days after Valentine's Day in 2003, Clayton Kershaw closed his locker and approached a classmate with brown hair and a vibrant personality. He stammered through a question that changed his life.

"Will you go out with me?"

Clayton was unsure how Ellen Melson would respond, but he was hopeful. The two freshmen did not know each other well. They were part of overlapping friend groups, including another couple who had encouraged them to date. They had chatted a few times on AOL Instant Messenger. His screen name was CTonga06, a play on one of the many nicknames he wore in his youth, ClayTonga. She was EllenMelon87. She was immersed in cheerleading and dance teams. He had just finished a season playing center on the Highland Park High freshman football team. She had recently graduated from braces. He resided in that bodily sweet spot of gangly chubbiness. They were a perfect match.

"Sure!" Ellen replied.

The conversation lasted about fifteen seconds. As she grew older, Ellen considered their pairing a gift. "Gosh, I bet the Lord just must have been smiling," she recalled. In the moment, though, it was no big deal. Clayton headed to the cafeteria to accept high-fives from his friends. Ellen went back to navigating the treacherous world of high school. They were, in truth, strangers. "I had no idea he was good at baseball," Ellen recalled. "When we started dating, we were fourteen years old."

The genesis of their attraction faded from their memories, in part because it grew difficult to remember life without each other. They smiled at each other's jokes. Clayton could laugh at himself, which Ellen appreciated. They didn't mind looking at each other. In the chaste matchmaking world of ninth grade, that was enough. "I think we just got along," Kershaw recalled. "I don't know why she wanted to hang out with me, though. I think I made her laugh every once in a while."

He maintained his sense of humor despite ongoing turmoil at home. Clayton split time between his mother and father, with Wednesday nights and every other weekend spent with Chris. Sometimes he sat by the window, waiting and wondering when his father would pick him up. He hated being late for practice, for school, for anything. And he hated that it wasn't his fault. The visits only grew stranger for Clayton as his father began to date, eventually marrying a woman who had children of her own. "I didn't want to deal with that," Kershaw recalled. By the time Clayton reached ninth grade, he had tired of the awkwardness. His visits with Chris became sporadic and eventually stopped. Chris attended his son's sporting events on occasion. But their time under the same roof ended.

As his father faded from his life, his mother faded from her own. In time, with the benefit of maturation, Clayton realized Marianne was dealing with depression. "She was pretty shook by the divorce," he recalled. She drew inward. Clayton recognized he had to become self-sufficient. He learned to finish his homework without prompting, to set his own alarm. Marianne fixated on paying the bills. Clayton could not afford to attend private school. Marianne decided to move into the Park Cities, the community encompassing Highland Park and University Park, about a ten-minute drive south from Preston Hollow. She wanted Clayton to benefit from Highland Park's school system.

The decision came fraught with cultural and financial consequences that shaped his journey into young adulthood.

*   *   *

Some referred to the Park Cities as "the bubble," a glistening rectangle of estates and green space encompassing Dallas Country Club, the campus of Southern Methodist University, and a Highland Park city hall that mirrored a Gothic Mediterranean villa with red-tiled roofing and burbling fountains. A 1994 story in *Texas Monthly* outlined the architectural grandeur: "French chateaux, Italian villas, Tudor manors." Nearly twenty years later, the *New Yorker* described Highland Park as a place known for "street after street of Gatsbyesque mansions." Others reached for more modern cultural markers. While reporting this book, I occasionally heard Highland Park described as a Texas-tinged *Beverly Hills, 90210*, a glitzy, affluent oasis tucked inside the city of Dallas.

A Dallas Independent School District official used different language. Highland Park existed as "that hole in the middle" of the city, a "separate school system, in the middle of this other school system." Highland Park Independent School District operated outside the scope of Dallas's control, with facilities that outshone those in the surrounding schools. The district benefited from wealth accumulation through the value of its homes. "Traditionally, Highland Park residents have taxed their property at a relatively low rate, yet because of the inflated price of their real estate, they have been able to afford one of the state's finest school districts," Dana Rubin wrote in *Texas Monthly*. The beneficiaries of this loop were almost exclusively white.

The author James M. Loewen has identified Highland Park as a sundown town, one of thousands of communities dotting the American landscape where it was considered unsafe for Black people to remain after dark. Built in the early twentieth century in a city abiding Jim Crow laws, Highland Park promised its residents even starker segregation: the district would function, according to a history published on

Highland Park's municipal website, "as a refuge from an increasingly diverse city." The district also used the slogan "Beyond the City's Dust and Smoke" to recruit new arrivals. Highland Park partnered with University Park to avoid annexation by Dallas and maintain its independence. The district restricted nonresidents from parks and tennis courts. "Highland Park . . . has been a leader in criminalizing ordinary behavior," Loewen wrote. "It may have more 'No' signs per capita than any other city in the nation." Those restrictions applied to its zoning, as well. Only small pockets on the outskirts of Highland Park permitted multifamily housing, according to a study from the Century Foundation, a liberal think tank: "In fact, more land is allocated for the Dallas Country Club than for multifamily housing."

The segregation persisted well beyond the Supreme Court's 1954 decision in *Brown v. Board of Education* and beyond the Civil Rights Act of 1964. After the Brown decision, residents in the Park Cities jettisoned the Black families who resided in the district as live-in gardeners and maids; a local alderman framed the firings as vital "so that Park Cities would not be confronted with white and Negro children attending school together." A Black student did not attend Highland Park High until 1974. When Marianne began renting in the district in the late 1990s, the schools were still overwhelmingly white. In 2003, the community newspaper *Park Cities People* caused a national stir with a story about the arrival of Highland Park's first Black homeowner: "Guess who's coming to dinner—and staying for a while?" Outside the bubble, the Park Cities were discussed with both envy and scorn as an enclosed bastion of white wealth.

"There's a lot of money in Highland Park," one rival high school coach said.

"Everybody there is extremely wealthy," one local youth coach said.

"If you're living a thousand miles away and you hear there's a good pitcher in Highland Park, Texas, your stereotype is 'Hey, he's a spoiled rich kid,'" one college coach said.

The reputation lasts into the present. In the summer of 2020, Kershaw vocalized his support for Black Americans during the protests after the murder of George Floyd. "We must unapologetically say that Black lives matter," he said in a video released by the Dodgers. That winter, Texas Rangers pitcher Taylor Hearn was discussing the scope of the movement within baseball. It was shocking, admitted Hearn, a Black man who had grown up just outside of Dallas, "for somebody from Highland Park to do something." The criticism frustrated Kershaw. "Yes, it has its flaws," he said. "It's very affluent. And there's all the drawbacks that come from that, like, people say it's pretty exclusive and all that. I do think the community itself is pretty special." He harbored little resentment toward Highland Park. The district, in his eyes, raised him.

*   *   *

For those families permitted entry into the enclave, Highland Park offered idyllic amenities. Jim Melson was studying to become a certified public accountant when he met Leslie Long at SMU. Jim had grown up in Houston. Leslie moved around a few times in her youth, uprooted by her father's corrugated box business, bouncing from Connecticut to Cincinnati before settling in Richardson, Texas. When Leslie was a baby, Bill Long rubbed the fuzz of his daughter's cheeks and coined a nickname: Peach. Leslie started dating Jim when she was a college senior and he was in grad school. After they married in 1978, Jim interviewed with New York accounting firms but decided to stay in Dallas. Their first child, a boy named Jed, arrived in 1982. More children followed: Ann, Ellen, and John. When Jed was entering first grade, the Melsons moved to Highland Park "because the school district is so good compared to the Dallas schools," Jim Melson recalled.

As a child, Ellen wore her emotions on her sleeves, which were often adorned with leopard or zebra prints. The first day at school usually ended in tears. Her family consoled her—if only so they could tease her about the outbursts as she grew older. Even as she dealt with the usual travails of adolescence, she liked to bring people together, inviting friends to sample the family's chocolate fountain and commune with Peach. Ellen raced home every afternoon in middle school to watch *Oprah*, dissecting each episode with friends the next day. When Oprah Winfrey visited Africa, Ellen found herself appalled by the conditions depicted on the show. "I realized more than ever that I was sheltered," she later wrote. "I had grown up in a bubble where poverty didn't exist." She dreamed of one day visiting the continent.

Ellen grew up in a tangle of siblings and cousins. The extended family once rented a bus for a three-week, eighteen-person tour of national parks across the western United States, complete with matching outfits and fanny packs. To teach the children a lesson about the dangers of gambling, Leslie took them to a casino and dropped a quarter into a slot machine. Except she won on her first spin. At home in Highland Park, Leslie kept an open-door policy for friends and family at dinner. "Her table always was set for twelve or fifteen people," Ellen recalled. They prayed before every meal.

Ellen's new boyfriend came from different circumstances. He had built up a robust social life, but almost all of it took place outside his home. Marianne found a home near the family of a boy named Josh Meredith, who had been on a soccer team with Clayton. "Obviously, renting a house in the Park Cities and trying to find a decently priced place, there weren't too many options," Kershaw recalled. "I'm sure she was like, 'Oh, this is the perfect location.' But she probably was trying to find what she could get." Clayton and Josh became best friends. Clayton often dined with the Merediths. He installed pegs on his bike so Josh could ride to school with him. Patrick Halpin, another kid in the neighborhood, joined the burgeoning squad. The band of boys hopping pools and mashing Nintendo 64 controllers expanded to become a lifelong crew: Carter English, Ben Kardell, Wade Prospere, and a rambunctious pair of twins, Charley and John Dickenson. Marianne baked chocolate chip cookies and let the kids stay up late playing hallway hockey. More often, they ended up elsewhere. "I was always bouncing around," Kershaw recalled. "I always ate dinner everywhere else."

The boys loved to compete. At Clayton's house, they battled on the Ping-Pong table, ignoring the bits of gum stuck underneath. When Clayton, Josh, Patrick, and Carter shared a lunch hour in high school, they played on Patrick's backyard basketball court. Clayton played defense "like it was two minutes left in the national championships, like, at all times," Halpin recalled. Clayton devised plays with Carter, picking and rolling to victory. "He didn't just want to win," Halpin recalled. "He clearly wanted to rip your throat out."

After dating for a little while, Ellen invited Clayton to meet her parents. He arrived with the number 52 shaved into his head, a spring football ritual. "My parents were like, 'Who's this person who you have brought into our household?'" Ellen recalled. She was mortified on one of their first dates when Clayton asked Jim Melson to buy them tickets to the R-rated thriller *The Life of David Gale*. The family got past the awkward stage. Jim often came home from work to find the young couple studying together as Leslie prepared dinner. Leslie sensed the boy did not often receive home-cooked meals. He inhaled her cooking. He lacked the material goods sported by the other Highland Park kids. Marianne was, as Jim recalled, "a saint, in so many ways," but she was stretched thin, her hours devoted to making ends meet. The Melsons filled some of that void. Clayton picked up Ellen for their first homecoming dance sporting moccasins with a hole in the toe. Leslie bought him dress shoes the next day.

In the summer, the Melsons retreated to Amelia Island, a tony resort town near Jacksonville, Florida. Leslie invited Clayton to accompany the family early in the relationship. Ellen was reluctant—she hadn't spent much time alone with her boyfriend. "I'm like, 'This is so awkward,'" Ellen recalled. "She's like, 'But I love him!'" Clayton splashed at the beach and jumped into photos with the extended Melson clan.

Later that year, Jed Melson stopped Clayton on the family's front
porch. Her face in her hands, Ellen watched through the window as
Jed warned her boyfriend not to break his sister's heart.

The two families only became more intertwined. The Melsons
invited Clayton and Marianne to join them for Thanksgiving and
Christmas. "That really helped show me what a family looks like," Kershaw recalled. The Melson kids teased their mother about preferring
Clayton over the others. "She really did take him on as our fifth child,"
Jim Melson recalled. That first Christmas, less than a year after Clayton had approached Ellen in the hallway, he found a message awaiting
him at the Melsons'. Hanging above the fireplace was a stocking with
his name on it.

*   *   *

Besides asking Ellen out, Kershaw made another crucial decision in the
second half of his freshman year. He quit the football team.

The legend of Kershaw's football career grew later in life, in part
because of one of his teammates. The freshman team had gone unde-
feated in 2002. Clayton split time with another boy at center. Far more
attention went to the quarterback: Matthew Stafford, a wunderkind
who had been flinging seventy-yard spirals since middle school, a
leader who had not lost a football game since sixth grade, a freshman
good enough to finish the season with the varsity. When Stafford was
in eighth grade, he told the varsity football coach at Highland Park, "I
want to win a state championship and play college football." He ended
up doing all that and much, much more—which made his schoolboy
teaming with Kershaw loom larger when the two men grew up to reach
the apex of different sports. They were friends through middle school,
with Matthew part of the crew shooting hoops and bouncing on the
trampoline at Clayton's house. One day Matthew fell and bashed his
head against the trampoline's metal edge. "He hit his head so hard on
that metal," Kershaw recalled. "He stuck it out. But he was pretty con-
cussed." Added Halpin, "He's the one who just happened to get

knocked off the trampoline, hit his head, and, like, had just a total meltdown. And then his parents came and picked him up."

Kershaw and Stafford took divergent paths in high school. Kershaw loved playing football with his friends. And he did not fear contact. When a scrum broke out against a rival, Kershaw dove into the pile and started swinging. But he was a five-foot-nine grunt and the repetitive interior violence came with its indignities. During one practice, according to a story in the 2003 Highland Park yearbook, Kershaw was long-snapping when the kicker booted the football with a lower trajectory than usual. The ball slammed into Kershaw's backside and bowled him over. "I thought it was really funny," John Dickenson told the yearbook, "but Kershaw did not."

The bigger problem was that football conflicted with baseball. The football team superseded other sports. If you weren't playing a different varsity sport in the spring, you had to participate in practice. When the baseball season started that spring, Kershaw was still on the junior varsity. If he wanted to thrive as a lineman, he needed to bulk up, expanding horizontally when baseball rewarded those who grew vertically. Halpin had recently walked away from football and encouraged Kershaw to join him. It was not a choice made lightly at a school like Highland Park, in a state like Texas. "Clayton," said freshman team assistant coach Reagan Dailey, "if you do that, that will be the worst decision you ever make in your life."

Freed from blocking sleds, Kershaw devoted his energy toward the diamond. He soon joined the varsity out of necessity. The senior class featured so few players that the team called up a crop of freshmen, including Stafford, who played shortstop. Kershaw slotted into the starting rotation behind Xerxes Martin, a crafty senior bound for Baylor. Martin's fastball rarely cracked the mid-80s. Neither did Kershaw's. But the baseball often went where he commanded it. "He had feel for pitches that freshmen and sophomores don't have," recalled Will Skelton, a pitcher two years ahead of Kershaw. "He was not yet overpowering. But he was still really good."

A spot on the varsity team came with perks. Each player was assigned a collection of cheerleaders, known as "baseball girls." Ellen volunteered for the role with her new boyfriend. She and her friends wore Clayton's jersey on game day. They decorated his room with posters. Ellen mixed him batches of puppy chow, a delightful concoction of Chex, powdered sugar, chocolate, and peanut butter. "Now that I think about it, I'm like, 'What?'" she recalled. The Highland Park Scots played at a lush, well-maintained ballpark called Scotland Yard. The players picked their own walkup music. Kershaw chose "Build Me Up Buttercup," the classic by the Foundations revived by *There's Something About Mary* a few years earlier. The song served as a tribute to Marianne, a Motown aficionado. It was also, Kershaw admitted, an attempt at humor. "I'd say he had a pretty carefree demeanor," recalled Martin. Kershaw appeared in the *Dallas Morning News* for various feats: a two-hitter against West Mesquite High, a fifteen-strikeout game against Wylie High. The season ended with Kershaw taking a playoff loss. The defeat did not diminish the impression Kershaw made. "He was definitely a very good freshman in the state of Texas," Martin recalled.

*　*　*

Within the insular community of Dallas baseball, Kershaw's talent was far from a secret. "He was the guy that at age twelve or so, you're hearing, 'This guy's really, really good,'" recalled Trent Appleby, who grew up in nearby McKinney. "And you hear that about other guys, but that's mostly because they got bigger, stronger earlier than everyone else." What separated Kershaw wasn't his size or his velocity. He excelled at the primary objective: getting people out. "He was just a really good pitcher," Appleby recalled.

Appleby came across Kershaw in the byzantine world of travel baseball, a spiderweb of various teams spread across the metroplex. By fifth grade, Kershaw was playing with kids from his neighborhood. "He was always the best pitcher," Meredith recalled. "Hitting the spots, throwing curveballs." From middle school into his early high school years, Kershaw joined Stafford on the Dallas Tigers, a local institution that included talented right-hander Shawn Tolleson, who lived nearby in Allen. Kershaw had more baby fat than height, more grit than velocity. He focused on locating his fastball and spinning his curve. At that age, Kershaw "didn't move very well," recalled Tigers coach Tommy Hernandez. "He played first and pitched for us. Really wasn't great at anything. It was just a solid kid." His mood shifted whenever he took the field. "He was a fun kid," Hernandez recalled. "But, man, when he was in between the lines, he was dialed in, trying to get better."

On occasion, Marianne took Clayton to an indoor batting cage in nearby Addison. The D-Bat facility was owned by Cade Griffis, who had played at Dallas Baptist and spent a season in the minors. D-Bat also sponsored travel-ball teams. Heading into the summer after Kershaw's sophomore season, Griffis was invited to meet with a group of parents. He walked into an impromptu job interview with Marianne, the Staffords, the Tollesons, and several other adults, all of them with children on the Tigers, looking for a new summer-ball team. "Basically, 'Tell us why we should play for you,'" Griffis recalled. Griffis convinced the parents to join D-Bat. He planned to install Stafford at shortstop. But Stafford had become QB1 at Highland Park as a sophomore. Stafford's father told Griffis about Matthew's slew of invitations to quarterback camps. Stafford chose the gridiron over the diamond. "I remember thinking, 'Man, you're five-eleven. You need to play baseball!'" Griffis recalled. "Boy, I was wrong about that one."

The others stuck around. Tolleson was the ace, overwhelming other teenagers with his slider. Kershaw was a solid sidekick. His curveball was less reliable, but he had grown six inches in between his sophomore and junior years. Kershaw and Tolleson bonded in dugouts and on trips across the state and beyond, kicking a Hacky Sack in hotel parking lots. They sweated over games of Ping-Pong or pickup basketball. "He's always had this ability to overcome a defeat, even if it seems like a defeat is inevitable," Tolleson recalled. If Tolleson pulled ahead on the basketball court, it didn't really matter that Kershaw lacked much of a handle and never left his feet when he shot. He tightened up on defense, backed down his opponent, and won. The same principle applied to even the most juvenile of pursuits, like wrestling in hotel rooms. "It's all fun and games until Clayton figures out he's losing," Tolleson recalled.

The team traveled to Chicago, to Houston, to Steamboat Springs, Colorado. Marianne Kershaw could not afford the expense; already she had begun to ask friends to loan her money to pay the bills required to stay in Highland Park. Griffis recognized the situation. Kershaw reminded Griffis of himself. As a boy growing up in Louisiana, Griffis lost his father. His mother taught school. Money was tight. Griffis underwrote Kershaw's travel, along with another parent who cut an extra check. "We've never talked about it," Griffis recalled. "Nor would I ever bring that up. But, yes, in so many terms, I funded his summer baseball. I knew he couldn't afford to do it. But he was such a good kid." Kershaw noticed the largesse. "I don't know this for a fact, but I know he probably let me play for cheaper than what I needed to play," he recalled.

Kershaw noticed lots of things, like the modesty of his circumstances, the sadness his mother felt. He was unsure how to handle her darkness after the divorce. As a teenager, he recognized baseball as an outlet. Here was a way to help himself. Here was a way to help his mother. At baseball games, he started to notice the college coaches in the stands. The game became more than a game.

"That's when I put more pressure on myself to do better," Kershaw recalled. "And I think it all culminated, like, as I got older."

*　*　*

The temperate climate of Dallas afforded Kershaw a boyhood spent outdoors. The first inklings of his faith stemmed from curiosity about the origins of the trees dotting the landscape. "It blew me away to look at the world around me—how could it have just come into being?"

Kershaw later wrote. "That didn't make any sense to me. I knew I wasn't here by chance. I knew the world was no accident." He believed in God, but he did not consider himself particularly religious. His family went through the motions: Methodist church every Sunday, plus Sunday school lessons. He viewed God as a great but distant king. "I knew I wanted Him in my life," Kershaw wrote, "but I also thought he could squash me like a bug."

Ellen changed his perspective. The Melsons were more devout than the Kershaws. Ellen and her siblings were fixtures at Highland Park Presbyterian Church. Ellen found her faith had deepened during a tumultuous year in eighth grade, when she frosted her hair and paired the bands of her braces with the color scheme of each upcoming holiday. The piddling stakes of middle-school drama are only understood by those who have already graduated middle school; in the moment, it just feels awful. Ellen felt wounded by teasing, betrayed by gossiping, overwhelmed by the awkwardness and cliquishness of it all. She dove into the Bible for support. "The Lord," she read in Psalm 103:8, "is compassionate and gracious, slow to anger, abounding in love." God, she realized, could be her friend. She could explain her hardships, her uncertainties, her dreams without worry of insult or dismissal. She often wrote her prayers in a journal, as if God were a pen pal who answered back without requiring ink or paper. Her faith helped her get through the year. (She received corporeal aid, too; her sister Ann stopped by the school to chastise the mean girls.)

Her worldview influenced Clayton as their relationship blossomed. He began to accompany the Melsons to church. In between pseudo-dates and after-school study sessions, they often talked about God. Ellen convinced Clayton to see God as she did: a friend, a loving father, someone you could commune with and entrust with your future. The message resonated as Clayton grappled with his financial insecurity. Beneath his insouciant surface, Clayton felt riddled with anxiety. The prospect of someone having his back appealed to him. He mulled it over as he read the Scripture and took part in Bible study groups with

Ellen. "I say I'm a Christian. I say all these things. But do I actually really believe it?" he recalled. "And I started thinking about it more and praying about it, and decided, 'Yeah, Jesus did what He said He did.' That helped me take the pressure off myself, in a sense. It's like, 'Okay, somebody else is in control of my life.'" His interpretation of the Scripture provided the lens through which he saw the world. As an adult, he identified as a "conservative Christian man," the sort of person who believed that everyone deserved God's love but also that gay marriage defied the Bible. He was a product of his environment, and a beneficiary of his environment.

During Kershaw's junior year, he came across the passage in a devotional book that became his mantra, Colossians 3:23: "Whatever you do, work at it with all your heart, as working for the Lord, not for human masters." He knew his family lacked the money to send him to the colleges eyed by his classmates. His best hope was baseball. The realization knotted his stomach and frazzled his mind. He could offload some of that worry into his burgeoning trust in God. But he could also do his own part. He could work at his craft. That meant sacrifices. And it meant changing how he told time. Most boys organized time based on a seven-day week, Sunday to Saturday. Kershaw decided to live within a cycle that began the day after he started and ended the next time he climbed atop a mound. He wanted to pitch without regret, knowing he had done everything within his power to be ready for each game. The schedule he undertook would evolve as he grew older. But that teenage zeal to dog no sprint, to skip no set in the weight room, to waste no day—that never left.

CHAPTER 4

TEAM USA

The morning after Santa Claus rode through Highland Park, Clayton Kershaw pulled his white GMC Denali out of his driveway and made the five-minute drive to his high school. He waved a fob at the entrance to Highland Park's indoor athletic center. He was long past the days of hopping fences to throw at Scotland Yard. The school granted him access to a facility carpeted with synthetic turf and lined like a football field.

The facility was empty save for a teenager kicking field goals. To prepare for the season, Kershaw was throwing four times a week, in addition to his regular lifting, conditioning, and physical therapy. He organized throwing sessions with local pitchers. These were not open-ended affairs. A few weeks later, Shawn Tolleson asked Kershaw when they could grab lunch. Kershaw was precise. He told Tolleson his session ended at 11:42 A.M., so noon would be fine. Kershaw showed up reeking of sweat.

In the past, a variety of big-leaguers had thrown with Kershaw. To receive an invitation felt like an honor and a privilege. Most of his throwing partners were gone now. Tolleson retired in 2019. Yu Darvish was spending the winter between Japan and San Diego. Chris Young had become the general manager of the Texas Rangers. Only one of his contemporaries remained: Brett Anderson, a burly, taciturn southpaw, whose career had been intertwined with Kershaw's since they were teenagers.

Kershaw was the first to arrive. The others straggled in. Anderson mumbled a greeting. They watched the kicker practice. His technique was odd. He stood behind the football and booted it without striding. It reminded the pitchers of their industry's mecca of biomechanical improvement.

"That's, like, the Driveline of kicking right there," Anderson said.

Kershaw ambled over.

"Can I try one?" he asked.

The kid stepped aside. Kershaw stood behind the ball, raised his right foot and took a whack. The ball barely lifted off the ground. It skittered into a soccer net beneath the uprights. Kershaw jogged back to the pitchers. "I was right there," he said.

Kershaw loosened his arm as the others chatted. Most of the talk centered around six-foot-seven right-hander Kyle Muller. The day before, he had been traded from the Atlanta Braves to the Oakland Athletics. Muller regaled the group with a story about how he had missed the initial phone call from Athletics manager Mark Kotsay. He had been too busy hunting.

Kershaw had walked away. "If there's a baseball in his hand," said Jamey Wright, a former throwing partner, "it's business." Kershaw scooped a weighted ball and knelt facing away from a wall. In one continuous motion, he flung the ball behind his back and off the wall, catching it with the same hand. The sound echoed through the facility. Then Kershaw stood up and farted.

Kershaw and Anderson stood eight yards apart and started to play catch. Anderson had sat out the 2022 season, but he was plotting a comeback, and his movements were still languid and leisurely. He made everything look easy. Kershaw grunted and thudded. He made everything look violent. As the distance between the two men separated, it was not hard to see why, seventeen years earlier, when they were both left-handed kids dreaming the same dream, scouts looked at them and felt sure about which one was going to make it.

* * *

In the summer of 2005, 144 teenage boys descended on Joplin, Missouri, a city tucked in the southwestern corner of the state. They came from Northern California and Southern California, from the Pacific Northwest and the suburbs of Miami, from the sprawl outside New Orleans and the Lower East Side of Manhattan. They represented the best of the best of the best of the American Amateur Baseball Congress and American Legion Baseball and all the other summer leagues in the United States. They were all there for the same reason: to compete in the tenth annual Tournament of the Stars and to represent the United States that September in the Pan Am Championships.

The boys were divided into eight teams. For a week, they played doubleheaders beneath the watchful eyes of Team USA officials, college coaches, and professional scouts. At night, they stayed with host families. Some of the boys were too confident or too naive to feel nervous about the showcase. Kershaw was not one of those boys. He noted all the evaluators in the stands. He recognized the significance of the opportunity.

He had not come to Joplin alone. Tolleson also made the cut. But the teams were drawn at random. Kershaw ended up with Anderson, who was already renowned for his surgical precision and his affinity for silence. His ratio of words to strikes was infinitesimal. Anderson was born into baseball. His father, Frank, was a Division I pitching coach, venturing from Texas Tech to Texas to Oklahoma State, where he took over as head coach in 2004. During a rain delay in one of Frank's games, preteen Brett amused himself by chucking a Nerf Vortex football until the rocket-shaped device landed atop the ticket office, remembered Trip Couch, who worked with Frank Anderson at Texas. "He was never a very good athlete," Couch recalled. "But good Lord, he had a great arm and he could hit a gnat's ass."

Anderson arrived in Joplin with renown. "Brett Anderson," recalled Team USA pitching coach Jason Hisey, "had the best high school command I've ever seen." He had committed to play for his dad after he graduated, but few expected him to ever get to campus. "He was just so much more polished than all of us," Kershaw recalled. Hank Conger, a catcher from Huntington Beach, California, had known Anderson since they were twelve. Conger inhaled every issue of *Baseball America*, keeping track of his contemporaries as the next summer's draft crept closer. The publication projected Anderson would be a top-ten pick. "To me," Conger recalled, "up until that point, he was the best left-handed pitcher, amateur pitcher, in that draft." Team USA was thrilled that Anderson committed to play. "At that age, if you can keep walks down, you're gold," recalled USA Baseball director of operations Ray Darwin. "And so Brett Anderson was, like, the stud."

Conger and the others were less familiar with Kershaw. Conger had seen his name, but usually paired with his D-Bat teammates. One night early in the trials, when the boys were still jittery, Conger settled behind the plate to catch Kershaw. Before the outing, Conger had received a thumbnail scouting report on Kershaw. Decent velocity from the left side, a bit erratic, big curveball. The report sold Kershaw short. The fastball was lively. The curve was "an absolute hammer," Conger recalled. Conger could not understand why Kershaw arrived in Joplin with so little hype.

Who the fuck is this guy? Conger wondered.

* * *

Clayton Kershaw occupied a position unique to his ability and his geography that summer. He was considered by college coaches, professional scouts, and accredited publications to be one of the better high school pitchers in the country. He was also the No. 3 starter for D-Bat. The travel-ball club included a prospect who would enter the spring as *Baseball America*'s No. 1 high school player in America. His name was Jordan Walden.

Walden lived in Mansfield, nearly an hour south of Highland Park. He displayed skills that made big-league teams salivate, even though Walden skipped the Team USA trials. He stood six-foot-four and weighed 185 pounds. His right arm looked blessed. He threw *hard*. When he surfaced at a Texas Christian University showcase that summer, scouts clocked him at 99 mph—harder than even Walden thought he could throw. Walden benefited from an odd delivery: he jumped down the slope of the mound. The leap closed the distance to the plate, which amplified his heater. "Nobody could touch him," recalled Mark Cohoon, Walden's teammate at D-Bat and Mansfield High. Yet when D-Bat coach Ken Guthrie needed to win, he preferred another of his pitchers. "Tolleson," he recalled, "was the go-to guy." To Guthrie, who had played a couple of seasons of pro ball, Tolleson already wielded a big-league slider. Tolleson "was absolutely just unhittable," recalled D-Bat catcher and future big-leaguer Cameron Rupp. "Shawn was the first guy I ever saw strike seven kids out in a row," Cohoon recalled.

Kershaw could not throw as hard as Walden. His curveball could not match Tolleson's slider. What Kershaw offered, D-Bat officials believed, was an intriguing combination of intelligence, aptitude, and ambition. "The biggest asset he had was how competitive he was," Guthrie recalled. He appeared willing to do anything to reach his ceiling. Earlier that summer, Kershaw received an invitation to the Area Code Games, a prestigious cattle call for schoolboy talent in Long Beach, California. Kershaw watched a presentation from Alan Jaeger, a former college pitcher whose unconventional methods had charmed big-league stars like Barry Zito, another lefty with a big curveball. Kershaw adopted Jaeger's slate of warmup exercises "to the letter," he recalled.

In addition to the showcases, the D-Bat boys played dozens of games that summer. There were midweek doubleheaders and weekend tournaments. There were always more innings than arms. "It'd be like, 'Hey, we're going to this tournament in Oklahoma City. We need two pitchers. Can you call a buddy?'" recalled Austin Goolsby, a catcher from Coppell, Texas. Before a tournament in Oklahoma, Guthrie surveyed the area for pitchers. One of his assistant coaches had scouted a left-hander who had recently moved from California. Guthrie called Greg Britton and asked if his son, Zack, was available. Guthrie picked up Zack at a Cabela's in Fort Worth—"back when that was okay to do, I guess," Britton recalled—and drove his new pitcher to the tournament. Britton lived in the rural town of Weatherford and didn't fit in with the wealthy Dallas kids. One of the first players who approached him was Kershaw. "If you need anything," Kershaw told Britton, "here's my number."

Britton slotted into the back of the rotation with Kershaw. "Shawn Tolleson and Jordan Walden were just so much better, at that age," Britton recalled. That weekend, Kershaw pitched in a preliminary game. Britton started the championship game. Around the third inning, Guthrie heard rustling in the dugout. "I want the ball," Kershaw kept muttering. Guthrie did not like his pitchers to throw more than once a week. He held off Kershaw until the final inning. Guthrie affixed a tight leash around Kershaw: if he threw more than twelve pitches, he was coming out. "And of course, he went out there and struck out everybody in less than twelve pitches," Guthrie recalled.

Kershaw cataloged slights. One time, Cade Griffis recalled, "Someone told him he had a horseshit pickoff move." Kershaw stewed about it all offseason. There was a game the next summer when he was mowing down the opposition. His fastball hovered around 85 mph, but that was still faster than most amateurs could handle. Griffis was admiring the procession of outs when Kershaw drilled a hitter. Moments later, Kershaw picked the runner off first base.

"Clayton," Griffis asked later, "did you hit that guy on purpose?"

Kershaw offered a sheepish smile. "I just wanted to see if I could pick him off," he said.

There was a sense, among some of the other D-Bat players, that Kershaw registered the distance between himself and his celebrated peers. He understood he was pretty good. He wanted to be great.

*   *   *

Baseball revolves around failure. It is designed to break the heart of the fan, but it breaks the will of its participants first. Failure touches every player. They fail because of inability and they fail because of fragility and they fail because of temperament. The lucky few overcome those failures. The overwhelming majority do not. For those, the cruelty of the game is often not that they failed. It is that there were so many days when failure seemed so unlikely.

In the summer of 2005, at the Tournament of Stars in Joplin, there were a handful of boys who appeared untouched by failure. They were the sort of players other players whispered about. When they took batting practice or threw bullpen sessions, everyone gawked. "They almost take on a mythical quality when you see them walking around," recalled Lars Anderson, an outfielder from the Bay Area.

Brett Anderson (no relation to Lars) was one of those. Shawn Tolleson was another. So was Grant Green, who had just hit .455 as a junior in Anaheim. Marcus Lemon, a shortstop from Orlando whose father was All-Star outfielder Chet Lemon, had hit .489 as a junior. Max Sapp, a catcher with thunderous power, had played in international competitions since he was thirteen. The studs carried themselves "like gods on a baseball field," Lars Anderson recalled.

As the trials progressed, for some of the mortals, Kershaw took on a similar stature. Like Anderson, like Kershaw, like so many of the boys in Joplin, Dwight Childs quaked with nerves. Childs, a catcher from the Bay Area, felt his confidence resurface when he smashed a fastball from Kershaw foul down the third-base line. "Then he threw me the nastiest curve—I swear to God this thing touched the clouds and came back down to my knees," Childs recalled. "I had never seen a curveball like this. I don't think anybody had, at this point."

But the brilliance from Kershaw was only occasional. During the trials, Brett Anderson was warming up near Team USA head coach Jerry Dawson. Anderson's location was so precise that he apologized to his catcher for missing his spot. "And he only missed it a foot," Dawson recalled. "Wherever you put it, it was there." Kershaw could not do that. "He was good," recalled Brandon Belt, a left-handed pitcher from Lufkin, Texas. "But he wasn't like the Clayton Kershaw everybody knows now." To Dawson, his delivery looked rushed, with his legs lurching forward before his left arm was ready. "At that point, he was having trouble throwing strikes," Dawson said. "But the stuff was above and beyond."

Dawson was one of the more decorated high school coaches in America. He had been at Chaparral High School, in Scottsdale, Arizona, for more than thirty years. Chaparral had won the state title five of the previous seven years. "He was a ball of fire," recalled L. V. Ware, an outfielder from Atlanta. Dawson paid particular attention to appearance. He forbade eyeblack, sunglasses on the bills of caps, gloves dangling from pockets. He considered cutting Dellin Betances, a six-foot-eight New Yorker, because he wore his cap sideways, but eventually relented. Dawson had assisted the national team the previous year. In 2005, he was joined by Hisey, a former minor-leaguer who was the pitching coach at Pima Community College in Tucson. The coaches sketched out a pitching staff for the tournament in Mexico. They determined Anderson should headline the rotation. The next man up was Tyson Ross, a six-foot-five right-hander from Oakland. He was a month older than Kershaw but a grade ahead. He had left freshman orientation at the University of California at Berkeley to attend the trials. Ross had played for Team USA the summer before, with a group that featured future All Stars Andrew McCutchen, Buster Posey, and Justin Upton. "Brett Anderson and Tyson were dominant," Ware recalled.

Rounding out the rotation were Betances, Kershaw, and Josh Thrailkill, a right-hander from North Carolina. Tolleson loomed as a multiple-inning relief weapon. Team USA officials could not envision a similar role for Kershaw. They had watched his pregame routine. It was a forty-five-minute ritual, meticulous in detail, but problematic in practice. "Because we can't do all this rigmarole, coming into the sixth inning," Darwin recalled.

After a week in Joplin, USA Baseball officials culled the group to forty. Those forty played another week of games. That group winnowed to twenty-six. The players dispersed to California and Miami and Texas. In late August, the team reconvened in Cobb County, Georgia, just north of Atlanta. There was another round of games against local kids and Team Canada. From there, Team USA finalized its twenty-man roster. The team bussed to the Atlanta airport. Kershaw had taken a handful of flights in his life. He was leaving the country for the first time, in a peculiar role that felt familiar: He was one of the best pitchers in America. But other boys were better.

*　　*　　*

A police escort greeted Team USA at Villahermosa International Airport. The early September heat felt oppressive as the players boarded buses bound for Villahermosa, the capital of Tabasco, hard by the Gulf of Mexico. At the hotel, kids pounded the sides of the bus. Dawson advised the players to sign autographs for children but not for adults. The atmosphere at the opening ceremony at Estadio Centenario was raucous. Police clutched AK-47s and AR-15s atop the dugouts, several players recalled. "Like, 'Am I in the Beatles right now?'" recalled Lars Anderson.

For the Americans, the environment presented more challenges than most of the opponents. USA Baseball officials fretted about rebels ignoring Dawson's curfew. They worried about rain disrupting the schedule. And then, of course, "You're always fighting the food battle when you go to those places," Hisey recalled. This was long before the days of meal prep and carefully plotted diets. Team USA gorged on chips and salsa for breakfast. After games, they devoured Domino's pizza, ferried to the hotel by a guy with a heater on the back of his moped. A few took advantage of the drinking age, which was eighteen. Others indulged in more mundane ways. Tolleson guzzled Fanta "like it was water," he recalled. Kershaw, Tolleson, and Brett Anderson ventured outside the hotel for street-cart tacos. They managed to avoid the batches that waylaid their teammates. "Oh my gosh, the street tacos just wrecked you," recalled Greg Peavey, a pitcher from the suburbs of Portland, Oregon. "They were good going down. And then about an hour later, you were done." The gastrointestinal distress was not limited to players. "I lived the last four or five days of that tournament on Imodium, pretty much," Hisey recalled. By the end, most of the traveling party subsisted on jars of peanut butter and jelly brought by Darwin.

The conditions were not ideal. Dawson spent one afternoon throwing batting practice behind a chain-link L-screen. The grass at one site looked "like it hadn't been cut in years," Ware recalled. To ready the field after one rain-drenched afternoon, stadium workers hauled canisters of gasoline and lit home plate on fire. The flames helped the grass dry. "And instantly, it was like, 'Play ball!'" Tolleson recalled. "I was like, 'We should remember that.'"

Kershaw tagged along with Tolleson "like a puppy dog," Darwin recalled. They passed the time kicking the Hacky Sack with Anderson and reading the Bible. They talked about what they might do in the Big 12 after graduation—even if all three hoped to go in the first round rather than to college. Kershaw could see why their hopes seemed more realistic than his own. When he watched how Anderson located, when he saw how Tolleson dominated, he noted where he could improve. "I always played with guys who were better than me," Kershaw recalled. "I think that's good. At the end of the day, it's good not to be the best all the time."

For the first week of the tournament, he watched his peers squash the competition. Dawson built his rotation so Anderson and Ross would be available for the finals. Kershaw slotted into the fourth spot. He passed the time in the bullpen. The boys ripped farts and cracked jokes. Tolleson amused the gang with his double-jointed elbows. "I think we lit someone's cleat on fire," Childs recalled.

The rain washed away Kershaw's start against Brazil. The game was rescheduled three days later. Kershaw lasted only four innings. He gave up three hits and walked four batters. It was the same story as the trials. He threw with a three-quarters arm angle that taxed his elbow. His delivery lacked consistency. Sometimes all the pieces clicked into place. And other times, his body moved too quickly. He looked skittish compared to Anderson, who struck out twenty-four of the fifty batters he faced in the tournament. A day after Kershaw pitched, Anderson gave up an early run against Panama. In the dugout, Anderson flung his glove against the wall and unleashed "probably fifteen of the most beautifully strung together profanities you could ever ask to hear from anybody," Dawson recalled. Dawson turned to his hitting coach: "If you can score two runs, this game's over." Team USA scored seven. Panama did not score again.

Kershaw watched Ross start the gold-medal game against Cuba from the bullpen. Team USA had not lost in the competition. The group had beaten Cuba a week earlier. But late in the game, the Cubans picked off a runner at second base and then manufactured the go-ahead run when they came up to bat. Dawson got ejected. He was never sure why. The language barrier did not help. (It should be noted that Dawson harbored congenital distaste for umpires. "I despise them all," said Dawson, who was still coaching at Yavapai College in Prescott, Arizona, in 2023.)

The Americans lost, 2-1. The adults took the defeat the hardest. The players were eager to return to the States with memories and souvenirs. After the game, the Americans traded gear with the Cubans. More than a decade later, Tolleson and Ware still hung Team Cuba jackets in their closets. Most of the players returned to the hotel. A few broke the curfew one last time. The next morning, at the airport, Darwin wished them the wisdom gleaned from the hangovers of youth. Back home, school had already begun. Ross would begin his freshman year at Berkeley. Most would be high school seniors: Kershaw in Highland Park, Anderson in Stillwater, Tolleson in Allen. They overflowed with wonder about what the next year might hold, and all the years thereafter.

"You knew that probably the majority of that group was going to be major-leaguers, like they always are with USA Baseball," Hisey recalled. "But you just never know what's inside of somebody. You always wonder: who has that X-factor?"

* * *

Seventeen years later, two alums stood ninety feet apart, inside Highland Park's indoor facility. Kershaw hopped forward and hurled the baseball. The throw went awry, a rarity even in this setting. Anderson jumped to catch it.

"Woo!" Kershaw said. "Nice!"

"Tore my rotator," Anderson deadpanned.

The two men finished and walked off the field. Kershaw attached an electronic stim machine to his left biceps. Anderson sank along the wall. He had played for thirteen seasons and made nearly $60 million despite a series of significant injuries. He talked about showcasing himself for professional scouts that winter. But he did not play in 2023.

While the minor-leaguers kept throwing, Kershaw and Anderson shared some laughs. I asked what they were trying to accomplish this early in the winter.

"Just to see how bad it hurts," Kershaw said.

They were young men with aged bodies. Both understood that every toss could be his last. Anderson had undergone Tommy John surgery and a pair of taxing back surgeries. Kershaw ended most seasons with debilitating pain. Every professional pitcher is an hourglass. Most of their sand had filtered to the bottom.

CHAPTER 5

1-2-3

On a January afternoon in 2006, Seattle Mariners scout Mark Lummus answered his phone and scoffed at an invitation to witness history. On the other end of the line was Skip Johnson, a coach at Navarro College in Corsicana, Texas. Johnson asked Lummus to come to the D-Bat facility in Addison, more than an hour north of Lummus's home in Cleburne. In the winter, Johnson moonlighted giving lessons. He was gaining a reputation as "a pitching whisperer," Lummus recalled, and wanted to show off his latest pupil.

"Skip, no," Lummus said. "I'll see him when the season starts."

Like plenty of scouts in the area, Lummus thought he knew about Clayton Kershaw. Good kid. Still pudgy. Decent fastball, big curveball. Not enough strikes. "He was a guy to keep tabs on," Lummus recalled, not much more. Lummus had played at the University of Texas with J. D. Smart, who was Kershaw's advisor. (To protect NCAA eligibility, agents were called "advisors.") Smart had been in his ear, too. Lummus was skeptical. In his estimation, Kershaw needed to sharpen his game in college.

Lummus oversaw eleven states for the Mariners. His time was precious. But Johnson insisted. The two friends trusted each other. Lummus perked up when Johnson referenced Seattle's place in the draft that June.

"Y'all pick in the top ten, right?" Johnson said. "Then you need to come see him."

"To see Kershaw?" Lummus said.

"Mark," Johnson said. "You need to come see this."

* * *

Arthur Ray Johnson was present at the creation of Clayton Kershaw's greatness. He did not inspire it. He did not sustain it. He did not brew the cocktail of anxiety and restlessness and desire that elevated Kershaw above his peers in the class of 2006. But Johnson, known as "Skip" since boyhood, was the man who unlocked the door for Kershaw. He shaped the delivery that tormented generations of big-league hitters.

They met before Kershaw's senior season at Highland Park. The weight of responsibility hung on Kershaw's shoulders. The draft was drawing closer. If he played well, he could net a signing bonus that could pay off his mother's debts. If he stumbled in his final year—or even worse, if he got hurt—his next step was less clear. Against that backdrop, Clayton and Marianne welcomed a procession of agents into their home. They hired Smart, a former big-league pitcher who worked with Hendricks Sports Management, the firm that represented Texas legends Roger Clemens and Andy Pettitte.

To Kershaw, part of Smart's appeal was "he seemed like the most normal of the people." Smart also understood Kershaw's financial situation. When Kershaw met with a representative of the high-powered baseball attorney Scott Boras, he was turned off by the suggestion that he attend college. The request was reasonable: most teams disliked offering sizable bonuses to high school pitchers. Boras had negotiated a $3.55 million deal for Wichita State pitcher Mike Pelfrey in 2005—the third-richest bonus in the draft, despite Pelfrey going ninth overall to the Mets. For amateur pitchers, many in the industry believed, the path to a life-changing bonus wended through college.

Kershaw did not think he could wait. "His mom was so nervous that he was not going to get a scholarship," D-Bat coach Ken Guthrie recalled. Her son felt the same anxiety. He recognized he could not afford to live far from home. Stanford offered him a 90 percent scholarship, but for the Kershaws, 10 percent of life in Palo Alto was too pricey. His recruitment boiled down to Texas A&M and Oklahoma State. Each extended Kershaw a full ride, a relative rarity for college baseball. Frank Anderson offered Kershaw a scholarship at a tournament in Stillwater, Oklahoma, in the summer of 2005. Kershaw opted to sign with A&M. He discussed rooming with Britton. A&M coach Rob Childress had an unexpected ally: the Melsons were Aggies. Jed and Ann had loved College Station. Ellen had her heart set on the same. Clayton committed to joining her—even if he wasn't sure he would ever make it to campus. "Even with a full scholarship, I didn't know how I was going to be able to go to college," Kershaw recalled. "There's stuff that costs money at college."

Every spring, top high school prospects confer with their advisors to set a price for their services. Advisors used colleges as leverage: *If you don't hit this number, my client is headed to the SEC.* But if you enrolled in a four-year school, you were not eligible to return to the draft for three seasons. So Kershaw asked Smart to bluff. He would accept any reasonable six-figure offer. If none came, Kershaw considered forgoing A&M for a junior college, where he could become eligible for the draft again in 2007.

Early in the season, Kershaw remained a second-tier prospect. "I never would have guessed he would do what he's done," recalled former Texas Rangers scout Randy Taylor. In December, *Baseball America* published a list of the top high school players. Jordan Walden, the 99-mph man, ranked No. 1. Brett Anderson landed at No. 3. Shawn Tolleson was No. 12. Kershaw landed at No. 32, in between a right-handed pitcher from Alabama named Cory Rasmus and a shortstop from Miami named Ryan Jackson. If he stayed healthy, he would be drafted. But there were dozens of kids ahead of him, plus an entire crop of college players. He was facing an uphill climb toward stabilizing Marianne's finances. Around the time *Baseball America* printed that list, Smart rang Arthur Ray Johnson.

*   *   *

"'I'm not the best pitching coach," Johnson insisted in January of 2023. "Don't get me wrong. I'm not sitting here blowing smoke, like I'm somebody."

Johnson spent years on the fringes. He grew up in Denton. He played for three small colleges in Texas. After earning a master's degree in education, he took over the Navarro program in 1994. He offered lessons to any kid old enough to wear a glove. He insisted he was unsure of his prowess as a coach until a few years later, when he plugged into his VCR a tape of Brad Hawpe, a pitcher he had been tutoring.

Holy shit, Johnson told himself as he rewound the footage, *look how much better he got.*

Hawpe spent nearly a decade in the majors, but as a hitter. Johnson had a more profound effect on the boy he met at Smart's request at D-Bat. Kershaw benefited from the wisdom Johnson had osmosed during his years coaching at every age level. Kershaw's path to the Hall of Fame began, in a sense, with an exercise Johnson devised for children. "It's probably the best drill to do for Little Leaguers," Johnson recalled. It was called the 1-2-3 drill. For years, Kershaw had thrown with his left arm lowered about 50 degrees, known as a three-quarters arm angle. A lot of lefties threw like that. It deceived hitters. It also hurt his arm while limiting his velocity. Johnson wanted Kershaw to elevate his arm closer to his head and use his six-foot-four frame to his advantage. Johnson told Kershaw to act like his hands and his right leg were attached by a string. With every pitch, Kershaw gripped the baseball in his left hand, tucked inside the glove covering his right. When his hands rose, so should the leg: one. When his hands descended, the leg would follow: two. Only then, Johnson instructed, should Kershaw's left hand leave the glove: three.

Kershaw practiced until his muscles absorbed the memory. Up. Down. Break. Up. Down. Break. One. Two. Three. His hands reached to the sky and his right knee ascended to his chest. When his knee straightened and lowered toward the ground, his hands followed suit and arrived at his chest. Only then did the two halves move in separate directions: he pulled the baseball from his glove with his left hand and swept it behind his left ear as his right leg stretched as far it could stretch toward the plate. The radar gun registered the difference: his fastball cracked the 90-mph barrier—and his arm didn't hurt. "It felt more effortless," he recalled. Kershaw repeated the movement in front of a mirror in his home. He practiced in the hallway at school. Up. Down. Break. Up. Down. Break. One. Two. Three.

The 1-2-3 drill mended another flaw. When scouts and Team USA officials watched Kershaw the summer before, he rushed to the plate, which sent fastballs flying out of control. The wildness reduced when he followed Johnson's blueprint. His two halves moved in concert, sharpening his command and improving his velocity. It was a remarkable tweak. It also gave him a trademark. "Skip was the inventor of the gathering pause that he has," Highland Park teammate Will Skelton recalled. To maintain his balance, at the end of the 1-2-3, Kershaw held himself in place, right foot in the air, momentarily frozen. In that instant, the baseball disappeared from the eyeline of hitters, only to emerge in a blur from behind his head.

In another drill, Johnson handed Kershaw a hockey puck. He told Kershaw to throw a curveball with it. Johnson emphasized two points: set in the back, throw it out front. The switch taught Kershaw "to throw with sick spin," Johnson recalled. Rather than bend, the curveball began to snap. Imagine a clock: the ball started at twelve and plunged to six, movement that could not be generated from Kershaw's old arm slot.

In Kershaw, Johnson found an eager pupil. But he did not find a wealthy one. After the first session, Kershaw pulled Johnson aside. "Skip," Kershaw told him, "I can't pay for a pitching lesson." Johnson told Kershaw to pay what he could, when he could. Johnson stuck to his word. "His dad gave me twenty dollars one time," Johnson recalled. "That was about it." And so Johnson trekked about an hour north from

Corsicana, twice a week, week after week, to sculpt Kershaw for free. "That's what we do," Johnson recalled. "That's what we're in coaching for." Johnson met Kershaw about fifteen times that winter. The sessions were a revelation. "Man," Kershaw recalled, "it just all came together." He elevated his arm angle, which lessened the strain. He found balance on the mound, which created more strikes. And his velocity rose, which figured to impress scouts. "It was like we were shooting skeet in the building, he was throwing so hard," Johnson recalled.

A month into the lessons, Johnson decided Kershaw was ready for an audition. He thought about Mark Lummus, who was helping Seattle decide about the fifth pick in the draft. Johnson gave his pal a call.

*   *   *

When Lummus pulled into D-Bat that January evening, he discovered Johnson had also invited Yankees scout Mark Batchko. The audience was still small. Lummus walked past an indoor soccer game until he found Johnson, Kershaw, Batchko, and a catcher, with Marianne watching in the wings.

The first thing Lummus noticed was the sound. The fastball exploded into the catcher's mitt, like a cannonade echoing off the walls. Up. Down. Break. Up. Down. Break. One. Two. Three. Lummus watched Kershaw pump strikes. "Do you want to throw some curveballs?" Johnson asked. Kershaw toed the rubber and unleashed one. Lummus listened as the pitch hissed through the air "like a buzzsaw." It possessed the sort of violent beauty that made jaded lifers swoon.

"Do it again," Johnson said.

Kershaw snapped off another.

And another.

And another.

Lummus noted the joy on Johnson's face, the bashful thrill emanating from Kershaw, the smile from his mother. Lummus pulled Johnson aside, eager to share his excitement and loose command of art history.

"This must have been what it was like to watch Da Vinci paint the Sistine Chapel," Lummus said.

Lummus looked down at his own arm. The hairs were standing up.

* * *

On the drive home, Lummus started making calls. He was enthralled with Kershaw—but he understood it would be hard to sell his superiors.

The Mariners had finished in last place in the American League West for two consecutive seasons. The team had not reached the post-season since 2001. Scouting director Bob Fontaine Jr. felt pressure from his boss, general manager Bill Bavasi, who felt pressure from his boss, CEO Howard Lincoln. Seattle "was trying to get back to winning ways as quickly as possible," Fontaine recalled. The No. 5 pick could not be a teenager who needed several years of minor-league apprenticeship. Lummus knew this. But what he had seen, inside that facility in Addison, made him think Kershaw might not be a project.

"I honestly think," Lummus told Mariners officials later that year, "that this guy has a chance to be as good as, if not the best, pitcher that's ever come out of the state."

* * *

In early February, another scout arrived in Texas. He checked into the Marriott near the Dallas–Fort Worth airport. Logan White, the scouting director for the Los Angeles Dodgers, did not intend to stay long. He had come to watch two pitchers. He was considering selecting either of them with the seventh pick in the draft.

White climbed into a car with Calvin Jones, his eyes and ears on the ground in the area. The two men had played together in Seattle's minor-league system. They spent a year riding buses through the Midwest and then another rumbling across California. White peaked in class-A baseball. Jones pitched two seasons in the majors. The Dodgers hired White to run the draft in 2001. A few years later, White hired Jones to scout Texas.

The first kid they saw was Jordan Walden, the right-handed stud from D-Bat. White watched Walden jump off the mound and wondered how he could stick as a starter. "Jordan Walden," White recalled, "had a rough delivery." High school hitters couldn't handle it—but maybe Walden's body couldn't handle it, either. The risk felt significant.

A day later, White and Jones drove an hour east, toward Terrell, Texas. Highland Park was scrimmaging there. A collection of rival scouts crowded behind the plate. On the field, Kershaw was doing his rigorous stretching routine. White slinked to the bullpen to watch. Later in life, as he reflected on that first look, White wondered if he merely served as an instrument of God, as if divine forces used him to deliver Kershaw to the Dodgers. Because after only a handful of pitches, White experienced a sensation akin to what Lummus felt.

"It doesn't happen very often," White recalled, "where your whole being, your whole being, just tells you, 'This guy is a dude. This guy is for real.'"

Kershaw threw only a handful of innings. He still lost the handle on the curveball. His delivery still looked stranger than the textbook recommendation. White could live with those imperfections. On the drive out of Terrell, the scouting director turned to his fellow former Wausau Timber.

"Man," White told Jones, "we've got to stay on top of this guy."

He wondered if he had seen the future of his franchise.

CHAPTER 6

SENIOR YEAR

A preseason story in the *Dallas Morning News* outlined the stakes for Clayton Kershaw's senior year at Highland Park. The team had a chance to go to the state tournament and Kershaw had a chance to break Xerxes Martin's school record of thirty-one career victories. He was part of a Highland Park pitching lineage that included Martin, right-hander Zane Carlson, and San Diego Padres starter Chris Young. Kershaw, wrote Tim MacMahon, "might be the best of them all." Kershaw told MacMahon he hoped to turn pro: "If it's the right situation, I wouldn't hesitate."

Early that spring, Kershaw and Patrick Halpin played catch at Scotland Yard. Halpin knew his pal had played ball all across North America that summer, and he knew Kershaw had taken pitching lessons during the winter. The progress remained hidden until Kershaw reared back and fired.

"I could tell that something was different," Halpin recalled. "In our little long-toss warmups, he was throwing it on a rope from the center-field wall."

The difference looked even more noticeable during Kershaw's bullpens. No longer did his fastball hover in the upper 80s. "Somebody gets a gun out there, like, 'Oh, my God, this is like 89 mph, touching 90, 91 every now and then,'" Halpin recalled. "All of a sudden, it's like, 93 to 95 mph."

Before he departed for spring training with the Padres, Young ventured to his alma mater, his six-ten frame conspicuous in the stands as he watched Kershaw pitch. "I could tell how electric the ball was," Young recalled. Over in Allen, Shawn Tolleson started to hear rumors. He watched a game at Highland Park, marveling at his friend: "I was like, 'Wow, what happened to you, in one winter?'"

* * *

Seen from a distance, through the dually intensifying perspectives of hindsight and nostalgia, Clayton Kershaw's senior season at Highland Park High unfolded like a dream.

He never lost a start. The alterations made by Skip Johnson led to devastation for opposing hitters. "My senior year, I don't know if there was a time that I threw harder in my life," Kershaw recalled. His statistics were astounding. He finished with an 0.77 ERA. He struck out more than two batters per inning. He pitched a perfect game in which he punched out every hitter. He made a steady ascent from intriguing arm to fringe first-rounder to a player worth evaluating by the team with the No. 1 overall pick. He made Mark Lummus's proclamation about his place in Texas history look reasonable.

But it was also a year in which Kershaw grappled with concerns about his performance, his health, and his finances. The pressure that had been building since he was a freshman only heightened. *This isn't just a game anymore,* he recalled thinking. *This could be my future.* When he became a star in the major leagues, his predilection for start-day turkey sandwiches served as an amusing quirk. But the reason Kershaw visited the local shop New York Sub for pregame meals was more elemental. "A turkey sandwich is the easiest thing to eat," he recalled. His nerves muted his appetite. On the day of his starts, usually on Friday evenings, he shuffled through the halls in a daze. "I had to go to class and take tests and quizzes, and I was like, 'Golly, I don't want to be here,'" he recalled.

Most of his friends and teammates only saw the image he projected: John Wayne on the mound, a goofball off it. A few of his closest pals understood his financial precarity. "My mom had borrowed money from friends of mine's parents," Kershaw recalled. "Which sucks, right?" The situation impacted his psyche. "They would have to ask people for things," Ellen recalled. "And I think that Clayton immediately, at a young age, just kind of felt this shame and this feeling of, 'What if I can never pay them back?'" Kershaw understood that the debts would have to be repaid through whatever money he made in the draft. "I knew I would need to help," he recalled. "But I didn't realize the extent of how much it was."

And so Clayton Kershaw's senior season at Highland Park High unfolded like a dream—and also as a window into the future. That season marked the first time Kershaw shouldered, in full, the burden of greatness. The weight would stay there for the entirety of his professional life.

"I think that's where all the nerves and pressure came," he recalled. "It meant a lot."

*   *   *

Deric Ladnier, the scouting director for the Kansas City Royals, owners of the No. 1 pick in the draft, stood on the bleachers above the Highland Park bullpen, staring down at Clayton Kershaw. On a rainy day in Dallas, the picture before him was clear. The fastball crackled with life. But it did not always arrive where the catcher set the mitt. The curveball was engrossing. But sometimes it bounced. "He was not an elite strike thrower," Ladnier recalled. "But he was an elite stuff guy." Ladnier watched Kershaw's delivery, the 1-2-3 movement that could be so captivating, and wondered where it might go wrong.

The Royals were in turmoil, spiraling toward another hundred-loss season. The team had not made the postseason since 1985. Owner David Glass decided to replace general manager Allard Baird with Braves executive Dayton Moore on May 31, a week before the draft. Ladnier remained in charge of the proceedings. His task required him to select a player who could aid the big-league club in the immediate future.

When it came to Kershaw, the reward was obvious. But so was the risk.

The Major League Baseball draft is far more volatile than its football and basketball counterparts. In those sports, if a top pick flames out, the offending franchise absorbs a lifetime of ridicule. Ryan Leaf and Darko Miličić became household names. You heard far less about Jeff Austin (MLB's No. 4 overall pick in 1998, the year Leaf signed with San Diego) or Kyle Sleeth (the No. 3 pick in 2003, the year the Detroit Pistons chose Miličić over Carmelo Anthony). The developmental path of amateur baseball players was less linear than in other sports: injuries were common, the professional schedule was more rigorous, and young players needed to learn to adapt from failure. The process was hard to predict.

And there was no athlete more volatile than a pitcher coming out of high school.

From 1996 to 2000, twelve high school pitchers were taken in the top ten. Nine never reached the majors. Josh Beckett—the No. 2 overall pick in 1999 who led the Florida Marlins to the World Series in 2003—was the exception. The rule applied to flameouts like Geoff Goetz and Josh Girdley and Bobby Bradley. To select a high school pitcher that early in the draft, many evaluators believed, felt like packing millions of your team's budget into a barrel and dropping a match. The first round of the 2002 draft featured four prep pitchers who became All Stars. But as scouts filed reports for the 2006 draft, the progress of the three pitchers selected ahead of that quartet loomed as a warning. Cincinnati had taken California righty Chris Gruler at No. 3. Baltimore chose Canadian righty Adam Loewen next. Montreal picked Texan Clint Everts at No. 5. Only a few years later, all three looked like busts. "If you get the right one, they usually end up being stars," Ladnier recalled. "But the probability of getting the right one is very slim."

Ladnier had gotten one of the right ones only a few years before. In the spring of 2002, Ladnier recalled, Baird wanted a college pitcher. After Ladnier saw Zack Greinke, a preternaturally polished right-hander from the suburbs of Orlando, he told his boss, "You're getting one. He's just eighteen years old." Ladnier could not offer the same assurance about Kershaw. Greinke repeated his delivery with metronomic precision. "It was like watching Greg Maddux pitch in high school," Ladnier recalled. But Kershaw? Ladnier wasn't sure he would throw enough strikes. And the allure of the other pitchers in the draft was strong.

The incoming class of college pitching looked like one of the best in recent memory. Andrew Miller, an imposing lefty from the University of North Carolina, won the Roger Clemens Award, college baseball's equivalent of the Cy Young. The other finalists included University of Houston lefty Brad Lincoln, who won the Dick Howser Award as the collegiate player of the year. The Golden Spikes Award went to a slender dynamo from the University of Washington named Tim Lincecum.

Even the players without hardware were impressive. Stanford righty Greg Reynolds intrigued evaluators with his six-foot-seven frame. Brandon Morrow, a right-hander from the University of California at Berkeley, "had one of the best true arms I've ever seen on a kid," Mariners scouting director Bob Fontaine recalled. The University of Missouri boasted Max Scherzer, a combative right-hander who mostly threw fastballs. There was also Miller's Tar Heel teammate Daniel Bard, University of Southern California righty Ian Kennedy, and University of Nebraska righty Joba Chamberlain.

And there was Luke Hochevar, who was pitching for an independent team in Fort Worth. A year earlier, he thought he was going to sign with the Dodgers. His saga toppled the first domino in a series of events that led to Clayton Kershaw falling into Logan White's lap. It was the sort of sequence that fortifies a man's belief in the divine. "To me," White recalled, "it was all part of God's plan, for him to be there."

* * *

Logan White made his living with his eyes. But as a child, he relied upon his hands. He once told a reporter he started working in the fourth grade. He washed dishes and swabbed bathrooms for $0.75 an hour. As he grew older, he baled hay and cleaned pigpens near his home in Portales, New Mexico. Even if he worked only two hours, his parents could use the money. His father roped cattle. He also played guitar and drank. His drinking worsened as White grew older. He took out his anger on his wife. The abuse lingered in White's memory. He pushed himself to succeed by thinking of his mother. He did not want to let her down.

Baseball took him to Western New Mexico University. Seattle chose him in the twenty-third round in 1984. He was a right-handed reliever with decent size but not much else. He wrecked his arm chasing his dream. He underwent six separate surgeries. The Mariners hired him to scout. He climbed the ladder: area scout for the Orioles, West Coast supervisor for the Padres, back to Baltimore for the same job. In December of 2001, Dodgers general manager Dan Evans named White as scouting director, the man in charge of running the draft.

In his years of apprenticeship, White developed a straightforward but challenging mandate: take the player with the highest ceiling who can get to the big leagues the quickest and stay the longest. This was not particularly easy to accomplish. It was the draft's eternal struggle. The entire enterprise was a crapshoot, hardened baseball men liked to say. In the early 2000s, teams like the Oakland Athletics targeted older, more developed college players to reduce risk. Some evangelized that trend. White was not one of them.

When White joined the Dodgers, he felt required to target All-Stars, not role players. He also understood that the Dodgers would be a competitive club. The franchise had picked in the top ten only twice since 1990. So White studied the previous ten years of the draft, to figure out where the All-Stars had come from outside of the top ten. He found players like Scott Rolen (a second-round choice from Jasper High in Indiana) and Jimmy Rollins (a second-rounder from Encinal

High in Alameda, California). "We needed to be really good at knowing the high school talent," White recalled.

He conditioned his lieutenants to dream large. In the summer of 2005, White indulged in a fantasy of his own. He believed that he had nabbed one of the best pitchers in the draft despite not picking until fortieth. Luke Hochevar, a six-foot-five, 205-pound righty, had just struck out 154 batters in 139.2 innings with 2.26 ERA for the University of Tennessee. His exploits merited him the Roger Clemens Award. His main blemish, in the eyes of baseball executives, was something called "signability issues." In plain English, the problem was his representation. Scott Boras excelled at prying dollars out of the industry's billionaire ownership class. Those owners employed general managers and scouting directors to curb Boras's demands. In the days leading up to the draft, teams found the proposed price for Hochevar—a $4 million bonus and a major-league contract—to be excessive.

And so Hochevar tumbled out of the top five, out of the top twenty-five, all the way to the Dodgers at No. 40. White gambled that negotiations could bridge the divide between his team's interest and Hochevar's desires. The sum that separated the two sides was a relative pittance, with a $1.7 million difference between the Dodgers' initial $2.3 million offer and Hochevar's perceived asking price. The talks stalled until they spiraled. After months without progress, Hochevar fired Boras, hired a new agent, signed an offer sheet with a $2.98 million bonus, got spooked, rehired Boras, and backed out. The Dodgers honored Hochevar's cold feet. Hochevar accused White of taking advantage of him. "Not signing Hochevar was so stressful, so hard on my family," White recalled.

The dispute was still ongoing in the summer of 2006. By then, Dan Evans was no longer the general manager. He had been replaced by Paul DePodesta, a former Oakland executive hired by new owner Frank McCourt. The Dodgers won the National League West in 2004, DePodesta's first year at the helm. Things fell apart the next season: the team won only seventy-one games, its lowest total since 1992. DePodesta and manager Jim Tracy were fired. McCourt hired Ned Colletti, who had spent more than a decade with the San Francisco Giants, as general manager. The losing netted Colletti the No. 7 pick in the next draft, the team's highest pick since 1993. He also inherited Hochevar's draft rights. He would not meet Boras's demands. "Do I feel the talent is worth the asking price?" Colletti told the *Los Angeles Times*. "I don't agree."

The Dodgers let Hochevar reenter the 2006 draft. The strife represented a rare misstep for White. He kept running the Dodgers' draft, despite the changeovers in ownership and management, because of his success identifying future All-Stars. "Sometimes," recalled Roy Smith, the team's former vice president of scouting and player development, "you just have an eye." In *Baseball America*'s preseason top one hundred prospects list in 2006, five were high school players drafted by White: Chad Billingsley, Jonathan Broxton, Scott Elbert, Blake DeWitt, and Matt Kemp.

In the spring of 2006, White's scouts descended upon Highland Park. Calvin Jones, the area scout, monitored Kershaw all season. Tim Hallgren, one of White's national cross-checkers, had been smitten since a preseason scrimmage. Gary Nickels, the Midwest coordinator, raved about Kershaw's competitiveness. The young lefty reminded Nickels of another southpaw, Steve Carlton, who winnowed his focus into a tunnel, so that "the only thing he cared about was from his eyes to home plate, as wide as the strike zone," Nickels recalled.

The results were hard to ignore. Kershaw struck out eighteen when Highland Park played West Mesquite. In April, he surpassed Martin's school record for victories in a two-hit performance. Highland Park clinched a spot in the playoffs during a game in which Kershaw homered twice—and struck out seven in five innings. Kershaw started at first base on the days he didn't pitch. When he was on the mound, he rarely ran the bases. The rulebook permitted teams to use a designated runner: usually Josh Meredith, who was still basking in the glow of winning the state title alongside Matthew Stafford and the rest of the football team.

Kershaw was beginning to reckon with all that was expected of the exceptional. The attention from pro teams, the chants of "O-ver-rated" at road games, the newspaper clippings. He was becoming a singular figure—opponents weren't playing Highland Park; they were playing Clayton Kershaw. Blending in with his friends became difficult. The scouts came to see him. When he left the game, they left the stands. Each start felt like a referendum on his draft status. To soothe himself, he repeated a passage from Paul's Epistle to the Philippians: "Do not be anxious about anything, but in everything, by prayer and petition, with thanksgiving, present your requests to God."

For once, not even the Melsons could offer much guidance. "We're not baseball parents," Jim Melson recalled. "We didn't have a clue." Jim and Leslie were unsure what would happen in the draft. But their youngest daughter had an inkling.

"It wasn't until even second semester of our senior year, when the people started talking about him being bumped up in the draft, that it really started to resonate with me," Ellen recalled. "Like, 'Oh my gosh, I don't think we're going to be going to college together.'"

* * *

Kershaw registered his new place in the baseball landscape one afternoon that May. He was at a friend's house when he saw the May 8–21 issue of *Baseball America*. The magazine promised "Big Changes" in its pre-draft rankings. The biggest change: Kershaw had become the No. 1 high school prospect in the country. "I was like, 'Oh, that's cool,'" he recalled.

His friends and peers were ravaged by the vagaries of the game: injuries, ineffectiveness, and aesthetic biases. Jordan Walden pulled a groin muscle early in the year. He decided to keep pitching. His velocity dipped, and so did the corresponding opinion of his future. Brett Anderson suffered from the withering gaze of professional scouts. As a senior, he stood six-foot-four and weighed 215 pounds. Evaluators questioned his athleticism. The balletic precision he demonstrated in his delivery mattered less than the puffiness of his face. The scouts lowered his ceiling.

What happened to Shawn Tolleson was the most devastating. Kershaw and Tolleson had been walking parallel paths. Tolleson made the varsity team at Allen as a freshman and benefited from the seasoning before his body developed. He devoted his summers to baseball. He studied swings on the diamond and the Bible off it. He even committed to Baylor for the same reason Kershaw signed with Texas A&M: Tolleson's girlfriend, Lynley, was going there. Like Kershaw, though, Tolleson never wanted to reach campus. He debated his future often with his parents. His father ran a successful veterinary practice. The Tollesons cared about education. Tolleson burned to play baseball. Before the season, they made a compromise. If Shawn was selected in the early rounds, his parents would let him turn pro. "And so in my head, I was like, *Got to be a first rounder, I've got to be a first rounder,*" Tolleson recalled.

When the spring began, Tolleson believed he had a chance. Twenty-five scouts attended his first scrimmage. An even bigger crowd flocked to see Allen face the Woodlands, a suburban Houston powerhouse. The matchup pitted Tolleson against potential first-round pick Kyle Drabek. "That," recalled Paul Goldschmidt, the third baseman for the Woodlands, "was a big game." In the third inning, Tolleson felt an ominous pop in his elbow when he threw a slider. In his heart, he knew what had happened. But he didn't want to freak out the scouts. He pointed to his ankle. In his final act as a high school pitcher, Tolleson faked a limp as he left the diamond, desperate to fool the evaluators.

The ruse unraveled a couple of days later. An examination revealed Tolleson had torn his ulnar collateral ligament. He required Tommy John surgery. His senior year was over. His first-round dreams were dashed. "We all make plans in our life that never work out how we think they're going to work out," Tolleson recalled. In time, he considered this a blessing. In the moment, he felt only sorrow.

"I felt bad for him," Kershaw recalled. "I felt really bad for him." He also felt that, despite this setback, Tolleson would be okay. "Shawn came from a good family," Kershaw recalled. "And it wasn't, like, going to make or break his life, getting drafted." Kershaw did not believe he had the same luxury.

*   *   *

As they did with potential advisors earlier in the year, Marianne and Clayton invited big-league officials to their home during the season. Chris Kershaw stayed on the periphery; on occasion he quizzed scouts about his son, but he didn't attend the at-home visits. The industry could ding a prospect for an imperfect family life. Kershaw declined to sugarcoat his. "He acknowledged that it wasn't an ideal situation," Lummus recalled. "He made it very clear it wasn't the end of the world, in his eyes."

Marianne never asked about money, Lummus recalled. She peppered him with different questions: Where would Clayton live? Who handled transportation? How would the team monitor him in the winter? When Diamondbacks scout Trip Couch watched Kershaw pitch, he thought, *What is there not to like about this guy?* A visit to the Kershaw home confirmed his ardor. "They lived in a smaller home there in Highland Park," Couch recalled. "I just remember being blown away about what a great kid this was."

Not every team developed that impression. Fragments of the meetings stuck with Kershaw. A Florida Marlins scout chided him for wearing shorts and a T-shirt. "He was like, 'It's a bad representation of who you are,'" Kershaw recalled. "And I was like, 'No, this is who I am.' Some of those guys were just stupid." In a meeting with the Pittsburgh Pirates, who had the No. 4 pick, he fielded a question on the infield fly rule. "I was like, 'I know what it is. Why do you care?'" Kershaw recalled.

Kershaw thought Pittsburgh might take him. The team had emailed him a battery of questions, a common practice at the time. His eyes glazed during the questionnaire. "Probably toward the end of them, I was just, like, click, click, click," he recalled. At the meeting, the

Pirates told him he had flunked the exam. They worried he wasn't competitive enough. "They said I had conflicting answers," Kershaw recalled. "Sorry. What do you want me to do? I'm not going to retake it."

The Dodgers took a different approach. White never visited the Kershaw home. He did not speak to Clayton or Marianne. Besides one brief conversation with Chris Kershaw, he avoided contact with the family. "The last thing I need to do is create attention," White recalled, lest the six teams drafting ahead of him wonder why the Dodgers were so hyped about this teenager with an unorthodox delivery. Calvin Jones made a brief at-home pitch. After exchanging pleasantries, he asked if Kershaw would sign if the Dodgers chose him in the first round. Kershaw said he would. Jones thanked the family for their time and left. The meeting lasted five minutes, Kershaw estimated. "I was like, 'Wow, you guys get it,'" he recalled.

J. D. Smart tried to prep Kershaw for the financial ramifications of his status. "How much would it take for you to sign?" Smart asked one afternoon over burgers at a local institution called Chips. Not much, Kershaw responded. "Enough to cover this lunch," he said. Smart relayed how much money Kershaw might merit if he went in the first round: $1.5 million. Kershaw felt his eyes well up. The sum astounded him. "I was like, 'Oh my, that's incredible. Take it!'" he recalled.

Kershaw's advisors conducted their own reconnaissance. Alan Hendricks called Logan White. They engaged in a typical conversation for that time of year, two seasoned fellows fishing for information, keeping it casual, toeing the line between candor and caginess. Hendricks mentioned a few of his clients and asked White's opinion.

"What do you think of Kershaw?" Hendricks said.

White did not want to tip his hand. He also did not want to lie.

"Well, I like him," White said.

"You like him?"

"Alan," White said, "I would definitely take him with our twenty-sixth pick."

There was no reason to believe Kershaw would last that long—at least until his outing on April 28 against Forney. In the second inning, he felt something give in his left side. Six weeks away from the biggest moment of his life, Kershaw had done something he feared he could not afford to do. He got hurt.

*   *   *

For three weeks, Kershaw did not pitch. The injury was not serious; he had pulled an oblique muscle, or a "chublique," as he later put it. But the layoff lasted long enough to spark hope in Mark Lummus. He wondered if the injury might scare other teams, and somehow cause the kid to fall to Seattle's second-round pick at No. 49. He was curious to see how Kershaw responded when he returned to action on May 19.

The Scots hosted Northwest, a high school in Justin about thirty-five miles west, in the Class 4A regional semifinal. Texans coach Che Hendrix hoped a strict pitch count might limit his usage. The first inning inflated Hendrix's hopes. Kershaw was rusty and rushed, aware of the scouts, aware of the stakes, aware that a hiccup might cost hundreds of thousands of dollars. He stuck to fastballs. The Texans fouled off a bunch. All three at-bats ended in strikeouts, but they took a while. "I'm not sure he threw a ball the rest of the game," Hendrix recalled.

Kershaw struck out the side in the second. By the third, Hendrix's optimism had faded. His boys were getting overrun. They still hadn't put a ball in play. He barged out of the dugout to upbraid the umpire.

"Everything can't be a strike," Hendrix said.

The umpire was insistent: "Coach, I've never seen anything like it. Everything is a strike."

Hendrix deflated. "God dang it," he said. "That's what I figured."

Kershaw struck out everyone in the third. He struck out everyone in the fourth. In the bottom of the inning, he smashed a home run. Then he went back to striking everyone out. The game ended when Highland Park triggered the ten-run mercy rule in the fifth. That left Kershaw's line pristine and preposterous: a five-inning perfect game. He faced fifteen batters and struck out all fifteen. He had eradicated any concerns about his health—and any chance he might still be available in the second round.

*   *   *

In the days leading up to the Class 4A Region II semifinal at Dr Pepper Ballpark in Frisco, the home of the Rangers' double-A affiliate, Corsicana coach Tracy Wood recited a mantra about the upcoming opponent. "When you're on deck, start swinging," Wood recalled. Before the first pitch, Corsicana junior Stayton Thomas tried to time up the heater. He felt it was his only chance. Thomas had admired Kershaw from afar while playing for the age group behind him at D-Bat. "We knew he was about to be a millionaire," Thomas recalled.

Depending on who you believe, Thomas may have diminished Kershaw's first bonus. Kershaw was erratic at the outset. Thomas followed Wood's advice: he ignored the curveball and waited for a full-count fastball. Kershaw obliged. Thomas was ready. He blasted the ball beyond the 364-foot sign in left-center field. This would not be another perfect game. Corsicana dogged Kershaw all evening. So did their fans. He heard the familiar "O-ver-rated!" chants. His bat saved his arm. He delivered a game-tying single in the second and launched a fourth-inning homer. Kershaw picked off a runner to escape a fourth-inning jam. Highland Park won, 8-3.

The shakiness did not dissuade Logan White. "Clayton's such a competitor, when you tell him, 'Oh, you didn't throw as good in that game,' he gets pissed at me," White recalled. "But I'm like, 'Clayton, don't get mad. I know the scouts. I know what people saw.'" As the years passed, Dodgers scouts told stories about the whereabouts of Pirates executives on that evening. Some said Pirates general manager Dave Littlefield was in Houston, watching Brad Lincoln dice East Carolina. Others remembered him in attendance in Frisco, where Kershaw couldn't land his curveball. White recalled teasing John Green, a Pirates scout who shared his affinity for Kershaw, at the airport the next day. "Greeny!" White said. "Nice game to have your guy at."

(I contacted Littlefield in October 2022. "I received your email," he replied. "Nothing personal, but I'll pass on the conversation." I tried to reach Pirates scouting director Ed Creech. A person who identified himself as Creech's son responded and indicated his father, now in his seventies, was "retired and not too interested in discussing baseball lately." Green did not respond to a message.)

The tale became part of Dodgers scouting lore. But Thomas had never heard the story about the alleged significance of his homer. He cackled over the phone when told. "I apologize, Mr. Kershaw and family," said Thomas, who played in the minors with Tampa Bay before becoming a high school coach. "But I guess you're welcome, Dodgers fans."

*   *   *

Two days after Thomas went deep but Corsicana went home, three coaches from McKinney North, a school about thirty minutes from Highland Park, drove south down US Route 75. They pulled into a McDonald's near the highway. Brandon Milam gathered his assistants and went inside to meet Scots head coach Lew Kennedy.

The aroma of breakfast enveloped them: Egg McMuffins and sausage biscuits, pancakes and artificial syrup, families gathered to commune after church. "Everybody else is enjoying their coffee and we're sweating bullets," Milam recalled. The two teams had been unable to agree upon the terms of their upcoming matchup. The rules offered a choice: a one-game series or a three-game series. Kennedy wanted a one-game playoff with Kershaw on the mound. Milam wanted three games. They settled it the way they did these things in Texas. They flipped a coin. (A week earlier, Kennedy had met Wood, the Corsicana coach, at a gas station. "Well," Wood said after he lost the toss, "it's been a good year.")

Back in McKinney, Milam's wife, Lesley, had asked her Sunday school students to pray about the toss. Her husband pulled out his lucky quarter. He handed it to one of his assistants, Brooke Court. He asked his other assistant, Ricky Carter, to call it.

"Tails never fails," Carter said.

Court flicked the coin. Heads represented annihilation, a one-night stand with the best pitcher in the country. Tails represented salvation, in a series that at least gave McKinney North a chance. The coin clattered off the table and to the floor. The coaches ducked underneath the booth for the verdict.

Tails.

The McKinney North coaches felt giddy. Milam's gears turned. He had a pair of strong pitchers: Trent Appleby, a junior bound for Texas Christian University, and Michael Bolsinger, a senior who had played for D-Bat. The familiarity bred overconfidence. "I want Kershaw," Bolsinger told the coaches. Milam shot him down. He had a better idea.

* * *

On May 31, 2006, Clayton Kershaw loosened up in the Dr Pepper Ballpark outfield. He progressed through his pregame stretching routine for what could be the final start of his amateur career. On the other side of the diamond, trickery was afoot.

Milam carried with him two lineup cards: one if Kershaw pitched, and another if he didn't. Milam told Appleby to warm up. Milam expected Kershaw to start, but he trained his eyes on the opposing bullpen to be sure. When Kershaw picked up a ball, Milam activated a seldom-used sophomore named Bryan Kinard, who had been alerted earlier in the week to his assignment. "Coach Milan came up to me, and he was like, 'Oh, hey, by the way, you got the first game,'" Kinard recalled. "And I was just like, 'Hold up. What?'" The young man played a sacrificial role. Milam intended to save Appleby and Bolsinger for the next two games. Highland Park scored six runs in the top of the first. Once again, Kershaw failed to land his curveball for strikes. He walked four in five innings—but Highland Park activated the five-inning mercy rule, 13-1.

Kershaw never pitched as an amateur again. Milam's gambit worked. McKinney North took the next two games. Kershaw reckoned with the closing of a chapter. Josh and Patrick and all the other guys were bound for college. Kershaw was waiting for the draft, unsure about the next step, saddened that his senior year was over. When McKinney North spilled out of its dugout to celebrate, Kershaw felt humbled, sure that his team was the one that should be advancing. He watched a dog-pile form on the diamond. That scene would become hauntingly familiar.

* * *

In the Highland Park yearbook, Chris and Marianne placed an ad congratulating their son. They listed twenty-nine nicknames—like "bunny, baba, booger," "claytonga, claytonia, kersh," "beanie boy, little bud, and sweet baboo"—before reminding him, "You'll always be our Clayton." It featured eight pictures, including Clayton as a baby, Clayton in his football uniform, Clayton playing baseball. In one photo, preteen Clayton and Marianne shared identical smiles. In another, Chris held infant Clayton, clad in overalls. Chris was grinning.

The ad featured no photos of Chris and adolescent Clayton. The Wednesday night visits had stopped. So had the occasional weekends. Chris had remarried. He was less reliable, less gregarious in the recording studio. Chris had a place in the Park Cities, then in Richardson, then elsewhere. "My dad bounced around a lot," Kershaw recalled. His son did not follow him. "In high school, I remember it getting weirder, and not spending much time together," he recalled.

Marianne took out a separate ad.

Clayton, I am so proud of you.
You are my sunshine.
Love, Mom.

CHAPTER 7

THE DRAFT

On June 5, 2006, two days after Logan White Jr.'s eighth birthday and one day before the Major League Baseball Rule 4 draft, Logan White told his son his plan. All those hours projecting the future, all those miles in rental cars, all those nights in discounted Marriotts—they all pointed toward this moment. White illustrated the landscape for his boy. He wanted Clayton Kershaw. There were several teams in the way. He had heard the Detroit Tigers, picking one slot ahead of the Dodgers, were torn between Kershaw and University of North Carolina left-hander Andrew Miller. But Kansas City might use the No. 1 overall pick on Miller. So White asked for a favor: "When you go to bed tonight and say your prayers, say a prayer that Clayton can get to us."

The next morning, friends crowded into Kershaw's home. Ellen came with her parents. About a dozen people showed up, including Chris. As the Kershaws waited for the draft to begin, Dodgers officials assembled in a Dodger Stadium conference room. Kershaw was No. 1 on the department's board. The only other player White considered was Long Beach State third baseman Evan Longoria. But White did not expect Longoria to escape the top five.

If Kershaw was not available, White did not intend to dip into the pool of college pitching. Max Scherzer, the University of Missouri right-hander, was represented by Scott Boras, who had handled the disastrous negotiations with Luke Hochevar. White had also ruled out Tim Lincecum, the lithe, electric pitcher from the University of Washington. Earlier in the summer, White had asked Dodgers executive Roy Smith to scout Lincecum. Smith marveled at Lincecum's ability but worried how he would age. "I feel the same way," White replied.

A couple of days before the draft, White invited another pitcher to Dodger Stadium. Bryan Morris, a right-hander from Tennessee, had spent the season at a local junior college. "You're not supposed to have pre-draft deals," White recalled. "But if you word it in a certain way, it's fine." Through some artful linguistics, White hammered out a backup plan. White could spend $2.3 million on the No. 7 pick. Morris was willing to sign for $1.8 million. If someone chose Kershaw in the top six, White decided, the Dodgers would take Morris and redistribute the money elsewhere.

White conveyed the potential $500,000 discount to Ned Colletti. There was a discussion about the merits of saving the money. White stumped for choosing Kershaw. (Colletti said he did not recall a debate.) They came to an agreement. If Kershaw was there, he would be a Dodger.

But would he be there?

*   *   *

In 2006, there was another difference between MLB's draft and its equivalents in the NFL and NBA. It was not televised. Executives followed a rudimentary internet broadcast. They worked the phones, calling agents, calling players, calling colleagues. Tim Hallgren, a Dodgers scout, was connected with other clubs. His canvassing produced hope. It came from an unlikely source: Hochevar, the Dodger who never was.

The Royals had ruled out Kershaw earlier in the spring. "As much as I don't like to admit this, Clayton would not have been a factor for us, picking No. 1 in the country," scouting director Deric Ladnier recalled. They deliberated between Hochevar and Miller. When the Royals chose Hochevar, a door opened for the Dodgers: The Tigers would have to decide between Miller and Kershaw. And the better bet, the executives knew, was almost always on the college arm.

The next few picks went White's way. Colorado opted for six-foot-seven Stanford righty Greg Reynolds, whose career would be marred by shoulder injuries. R. J. Harrison chose third for the Tampa Bay Devil Rays. Harrison had scouted Kershaw twice. He saw the same things Ladnier saw, the allure and the inconsistency. He picked Longoria, who won the American League Rookie of the Year award in 2008 as the club evolved into a low-budget marvel. "There are some times you wake up in the middle of the night, in a cold sweat, wondering why you did something that didn't work out well," Harrison recalled. "In this case, I don't lose that much sleep. Because we picked a guy who ended up being the face of our franchise for ten years. As a scouting director, I probably never made a better pick."

The Pirates could not say the same. Owner Kevin McClatchy preferred college players to high schoolers, which handcuffed general manager Dave Littlefield. "Dave wasn't going to be able to take a high school pitcher," recalled one person familiar with the situation. Pittsburgh selected Brad Lincoln, the University of Houston pitcher. Later in his life, Kershaw pondered his good fortune in avoiding Pittsburgh. "I remember pitching one game and my curveball wasn't good, so that was, like, the final straw from them," he recalled. "So, great. I'm glad I'm not there."

Up next were the Mariners. The early insight gleaned by Mark Lummus did not outweigh the mandates from ownership. Bob Fontaine Jr., the scouting director, opted for Brandon Morrow, the pitcher from Cal. The choice agonized Lummus. But he understood. "He did the right thing," Lummus recalled.

The dominos had toppled exactly as White desired. Only Detroit stood between Kershaw and the Dodgers. "If Andrew Miller wouldn't have been there, Clayton Kershaw wouldn't have been a Dodger," former Tigers general manager Dave Dombrowski recalled. But Miller *was* there, in part because Hochevar had not signed the year before.

Six teams had the chance to take Kershaw. All six passed. The seventh would not.

A small bit of drama remained. White took a timeout, an option back in those days, to pause the clock for five minutes so he could haggle with Hendricks about a bit of contractual arcana that Dodgers owner Frank McCourt required and agents detested—a clause requiring a player to return his bonus if he quit the sport. Gary Nickels stayed on the phone with a Dodgers staffer posted by the fax machine. Once the paperwork came through, Nickels signaled to White. They were good to go. With the seventh pick in the 2006 draft, the Dodgers selected Clayton Kershaw, a left-handed pitcher from Highland Park High School in Dallas.

Moments later, the landline at Marianne Kershaw's house rang.

* * *

The phone kept ringing for a while. When Kershaw heard the news, he raised his arms to the sky. Rob Childress, the Texas A&M coach, called to bid his prized recruit farewell. Cade Griffis, the D-Bat owner, heard Kershaw's voice crack over the phone. Kershaw took a few more calls, absorbed some backslaps and high-fives. "A lot of happy tears," Patrick Halpin recalled. Then Kershaw celebrated with his friends: he might be a budding millionaire, but he still couldn't beat his pals in *Halo*.

The bliss was temporary. When Kershaw signed his first professional contract with the Dodgers, he received a $2.3 million bonus. He thought he was financially set for life. He felt, ever so briefly, a sense of relief. It did not last long. He could not believe how much he had to pay his agent. Then he had to square his mother's debts. Over the years, Kershaw learned, Marianne had borrowed about $15,000 from the parents of her son's friends. Clayton paid back the money. But the loans had stressed those relationships. Some of them fractured. Marianne still had bills to pay. His father also asked for help. Relief gave way to reality.

The stress crystallized something for Kershaw. He had strived toward this goal, the salvation of the draft. He had reached that goal. Out of all the boys who played high school baseball in 2006, Kershaw was the first one chosen. The draft deepened Kershaw's belief in God's providence. "That was when my faith started getting stronger, when I saw the fruits of that," he recalled. But he had not solved all of his family's problems.

Now, he told himself, *I've got to make it to the big leagues.*

* * *

Because Kershaw signed so quickly, the Dodgers wanted him to start pitching before the minor-league season ended. The franchise indoctrinated him into the organizational culture that summer. Two weeks after the draft, he was booked on a flight to Los Angeles.

As his departure neared, Kershaw was scrambling. "I didn't have a suitcase," he recalled. "Didn't have nothing." Leslie Melson came to his house bearing supplies. She purchased him new socks, new underpants, deodorant, toiletries. She packed them inside a new set of luggage. The Melsons bought Kershaw a laptop so he could chat with Ellen. Leslie gave him some cash, in case he needed it. "I don't know what I would have done without Ellen's parents packing me, basically," Kershaw recalled. The memory made Jim Melson blink back tears. "Leslie was the epitome of a mother," he recalled.

Kershaw said goodbye to Marianne and his friends. He was unsure when he would be home. Ellen was headed to summer classes at Texas A&M. They planned to reconnect when they could—whenever that was. Then he stepped out of his childhood and boarded a plane for the West Coast.

A whirlwind awaited him. In Los Angeles, he met another of the team's teenage first-round picks, Preston Mattingly, the son of the former Yankees star, Don. The two newfound professionals shared a car service to Dodger Stadium. They toured the clubhouse and the offices. They met Hall of Fame manager Tommy Lasorda and legendary broadcaster Vin Scully. Kershaw sat with Colletti, the mustachioed Chicagoan who ran the franchise's baseball operations department. Kershaw pulled a crisp Dodgers jersey over a baggy blue button-down while being introduced before a game. Mattingly gawked as he listened to Kershaw's stats. "I remember just looking over and being like, 'Oh my God. Who is this guy?'" Mattingly recalled.

The teenagers caught another flight. Kershaw and Mattingly had been assigned to the lowest domestic affiliate in the Dodgers system, the Gulf Coast League, on the east coast of Florida. Upon arrival, they hopped into a van and headed toward a sleepy town called Vero Beach. They rolled past palm trees and pulled into a parking lot. Kershaw carried a dream in his heart and a goal in his mind: he wanted to reach the majors by his twenty-first birthday. The first step came when he exited the van and set foot in Dodgertown.

*   *   *

Branch Rickey founded the place. In the late 1940s, Rickey, the Brooklyn Dodgers president, was searching for a training locale. A fellow named Bud Holman showed him an abandoned World War II naval station a few hours north of Miami.

"There among palms, palmettos, scrub pines, and swamp," Roger Kahn wrote in *The Boys of Summer*, "he made a world."

Rickey ordered the construction of baseball diamonds, batting cages, and sliding pits. Bullpen mounds sprouted across the facility. The barracks housed the entire crew. Rickey had devised the modern farm system; the spring-training complex was another innovation. It was a baseball paradise, but only in theory: Black players still dealt with the degradations of Jim Crow. Rachel Robinson, Jackie's wife, told Kahn about being barred from shopping with the white wives. Kahn once asked pitcher Joe Black, a Black man from New Jersey, how he felt about spring training in the South. "I can't tell you," Black said. "They won't let me in."

The legacy of Dodgertown was checkered. But it still served as part of the franchise's connective tissue. "Walking around Dodgertown," former Dodgers prospect Wesley Wright recalled, "it's like walking into history." Inside Championship Hall, a mural of World Series rings greeted visitors: "Six Dodger World Championship teams started here!" On an adjacent wall, the champions were listed: 1955, 1959, 1963, 1965, 1981, 1988. Young hitters like Mattingly took the same diamonds that Robinson and Pee Wee Reese and Duke Snider once graced. Young pitchers like Kershaw traced the steps of Sandy Koufax and Don Drysdale and Don Sutton. "You just think about all the greats who have been on that same field," former Dodgers prospect James McDonald recalled. By the time Kershaw and Mattingly arrived, the town had begun to show its age. On the drive from the airport, Kershaw noticed weathered street signs and scant traffic. He was entering an isolated, insulated world.

Kershaw roomed with Kyle Smit, a skinny fifth-rounder from just outside Reno, Nevada. Smit was a quiet kid, overwhelmed by the transition. He had never spent much time on his own. He found his new roommate to be friendly. Smit was not awed by Kershaw's stature, mostly because he wasn't aware of it. "I actually had no idea," Smit recalled. "I didn't really find out until like two weeks in. I was like, 'Holy shit. He's legit.'" By that point, Smit recognized that Kershaw operated on a different plane. "I just showed up and played," Smit recalled. Kershaw conducted his lengthy stretching routine before he threw. In between outings, he studied the primitive hitting charts of opponents. He looked comfortable clanging and banging in the weight room. He never appeared to tire. "He was way above everybody else, way above me," Smit recalled.

The minor-league system functioned as a thresher. There was precious little wheat and an abundance of chaff. Almost all of the players who wore uniforms and called themselves professionals would never appear in the big leagues. In the majors, salary created the distinction between stars and scrubs. In the minors, where teams like the Dodgers paid all Gulf Coast League players about $300 a week, the caste system developed based upon a player's signing bonus. In the summer of 2006, Kershaw stood atop the pyramid in Vero Beach. He had received the largest bonus in Dodgers franchise history. Mattingly signed for $1 million. The prices shriveled in the later rounds. Selected 136 picks after Kershaw, Smit drew a $175,000 bonus. Trayvon Robinson, a tenth-round pick in 2005, signed for $50,000.

Then there were guys like Dave Preziosi. He went undrafted out of Boston College. Nearly twenty years after his career ended, he could recall his bonus to the exact decimal point: "Nothing," he said. "Zero dollars." In a way, signing with the Dodgers cost him $800: he had been playing in Germany and paid for his flight home. Preziosi belonged on the Island of Misfit Toys. His fastball resided somewhere in the 70s. He threw sidearm. And his delivery was, in a word, strange. "I had a really funky motion where I kicked my glove and brought my body momentum down to really get down low," he recalled. His claim to fame was striking out Red Sox slugger David Ortiz with a 55-mph slider in an exhibition. "He had never seen something that slow," Preziosi recalled.

Preziosi knew his time was borrowed. But for one summer, he could baffle teenage hitters in the Gulf Coast League. Preziosi compared his statistics to those of the golden boy. "I would be like, 'You signed for $2.3 million, and I didn't sign for anything—and I have a better ERA than you,'" Preziosi recalled. Kershaw usually laughed it off. But one afternoon, pestered one time too many, Kershaw snapped: "At least I don't have to resort to kicking my glove to extend a baseball career that's clearly going nowhere!" Preziosi burst out laughing. Kershaw apologized immediately. Later in the summer, when Preziosi got lit up, he stewed in the clubhouse. His mood improved when he saw Kershaw cackling.

The players lived together in a collection of bungalows. When the Melsons came to visit, driving from Amelia Island, they were taken aback by the spartan setup. "Two beds, a bathroom," Smit recalled. "Pretty much like a Motel 6." The team provided three meals every day. There were games during the afternoon. At night, the guys lounged around the complex. They held Xbox tournaments in *FIFA* and *Madden*. If Mattingly drove to Taco Bell, Kershaw tagged along. They cashed paychecks at the nearest Walmart. Sometimes they went bowling. A trip to the mall represented the height of excitement.

Kershaw stood out while fitting in. The talent blinded his teammates during the day. In the evenings, though, "You would never realize that he was the one on the team who had just signed a massive contract," recalled Jason Schwab, an outfielder from New Orleans. Kershaw didn't brag about his fastball or his bonus. He never swore. If he teased people, he kept it gentle. Kershaw, recalled Trayvon Robinson, was "a sweet guy. If he saw a roach, he probably wouldn't step on it. He'd walk around it."

That kindness did not apply to opposing lineups. "When he pitched," Schwab recalled, "you weren't going to have much to do, and it was going to end quick." After one game, Mattingly called his father, then the Yankees hitting coach. "Dad," Preston jested Don, "we've got a guy who can beat you guys right now." He was so good that the others wondered why he shared the field with them. Robinson watched Kershaw's first bullpen after he signed. "It was like, 'Nah, he ain't going to be here long,'" Robinson recalled. The catcher behind the plate felt the same way. *This kid doesn't belong here,* thought Kenley Jansen, a hulking backstop from the Caribbean island of Curaçao.

Kershaw appeared in ten games that summer. He struck out 54 of the 144 batters he faced. He posted a 1.95 ERA. "He looked like he didn't belong in that league," recalled Daniel Murphy, a recent draft pick of the New York Mets. Kershaw even recorded a save, pitching to Jansen to close a playoff game. His relief appearance upset some in the organization, who wondered why the Dodgers would risk his health for a minor-league title. "I was pissed," White recalled. When the season ended, the Dodgers sent Kershaw to Arizona's instructional league. He roomed with Mattingly in Peoria. The posting felt like an extension of the Gulf Coast League: baseball during the day, *FIFA* and *Madden* at night. Again Kershaw's presence confounded his peers. "I was just like, 'Man, why is this dude here?'" Robinson recalled. "I'm here trying to switch hit. What does Kershaw need to work on?"

The Dodgers assigned Kershaw a task that would bedevil him for the rest of his career: they wanted him to learn a changeup. His two-pitch mix, the fastball and the curveball, was good enough against low-level competition. But the Dodgers did not expect Kershaw to stay in the minors for long. He needed a third option. When executed properly, the changeup upsets a hitter's timing. If paired with a heater like Kershaw's, Dodgers officials figured the combination could be overwhelming.

Except Kershaw could not throw it. At least, he could not throw it to a standard he felt acceptable. The pitch required differentiation in the movement of his wrist when he released the baseball. He threw it and threw it and threw it. And still the pitch stank. He told team officials he wanted to junk it and focus on the two pitches he had. Marty Reed, the organization's minor-league pitching coordinator, gave him a directive: one of the first two pitches Kershaw threw to each hitter *had* to be a changeup.

The mandate did not build Kershaw's confidence. It only irritated him. After one game, Kershaw approached Reed and apologized. Kershaw was embarrassed to have walked so many batters. Reed told him not to worry about it—this, he explained, was a learning experience. No, Kershaw insisted, he needed to be better.

One night Reed took Kershaw out to dinner and asked about his goals: Who do you want to be? What kind of career do you want? Kershaw did not mention the legacy of the Dodgers. He did not list players he intended to emulate. He told Reed he hoped to reach the major leagues. He wanted to provide for his mother. And he wanted to work at his craft with all his heart.

* * *

When he returned to Texas after the season, Kershaw bought a car. He had never owned one before. A couple of years earlier, his father had loaned him his Ford Explorer. Clayton drove it for a while, without insurance, before Chris took the car back. Now that Clayton had money of his own, he knew exactly what he wanted. He paid $37,000 for a black Ford F-150 King Ranch truck with leather interior. "My dream car," he called it.

One day in February 2007, Kershaw pointed the truck south toward College Station. Clayton and Ellen had stayed in touch through phone calls and emails during the season. In her first month on campus, she pledged a sorority, Chi Omega. When Kershaw came to visit, he felt out of place. "Where do you go to school?" other kids asked. "I don't go to school," Kershaw replied, without further explanation. Ellen begged him to reveal his profession, lest her new friends wonder why she was dating a burnout. He once told one of her sorority sisters that he worked at Walmart. He slept on couches across Texas A&M's Greek community. He could usually only handle two nights there before he wanted to leave.

Yet they had found an equilibrium. After a couple of months apart, Ellen realized she could manage the distance. "Everybody's under the impression, like, 'You're going to want to be single in college,'" she recalled. "That was not me. I was not, like, vying to be single and date around." So they made the most of their time together. For one theme party, they dressed up as Clark and Ellen Griswold. On that February trip, they stayed up chatting at her sorority house until early in the morning. Neither was drinking, they both said. Kershaw crashed upon some nearby furniture before getting up early to head home.

Kershaw only slept for a handful of hours. He was not yet a coffee drinker. On the highway, his eyes closed.

"I fell asleep and hit those grooves on the side of the road," Kershaw recalled. "And it woke me up. And I went *voom*."

The truck flipped twice. Kershaw emerged with a single scratch on his arm. He shuddered to think what could have happened. In his truck was one of his forearm weights, a ten-pounder attached to a pole. "And it was just flopping around in my back seat," he recalled. "Could you imagine if that had . . ."

His dream car was totaled. He never drove it again. But he was fine. The paramedics took him to a hospital near the campus. Ellen was chatting when her phone rang. When she saw her boyfriend's name, she declined the call. She figured Kershaw wanted to kill time on his drive. Then he called again. And again. Eventually she answered and raced to see him.

Later that day, Kershaw called Logan White to explain the accident. He needed to shrug off his brush with mortality to prepare for his first full professional season. Even after more than a decade had passed, after he had matured and become a parent, he struggled to place the accident into perspective.

"What did I take from that experience? I don't know," Kershaw recalled. "Don't fall asleep driving? I don't know. I really don't know. Just a miracle."

* * *

The palm trees rustled along Jackie Robinson Way one morning in the spring of 2023, at the facility that used to be Dodgertown. The Dodgers pulled up stakes for the Arizona desert in 2008. The facility remains in use, a youth sports complex that doubles as a semi-abandoned shrine. The morning was quiet save for the occasional golf cart zooming across the streets dedicated to Dodgers legends—Sandy Koufax Lane, Vin Scully Way, Avenida Jaime Jarrín. The meeting room dedicated to longtime manager Walter Alston featured a Ping-Pong table, a Skee-Ball machine, and an unplugged *Transformers* pinball machine. A pile of mattresses occupied a corner of Koufax's meeting room.

A creek ran through the center of the complex. On one side sat the barracks, the cafeteria, all the fields and mounds populated by the minor-leaguers every spring. On the other side was Holman Stadium, where the big-leaguers played. A little footbridge connected the two banks. To cross that bridge, as a Dodger, meant access to life-changing wealth and endless possibility. To cross that bridge meant to leave others behind.

The Dodgers traded Smit in 2010. He never reached the majors. Robinson was traded a year later to Seattle. He played in parts of two seasons with the Mariners and hung around the minors for a decade. Preziosi was released in the spring of 2007. He pitched in Italy for a summer before coming home. After the Dodgers cut him, Preziosi wrote letters to Kershaw and Mattingly: *You guys are really special,* Preziosi recalled writing. *Use your platform to do something great in life, not just in baseball.*

CHAPTER 8

THE BRIDGE

In the spring of 1993, while scouting for the San Diego Padres, Logan White signed a Texas Christian University southpaw named Glenn Dishman. He was the sort of undrafted player who could have washed out within months, but he did not. Just two years later, Dishman made it all the way to the majors. He hung around for parts of three seasons. Like White, he damaged his arm in the process. Like White, he decided to stick with baseball even after he could no longer throw one.

Dishman coached for a season at TCU and another at a small college in California. When Dodgers farm director Terry Collins was looking for a minor-league pitching coach, White recommended Dishman. He spent the summer of 2005 at the Dodgers' class-A affiliate in Columbus, Georgia. He graduated the next year to the Florida State League in Vero Beach. He figured another promotion was likely in 2007. While coaching winter ball in Hawaii, Dishman learned his next assignment: a demotion to the class-A Great Lakes Loons. Dishman wondered what he had done to earn a frigid spring in Michigan.

"We've got this left-hander named Kershaw there," assistant farm director Chris Haydock told him. "And we want you to go there with him."

Dishman's job was to help Kershaw cross that bridge at Dodgertown.

*   *   *

After flipping his car, Kershaw returned to Vero Beach in 2007 for his
first spring training. Under Ned Colletti's watch, the Dodgers had
returned to the playoffs in 2006. The organization expected to contend
again. The exploits of a teenage prospect, even with Kershaw's potential, didn't register for the big-leaguers. Among the farmhands, though,
the word was out: "You could just tell there was something different
about him," pitcher Cody White recalled.

Kershaw fit into the tableau of Dodger blue, showing off his arm
during the day, cracking jokes at night. He didn't crow about his status.
He never flashed any money. He finished the same drills, completed
the same conditioning tests. "He so desperately just wanted to be one of
the guys," recalled A. J. Ellis, who met Kershaw that spring. He
embraced the comfort of a five-day routine. He made the weight room
his second home. He strolled the barracks gobbling massive portions of
soft serve. "And everyone would be like, 'There goes our first-rounder,
crushing ice cream,'" Ellis recalled. One day, the players discussed cin-
ema. Kershaw delighted in the stunts of Johnny Knoxville, Steve-O,
and Bam Margera. He was less keen about swearing. Ellis had never
heard of *Jackbutt.*

Kershaw's presence made others question themselves. The Tigers
had drafted Paul Coleman out of Pepperdine in the ninth round in
2005. But he had been pitching with a torn labrum in his left shoulder.
After he flunked his physical, Coleman returned to college, where he
had been the West Coast Conference pitcher of the year. His interest in
analytics earned him the nickname "Fibonacci." After the Dodgers
picked him in the twelfth round in 2006, he debuted with the team's
single-A affiliate in Ogden, Utah. He thought he had a chance.

The next spring, he threw with Kershaw.

The session left Coleman shaken. He called his parents. "I'm scared to play catch with his curveball," he told them. His parents mentioned his college exploits to buck him up. They tried to tell him he was just as good as all the other players there. No, Coleman insisted. He was not. If someone like Kershaw set the bar, he could not clear it.

The astonishment was not limited to players. In a meeting that spring, pitching coordinator Marty Reed thought back to the draft and shook his head. "There's no way," Reed told the group, "there's six kids better than this kid."

*   *   *

Kershaw entered the season ranked the twenty-fourth best prospect by *Baseball America*. The publication slotted him between Adam Miller, a pitcher with Cleveland who never made it, and Billy Butler, a hitting savant for Kansas City who spent a decade in the majors. Kershaw would not sneak up on anyone in 2007. But he was far from a finished product. The road from the draft to The Show was filled with promising pitchers who faded after ballyhooed debuts.

It fell to Dishman, the pitching coach, to deliver the organization's decrees. "Immediately," Dishman recalled, "you knew he was different than everybody else." Dishman once crouched behind the plate for a bullpen session. Kershaw unleashed his curveball. That pitch dove with such abruptness, Dishman recalled, that he "almost killed myself trying to catch one of those." Outside of the ability, the kid understood the game's fundamentals. He never slacked off. And he listened when Dishman offered advice—even about the elusive changeup.

When Kershaw played catch, he threw the changeup. In his bullpen sessions, he threw the changeup. But during games, he pocketed it. He did not want to give up runs using a pitch that wasn't his best. Which meant that on certain days, when he could not control the curveball, he would attack hitters with only one pitch. In the Midwest League, his fastball was devastating on its lonesome. "His stuff pretty much overmatched the league," Great Lakes manager Lance Parrish recalled. When Kershaw appeared at the prospect showcase known as the Futures Game that summer in San Francisco, the broadcasters raved about his curveball. "You hear the announcer say, 'Oh, he has the best curveball in the minor leagues, per *Baseball America*,'" Preston Mattingly recalled. "We were just like, 'He does?'" They had only ever seen him throw fastballs.

Early on, Dishman noticed a pattern. Kershaw blamed himself for everything that went sideways while he was on the mound. To succeed as a starting pitcher requires a reliance upon others: the catcher, the defenders behind you, the umpire, the caprice of batted-ball luck. Sometimes things went awry that were not his fault. A grounder might shoot past a defender who would never make it to the majors. An inexperienced umpire might miss a call on Kershaw's curveball. The opponent might produce a broken-bat flare for a hit. Whenever this happened, Kershaw fumed. And he understood only one way to extricate himself. "If he ever got into any trouble, he'd try to go to ludicrous speed," Dishman recalled. The approach was foolish. Kershaw risked injury by overthrowing his fastball. He also lost his command. As he rose through the ranks, Dishman explained, Kershaw needed to stay within himself to stay within the strike zone.

The player-development staff built guardrails for Kershaw. Reed mandated Kershaw throw fifteen changeups every single game. That was just about the only rule that Kershaw chafed against, Parrish recalled. At nineteen, Kershaw was the youngest pitcher on the Loons. He was goofy but grounded, respectful with elders, courteous with strangers. When pitcher Steve Johnson's mother visited, she raved about Kershaw's politeness. Parrish, an eight-time All-Star catcher, never had to fine Kershaw for tardiness or chastise lackadaisical effort. "He was just one of those guys who you dream about having on your team," Parrish recalled.

In Midland, Kershaw grew close with Coleman, pitcher Josh Wall, and outfielder Scott Van Slyke, whose father, Andy, had been an

All-Star with the Pirates. The players bonded over their faith. They tended to view the game through the same prism. And, crucially, almost all of them had significant others. "There's guys who come to the ballpark and go out every night," Coleman recalled. "And there's guys who go back and hang out with each other and call their girlfriends." Kershaw fit into the latter group. "He was always on the phone with [Ellen]," Cody White recalled. "They might as well have been married."

The maturity had its limits. The players launched water balloons from hotel balconies and risked the stability of their joints on the basketball court. Kenley Jansen, the catcher from Curaçao, had grown up idolizing Los Angeles Lakers center Shaquille O'Neal. He liked to believe he could replicate the Big Aristotle's moves. He woofed about it with Kershaw until they agreed to duel. Kershaw and Jansen met at the backyard hoop of Jansen's host family. The catcher had been "talking so much crap," Jansen recalled. Then he realized he had unleashed something within his teammate. "You could tell, his face," Jansen recalled. "He got so competitive, so locked in, so serious." Jansen stood about an inch taller than Kershaw. He outweighed him by a decent amount. But Kershaw still backed him down in the post. "He beat my ass in basketball," Jansen recalled.

Kershaw rarely took part in hijinks at the ballpark. When he was there, he lived inside the cycle, the routine he had fashioned in Highland Park. Before every home start, he picked up a turkey sub at Quiznos. The cycle sustained him while he raged at his inability to throw the changeup. It grounded him when he overpowered opponents with his fastball. To Dishman, the adherence to the routine separated Kershaw from the pack. "You could tell he wanted to be the best in the world," Dishman recalled.

"A lot of kids are just like, 'Oh, I want to be the best. I want to be an All-Star. I want to win a Cy Young,' or something like that," Dishman explained. "But he's one of the ones that was willing to sacrifice mentally and physically beyond everybody else to do it."

* * *

A month after the Futures Game, Marty Reed traveled to Jacksonville for Kershaw's arrival in double-A. Reed pulled aside A. J. Ellis, who was seven years older than Kershaw and playing at the level for the second consecutive year. Reed wanted Ellis to guide Kershaw, who was skipping the class-A California League. Ellis also needed to enforce the organization's directive: fifteen changeups per game, no matter what.

Ellis listened to orders. He threw an arm around Kershaw when he got to town. Ellis was a burly, congenial fellow, quick with a quip in a motor-mouthed drawl that included a taste of his native Kentucky. He recognized his own limitations. He wanted to help. Ellis began a lecture about the challenges of double-A, the proving ground for prospects, a league stocked with actual talent, when the kid cut him off.

"Have you heard about this fifteen-changeup thing?" Kershaw said. "Let's get them out of the way as fast as possible."

"What?" Ellis said.

"Just get them out of the way as fast as possible," Kershaw said. "I'll throw my fifteen and then we can pitch."

In the years to come, Ellis raved about Kershaw's intensity, stubbornness, and dedication to routine. It took time for the dedication to become apparent. But he saw the intensity and the stubbornness right away. Before one of their first outings, Kershaw kept missing the target while warming up.

"Hey man, relax!" Ellis said. "Just relax!"

Kershaw pointed his glove at Ellis and screamed, "You relax!"

Despite the early hiccups, Ellis felt comfortable as a mentor. At twenty-six, he was one of the older guys on the team. He was the sort of player who had spent his career being overlooked. Before he met Kershaw, he never harbored big-league dreams, because the game had rarely given him a reason to harbor them. He went undrafted after hitting .371 as a junior at Austin Peay State University, in Clarksville, Tennessee. A year later, the Dodgers took him in the eighteenth round. For his first full-season assignment, in 2004, the Dodgers sent him to Vero

Beach. The affiliate also had twenty-one-year-old catcher Russell Martin, a converted third baseman from Montreal, who was being groomed as a franchise cornerstone. Martin was going to play most of the games. No one cared about his backup. Ellis only caught every fifth day. He usually worked with Chad Billingsley, another high school pitcher taken in the first round by Logan White in 2003. After several outings together, Ellis figured they were a partnership. One day Vero Beach manager Scott Little called Ellis into his office to relay that Ellis would catch Billingsley's next start.

"Oh, I know," Ellis told his manager. "I figured as much."

Ellis got up to leave. Little asked him to stay.

"Do you know why you catch Chad?" Little said.

Ellis thought he had an idea: Billingsley needed guidance and Ellis could provide it.

"You catch Chad," Little said, "because on the day he pitches, I don't need any offense."

The game humbles some when they are young, some when they are old, and some just about all the time. Ellis fit into the third category. He dove into his role as Billingsley's caddy. Teammates called them Chappie and Gus, the battery mates from *For the Love of the Game*. The pair did not stay together for long. Billingsley graduated to double-A Jacksonville that summer. Ellis stayed in Vero Beach. He spent all of 2005 there, too. Martin became the star the Dodgers envisioned. In the offseason, Ellis gave baseball lessons and worked as a substitute teacher. One winter he did data entry for a doctor's office. His wife, Cindy, worked for a catering company in Wisconsin. She handled the bills while her husband was a minor-league pauper. In 2006, the Dodgers promoted Ellis to double-A—only to leave him there for another season. By the time Kershaw arrived, Ellis was realistic. The Dodgers did not view him as part of their future. Through Kershaw, though, Ellis figured he could still influence that future. "A. J. became that big brother figure for him," recalled Wesley Wright, who pitched for Jacksonville that summer.

During the last few weeks of the season, the rest of the Suns witnessed Kershaw's duality: the intensity of his work ethic and the silli-
ness of his personality. There were no Quiznos nearby, so he patronized
Firehouse Subs for his pregame turkey sandwich. The players sometimes teased him about his perceived lack of athleticism. How, Kershaw was asked, had he played offensive line in high school? Whenever
someone pulled out a football, Kershaw insisted on running patterns to
show he had left behind his days as a center. He sprinted as fast as he
could in conditioning tests. And he pounded the outfield grass whenever his schedule demanded it, running in the ungodly Florida humid-
ity. Reed kept an eye on Kershaw during his early days in Jacksonville.
Kershaw looked gassed. His bullpen sessions weren't sharp. Kershaw
conceded to Reed that he felt run-down. Reed told Kershaw to listen to
his body. He didn't need to drive himself into the dirt in between starts.

After the season, Kershaw called Reed to thank him. He had cut
back on his running and finished strong. It was the sort of advice he
would struggle to accept for the rest of his career.

*   *   *

To be a top prospect is to see your name mentioned in trade rumors. In
the summer of 2007, the Texas Rangers asked about Kershaw while
shopping first baseman Mark Teixeira. In the winter, the Florida Marlins asked about Kershaw in exchange for slugger Miguel Cabrera.
Same story with the Minnesota Twins and ace Johan Santana. These
teams targeted Kershaw as part of a package, often bundling him in
their dreams with Chad Billingsley and Matt Kemp, both of whom
had just finished their second big-league seasons. The talks never got
far.

Érik Bédard was not the same caliber of player as Teixeira, Cabrera,
or Santana. But Bédard, a Baltimore Orioles lefty, was a safer bet to aid
the Dodgers in 2008 than a double-A teenager. And he had stymied
the New York Yankees in recent years. That mattered in Los Angeles
because after the 2007 season, Colletti hired Joe Torre, who had won

four World Series in the Bronx, to replace manager Grady Little. Torre brought a fleet of Yankees coaches with him. The group cared more about contending than nurturing the farm system. They hadn't heard much about Kershaw. "I don't think any of us really knew who he was, because we weren't in the organization," recalled Mike Borzello, a former Yankees bullpen catcher whom Torre brought to Los Angeles. Torre suggested pursuing Bédard. Members of the player-development department blanched when they heard whom Baltimore wanted in return: Kemp and Kershaw.

In hindsight, the Dodgers benefited from what Orioles president of baseball operations Andy MacPhail described as organizational chaos. MacPhail found Frank McCourt's Dodgers to be "frankly, an unreliable partner." One day, Kershaw or Kemp was available. The next day, only one of them was. The day after that, neither. MacPhail couldn't figure out if Colletti wanted a deal but McCourt wouldn't allow it, or if McCourt was pushing and Colletti was trying to pump the brakes. (Colletti said he recalled "very little" about the discussions.) MacPhail said the talks never gained much traction. He dealt Bédard to Seattle for a package built around future All-Star outfielder Adam Jones.

Kershaw—and Kemp—remained in Dodger blue.

"There were a few times when his name came up in trades," White recalled. "And you can imagine what I said every time: No, no, and hell no."

*   *   *

A month after Bédard went to Seattle, Torre and his lieutenants learned why moving Kershaw would have been disastrous. The Dodgers hosted the defending World Series champion Boston Red Sox on a Sunday afternoon, March 9, 2008, in front of the largest crowd in the history of Holman Stadium, a group of 9,291 unaware they were about to witness the launch party for a phenom. As the fourth inning began, Red Sox first baseman Sean Casey gazed out at a lanky, baby-faced southpaw wearing No. 96 with no name written across his back.

"What do you got on this guy?" Casey asked hitting coach Dave Magadan.

"I got nothing," Magadan replied.

Casey had spent more than a decade in the big leagues. He made a few All-Star teams. But it was his first spring with Boston, and he didn't want to embarrass himself. Any insight couldn't hurt. He found manager Terry Francona. "Just some rookie they're looking to give innings," Francona offered.

In a sense, that was true. Kershaw was still a few days from his twentieth birthday. That January the Dodgers had invited him to a two-week prospect mini-camp at Dodger Stadium. The players listened to speeches from Torre and Tommy Lasorda. Phil Jackson opened up a Lakers practice, where the group gawked at Kobe Bryant. They went to dinner with former UCLA coach John Wooden, the Wizard of Westwood. Back at Dodgertown, Kershaw tried to maintain a low profile. It wasn't easy. "There was just this aura around him," the sort of player who "demands attention, respect," recalled Blake DeWitt, who had played with Kershaw in Jacksonville the previous summer. In time, his peers understood, Kershaw would cross the bridge and leave the minor leagues behind. And not all of his friends could come with him. That spring, Paul Coleman asked the Dodgers for his release. His arm in agony, he could barely break 80 mph with his fastball. He never played again. After hitting .210 with Great Lakes, Preston Mattingly repeated the level in 2008. He never made it to double-A.

Kershaw was bound for greater things. The player-development staff preached patience. Once Torre saw his arm, though, patience would be hard to practice. One morning, Logan White asked Torre to accompany him to watch the minor-leaguers. The invitation came with a warning. "When you see him," White explained, "you're going to want to keep him." In late February, Kershaw logged an inning in a simulated game. Torre sauntered over. "Stay healthy," Torre said. His career could be long and prosperous, Torre continued, if his body cooperated. "Nice to meet you," Kershaw replied.

On March 4, Kershaw crossed the bridge to play with the Dodgers for the first time. "We're going to bring the kid over," Colletti told Torre and pitching coach Rick Honeycutt. "But you cannot fall in love today." The outing did not start well. Facing the lowly Washington Nationals, Kershaw served up a homer on his third pitch and then loaded the bases. Torre let Kershaw douse the flames. Kershaw stayed within himself and stayed within the zone, as Dishman had counseled. He struck out one batter with a 97-mph fastball and froze another with a curveball. Torre appreciated that Kershaw did not collapse. Don Mattingly recalled Preston's boast from the summer of 2006 about Kershaw's chances against the New York Yankees. "You may have been right," Don told his son. "He probably could have beat us."

Five days later, the Dodgers afforded Kershaw another opportunity. The Red Sox had flown across the state from their spring-training home in Fort Myers for a trip along Florida's east coast. Francona brought most of his regulars with him, so a decent challenge awaited Kershaw: four-time All-Star third baseman Mike Lowell, former Dodger J. D. Drew, and Casey, a garrulous left-handed hitter known as "The Mayor."

Casey did not have long to prepare. Lowell popped up to second base. Kershaw broke Drew's bat on a grounder. Left clueless by his coaches, Casey trotted to the plate. He stared across the distance, sixty feet and six inches, at a young man he would never forget. Kershaw brought his hands skyward, his leg rising in synchronicity, as if attached by a string. The limbs descended in the same uniform motion. And then the baseball emerged from behind his head, hidden by the angle of his delivery. "It just came out different and just got on me so quick," Casey recalled. The fastball nicked the outer edge of the zone. Strike one. Casey looked toward the home dugout. Torre and third-base coach Larry Bowa were laughing at him.

Bewildered, Casey stepped back into the box. Kershaw wound up once more and fired. It was another fastball. Casey still couldn't see it, couldn't touch it, couldn't do anything. Strike two. Then Kershaw flung a curveball. "No doubt it was a strike," Casey recalled. The umpire disagreed. Undeterred, Kershaw tried another curve. This one was beautiful and undeniable. The baseball hovered near Casey's chest before it tumbled toward the ground. The pitch triggered something in Casey's cerebellum, because his knees buckled, as if he intended to swing but could not spark his limbs in time. The bat never left his shoulder. "It literally felt," he recalled, "like I had just got abused." Kershaw was jogging off the mound before the umpire signaled the strikeout. In merely ten pitches, he had vanquished three accomplished hitters on the defending world champions. And the majesty of his last pitch, that incredible bender, registered in Vin Scully's broadcast.

"Ohhh, what a curveball!" Scully gushed. "Holy mackerel! He just broke off Public Enemy No. 1."

Back in the dugout, Casey fumed as his teammates razzed him.

"You don't know who that guy is?" Casey asked his manager.

"No," Francona said. "But I'm just glad I'm not you."

Casey grabbed his glove and headed to first base. Along the way, he crossed paths with Bowa, who covered his face with his cap to hide his laughter. Casey kept asking about Kershaw's identity "like it was a frickin' superhero: Who was that masked man?" At third base, Lowell told Bowa it looked like Kershaw was throwing aspirins. The astonishment was not limited to the Red Sox dugout. "Everybody was like, 'Who is *this* guy?'" recalled Dodgers outfielder Juan Pierre. "I was like, 'He's better than anybody we've got on our staff now.'"

Inside the Dodgers dugout, Kershaw looked giddy. With the help of Dishman and Ellis and Reed, he had crossed the bridge. It would be the responsibility of a new mentor to make sure he could stay. As Kershaw beamed, Honeycutt sat beside him. He had news to share: Kershaw would spend the rest of the spring at big-league camp. In time, Honeycutt would spend hours counseling and cajoling Kershaw. He would teach Kershaw the pitch that changed his career. He would also suffer alongside Kershaw. For that moment, though, inside the dugout on the other side of the bridge at Dodgertown, Honeycutt allowed himself to dream. *This kid,* Honeycutt thought, *is going to be special.*

Kershaw ran down the right-field line, through the Dodgers bullpen and out of sight. He knew how to celebrate his achievement. He wanted to use the major-league team's weight room.

CHAPTER 9

THE SHADOW OF SANFORD

The door swung open, and a silver-haired eminence entered the Dodger Stadium conference room. He wore a blue pullover, dark jeans, and black sneakers that emphasized comfort over couture. He looked eighty-seven going on sixty-five. His bearing was more genial than regal, despite his ability to cause a ruckus at a card show or a convention, despite the mob that would swallow him if he climbed a flight of stairs and walked the ballpark's concourse.

Then Sandy Koufax extended his right hand.

"Have you ever seen Sandy's hands wrapped around a baseball?" Clayton Kershaw once asked. The legend of Koufax bloomed for many reasons—spiritual, technical, philosophical. Some of it was just genetics. "He doesn't have hands," a teammate replied. "He has paws."

Koufax pulled up a chair. To his right, a framed illustration hung along the wall. In the painting, Jackie Robinson, clad in a white shirt and blue tie, smiled beside a southpaw from Brooklyn, the man with The Left Arm of God, grinning in his crisp, No. 32 uniform.

Every pitcher at Dodger Stadium lives in the shadow of Sandy Koufax. Even, at times, the man himself.

* * *

The comparisons started at the beginning. Sometimes Dodgers people blamed the press. When the Dodgers selected Kershaw, a left-hander with a hellacious overhand curveball, the writers likened him to the franchise's most famous left-hander with a hellacious overhand curveball. But Dodgers officials indulged the temptation. "I'm the one who opened my mouth and said he reminded me of Koufax," Joe Torre recalled. He wasn't the only one. Marty Reed, the minor-league pitching coordinator, sat in a meeting at the end of 2007 with the brass. "I don't know if I should say this," he told the group. "But he might be the closest thing to Sandy Koufax." By the spring of 2008, the sentiment was not limited to private discussion. "You're praying he's Koufax," Logan White told the *Press-Enterprise* of Riverside, California.

In those years, Koufax still roamed Dodgertown each spring. Rick Honeycutt, who had become a Koufax disciple while pitching for the Dodgers in the 1980s, encouraged his friend to check out the team's top prospect. "Wait 'til you see this kid," Honeycutt said. Koufax kept his interaction with Kershaw brief. "Good luck," Koufax told him.

This was the land of hopes and prayers that Kershaw inhabited that spring, after he humbled Sean Casey, after Vin Scully compared his curveball to John Dillinger's tommy gun, after he crossed the bridge to big-league camp. He was still a teenager. He could only throw two pitches. He had pitched in four games above class-A baseball. And yet the team openly wondered if he could grace the celestial plane established by Koufax, the organization's patron saint of pitching, the three-time Cy Young Award winner who walked away from the game at thirty, the living deity still worshipped from coast to coast.

All that stood between Kershaw and the chance to emulate Koufax was the Dodgers front office. Ned Colletti had authorized Kershaw's rapid ascension through the minors the previous year. But he held the line when Joe Torre's staff clamored for Kershaw to break camp with the big-league club. "I remember Larry Bowa going, 'How about the Kershaw kid? Why don't we just take him?'" recalled catching coach Mike Borzello. "And Ned's like, 'No, no, no. He's not ready yet.'"

The Dodgers sent Kershaw back to Jacksonville. To ease his passage out of the minors, the team promoted Glenn Dishman, his pitching coach in Midland. The organization intended to challenge Kershaw while treating him with care. It was a delicate dance. Dishman maintained steady dialogue with Colletti and Reed. There were the usual changeup quotas. Dishman monitored Kershaw's pitch count closely. The Dodgers did not want Kershaw to expend too many bullets against the Tennessee Smokies or the Montgomery Biscuits.

Kershaw chafed at mandates. On the endless bus rides, he would tell fellow pitching prospect James McDonald he was sick of changeups. He toiled with the pitch, often against his will, to satisfy superiors who he believed did not understand his body as well as he did. "He would get frustrated with it, when they were trying to force him to do things," McDonald recalled. "He was just like, 'I'm not throwing it. I'm done doing that. I'm going to be Kershaw. I'm not trying to be who they want me to be.'" He disliked being told what to throw before the game, rather than choosing during the heat of competition. "If I had his fastball, why wouldn't I want to throw it by people?" Dishman recalled. The pitch counts were tougher to argue against. The Dodgers were training Kershaw to be able to throw a hundred pitchers or more in a game in the majors. But the club did not want to overexpose him in less consequential settings. All teams faced this conundrum when developing pitchers: how do you build stamina without risking injury? Kershaw believed the only way out was through. "You know I can go further than that," he would say after being informed he could only throw five innings or seventy-five pitches in a given outing. Dishman counseled Kershaw about the big picture. The message did not always land. "It was always a tough day when you knew Clayton was only going to have a certain amount of pitches," Jacksonville manager John Shoemaker recalled.

Kershaw grumbled while abiding by the restrictions. He had thrown 122 innings in 2007; the Dodgers did not want him to exceed 170 in 2008. In his first month in Jacksonville, he pitched into the seventh just once. The Dodgers responded by skipping his turn in the rotation and giving him ten days off. The handcuffs did not hamper his results. He was striking out about a batter per inning. His command improved. He discovered that he did not need to chase strikeouts. If he threw his fastball or his curveball in the zone, Cody White recalled, "People just couldn't hit it." To Shoemaker, Kershaw personified what Tommy Lasorda, the organization's cartoonish sage, used to tell prospects: "Walk out onto the field and act like you're the best ballplayer on the field—but just don't tell anybody about it."

Kershaw's presence brought heightened attention to the club. "It wasn't just the Jacksonville Suns," recalled outfielder Adam Godwin. "It was the Jacksonville Suns and Clayton Kershaw Show." Kids at the Baseball Grounds of Jacksonville hounded him for autographs. So did the ladies; teammates occasionally teased Kershaw for refusing to chat up women who sought his acquaintance. When the Suns auctioned the players' pink jerseys for breast cancer awareness, Kershaw's led the bidding at $800. He stayed humble, several remembered. He drove a Chevy Tahoe purchased with insurance money he recouped after flipping his dream car. One afternoon, a few players ventured to the outlet malls. Kershaw found a pair of Under Armour sneakers he liked on sale for $49.99. "I like these," Kershaw told Godwin. "I'm not going to get them, though. They're too expensive." Godwin thought Kershaw was kidding. Then he watched him leave the store. A similar scene had unfolded at a Sunglass Hut in Florida in 2006. "There was a pair of Oakley sunglasses for $100," Dave Preziosi recalled. "And he just couldn't justify paying that money."

Teammates needled Kershaw for his refusal to part with a buck. In Midland, he slept on Walmart air mattresses until they collapsed under his weight. He exchanged the busted mattresses for new ones. "It was very unethical," Kershaw recalled. "But I did it. I tried to live as cheap as possible." He heard cracks about his disdain for pants, his limited rotation of free Under Armour polo shirts. "He doesn't dress overly loud like, 'Look at me, look at me,'" Trayvon Robinson recalled. "I don't think he owns a chain, to be honest. His personality doesn't spark like, 'Okay, I'm going to get a two-hundred-thousand-dollar car.'" (Kershaw did wear a diamond-encrusted cross in the majors. "I'm not cheap anymore, I don't think," he said. "But I definitely have no interest in buying, like, the finer things.")

Kershaw rented a condo near the ballpark with McDonald and pitcher Brent Leach. "We always joked with Clayton that he was the cheapest guy," McDonald recalled. "Like he didn't want to spend nothing. 'This TV is going to be a small TV.' 'We don't need cable.' He was always smart, realistically, about spending." McDonald wondered why Kershaw didn't splash his bonus money around. In time, Kershaw told his roommate about his childhood.

"When he was growing up, he didn't have his father in his life like that," McDonald recalled. "It was his mom. So he did whatever he could to help her, and make sure she was going to be all right."

*   *   *

In late May, the Suns took a seven-hour bus ride from Jacksonville to Zebulon, North Carolina. Kershaw was slated to make his tenth appearance of the season. He had struck out forty-five batters in 42.1 innings, with a 2.34 ERA, but innings restrictions had prevented him from recording an actual victory. After Kershaw retired the side in the first inning on May 22, Shoemaker sidled up to him.

"You're done," Shoemaker said.

Kershaw protested. Shoemaker did not budge. Dishman offered no explanation. Kershaw retreated to the clubhouse and iced his arm. He had eight innings to stew. He racked his brain. What could this possibly be about? The answer should have been obvious. A couple of weeks earlier, the Suns reorganized their rotation so Kershaw would make his big-league debut on May 17. Then Kershaw surrendered five runs and couldn't finish the fourth inning against the Mobile BayBears. The Dodgers delayed his promotion. Kershaw wondered if he had botched another opportunity.

After the game, Shoemaker called Kershaw into his office and handed him a phone. On the line was Colletti: the Dodgers needed Kershaw to start in three days. Colletti asked Kershaw to keep the news quiet. Kershaw wanted to play it cool, but his head was swimming. Once he stepped outside the clubhouse, he opened his phone.

"Ellen, don't tell anybody," he said. "But I got called up."

Then he told her to tell everybody. His mom. Her parents. His friends. He asked her to search his closet for his suit; he only had shorts and T-shirts with him, and he didn't want to look ratty when he reached the majors.

By the next day, the other Suns had figured out what was going on. He stood apart from the group, even if they considered him part of it. "It's like, 'Hey, they're going to call Kershaw up, and I'm going with him!'" Godwin recalled. "We all had dreams and goals and missions." Kershaw was much closer to fulfilling his ambitions than the others. As he headed to the airport, he started thinking about his first opponent, the St. Louis Cardinals. His excitement gave way, ever so slightly, to fear.

* * *

A car picked Kershaw up at Los Angeles International Airport and hustled him to Dodger Stadium. Inside the clubhouse, the inner sanctum of the best of the best, he dropped his duffel bag and gawked at the cleanliness, the orderliness, the stars gathered around him. The team gave him a locker next to veteran pitcher Jason Schmidt, a three-time All-Star with the San Francisco Giants who was midway through a disastrous Dodgers tenure. The club had signed Schmidt for $47 million, only for Schmidt to show up with an injured shoulder. When Kershaw debuted, Schmidt couldn't really throw. But he could still pull a prank.

Jazzed about his opportunity, unsure of his surroundings, Kershaw reached into a locker and grabbed a jersey. It was not his. Schmidt saw the rookie sporting a No. 29 with SCHMIDT on the back and told his teammates to dummy up. Schmidt put on Kershaw's No. 54. When the players lined up for the national anthem, Schmidt instructed Kershaw to stand beside him. The big screen at Dodger Stadium showed Kershaw's face. And then it cut to the back of his jersey, where another man's name was spread across his shoulders. The crowd and the rest of the players cracked up. Kershaw thought the song would never end.

After the game, he met his friends at his hotel. Ellen had come through. A twenty-three-person fleet had made the trip from Texas. Marianne Kershaw and Leslie Melson were there. Kershaw gabbed with his crew before heading to bed. Alone in his room, he thrashed around, staring at the tableside clock. After a while, he called Ellen, who was staying in a separate room at the hotel. She calmed him with their shared belief that God controlled his fate the next day. Kershaw felt his heart rate slow. After they said goodnight, he managed to get a few hours of rest.

In the morning, he sat alone in the Dodgers clubhouse, overwhelmed with the swirl of emotions. In the years to come, he leaned into the comfort of his routine to ease his mind. But on his first day, he rode the waves. He was too amped to notice the hoopla, his starring role in this seismic event in franchise history. Koufax offered encouragement before he took the mound. In the dugout, Kershaw felt his heart hammering in his chest. He remembered what Ellen had told him. He said a few words, which he would repeat before every subsequent start: "Lord, whatever happens, be with me. Be my strength."

Across the field, the St. Louis hitters were unsure what to expect. The scouting report on Kershaw was brief. A few players studied video clips. Cardinals outfielder Rick Ankiel approached his agent, Scott Boras, who frequented games at Dodger Stadium. Seven years earlier, Ankiel had been a phenom, a pitcher whose left arm supplied lightning. A mysterious inability to throw strikes nearly ended his career before he reinvented himself as a hitter. He knew Boras, who had been unable to convince Kershaw to attend college, kept tabs on all the top prospects. "He's the next Rick Ankiel," Boras said. Ankiel and his teammates scoffed. "We're like, 'He ain't no Rick Ankiel,'" infielder Skip Schumaker recalled. Under future Hall of Fame manager Tony La Russa, the Cardinals possessed a pride that bordered on haughtiness. "Our whole thing was 'We're not going to get beat by a twenty-year-old. We're the Cardinals,'" recalled infielder Aaron Miles.

Schumaker, the St. Louis leadoff hitter, had spent his entire career as a Cardinal, a modestly talented ballplayer who maximized his talents, molded by a player-development system designed for La Russa. Schumaker figured Kershaw would be too nervous to throw anything but fastballs. At 1:10 P.M., Kershaw wound up to pitch in the majors for the first time. His legs and hands rose in concert. Up. Down. Break. One. Two. Three. The fastball disarmed Schumaker. "It came from a spot where I just could not see it," Schumaker recalled. The video had not prepared him for this. He hung around for seven pitches, fouling off four, before Kershaw pumped a 95-mph fastball past him.

Inside the dugout, Schumaker spotted Ankiel. "Ricky," he said, "he's better than you."

Kershaw permitted himself a smile. His first big-league strikeout resided in the record books. He extended his glove to catcher Russell Martin. Martin tossed the ball toward the dugout, where it could be commemorated.

"Can I have the ball back?" Kershaw said.

"Relax," Martin said. "Here's a new one."

The rest of the inning demonstrated the challenge ahead. Unable to locate his fastball, Kershaw walked outfielder Brian Barton. Up next was Albert Pujols, an imperious slugger who had already won one National League MVP award and would win two more. He excelled by combining patience with power. He waited for mistakes and then punished them. With a full count, Kershaw thought he might surprise Pujols with a curveball. Pujols smashed it for a run-scoring double. Kershaw chuckled to himself. This, he realized, would not be easy.

His first inning lasted thirty-two pitches. St. Louis ground pitchers to dust through tenacity. The Cardinals could not crush his fastball.

But they could nick it, redirect it, do anything to keep Kershaw working. He responded by challenging them in the zone. "Every once in a while you face a kid making his debut and you just instantly know that it's not normal," reserve infielder Adam Kennedy recalled. In the sixth, Kershaw gave up another run, but he finished the inning with the game tied and a pitching line worth savoring: six innings, five hits, two runs, one walk, and seven strikeouts. He did not collect a win, but the team did. Kershaw cheered from the dugout as outfielder Andre Ethier delivered a walk-off hit in the tenth inning.

After the game, Kershaw met Ellen, Marianne, Leslie, and the rest of the Highland Park contingent. He had changed into an orange T-shirt and the navy suit Ellen brought. The gang posed for pictures with all their friends, the happy couple in the center of an Aéropostale ad. When Leslie returned home, she told her husband she sensed things between Ellen and Clayton were getting serious.

Kershaw bid the group farewell and boarded a bus to the airport. His friends were going home. He was headed to Chicago and New York. Most of his buddies had just finished sophomore year in college. He was the youngest pitcher to debut in the majors that season. He was the first member of Team USA to do so. Tyson Ross was a junior at Berkeley. Shawn Tolleson was just getting back on the mound at Baylor. The Diamondbacks had traded Brett Anderson that winter; he was pitching for one of Oakland's class-A teams.

Kershaw had beaten his goal, to reach the majors by his twenty-first birthday, by 298 days.

"This is a dream come true," he said after the game.

He had made it.

*   *   *

Except he hadn't.

Every day someone reminded him he was a neophyte. The lessons came from teammates and opponents alike. For his second start, Kershaw pitched against the Mets at Shea Stadium. It was his first trip to

New York. In the days before the game, he toured Yankee Stadium. He also received a new uniform number. Utility infielder Mark Sweeney had been wearing No. 22, the digits of Kershaw's childhood favorite Will Clark. A team official mentioned Kershaw's preference to Sweeney. At thirty-eight, playing on his seventh team, Sweeney had no relationship with No. 22. He understood Kershaw's future importance with the franchise. But he could not help himself. Minutes after the clubbies stitched Kershaw's name onto a No. 22 jersey, Sweeney told Kershaw how much the number meant to him—Sweeney's grandfather had worn it, the vet told the kid. Kershaw mumbled and ran his fingers through his hair. Then Sweeney revealed his grandfather had never even played baseball.

After 2007, when clubhouse discord expedited Grady Little's departure, Colletti hoped Torre would settle things down. Torre brought gravitas and perspective. But he was not a hall monitor. The room was still split between the homegrown Dodgers—Billingsley, Kemp, Martin, and now Kershaw—and the veterans, almost all of whom had been raised in other organizations. Nomar Garciaparra had won two batting titles and made six All-Star teams. Andruw Jones had won ten Gold Gloves in center field. Jeff Kent was a five-time All-Star and four-time Silver Slugger at second base. Derek Lowe and Brad Penny each had a World Series ring and two All-Star appearances to his name. "There were some massive, massive names and some massive egos," A. J. Ellis recalled.

To Ellis, who arrived later that summer, it felt like the older players scanned the clubhouse with magnifying glasses, thrilled to find any infraction. It could be a mistake on the field. It could be a violation of the dress code. It could be speaking out of turn—or even speaking at an improper volume, a practice known as "loud talking." "It was a little bit intimidating," McDonald recalled. "You felt awkward. You didn't feel like you were a part of it." Some of the treatment was goofy; rookie reliever Cory Wade had to haul a bag of candy and a cooler of drinks to the bullpen. Some of it felt sinister; McDonald saw his glove scorched on an electric stove because he refused to entertain a group of elders.

On an individual level, the vets could be friendly. But as a group, they commanded respect and declined to offer much in return. "Not many people gave me the time of day," Kershaw recalled. The public might have viewed Kershaw as a potential savior. The veterans saw him as just another kid trying to take someone else's job. "It was tough on him," recalled outfielder Juan Pierre. That was how they had been raised. They thought it best to treat the next generation the same. "The thing you learn as a rookie is 'Shut up and speak when spoken to,'" recalled Scott Proctor, who played for Torre with the Yankees before joining the Dodgers. He enforced the same principles with Kershaw. "What the younger guys didn't understand," Proctor recalled, "was they're trying to test you to see, when it comes down to the playoff run, do you have the cojones to stand up and fight through it?"

So a skeptical group watched Kershaw, clad in his new No. 22 jersey, take the mound on May 30 against the Mets. In the first inning, he surrendered the first home run of his career, to light-hitting second baseman Luis Castillo. The Mets scored four runs against him. He could not finish the fourth. A learning experience, he called it. There were more lessons ahead. He gave up two runs to Colorado in five innings in his third start. His fourth time out, he made it into the sixth against San Diego. He completed four innings against Detroit, five innings against Cleveland, four innings against the White Sox. "He was a run-of-the-mill, hard-throwing young lefty," Cleveland third baseman Casey Blake recalled. The mediocrity produced grumbling within the Dodgers front office. Tim Lincecum, the slender right-hander taken three picks after Kershaw in 2006, was on his way to winning the National League Cy Young Award that year. Kershaw could barely get past the fifth inning. He lacked fastball command. He didn't trust his changeup. And his most celebrated pitch, the heralded Public Enemy No. 1, had gone into hiding. "The problem was he couldn't command his curveball consistently," Borzello recalled. "So he's going, like, four innings, five, tops. Which nowadays is almost acceptable. But back then, it was not."

On July 1, Kershaw took the mound at Minute Maid Park in Houston, close enough to Highland Park that his friends could make the drive. Kershaw departed with two outs in the sixth, charged with three runs. He had made eight starts and never won a game or thrown a pitch in the seventh inning. His ERA was 4.42. He was walking too many hitters, not because he feared throwing strikes, but because he rushed his delivery and lost control. He was still trying to *throw* his way out of trouble, rather than pitch. His short outings drained the bullpen. A day later, Kershaw was leaving some tickets for his pals when he was called into Torre's office. He found Torre, Rick Honeycutt, and assistant general manager Kim Ng waiting for him. A three-person tribunal was never good news for a rookie: Kershaw was demoted back to Jacksonville. "That wasn't a happy conversation," Torre recalled. Kershaw barely listened as Torre explained the club needed to open a roster spot as veteran Hiroki Kuroda returned from an injury. "He didn't want to hear what he needed to work on," Torre recalled. The manager sugarcoated the message by framing the decision as a reflection of the mechanics of the roster rather than Kershaw's performance. Kershaw didn't really care. He did not feel like he was failing those around him. He felt like he was failing himself. He had been a big-leaguer. Now he wasn't.

*   *   *

Five weeks earlier, Adam Godwin, James McDonald, and the rest of the Jacksonville Suns had gathered around a television in Zebulon, North Carolina, and watched Kershaw stand tall against the Cardinals. They figured if they ever played with him again, it would be in Los Angeles. On a bus ride to Mobile, Alabama, they learned they were mistaken. Before the demotion, Kershaw had experienced only an upward trajectory. He had gone from the No. 3 starter on his travel-ball team to a likely first-round pick to a potential successor to Sandy

Koufax. Along the way, he dealt with only episodic bouts of failure, blips here and there, nothing as demoralizing as this. "We were all like, 'What kind of Kershaw are we about to get?'" Godwin recalled.

In Mobile, Kershaw reconnected with Dishman. The coach could sense Kershaw's frustration. For the first time in a long time, Kershaw had not met his own standard. He had been average, and that was unacceptable. Dodgers officials told him his issues stemmed from execution, not talent. If he trusted his arsenal, if he controlled his pitches a little bit better, he could cut down the walks and last deeper into games. "Let's tighten things up so that when you go back, you stay, and you don't ever come back to the minor leagues," Dishman told him.

The exile only lasted a few weeks. Kershaw made three starts for the Suns, permitting two runs in eighteen innings, before the Dodgers needed him again. But he was gone long enough to recognize the difference between chartered flights across the country and overnight bus trips along the highway. He had to prove to his team he was good enough to never ride the bus again, to remain on the other side of the bridge. And he had to prove it to himself.

*   *   *

When he got back to Los Angeles, Kershaw asked an old teammate for a favor. Paul Coleman, the former Pepperdine star, was recovering from a shoulder injury. He had realized a career in baseball was unlikely. He lived in downtown Los Angeles with his wife, a medical resident at the University of Southern California. Kershaw wondered if Coleman had enough space at his apartment for a roommate.

For players shuttling back and forth between the majors and the minors, housing was tricky. Kershaw couldn't rent a place of his own, because one bad start might get him relegated to Jacksonville or triple-A Las Vegas or some other outpost. For a while, he lived at a Pasadena hotel. When Shawn Tolleson visited that summer, he slept on a cot inside Kershaw's room. "Everything that he owned fit into this little duffel bag," Tolleson recalled. Kershaw filled the bag for road trips and emptied its contents at the hotel when the Dodgers returned to Los Angeles.

Kershaw called Coleman because he sought stability. The Colemans were happy to have help with the rent on their three-bedroom spot with gated parking near Staples Center. Kershaw made an ideal roommate. He didn't throw parties or make a mess. He rarely saw his landlords; the Colemans left the apartment early in the morning, while he slept until noon and often didn't get back from the ballpark until nearly midnight. He walked downtown without being recognized. He crushed barbecue chicken pizzas at California Pizza Kitchen. He found a new chain, Subway, for his turkey sandwich.

"You ever heard of Jersey Mike's?" Coleman once asked.

"No," Kershaw said. "I'm a Subway guy."

For the Dodgers, Kershaw faded into the background that summer. Star power propelled Los Angeles, and Kershaw was too green to supply it. Colletti had found another source, a slugger capable of filling the seats at Chavez Ravine and filling new teammates with awe. On August 1, Torre introduced Kershaw to Manny Ramírez, the dreadlocked slugger Colletti had just acquired from the Red Sox. By the summer of 2008, the thirty-six-year-old outfielder had made twelve All-Star teams, notched nine Silver Slugger Awards, collected two World Series rings—and completely worn out his welcome in Boston. He had a reputation for preposterous behavior—"Manny being Manny" went the saying—but his actions had turned more volatile. Before the Red Sox got rid of him, Ramírez fought with teammates and toppled a sixty-four-year-old traveling secretary.

Colletti gambled that Ramírez would thrive in new scenery. Ramírez embarked on a torrid stretch that captivated the South Bay. Dodger Stadium became Mannywood. He hit .396 in fifty-three games with seventeen home runs. He lengthened the lineup and reduced the stress on younger hitters like Ethier and Kemp. Ramírez, McDonald recalled, "Always talked to the young guys, made us feel comfortable." His presence also eased tension in the clubhouse. The room could be a cold place. When Casey Blake joined the Dodgers that summer, acquired from Cleveland in exchange for catching prospect Carlos Santana, the reception was muted. "It's not like they were rushing up to meet me or introduce themselves to me," Blake recalled. Cleveland had banned cellphones in the clubhouse. Blake walked into a room of dudes gabbing on the phone. The players kept to themselves; Blake discovered they didn't even play poker. (When Blake started a game, Kershaw declined because the $100 buy-in was too expensive.) Ramírez changed the atmosphere. "I really felt like he cared about me as a person and as a player," Blake recalled. "If I had a bad game, he'd come and sit down next to me and say, 'Hey, you're going to hit four tomorrow.'"

As Ramírez swatted dingers, Kershaw stayed in the rotation. He recorded the first win of his big-league career—and his first win of 2008—with six scoreless innings against Washington on July 27. Ten days later, he completed the seventh inning for the first time. In his final thirteen starts of the season, his ERA was 4.24, only a touch better than it was when the team demoted him. (That August, he spent a few days with triple-A Las Vegas as a procedural move. Kershaw told reporters he never set foot in the casinos.) His improvement pleased Dodgers officials. They would rather see him give up hits than walk the park. His behavior appeased his veteran teammates. He did not brag when he succeeded. He did not sulk when he failed. "He earned respect because of the way he carried himself," Sweeney recalled. Save for a few stumbles, like a four-run outing in September against Max Scherzer, taken four spots after him in 2006 by the Arizona Diamondbacks, Kershaw avoided abbreviated starts that sapped the bullpen. At times, Torre extended him too *much* leeway. Colletti seethed when Torre sent Kershaw out for the eighth inning, for the first time in his career, up seven runs against San Diego on September 2. On his drive home, Colletti's phone rang. "Boss," Torre said, "I'm sorry." "You've got to be careful with this guy," Colletti replied.

Kershaw kept his eyes peeled. He noticed that Derek Lowe ventured to the bullpen on the day before his starts. Lowe climbed the mound without a baseball and practiced his delivery. The practice, known as "dry throwing," allowed Lowe to visualize his upcoming outing. Kershaw incorporated that into his routine. When Colletti traded for Greg Maddux, the forty-two-year-old, four-time National League Cy Young Award winner, Honeycutt encouraged Kershaw to pick the sage's brain. "This guy's different," Honeycutt told Maddux. In the final weeks of the season, Kershaw sat beside Maddux during games. He impressed Maddux with his dedication to the ancillary parts of the job. Kershaw cared about fielding his position, getting down bunts, running the bases. "The little things," Maddux recalled, "were important to him."

Ramírez slugged the Dodgers into the postseason past mediocre competition in the National League West. Kershaw stayed on the periphery as the team downed the Chicago Cubs in the National League Division Series and then dueled with the Philadelphia Phillies in the National League Championship Series. Kershaw was less reliable to Torre than the trio of Lowe, Billingsley, and Kuroda. He pitched out of the bullpen as the eventual champion Phillies squashed the Dodgers in five games. In Game 2, he made his postseason debut, recording five outs after Philadelphia wrecked Billingsley. Three days later, Torre asked him to protect a one-run lead. Kershaw could not. Unable to command his curveball, he walked leadoff hitter Ryan Howard and permitted a single to outfielder Pat Burrell. Howard scored after Torre yanked Kershaw. The lead, the game, and eventually the series were lost.

"Just one of those things," Kershaw said afterward, "you can't explain."

He could not have known how often he would have to answer questions like those, to explain failure in October, for the rest of his career.

* * *

When Sandy Koufax was twenty years old, he moldered on the Brooklyn Dodgers bench. He rarely pitched. If he fell behind a batter, manager Walter Alston called the bullpen. He was only on the roster because he received a $14,000 bonus when he signed after his freshman year at the University of Cincinnati. He was a "bonus baby," the equivalent of a first-round pick before the implementation of a draft. Brooklyn had to carry him on the roster for all of 1955 and 1956. When Brooklyn beat the Yankees in the 1955 World Series, Koufax was a uniformed spectator. When the Yankees recaptured the crown the next October, Koufax played the same part.

A distance of more than five decades separated the twenty-year-old Koufax and the twenty-year-old Clayton Kershaw, but the similarities extended beyond which pitches they threw and which hand they threw them with. Koufax did not want to slink home to his neighborhood in Brooklyn and ride the train with all the work-a-day straphangers from Bensonhurst. Kershaw did not want to flame out and leave his mother strapped with bills in Highland Park. But Kershaw was not measured against the reality of Koufax, who required six years of seasoning before becoming an icon. Kershaw was measured against the legend of the man who could stop a crowd decades after he retired, the man immortalized across the industry and the nation, the man whose statue stood at Dodger Stadium in 2023. Kershaw insisted the comparisons never affected him. He set his own standards. And he considered Koufax a friend.

In the spring of 2010, as Kershaw prepared for his third season, Torre invited him to a charity event. On a flight to Los Angeles, the manager arranged for Kershaw to sit beside Koufax. They talked for hours. "You couldn't get a sheet of paper in between the two of them," Torre recalled. Kershaw felt honored by the elder's wisdom. Koufax appreciated Kershaw's intensity and humility. "He always tries to get better," Koufax said. "He never stops trying to get better. He still does."

In time, Koufax understood that Kershaw defined success the same as he did. A pitcher was supposed to finish what he started.

"My feeling is competing is not tearing up water coolers," Koufax said when he sat down for an interview in 2023. "It's being there at the end. Last man standing."

Koufax stood up and extended his massive paw once more. His time was brief. His affection for Kershaw was apparent in his willingness to grant an interview. Koufax ambled away with public-relations maestro Steve Brener.

"You never wanted to give up the baseball, did you, Sandy?" Brener said.

"None of us did," Koufax said. "It was a different game."

CHAPTER 10

HOOKING THE SEAM

On a May 2009 afternoon in Philadelphia, seven weeks after he turned twenty-one, Clayton Kershaw walked into the visiting manager's office at Citizens Bank Park. One night earlier, the Phillies had pilloried him, scoring four runs in five innings, benefiting from Kershaw's recurring inability to throw strikes. Kershaw understood what an invitation to sit with the skipper usually meant. He suspected he was being demoted—maybe from the starting rotation, maybe from the team itself. Joe Torre had another idea in mind. He decided to stage an intervention.

Seven starts into his second season, Kershaw was teetering on the brink of a return to the other side of the bridge. The offseason departures of veteran pitchers Derek Lowe and Brad Penny created an opening for Kershaw. He had responded with a 5.21 ERA midway through May. He displayed the same maddening qualities from his rookie year. His fastball sizzled and his curveball popped eyes, but he failed to command either. His changeup remained toothless. Ned Colletti suggested a return to the minors. Torre asked to extend Kershaw a little more rope. Kershaw reminded Torre of his former middle infielders in the Bronx. Like Derek Jeter, like Robinson Canó, Torre appreciated how Kershaw handled misfortune. He deserved a chance to grow in the majors.

Inside Torre's office, Kershaw sat with his manager, pitching coach Rick Honeycutt, and hitting coach Don Mattingly. Kershaw had appeared in twenty-eight big-league games. The three coaches had combined to play in fifty-three big-league seasons. Torre figured their collective wisdom might break through. He lobbed Mattingly a question.

"If Clayton was pitching today," Torre began, "how would you face him?"

Mattingly had been one of the finest hitters of his era, Donnie Baseball in the Bronx, a six-time All-Star and nine-time Gold Glover at first base. He unspooled a devastating scouting report. He would cut the plate in half, because he knew Kershaw only threw inside, Mattingly explained. He would ignore the curveball, because he knew Kershaw could not command it. He would disregard the changeup, because he knew Kershaw did not trust it. He would focus on the inner half and wait for heaters. "He has one pitch," Mattingly explained. "Hit the fastball. It's not that hard."

Torre opened the floor to Kershaw.

"Do you know what you need to do?" Torre said.

"I know," Kershaw said. He had been hearing about this for weeks. Months. His whole brief big-league career, really. "I need to throw my curveball for strikes."

Torre was patient but firm. The coaches appreciated the kid's obstinance. All the great ones, they thought, exhibited some level of defiance, some refusal to deviate from their internal compass. "That's how they got to be good," Honeycutt explained. "They are stubborn in their belief, and their belief in themselves." Kershaw had a chance to be one of those. But he wasn't yet. To flourish, Torre explained, he required adaptation.

"You need to figure out a third pitch," Torre said.

*   *   *

He had heard this mantra ever since the Dodgers drafted him. The changeup galled him. He could not make the pitch meet his standard.

It was not for lack of effort, he believed. When he threw his fastball and his curveball, his left wrist flicked naturally across his body. To throw the changeup, he needed his wrist to snap in the other direction, a process called pronation. "I can't pronate," Kershaw explained. "I don't know how to do it." Yet he kept trying, all through the spring of 2009, at the behest of the organization. Lefties were supposed to throw changeups, and Kershaw aspired to be the best left-handed pitcher he could be.

For the Dodgers, 2009 was a year of transition. The team no longer trained at Dodgertown. Frank McCourt had found a new home outside the city of Glendale, Arizona, called Camelback Ranch. The Dodgers shared the complex with the Chicago White Sox. Grimy barracks and muggy Florida weather were replaced by clear skies and new facilities. The decisions made by McCourt and his wife, Jamie, would have dire consequences for the Dodgers in the coming years, but in the spring of 2009, there was still tranquility. In that first year in the desert, Honeycutt hooked Kershaw up with Koufax. "How can you not?" Honeycutt recalled. Honeycutt was curious if Kershaw could replicate some aspects of Koufax's delivery, the famed catapult that delivered his fastball and curveball, "the kinetic equivalent of E. B. White's 'clear, crystal stream' of the English language: honed, pared down, essential," Jane Leavy wrote in her biography of Koufax. The man told Kershaw the keys of his movement, like anchoring his left leg to the rubber, his right hip propelling him toward the plate.

The actions did not come naturally to Kershaw. He radiated dissatisfaction with the process, his frustration apparent to Randy Wolf, a kindly ten-year veteran lefty signed to fill out the rotation. One day in the weight room, Wolf encouraged Kershaw to trust his instincts. "One thing I've learned," Wolf told him, "is you don't really learn from freaks." No one could be like Koufax, Wolf explained. But Wolf had been around long enough, and seen enough of Kershaw, to recognize something else. In fifteen years, Wolf continued, there would be kids lifting their hands and feet in a fluid motion and pausing before exploding toward the plate. They would try to imitate Kershaw. And they would fail. "Because you're a freak," Wolf said.

Kershaw turned twenty-one that spring and bought his first beer; he sipped it for a while but declined to order a second. He showed his age in other ways. Over the winter, he bought a townhouse near Highland Park. He purchased a Ping-Pong table as his first piece of furniture. A dry-erase board for scorekeeping hung nearby. Searching for a haircut that summer, he fretted he could not find a Supercuts. The nearest salon tried to charge him $42. "How much for a buzz cut?" Kershaw countered. He haggled for a $24 shaved head.

His youthful obstinance was less amusing when it came to the game. Because he never cut corners, because he trusted the five-day cycle, he thought he knew best. After one shoddy outing at Dodger Stadium, Kershaw walked to the parking lot with Mike Borzello. Kershaw asked Borzello for a diagnosis. "You can't throw a curveball for a strike," Borzello said. When he missed with the curveball, he always came back with a fastball. The heater was special enough that even big-league hitters couldn't always handle it. But they could foul it off, drive up his pitch count, and wait for a mistake. Borzello suggested Kershaw throw a different type of curveball, one that sacrificed some of that beautiful movement, the spin that made Scully swoon, in exchange for one that could reliably land in the strike zone. Kershaw did not like that idea.

"I've always thrown my curveball one way," Kershaw said. "I've always thrown it as hard as I can."

Borzello chuckled. "Against who? High school kids? A-ball?" Borzello said. At this level, Borzello explained, starters needed off-speed pitches they could control. Borzello warned him of the consequences. "If you can't do that here, then you're not going to survive," he said. "You're going to be a reliever."

After meeting with Torre, Honeycutt, and Mattingly after several weeks of getting pounded, Kershaw understood the stakes. He refused to mess with his curveball. The changeup eluded him. That left one other option. He asked Honeycutt about a slider.

*   *   *

Rick Honeycutt grew up outside Chattanooga, Tennessee, and wore the orange and white for the University of Tennessee Volunteers in Knoxville. He spoke as if each syllable had been dredged through the Chickamauga Dam. He debuted in the big leagues at twenty-three. He retired at forty-two. In the intervening years, he made an All-Star team in Seattle, collected an ERA title in Texas, and won a World Series in Oakland. He had been a top-tier starter and he had been a second-rate reliever and he had been everything in between.

To Honeycutt, his most transformative experience came after the Rangers traded him to the Dodgers. His first spring at Dodgertown in 1984 blew his mind. He lapped up conversations with pitching coach Ron Perranoski, minor-league manager Dave Wallace, and an occasional spring instructor named Sandy Koufax. "I felt like I learned more in two to three weeks in spring training, just being around Sandy and Dave and Perry, than I had in my whole life," Honeycutt recalled. In 2001, Wallace called him about rejoining the organization as a minor-league coach. Honeycutt felt the Dodgers had "gotten away from who we were" during the late 1990s, after the O'Malley family sold the team to Rupert Murdoch's Fox Entertainment Group. Honeycutt joined the big-league staff as Grady Little's pitching coach in 2006. Torre kept him around because Honeycutt connected with players and understood the organization's history. "When I got hired, I wanted to bring back the influence of the past," Honeycutt recalled. He favored humility over histrionics. He rarely yelled. He excelled at convincing even the obstinate to trust him.

Honeycutt had learned his slider grip from former Yankees pitcher Mel Stottlemyre. The slider was a simple pitch, less picturesque than a curveball but easier to command, breaking down and away toward the pitcher's glove side. The grip was similar to that of a four-seam fastball, with the index and middle fingers overlaid on the ball's red seam and the ring finger anchoring a few inches away. To make the ball move, the pitcher rotated his fingers, ever so slightly. Koufax taught Honey-cutt how using pressure points tightened the spin. Koufax created a vise between his middle finger and the knuckle on his ring finger. He called it "hooking the seam."

In the spring of 2009, as Kershaw searched for a third pitch to stabi-lize his career, Honeycutt offered to pass down what he had learned. "Clayton was a little stubborn about it," Torre recalled. "But Clayton just loved Rick Honeycutt." Kershaw did not need something that dropped jaws like his curve. He just needed something he could throw for strikes. Honeycutt displayed his slider grip and preached the princi-ples he learned from Koufax, especially the pressure point. He told Ker-shaw to hook his middle finger deep into the seam. "I want you to feel like you're pulling down, not across the ball," Honeycutt stressed. Ker-shaw held the baseball in his left hand and mimicked the grip. Unlike the changeup, the slider did not force Kershaw to pronate. His wrist flicked just like it did with his other two pitches. All the slider required, he discovered, was power. He threw the pitch as hard as he could and the grip took care of the rest. Kershaw tried it in between his starts and liked the shape. But he wasn't sure it was ready. There were so many people in his ear—Honeycutt, Torre, Borzello, even Wolf. "The slider's going to be so much easier to command," Wolf told Kershaw. Explained A. J. Ellis, "He's a late listener. He hears what you say. Because he's a stubborn person—probably another attribute that makes him great, but also makes him a *joy* to work with. But he'll come around to things."

Kershaw delayed the implementation of the pitch for a few weeks. On May 17, in his first start after the meeting in Torre's office, he car-ried a no-hitter into the eighth inning against the Florida Marlins. The bid looked serious enough that Honeycutt ducked into the Land Shark Stadium clubhouse and called Colletti for instructions. At a certain pitch count, Colletti insisted, Honeycutt had to intervene. The game prevented any controversy. Kershaw yielded a leadoff double in the eighth and exited immediately. Honeycutt and Torre exhaled—and then gushed afterward. "He's got the Koufax dominance," Torre said.

Except five days later, Kershaw took a step back. He walked four in five innings against the Los Angeles Angels. In Colorado, the Rockies scored three runs in six innings. "You could tell there was a discontent within him," Wolf recalled. "No matter how he pitched, you could tell he was like, 'Okay. I can do better than that.'" After the game at Coors Field, the Dodgers flew to Chicago. Borzello was catching Chad Billingsley in the bullpen located down Wrigley Field's first-base line when Kershaw walked over. After Billingsley finished, Kershaw asked Borzello to stick around.

"I've got a slider," Kershaw said. "I want you to see it."

* * *

Mike Borzello was Zelig in a chest protector. In the summer of 1997, Borzello was playing catch with Yankees reliever Mariano Rivera when the pitcher's fastball darted without warning. The mysterious movement fostered Rivera's Hall of Fame cutter. Nearly twenty years later, Borzello was coaching for the Chicago Cubs when the franchise ended its 108-year World Series drought. In between those milestones, Torre brought Borzello with him to Los Angeles.

Torre grew up in Brooklyn with Borzello's father, Matt. Later in life, Torre and Matt Borzello ran a Southern California summer baseball camp for fifteen years. Mike went undrafted out of California Lutheran University but signed with the St. Louis Cardinals in 1991, where Torre was the manager. Several years later, when Torre was managing the Yankees, he invited Borzello to become a bullpen catcher. Borzello was driving a truck for his father at the time. Torre opened doors, but Borzello kept them open. He possessed an intuitive understanding of swings and became an early adopter of video analysis. Borzello was raised in the Los Angeles suburb of Tarzana, an eighteen-mile jaunt on the 101 from Hollywood, and he told stories with a cinematic flair and an ear for dialogue. He spoke his mind. "Some guys think he's abrasive," former Cubs manager Dale Sveum said, "but he's just brutally honest." He made an ideal witness for the unveiling of Kershaw's slider.

Borzello understood how a small change could transform a career. And if the pitch stank, Borzello wouldn't be afraid to say so.

Borzello suggested Kershaw warm up with fastballs. Kershaw went through his motion. Up. Down. Break. The four-seamer displayed its usual life. Then Borzello called for a slider. Up. Down. Break. The pitch that emerged from Kershaw's hand resembled a fastball until the moment before it arrived in Borzello's glove. The average slider tended to make a diagonal dive, usually with more horizontal tilt than vertical descent. This ball was different. It plunged toward the earth like a split-fingered fastball, with little horizontal movement. "Like, it vanished," Borzello recalled.

Kershaw made an inquisitive face, casting for approval.

"Do that again," Borzello said.

Up. Down. Break. The second slider charted the same course. *Jesus,* Borzello thought. Kershaw repeated his delivery and repeated the outcome. He felt the control he craved, the sensation that eluded him with his curveball. The ball went where he wanted it to go. "I could miss a little bit and still be close," he recalled. After a few more, Kershaw asked Borzello for his input. "Are you kidding me?" Borzello said. "If you can do that off a mound, that's game-ready." Kershaw looked unsure. It was hard to fathom he had conjured a new third pitch so quickly. "We'll see," he said.

Borzello was not the only fortunate spectator that weekend at Wrigley. An injury created a temporary opening on the roster for A. J. Ellis. He had been toiling at triple-A Albuquerque, blocked in the majors by Russell Martin and the veteran backup Brad Ausmus. A day after Kershaw tested the slider, Borzello pulled Ellis aside. He needed Ellis to catch Kershaw's bullpen session and analyze the new pitch. "Is he going to let me?" Ellis asked.

When Kershaw returned to the bullpen, Ellis crouched behind the plate. Honeycutt monitored Kershaw. Borzello stood next to Ellis. When the first slider arrived, Ellis looked up at Borzello, incredulous. "What'd I tell you?" Borzello said. The ball kept disappearing. From afar, the pitch did not look like much. Up close, it was a marvel. "It's hard to explain unless you've caught," Borzello recalled. "It's hard because you don't see spin." The catcher and the instructor maintained the dialogue, wondering if they could believe their eyes. Even Honeycutt, a far more reserved observer, registered his approval. This might be the answer to Kershaw's problem, the off-speed pitch he could land for a strike and throw when he trailed in the count. "It was supplying exactly what we were trying to do," Honeycutt recalled.

The group gathered after Kershaw finished throwing.

"What do you got on the slider?" Kershaw asked Ellis.

"It's game-ready," he said.

That sent Borzello into a tizzy.

"I told you!" he said. "I told you!"

"Relax," Kershaw said. He had been down this road before. "I'm telling you," Ellis said, "that is unbelievable." Honeycutt was less effusive but still encouraged. He liked the shape of the pitch. He liked the depth. And he liked how different it looked.

Kershaw could already hide the ball using the delivery Skip Johnson taught him. The angle of his arm, combined with the grip Honeycutt showed him, created a weapon that few other pitchers could emulate. "I can't emphasize enough how unique his slider is, compared to the rest of baseball," Honeycutt recalled. The singularity of the offering opened another door for Kershaw. He had something no one else really had. Hitters relied on muscle memory. Their eyes recognized the incoming pitch and their body reacted. But what happened when they faced something they could not recognize?

CHAPTER 11

THE PROPER BALANCE
FOR EVERYTHING

Clayton Kershaw was about to embark on one of the most devastating runs made by a starting pitcher in modern baseball history. He threw his first slider in a game on June 4, 2009, in Philadelphia. His ERA over his final twenty-one outings that season was 2.03. Kershaw was entering a phase in which he was, in the words of teammate Nathan Eovaldi, "untouchable." A generation of pitchers would study him, unable to replicate his arsenal. A generation of hitters would tremble in his wake, unable to decode his attack. His time as a prospect with potential was about to end. His reign as the best pitcher in baseball was about to begin.

But for the Dodgers in 2009, Kershaw was still a character actor in Manny Ramírez's starring production. Ramírez was inscrutable, insufferable, unstoppable. After the Dodgers were eliminated in 2008, Bill Plaschke of the *Los Angeles Times* asked Ramírez if he wanted to stay with the team. "We'll see," Ramírez replied. His free agency dominated the winter. Ramírez lounged at his home in Florida, waiting for the Dodgers to meet his price. Several weeks into spring training, Ramírez inked a two-year, $45 million contract and reported to Camelback Ranch. He terrorized pitchers that April as if nothing was amiss.

Around 1 A.M. on May 7, Ned Colletti got a call from Frank McCourt: Ramírez had tested positive in spring training for elevated levels of testosterone. Ramírez blamed medication he used for a "personal health issue." Major League Baseball levied a fifty-game suspension. "It's a dark day for baseball, and certainly for this organization," Colletti told reporters. (Two years later, Ramírez failed another test and retired rather than serve a hundred-game suspension. The offenses effectively scotched his Hall of Fame candidacy.)

The tumult captivated the public but did not derail the club. Matt Kemp and Andre Ethier each won Silver Slugger Awards. Jonathan Broxton, an overpowering closer, made his first All-Star team. Randy Wolf stabilized the rotation as Kershaw rounded into form. Ramírez clubbed the baseball after he returned from suspension in July. One afternoon that September, Ramírez was taking batting practice at Dodger Stadium. "Back in my youthful sprightly days, I liked to run around the outfield," Kershaw recalled. Ramírez flicked a ball into right field. Kershaw gave chase. He was sprinting, unaware of his surroundings, when he smashed into the wall. He tried to play off the pain; young players were not welcome in the training room. But Brad Ausmus had seen the collision.

"Go inside," Ausmus said. "You did something."

Kershaw sat out two weeks with a separated right shoulder. "Yeah," he recalled, "that was stupid." The Dodgers won ninety-five games, more than any other club in the National League. The first postseason round was a breezy, three-game sweep of the St. Louis Cardinals. Kershaw made his first postseason start. He scattered nine hits but held St. Louis to two runs in 6.2 innings. He could barely swing a bat with his bum shoulder. On the mound, "it was okay, but I wasn't getting to where I needed to" in his delivery, he recalled. He departed with the Dodgers trailing, but watched from the bench as the team fashioned a walk-off rally in the ninth.

A week later, Kershaw took the mound for Game 1 of the National League Championship Series. The Philadelphia Phillies were the reigning world champions, with a formidable lineup and unshakable confidence: Ryan Howard, the imposing first baseman, had won the National League MVP in 2006. Jimmy Rollins, the irrepressible shortstop, won the same award a year later. And Chase Utley, the five-tool second baseman, was the best of the bunch. Philadelphia held psychological sway after eliminating the Dodgers the year before. Wolf compared it to a horror movie: the Dodgers played as if waiting for a monster to jump out of the closet.

They did not have to wait long. Kershaw protected a 1-0 lead into the fifth inning, when veteran outfielder Raúl Ibañez led off with a single. From there, Kershaw unraveled. He threw a wild pitch and issued a walk. A visit from Rick Honeycutt had no effect. Kershaw served up a three-run homer to catcher Carlos Ruiz. The spiral only continued. Kershaw walked the opposing pitcher, Cole Hamels, on four pitches. Two more wild pitches followed. Utley walked. Howard clubbed a two-run double. Kershaw could not control the pace. He ignored the advice offered to him by so many—from Honeycutt to Mike Borzello to Glenn Dishman—about slowing the game down. Kershaw tried to overpower a lineup he could not overpower. His fastball did not faze them. He could not locate his curveball. And his slider did not scare the Phillies. "The early slider that he was throwing wasn't very good, to be honest with you," Utley recalled. "You could see the rotation fairly early." (Utley had a knack for seeing things. When he joined the Dodgers years later, he revealed a secret to his new teammates: Back in 2008 and 2009, the Phillies often knew what was coming. They had stolen the Dodgers' signs from second base.)

At last, after Howard's double, Torre intervened. Kershaw clutched a towel in the dugout and stared between his cleats. He was too young to take the blame for the loss; in the next day's *Times*, Plaschke flogged Torre for laissez-faire stewardship. "Kershaw will probably be a No. 1 playoff starter for the next several years," Plaschke wrote. "But for now, he is still learning his craft, and still needs to be saved from himself." Kershaw blamed himself for not tempering his pace and defusing the threat. "I'm trying to see all these bumps in the road as part of the process of becoming the man and pitcher I want to be," he later wrote. The process could be painful: "I sometimes wish the Lord were not quite so faithful to remind me, 'Clayton, you don't have it all figured out.'"

Kershaw never got a second chance to start against Philadelphia. After winning Game 2, the Dodgers got blasted in Game 3. In the fourth game, Broxton blew a save against Philadelphia for the second consecutive postseason. "You got the impression that you could smell burned toast against the Phillies," Wolf recalled. Facing elimination, Kershaw was rested and ready. In the days before Game 5, he approached Torre in the weight room. Torre rode an exercise bike and read the newspaper while wearing headphones. Kershaw was stalking the room "like a caged animal," Wolf recalled. Torre looked up. Kershaw asked if he would start Game 5. "No," Torre said. "You're out." The Dodgers went with Vicente Padilla. He gave up six runs. Kershaw permitted two more in relief. Another season ended with opponents forming a dogpile. "Those experiences," he wrote, "keep my competitive heart humble."

* * *

One night that winter, exhausted after riding roller coasters all afternoon at Six Flags with Kershaw, Ellen Melson wept inside her childhood bedroom. They were supposed to get dinner that night, but the particulars did not matter. She was convinced her boyfriend was blowing it.

Ellen had visited Kershaw in Los Angeles in 2009, the summer before her senior year at Texas A&M. Kershaw was still living with the Colemans downtown, but he was pitching well enough to envision a future in the city. For the first time, the couple discussed marriage. Ellen had a life of her own back in Texas: she was majoring in communications and engaging in campus philanthropy. During the summers, she worked as a missionary with orphans of the AIDS epidemic in Zambia. With graduation coming, she wanted to be near Kershaw. But she did not want to uproot herself for someone who wasn't ready to commit.

After the season, Ellen waited and hoped for a proposal. To her dismay, Kershaw kept dismissing the topic. Unbeknownst to Ellen, Clayton called her father and asked to meet with him so he could stammer a request for his daughter's hand. The nervousness amused Jim Melson before he gave his approval. Kershaw consulted Ellen's older sister, Ann, while designing the grand gesture. When he invited Ellen on that post-roller-coaster date a few days before Christmas, she missed the obvious signals: Clayton, the guy who loathed pants, arrived in a new suit, his beard Bic'd, in a white stretch limousine. They drove around Highland Park, admiring the holiday lighting, before dining downtown. Ellen was still in the dark about the purpose of the evening when Clayton asked the driver to stop at his townhouse before dropping Ellen off.

As she approached the door, Ellen saw a glow through the windows: Christmas music, greenery, lights. Snow crafted from dry ice covered the floor. Upstairs, beneath the tree, sat a single box. Ellen opened it and found a Santa Claus figurine holding her engagement ring. Ellen wept again—happy tears this time. A party was waiting for them back at the Melsons'. They discussed a date for the wedding. Of course it would be during an offseason.

*   *   *

In the spring of 2010, as the Dodgers gathered at Camelback Ranch to start another season, Kershaw asked Logan White for a favor. The draft was a few months away. Kershaw wanted White to check out an old travel-ball teammate. "I didn't know who the heck Shawn Tolleson was," White recalled.

Most of the other star pitchers from Team USA and D-Bat had reached the majors. Brett Anderson made thirty starts for Oakland in 2009. Tyson Ross debuted for San Diego in the spring of 2010. Jordan Walden, the flamethrower who fell from No. 1 in the country to the

twelfth round, played with the Angels that summer. But Tolleson was
floundering at Baylor. In college, as he recovered from Tommy John
surgery, he never recaptured the hellacious slider that made him Team
USA's relief ace. "They just assumed that I was going to just remember
everything that got me to that level," Tolleson said. "And I didn't
remember any of it." He went 2-7 with a 5.17 ERA as a senior. He had
begun applying to dental and medical schools.

On Kershaw's recommendation, White sent a scout to vet Tolleson.
The report was skeptical. The Dodgers logged Tolleson into their draft
database. And then White forgot all about him. At least until the day
of the draft, when White invited Kershaw into the conference room
with all the scouts. "How about my buddy Tolleson?" Kershaw asked.
"Where do you got him?" White confessed that Tolleson had slipped
from his mind. But in the thirtieth round, the Dodgers took a flier.
Tolleson signed for $10,000 and reported to the team's rookie-ball affil-
iate in Ogden, Utah. A couple of years later, he made the majors. A
couple of years after that, he saved thirty-five games for a Texas Rangers club that made the postseason. He hurt his back and then he underwent a second Tommy John surgery, which effectively ended his career.
But he still made about $5 million more than he expected. "Who knows
what my life would have ended up like?" Tolleson recalled.

Kershaw and Tolleson stayed close over the years. They hung out
during the winter and traded stories about their kids. Tolleson knew,
because White had told him, that Kershaw kickstarted his career. But
Tolleson never asked Kershaw about the draft. And Kershaw never
mentioned it.

*　*　*

In the final years of McCourt's reign, Dodger Stadium fell into disre-
pair. The franchise nearly capsized after McCourt and his wife, Jamie,
divorced in 2009. McCourt had always operated the Dodgers like a
man outrunning his creditors. A culture of ass-covering pervaded the
environment. After the divorce, funding for players, personnel, and

stadium repairs dried up. Dodger Stadium became a metaphor for decay. The elevators crawled. There was only one batting cage inside the stadium. The Dodgers shared a weight room with the visiting team. Orlando Hudson, a four-time Gold Glove second baseman, was playing for Arizona when he first met Kershaw among the weights. A year later, Hudson signed with Los Angeles. Kershaw reminded Hudson of his former teammate, the maniacally focused Roy Halladay, who won Cy Young Awards in both Toronto and Philadelphia. Barely past the drinking age, Kershaw brought youthful exuberance to his dogmatic routine. Kershaw was "always sweating," Hudson remembered. "Like, 'dude, what are you doing now?' 'I just finished running.' Two hours later: 'Dude, why are you sweating *now*?' 'I just got out of the cold tub.' Jeez almighty! I loved that. That wasn't for show. He did it *every single day*."

Kershaw was learning to optimize his time. His bullpen sessions became more efficient. At the outset of his big-league career, Borzello recalled, "It was like a young stallion. You let him out, he's just running all over the place." Borzello alerted Kershaw to the importance of commanding his pitches in that setting. He encouraged Kershaw to spot a good, low fastball, hammering the portion of the zone that Kershaw would live within. The sessions became tidy, thirty-four-pitch affairs, with attention paid to repeating his delivery rather than maximizing his velocity. He did not linger on shaky sessions or gloat about pristine ones. He checked the box and took the next step in his day. "It didn't matter whether good, bad, or indifferent, he would leave it there," Honeycutt recalled.

Honeycutt had noticed Kershaw was tipping when he pitched out of the stretch with runners on base. Kershaw gripped the baseball tight when throwing a fastball, but his glove expanded when he rummaged around for an off-speed grip. Honeycutt suggested Kershaw raise his hands and pause to breathe as he nestled into the grip. The movement disguised his intentions and alleviated tension in his shoulders. Kershaw no longer stood frozen save for telltale movement in his glove. In time, the maneuver became a signature. Kershaw raised his hands higher and higher, until they were fully extended, pointing toward the sky as he exhaled.

Kershaw often heard suggestions from coaches or executives or teammates. He discarded most, but applied the ones that made sense. "Early on, at that level, you'll try to do everything a coach tells you to do," recalled former Dodgers first-round pick Blake DeWitt. "And some guys just keep saying 'yes' and 'yes' and 'yes,' and they keep going down this trail that eventually leads them to forgetting who they are as a player." Kershaw, DeWitt explained, "was hard-headed enough that he knew what made him great, and he was going to stick with it, whether somebody wanted him to be like that or not."

Torre rewarded Kershaw with trust. In 2009, Kershaw reached the one-hundred-pitch mark in sixteen of his thirty starts. A year later, he did so twenty-seven times. He analyzed the charts devised by Honeycutt for game plans. Kershaw sought basic but crucial information: Which hitters were aggressive early in the count? Where were the sweet spots? Where were the holes? He memorized that information before games. Success begat conviction which begat more success which begat more conviction. "He fully believed," Brad Ausmus recalled, "when he was standing on the mound that he was going to get you out, no matter who you were."

* * *

On July 20, 2010, Kershaw dueled for the first time with the pitcher considered the best in the National League West. The crown would soon not belong to anyone besides Kershaw, but Tim Lincecum had earned his keep. As Kershaw scuffled through his first two seasons in the majors, Lincecum, a five-foot-eleven, 170-pound dynamo taken at No. 10 in the 2006 draft, entranced with his whirling-dervish delivery, an "engineering marvel," in the words of *Sports Illustrated*'s Tom Verducci, who "generates outrageous rotational power—the key element to velocity—only because his legs, hips and torso work in such harmony."

The harmony produced consecutive National League Cy Young Award trophies in 2008 and 2009. It also produced considerable agita in the Dodgers front office. "I remember Ned vividly saying, 'How'd you guys pass on Lincecum?'" Dodgers scout Tim Hallgren recalled. They had their reasons. When Roy Smith and Logan White discussed Lincecum before the draft, they agreed he offered high reward but incredible risk. The marvel of Lincecum's delivery relied upon the ridiculous quickness of his right arm, a quality no pitcher could maintain for long. "I remember thinking, if he loses just a little bit of arm speed, he's screwed, at that size," Smith recalled. In his first two seasons, Lincecum averaged 94 mph on his fastball. He lost some velocity in 2009. He was losing even more in 2010. The electricity was flickering out of his undersized frame.

On that July night, when Kershaw and Lincecum shared the mound for the first time, the matchup still qualified as marquee. In the first at-bat, while jockeying for the inner half of the plate, Kershaw hit Giants outfielder Andrés Torres on the left hand with a 91.3-mph fastball. There was history between the two sides. There was always history between the Dodgers and the Giants. A few months earlier, Padilla had broken the jaw of Giants outfielder Aaron Rowand with a pitch. After Kershaw clipped Torres, Lincecum flung three inside pitches at Kemp. The third finally drilled Kemp in the back.

When the umpires threatened both benches with ejections, Dodgers bench coach Bob Schaefer hollered his displeasure. He was not the only one fuming in the dugout. Even on the days he did not pitch, Kershaw hung on the railing, rooting for his teammates. "That guy is Mr. Dodger," former teammate Jamey Wright recalled. To see his brethren get bullied, on a day when he had control of the baseball, activated the same protective instincts that once found him throwing haymakers in a freshman football scrum.

Kershaw approached Torre and Schaefer.

"Joe," Kershaw said, "I'm getting somebody."

Retaliation was foolish, Torre explained. The Dodgers could handle this down the road. They would see the Giants again. Wisdom dispensed, Torre left to grab a cup of water. Kershaw was unmoved.

"Schaef," he told the bench coach, "I'm getting somebody."

Schaefer offered the same spiel. An inning later, San Francisco reliever Denny Bautista brushed back Russell Martin. Martin spun out of the batter's box. Schaefer went, as he put it, "ballistic." The umpire ejected him. On his way through the dugout, Schaefer saw Kershaw. "I'll see you in a little while," Kershaw told him.

With his first pitch in the seventh, Kershaw smoked Rowand in the hip. The umpire sent Kershaw to the showers. There were no histrionics or feigned protest. The crowd gave him a standing ovation. "To me," Schaefer recalled, "he's been a special guy ever since." Schaefer coached in the majors for nearly fifteen seasons. He had a theory about the intersection of talent and desire. "Some players," he explained, "are afraid to be good." They feared the attention. They struggled with expectations. They shied away from the work. Clayton Kershaw, he decided, was not like that.

"He had the goal of being the best in the game," Schaefer recalled. "A lot of people do in their own mind, but by the same token, they realize their own limitations. And Kershaw wouldn't let any limitations get in his way."

*   *   *

On December 4, 2010, seven years, nine months, and fifteen days after Kershaw first approached a girl with brown hair in the halls of Highland Park High, he stood at the altar of Highland Park Presbyterian Church. That same woman was walking toward him.

All those years later, after family trips with the Melsons plus countless calls and emails connecting his baseball world with her college life, Ellen still made him laugh. She exuded optimism and expanded his boundaries. "The best word to describe Ellen is just joyful," Kershaw explained. "She's so joyful and positive and enthusiastic." In Kershaw, Ellen found ballast. "I want to see the world through rose-colored glasses," Ellen explained. "Part of that is because I know I have the security of Clayton, who is going to check all the boxes and make sure that we're in a good place, and measure all the risks. I just get to look at the rewards." They complemented each other. "If there were two of us with heads in the clouds, it wouldn't work," Ellen explained.

The bride wore a strapless gown of silk taffeta. The groom wore a white tie and a daffy smile with his black tuxedo. Ellen's sister, Ann, was the matron of honor. Josh Meredith chaired a group of groomsmen that included several Highland Park friends, Tolleson, and Ellen's two brothers. The list of ballplayers in attendance included James McDonald, Preston Mattingly, and Paul Coleman. After the ceremony, the group repaired to Royal Oaks Country Club for the reception. The bar served Lasorda Family Wines. A choir sang Christmas carols. The couple's first dance deviated from tradition. A few days before the wedding, they were stumped. A classic ballad would not fit their vibe; they would have felt out of place plodding along to "Wonderful Tonight." Ellen thought back to her childhood passion. "I think we should choreograph a dance," she told him. And so it was that, on the day of his wedding, Kershaw switched into sneakers and strutted through the routine Ellen put together for Usher's "DJ Got Us Fallin' in Love." "I don't know how I convinced him to do it, but he did it," Ellen recalled.

For the honeymoon, they betrayed their age. They googled "all-inclusive resorts in Mexico," and ended up in Playa Mujeres. They sipped fruity drinks by the pool and Kershaw hurled baseballs at pillows to keep his arm fresh. A few weeks later, Clayton accompanied Ellen to Zambia for the first time. In the months leading up to the flight, Ellen sensed Kershaw's anxiety. He was not worried about the mission or the prospect of catching malaria. He did not want to disrupt his throwing program. He stuffed a padded mat onto the plane. Once in the country, he commissioned a welder to build a frame for the pad.

When they arrived in the capital, Lusaka, they met some of the children Ellen knew from her previous trips. A crowd of kids gathered. Some gawked at Kershaw; Ellen wondered if they had ever seen a white guy who was that tall. She squeezed her husband's hand. "This is incredible," he told her. The trip deepened his faith and bettered his understanding of Ellen's affinity for the country. He felt moved as he listened to the Zambians sing at mass. "Ellen had always told me that she thought worship in Zambia was a picture of what worship in heaven would look like," he wrote. "In that moment, I knew what she was talking about."

Kershaw maintained his workout schedule. He ran on dirt roads. He peppered the mat with pitches. Another guy on the trip had played high school baseball, so Kershaw deputized him to play catch. The two trips prepared Ellen for what future vacations would require.

"I wish that sixteen years ago I had just learned to catch him," Ellen recalled. "Because it would make our traveling so much easier if I could just do that."

* * *

In the winter, when he wasn't throwing to pillows, makeshift targets, or gym class heroes, Kershaw canvassed Dallas for pitchers to join him at Highland Park High's indoor facility. The crowd varied from high school friends to big-league starters. Brandon McCarthy, a Texas Rangers right-hander, joined the crew one offseason. He received a firsthand education on why Kershaw was terrorizing hitters. When he set a target, Kershaw connected. McCarthy just could not track the ball's arrival. "I remember that standing out quickly, like, 'Oh, that's why you can't really hit this. You can't pick it up,'" McCarthy recalled.

One afternoon, McCarthy stood beside Will Skelton, Kershaw's former Highland Park teammate, who was finishing up his career at Sam Houston State. Skelton noted that Kershaw's velocity was deceiving. His average fastball clocked at 93 mph, but the ball seemed to be moving faster than that. "I would love for someone to do an analysis of how many more rotations his ball does at sixty feet than mine," Skelton told McCarthy.

In the years to come, the fleet of aerospace engineers and spreadsheet wizards and analytically observant *Moneyball* acolytes who populated baseball front offices would be able to provide an answer: Kershaw's over-the-top delivery created tremendous amounts of backspin. The easiest way to explain this phenomenon is to consider an airplane. When a plane takes flight, the airfoil creates upward force beneath the wings. Backspin on a baseball works in the same way. The idea of a "rising fastball" is a myth. No human can generate enough force for that. But a pitcher like Kershaw could produce enough backspin to fight gravity for longer. His fastball descended later than most, which created perceptual confusion for hitters. "His fastball was such a difficult pitch to hit in his prime," recalled Cincinnati Reds first baseman Joey Votto. The heater did not travel on an expected path. "God dang, dude," recalled longtime outfielder Reed Johnson, who specialized in facing left-handed pitchers. "It just gets on you more than other guys."

"He had one of those fastballs that nobody really knew how to quantify," recalled Matt Carpenter, who would become Kershaw's nemesis with the St. Louis Cardinals. "You just knew it was way harder than what [the velocity] said."

Kershaw preyed on the weaknesses of hitters' vision, motor skills, endurance, and, ultimately, memory. They could not recognize what he was throwing. They could not react in time to discern between the fastball and the slider. They could not match his intensity. And they struggled to catalog his arsenal, because so few pitchers pursued hitters like Kershaw.

The slider unlocked everything. Opponents could not just hunt his fastball. In 2011, he increased the velocity of the slider from 81 mph to 84, which tightened the pitch's spin and further disoriented hitters. The pitch would increase in speed as the years passed. "You could not see the spin whatsoever," Utley recalled. "It looked like a fastball out of his hand. You think you're going to make contact with it, and it disappears."

Kershaw subverted the expectations for left-handed pitchers. He picked the brains of elders like Tim Wallach, a five-time All Star who joined the Dodgers coaching staff in 2011. Wallach believed right-handed hitters oriented themselves to look away against left-handed pitchers, because lefties often feared throwing inside. Kershaw staked a claim for the inner half of the plate. "And that's a big advantage, because most lefties can't do that," Wallach explained. To Yasmani Grandal, a catcher who debuted with San Diego in 2012, "it was almost like you were hitting against a righty."

David Wright, the Mets' star third baseman, was a compact man who loved to extend his arms over the plate and wallop lefties who threw fastballs and changeups away. Kershaw did not afford that luxury. "In the most humble way that I can say it, there were very few lefties in the game that I wasn't looking forward to facing," Wright recalled. "I loved hitting against lefties. I always felt confident against lefties. I matched up well against any lefty—but Clayton was one of the guys where it was like, 'Ehh . . .'" Kershaw hammered that lower inside quadrant with relentless, ruthless repetition. "He would just expose you," Wright recalled. "You knew he was going to throw it there. And it was one of those things where he would just throw it there, throw it there, throw it there. If you take it, he could throw it for a strike. If you tried to swing, you'd be icing your thumbs for the next week." And if you loaded up for a fastball, Kershaw countered with the slider. "You can legitimately swing and it would hit you in the shin," Wright recalled.

Left-handed hitters had it even worse. Kershaw pounded the same quadrant, low and away to their vantage point. "There was just no way to be able to see the pitch and react to it," recalled Brandon Belt, the former pitcher from Lufkin, Texas, who eventually became the San Francisco Giants' first baseman. Belt recorded his first career hit, an infield single in his first career at-bat, against Kershaw on Opening

Day in 2011. "It's just unfortunate it was my last hit I got off him," Belt recalled. He was barely kidding: Belt managed three hits in his next sixty-six at-bats against Kershaw. He felt like Kershaw was toying with him, always a step ahead. "It was like a never-ending puzzle that you couldn't figure out," Belt recalled.

The symphony of the fastball and the slider forced hitters to focus on Kershaw's particular quadrant. Which meant that even if Kershaw threw a sloppy curveball over the plate, it was often taken for a strike. "That surprise factor locks guys up," explained two-time American League Cy Young Award winner Corey Kluber.

The three-pitch mixture inspired comparisons to icons. The fastball reminded Honeycutt of Mets Hall of Famer Tom Seaver's. The slider reminded Mark McGwire, who first saw Kershaw while coaching with the Cardinals, of the disappearing bullet thrown by Yankees ace Ron Guidry. And the curveball reminded everyone of Koufax's. Most pitchers racked up strikeouts by getting hitters to chase. Kershaw did not need to leave the strike zone. "Kersh automatically had pitches for swing and miss," Honeycutt recalled.

Kershaw intimidated his foes. "He's an at-bat where you're probably almost never going to get hit by a pitch," Votto recalled. "But you feel scared." He exhausted them. "He makes you make a decision on every pitch," recalled Paul Goldschmidt, a cornerstone first baseman for Arizona and St. Louis. "His slider misses are barely down. I always felt like facing him, you maybe had one pitch to hit in three at-bats." And he confounded them. When Kershaw pitched out of the stretch, he slid toward the plate, a subtle maneuver where "you can't really tell he's gaining ground until you see his arm," Colorado Rockies outfielder Charlie Blackmon recalled. It was easy to swing under the fastball, which never sank like expected. "You miss the pitch and you're not sure why," Blackmon recalled.

In time, rival clubs would siphon wisdom from Kershaw's success. But in that era, most of Kershaw's peers threw pitches that deviated on a horizontal plane. Changeups, sliders, two-seam sinkers, even curveballs—all of them tended toward diagonal movement. But Kershaw's fastball created the perception of ascent paired with a curveball that tumbled toward six o'clock. In between, there was the slider, which dropped like the curveball, but later and with less break. Hitters grumbled as they walked back toward the dugout, unable to process what had happened. "The theory is hitters build up a mental model based on all the pitchers they've seen," one former Dodgers analyst explained. "So if your pitch mix is unique, then a hitter doesn't have a great mental model of it. And because of how vertical Kershaw's pitch separation was, hitters don't have a great mental model of that, just because no one does it like that."

"There were so few guys like him," Reed Johnson recalled. "By the time you feel like you've figured him out, your career's over."

*   *   *

On Nov. 17, 2011, the Dodgers staged a coronation for Clayton Kershaw. His individual brilliance brightened a year of collective failure and institutional shame. After the first game of the season, a pair of Dodgers fans assaulted a San Francisco Giants fan named Bryan Stow in an ill-lit Dodger Stadium parking lot. Stow spent months in a medically induced coma; his plight offered a "sobering reminder," as the *New York Times* put it, that the ballpark "no longer seems to fit its former image, and that many fans have become uneasy going there." In April, the *Los Angeles Times* reported McCourt needed a $30 million loan to make payroll. A few days later, citing "deep concerns regarding the finances and operations of the Dodgers," commissioner Bud Selig announced Major League Baseball was assuming control of the team. Later that summer, the franchise declared bankruptcy.

A slew of injuries decimated a roster made threadbare by McCourt's parsimony. The fleet of prospects drafted by Logan White ran aground. Russell Martin left in free agency. Jonathan Broxton never recovered from his October bludgeoning by Philadelphia. Chad Billingsley posted the worst ERA of his career. A new wave was not coming behind them. McCourt had hollowed out the budget for international free agents and White had placed a series of losing first-round bets on high school arms like Chris Withrow, Ethan Martin, and Zach Lee.

The bleakness meant the franchise celebrated its individual triumphs, in the form of Kershaw and Kemp. Kemp rebounded from a vexing 2010 campaign in which he squabbled with Joe Torre's coaching staff. He flourished after Don Mattingly became the manager in 2011. Kemp stole forty bases while leading the National League with thirty-nine homers and 126 RBI. Yet he finished second to Milwaukee Brewers slugger Ryan Braun in the National League MVP award voting. The snub looked worse when ESPN reported Braun had tested positive for a performance-enhancing drug earlier that season. Kemp still rode his runner-up campaign into an eight-year, $160 million contract.

The 2011 Dodgers never found traction outside of dominance from Kemp and Kershaw. In early September, the schedule pitted Kershaw against Lincecum for the fourth time that year. The Dodgers won each game by one run. Lincecum would finish sixth in the Cy Young voting in what would be his last elite season. By then, Kershaw had surpassed him. On that September afternoon in San Francisco, with Kershaw in his usual smolder while blanking the Giants, Josh Lindblom sat beside Ellis on the bench. At the time, baseball clubhouses were riven with debate about a new movie from Christopher Nolan chronicling the ravages of dreams and memory. "How much money," Lindblom asked Ellis, "to go up to Clayton and ask him what he thinks about the ending of *Inception*?"

Unperturbed by questions about Leonardo DiCaprio's spinning top, Kershaw struck out nine in eight innings of one-run baseball. The game helped him capture the pitcher's triple crown: he led the National League in wins (21), ERA (2.28), and strikeouts (248). He ran away with his first National League Cy Young Award, capturing twenty-seven of thirty-two first-place votes from the Baseball Writers' Association of America ahead of Philadelphia's duo of Roy Halladay and Cliff Lee. At twenty-two, Kershaw became the youngest pitcher to win the award since twenty-year-old Met Dwight Gooden took New York by storm in 1985.

At the Dodger Stadium ceremony, the team displayed the franchise's seven prior Cy Young Award winners on video boards across the second deck. These were the icons that once adorned the walls at Dodgertown: Newcombe. Drysdale. Koufax. Mike Marshall. Fernando. Orel. Eric Gagné. Kershaw stared at the names and took stock. He did not yet consider himself worthy of inclusion. All around him in Los Angeles was chaos. But Kershaw had found—in his relationship, in his career, in his faith—the proper balance for everything. He was about to strike it rich in his first round of arbitration. A reporter asked him how he might top the past twelve months, when he married his high school sweetheart and captured pitching's highest honor.

Only one thing, he realized, was missing. He had begun to dream about a stage the Dodgers had not stood upon since 1988.

"A second anniversary," he replied, "and a World Series sounds pretty good."

CHAPTER 12

DEUS EX GUGGENHEIM

The thumbnail ownership history of the Dodgers goes something like this: Walter O'Malley, a Bronx-born attorney and investor, paved baseball's path of manifest destiny by uprooting the Brooklyn-based club, a beloved team two years removed from a championship, and moving the franchise to Los Angeles before the 1958 season. Forty years later, O'Malley's descendants, after presiding over championships in 1981 and 1988, sold the team to Rupert Murdoch's Fox Entertainment Group. Murdoch took the team on a road to nowhere; the Dodgers never made the playoffs under Fox's management. Murdoch got out in 2004. Enter Frank McCourt, the Bostonian parking lot impresario who scandalized, embarrassed, and ultimately bankrupted the franchise.

There were signs of trouble before Frank's marriage to Jamie, an attorney, imploded on the eve of Clayton Kershaw's start against Philadelphia in the 2009 National League Championship Series. McCourt had bought the club with a $430 million bundle of borrowed cash, none of it his own. T. J. Simers, the acerbic Los Angeles Times columnist, christened him "penniless Frank McCourt." The owner lived up to the billing. In 2008, McCourt financed a $118.6 million payroll on Opening Day, a hefty sum for that era, but still $90 million less than the Yankees. After the team made the franchise's deepest postseason run since

1988, McCourt slashed the payroll by about $18 million. "No matter what I said," Ned Colletti wrote, "no matter how much I argued and pleaded, I kept hearing the same thing: 'The money's not there.'"

Where had it gone?

An examination of Jamie's divorce petition in the *Los Angeles Times* by baseball writer Bill Shaikin revealed the couple's indulgence in $400 dinners and $5,000 hotel rooms. Jamie drew a $2 million salary as the Dodgers chief executive officer. She estimated Frank paid himself somewhere between $6 million and $8 million a year. A subsequent filing by Frank accused Jamie of deputizing Dodgers officials to draw up plans for public office. One line from "Project Jamie" read: "Goal: Be Elected President of the United States."

Before their relationship sundered, Frank and Jamie functioned as a hustling power couple. They accumulated real estate. *Vanity Fair* tallied up the purchases: $21.3 million for a villa near the Playboy Mansion in Holmby Hills. The couple spent $6.5 million on another house nearby. A plot of land in Cabo San Lucas cost $4.7 million and another in Yellowstone cost $7.7 million. The Malibu beach house cost $27.3 million; the next-door bungalow cost $19 million. Then there were the renovations, including uprooting the kitchen of their Massachusetts home and depositing it into the Holmby Hills property. The couple paid a hairdresser $10,000 a month. There were drivers and security staffers, flights on private jets.

And there were some expenditures that defied belief.

* * *

As the divorce unfolded, the *Times* obtained a puzzling collection of emails. The messages contained phrases like, "diagnosed the disconnects" and "V energy," which did not make much sense. It took time to unravel the thread. The emails were written by a McCourt consultant about a septuagenarian Russian physicist named Vladimir Shpunt. His presence on the payroll was hidden from other Dodgers executives. Shpunt worked for the team for five seasons. He attended one game.

Otherwise he sat at home in Massachusetts and attempted long-distance transfers of positive energy. Or, more simply, the McCourts paid him to think happy thoughts.

The tale was so bewildering that Shaikin expected the McCourts to deny it. Instead, Frank blamed Jamie and Jamie blamed Frank. One of Jamie's attorneys told Shaikin that Shpunt was paid six-figure bonuses "and even higher" when the Dodgers reached the postseason. Shpunt had aided Jamie as she recovered from an eye infection, which eventually led to his hiring. After months of hesitation, Shpunt agreed to meet Shaikin at his Boston home. Shpunt offered coffee and chocolate before explaining his methods. "It seems like praying, or a magical way," Shpunt said. "There is no magic."

When Shaikin's story ran, in the summer of 2010, the fallout shamed the organization. There was a memorable exchange between Joe Torre and the *Times* beat writer Dylan Hernández. Torre deflected increasingly absurd questions about whether "long-distance energy transfers" were considered cheating. Hernández suggested that Shpunt might have been more valuable than the manager. Torre maintained a smile. "I'm against domestic violence, but you're not a member of my family," he said.

Near the end of that season, Torre asked Colletti to stop by his office. "Boss," Torre said, "I think I've had enough." Torre took a job with commissioner Bud Selig. Torre had good timing. The 2011 season represented a nadir for the Dodgers: the assault on Bryan Stow, the struggles to meet payroll, the intervention by Selig, the declaration of bankruptcy, the extended food fight between McCourt and the league. At one point, McCourt called Selig "un-American." MLB later accused McCourt of "looting" more than $189 million.

Most of the players ignored the tumult. The season was long and stuff happened: sometimes you win, sometimes you lose, sometimes the owner goes broke. On the night McCourt declared bankruptcy, Hernández bumped into Kershaw and A. J. Ellis at a bar in Minneapolis. The recent financial history of the *Times* had also been checkered.

Hernández bought a round of beers. "Welcome to the bankruptcy club, friends," he said.

The executives were less insulated from chaos. Colletti took pains to not insult McCourt. In private, several former Dodgers officials said, Colletti could be abrasive, capable of lashing out at underlings. But Colletti also operated under constraints unbefitting a franchise with the prestige of the Dodgers. Even before the money ran out, McCourt meddled. Colletti loathed sitting down in McCourt's office, because the conversation might last hours. McCourt scotched a potential trade in 2008 for Cleveland ace CC Sabathia because of a $4 million salary discrepancy. He stoppered the vital pipeline of Latin American amateurs. He denied Colletti permission to award raises.

It was a bad time. Within that maelstrom, Kershaw was the rare player who calmed Colletti. "When you're the GM of an organization," Colletti recalled, "people would say, 'What kind of day did you have today?' And I'd say, 'I had a great day today.' 'Really? What happened?' And I'd say, 'Nothing.'" In the spring, he did not have to worry about Kershaw reporting out of shape. In the summer, he did not wonder if Kershaw might fight a teammate. In the winter, he did not need to scan the police blotter for Kershaw's name. Not many people, in those days, helped Colletti sleep. Kershaw did.

* * *

In November 2011, Frank McCourt agreed to sell the Dodgers. He paid Jamie $130 million to settle the divorce. The sale figured to offset that payment. McCourt managed to divert the process through federal bankruptcy court and conduct an auction in March 2012. The list of suitors included Dallas Mavericks owner Mark Cuban, talk-show titan Larry King, and real estate scion Jared Kushner. The finalists were St. Louis Rams owner Stan Kroenke, billionaires Steve Cohen and Patrick Soon-Shiong, and an eclectic group fronted by Lakers legend Magic Johnson.

Johnson supplied his group's star power. Stan Kasten, a former Braves and Nationals executive, provided the baseball guidance. But

Mark Walter, a relatively anonymous Chicago financier, delivered the money, as the head of Guggenheim Partners. Walter had linked up with Kasten a year earlier while exploring a bid for the Houston Astros. Before McCourt's auction, Walter met McCourt in a Manhattan hotel conference room and offered $2.15 billion plus interest in the land surrounding Dodger Stadium. Cohen had already put forth a $2 billion bid. Guggenheim's offer came with a caveat: McCourt had to accept, right then, or Walter would walk. McCourt took the deal. (Cohen ended up buying the New York Mets in 2020 for $2.4 billion. Soon-Shiong, in a twist, bought the *Times* in 2018.)

For the Dodgers, a new day had dawned.

* * *

A strange thing happened to A. J. Ellis, in the spring of 2012, before Guggenheim rescued the franchise: the Dodgers named him their starting catcher. He turned thirty-one that April. He had spent nearly a decade in professional baseball, pawing for footholds all the while. For once, Ellis had a few things working in his favor. The Dodgers had no elite catchers coming through their minor-league system, and no money to acquire an alternative. Colletti lacked the funds for 2011 starter Rod Barajas, who signed for $4 million with Pittsburgh. "Thank goodness we were bankrupt and couldn't afford anybody," Ellis recalled. He maximized his offensive potential by understanding his limitations, cutting down on swings and taking walks. And he had grown close with the team's most important player.

Because Ellis played sparingly in the previous two seasons, he had become Kershaw's pre-game training partner. He caught his bullpen sessions. When Kershaw ran, Ellis tagged along. He audited the pre-start meetings between Kershaw, Rick Honeycutt, and the starting catcher. When Ellis slumped at the plate, Kershaw grabbed a bat and counseled about simplification. "If it's inside, pull it," Kershaw reminded his pal. "If it's down the middle, hit it up the middle. And if it's away, hit it the other way." Ellis rolled his eyes; not every task was as simple as Kershaw made it seem. During games, the duo talked shop in the dugout. Kershaw often asked Ellis if a starting pitcher could be a leader. Sometimes Kershaw asked Ellis about being a father on the baseball schedule. In spring training, they attended the team's Bible study group. During the season, they went to nondenominational chapel meetings. "Our shared faith played a lot into it," Ellis recalled. "Our ability to be vulnerable with each other, our ability to pray for each other, to share stuff we were struggling with away from baseball."

Kershaw opened up about his childhood. Ellis shared his fears about the fragility of his career. Kershaw revealed one tenet of his faith: he did not think God cared if he won or lost. The other team, he figured, was praying just as ardently as he was. "But He definitely cares how we respond afterward," Kershaw would tell Ellis. Did you hog credit after victories but shirk responsibility after failure? Kershaw believed that mattered more than the result on the field. When things went well, he deflected praise. When things went poorly, he accepted blame.

Along with Honeycutt, Ellis formed Kershaw's inner circle. Ellis came to understand the importance of Kershaw's adherence to the five-day cycle. The rituals comforted him. Ellis thought all that work generated confidence that overrode Kershaw's anxiety: "Like, 'I know what I've done this week to win this game. And I know you're not prepared to win. I'm prepared. Good luck.' And I think he needed that."

In 2012, for the first time, Ellis caught the majority of Kershaw's starts, thirty of the thirty-three. They formed a partnership that fortified them for several years—and would later exasperate a new crop of Dodgers officials. Before 2012, Ellis had witnessed Kershaw's dedication to the cycle, how much he studied opponents, how carefully he choreographed his approach. Now he absorbed some of his reflective glory. "Everyone would always give me so much credit: 'Oh, you called such a good game for Clayton,'" Ellis recalled. "He gave me the stage directions before we went out there. I knew exactly how he wanted to even *sequence* the guy."

The reason Kershaw liked throwing to him, Ellis reflected, was because he embraced Kershaw's vision. And he knew his friend well enough to recognize those rare occasions "when the train wasn't on the track," Ellis recalled. Ellis felt he earned his paycheck by using his intuition when the slider wasn't cooperative or the curveball was skittish. "The rest of the time I was just following what he was convicted in," he recalled.

*　*　*

On August 25, 2012, Kershaw was on the mound and Ellis was behind the plate at Dodger Stadium. But for once, Kershaw was not the starring attraction. Earlier that day, Walter had chartered a private jet at Logan International Airport in Boston to pick up a group of new Dodgers whose arrival demonstrated Guggenheim's desire to win. The new owners had already infused money into the organization. There were minor but crucial upgrades, like the renovation of the ballpark's family room. "Everything was new," Ellis recalled. "Big-screen TVs all over the place. New toys. Like, 'Wow, these guys are really serious.'" There were expenditures on players: an $85 million extension for Andre Ethier. A trade for All-Star shortstop Hanley Ramírez. A $42 million deal for Cuban outfielder Yasiel Puig, whom Logan White had only seen take batting practice once.

Kasten learned the value of homegrown stars while running the Atlanta Braves during their dominant 1990s run. He believed the Dodgers could create a developmental conveyor belt that sustained the organization. But that process would take years. "We had a fanbase that had earned an immediate team," Kasten recalled. So the trade made that August trumped all the other moves. Kasten and Colletti used Walter's money to absorb $250 million in salary from the Boston Red Sox. The deal included three-time All-Star pitcher Josh Beckett; four-time All-Star outfielder Carl Crawford, who was recovering from Tommy John surgery; and utility infielder Nick Punto. But the prize aboard Walter's jet was Adrián González, a five-time

All-Star who had grown up in San Diego and tormented the Dodgers with the Padres. His reputation in Boston had soured after the team collapsed in 2011. But his appeal to the Dodgers was obvious, as a Mexican American star who remained one of the best hitters in the sport. When Kasten took over, he encouraged Colletti to "think bold" about players the Dodgers had not been able to afford under McCourt. Colletti put González atop his list.

The deal was essentially finalized on August 24, pending MLB's approval process for such a significant salary dump. The Dodgers were still in a celebratory mood as fans piled onto the field for the usual Friday night fireworks. Ellis noticed Walter wandering underneath the pyrotechnics. "We got Adrián González," Walter kept saying. "We got Adrián González."

*   *   *

In September, the Dodgers traveled to San Francisco for a pivotal series. Despite the additions of González and Ramírez, despite the spending by Guggenheim, despite the usual brilliance from Kershaw, the Dodgers trailed in the National League West by four and a half games. The team needed this series to have a shot at the postseason. On the first night of the weekend, two days before his scheduled start, Kershaw cut short a workout. His groin was bothering him. "I couldn't walk," Kershaw recalled. "I would take a step and get this shooting pain in my nut."

The team thought he had developed a hernia. An MRI revealed something wrong with his right hip. After every pitch, Kershaw landed on his leg, where all the weight from his delivery transferred. He had dealt with plantar fasciitis in his right foot earlier that season. This condition was more alarming. The Dodgers scratched him from the Giants series. Given two extra days of rest and a cortisone injection, Kershaw limited Arizona to one run in seven innings. But each step agonized him.

With their postseason chances dwindling, the Dodgers kept Kershaw off the mound. On September 17, with the rest of the team in Washington, DC, Kershaw visited Bryan Kelly, a hip specialist at the Hospital for Special Surgery in New York. Kershaw had torn the labrum in his hip, which was exacerbated by an abnormality with his joints. Kelly prescribed an ultrasound-guided cortisone injection and the addition of hip flexibility exercises to the five-day cycle. "I really haven't had problems with it since that cortisone shot," Kershaw recalled.

A day later, Kershaw rejoined the team at Nationals Park. He was not in a good mood. Hernández had written a story explaining that if Kershaw underwent hip surgery, he would likely be out until May. Kershaw confronted Hernández. He felt injuries were private. Hernández countered that the ticket-buying public deserved to know if the team's best player was available. It was the sort of intractable disagreement that Kershaw would repeat in later years, as his body broke down. When he saw a group of reporters in the dugout later that week, he blew them off. "Oh, you clowns are out here?" he said. His frustration stemmed from more than his press clippings. Team officials were against letting him pitch again. After Kershaw lobbied his way into a bullpen session, Hernández approached, wary of another argument. "He just started talking as if nothing happened," Hernández recalled. Locked into the cycle, Kershaw had decided the fight was not worth it.

A day later, Kershaw called Colletti. Kelly had told the team Kershaw was not risking further damage to his hip. But the rewards felt meager. The Dodgers were out of it. Kershaw did not see it that way. "You've got to let me pitch tomorrow," Kershaw told Colletti. He promised that if he felt the slightest twinge in his hip, or any other portion of any other appendage, he would leave. Colletti gave his blessing. Kershaw walked five Reds but limited the team to one run in five innings. In his final two outings of the year, he struck out eighteen in sixteen innings of one-run baseball.

Kershaw made an admirable defense of his National League Cy Young title. His primary challenger had emerged from obscurity. Robert Allan "RA" Dickey had spent most of his professional life getting kicked in the pants. The Texas Rangers chose him in the first round of the 1996 draft, only to slash his bonus when doctors discovered his right elbow was missing an ulnar collateral ligament. For several years, he was a dud with a mediocre fastball. To salvage his career, he learned a knuckleball. Dickey bounced from Texas to Milwaukee to Minnesota to Seattle in the Rule 5 draft and back to Minnesota before signing with the Mets for 2010. Something clicked for Dickey that summer in Flushing. His mid-70s knuckler clocked about 10 mph faster than the flutterball mastered by Red Sox veteran Tim Wakefield. Dickey's pitch did not float. It stung. In 2012, Dickey assembled a season that, in some ways, surpassed Kershaw's. Dickey completed five games, with three shutouts. Kershaw pitched two shutouts but completed no other games. Dickey won twenty games on a crummy team; Kershaw won fourteen with a better supporting cast. Dickey threw 233.2 innings, six more than Kershaw. And he struck out 230 batters—one more than Kershaw.

When the ballots were cast in October, Dickey received twenty-seven of thirty-two first-place votes. Kershaw netted two. He blamed himself, for getting hurt.

"I should have won, anyway," Kershaw recalled, "but it cost me the Cy Young Award."

He collected a more meaningful piece of hardware that October. His trip to Zambia had not been a one-off. He and Ellen helped build an orphanage in Lusaka. They founded a charity called Kershaw's Challenge, which aimed to aid children in Africa and the United States. MLB recognized him with the Roberto Clemente Award, the sport's top humanitarian honor. At twenty-four, Kershaw was the youngest winner in the four-decade history of the award.

*   *   *

In the first week of December, the non-uniformed members of the baseball world poured into the Gaylord Opryland Resort & Convention Center, a biodome on the outskirts of Nashville that regularly hosts the Winter Meetings, the industry's offseason bazaar. It was the sort of event that everyone—the executives, the agents, especially the reporters—loathed; a once productive conference rendered obsolete by modern technology and overcooked by social media's rumor mill. Most of the attendees would have preferred to just stay home and conduct business on their phones.

Within that milieu, Stan Kasten stood out. He was the rare executive who actually left his suite. He liked to banter with reporters, agents, with anyone who crossed his path; Kasten did not always claim to be the most intelligent person in the room, but he was never afraid to point out who he thought was the dumbest. In later years, after the Dodgers became a juggernaut, reporters wisecracked that Kasten showed his face in the lobby because he had nothing to do. But in the winter after 2012, Kasten was still piloting the organization's revival. The Guggenheim group was flush with cash. Before the offseason officially began, the team threw $22.5 million at Brandon League, a middling reliever. In Nashville, Kasten and Colletti were pursuing a pair of pitchers to surround Kershaw: Zack Greinke, a former American League Cy Young Award winner, and Hyun-Jin Ryu, a Korean Baseball Organization star.

Kasten was strolling through the lobby when he bumped into two agents with keen interest in his whereabouts: Casey Close, the baseball head at Excel Sports Management, and his new lieutenant, J. D. Smart. Earlier that year, Smart had joined Excel. He brought with him Clayton Kershaw, who could become a free agent after the 2014 season. Excel also represented Greinke, so Kasten and Colletti treaded carefully. Anything offered to Greinke could be leveraged in discussions about Kershaw. The agents knew that, too. "They see me, 'Oh, the piggy bank's open!'" Kasten recalled.

The days of Frank McCourt's penny-pinching and legal squabbling had ended. A week after Nashville, the Dodgers inked Greinke to a six-year, $147 million deal, the largest ever free-agent contract for a pitcher. The team forked over $36 million for Ryu the next day. The Excel suits had reason to lick their chops. The bank was open, and Kershaw was well situated to break it. Inside the Dodgers front office, Kasten had a loftier ambition. The team did not just want to prevent Kershaw from reaching free agency. They wanted to make him a Dodger for life.

CHAPTER 13

THE FIRST SUMMIT

The man in the hospital bed had once cradled Clayton Kershaw in his arms and lifted him toward the sky. They shot countless rounds of hoops together. They shared the same angular jawline and sandy brown hair. But Chris Kershaw and his only son were not close, not anymore, and they never would be again. "They hadn't seen each other in years," Ellen Kershaw recalled. "They hadn't talked in years." And their resemblance dimmed as Chris succumbed to his demons.

In the early months of 2013, before he reported to Camelback Ranch for another season, Kershaw reopened a door he had long ago closed. At Ellen's encouragement, he met his father. The circumstances were somber. Chris was dying. Clayton had come to say goodbye. "I think I just needed to see him," Kershaw recalled. "I didn't want to see him, because he was a mess."

After the divorce, Chris had remarried. But he had not prospered. He kept drinking. His health deteriorated. He developed diabetes. He had problems with his taxes and problems at work. He showed up late to the studio and missed deadlines. He lost the ability to hit the high notes. The clever guy with precise diction and exquisite timing faded away. "It was sad to see the deterioration of it," recalled Jonathan Wolfert, Chris's boss. Chris never attended one of his son's games in the majors. "He really couldn't share it with Clayton, because Chris had screwed up so much," Wolfert recalled. Wolfert once noticed Chris watching Clayton on television in his office. "I'd like to call him and congratulate him," Chris told Wolfert, "but he never calls me back."

"He would always hit me up for money and call me all the time," Kershaw recalled. "That was hard. It wasn't fun. I always felt bad that I didn't give him as much as I should have, or needed to." Kershaw was not sure what to do. "Honestly, I didn't answer his calls for a lot of years," he recalled. "Because it was never a check-in. It was always for something."

But Ellen took calls from Kershaw's stepmother, who reached out that winter about the gravity of Chris's situation. Ellen and the couple's pastor, Ron Scates, persuaded Kershaw to visit the hospital. Scates accompanied him. The three men talked about faith. The son attempted to find closure.

"He was, like, a shell of himself," Kershaw recalled. "But I at least got to go and say goodbye, basically. I don't know if that was important or not. But it probably needed to happen."

*   *   *

A 7 A.M. alarm jolted Kershaw out of the bed he shared with Ellen at their home in Los Angeles on April 1, 2013. A familiar anxiety coursed through him. It was the first day of a new season, and his first fifth day of a new season. His motivation had shifted. Before the 2012 season, he signed a two-year, $19 million contract that bought out two years of arbitration. The money aided his mother and eased his mind. "I was like, 'Okay, I'm good for life. I'm set,'" he recalled. "Not the same feeling as, like, winning a World Series, but that burden of providing for your family, I think there was some relief in that." But he still felt drawn into the cycle, unable to shake loose from its hold. "The mindset changed," he explained. "You always find something to compete for." He had made his money. He had established himself as a star. All that remained was winning baseball's ultimate prize.

By the spring of 2013, the Dodgers looked ready to contend. The price was steep. On Opening Day, Mark Walter's Guggenheim group unveiled a roster that cost $216.7 million, more than twice as much as the payroll in 2012, Frank McCourt's last spring. The New York Yankees still sported baseball's most expensive team, but the Dodgers would claim that crown a year later. For now, second place in spending heightened expectations. The writer Molly Knight was working on a book about the team. The title said it all: *The Best Team Money Can Buy.* The tab stemmed from the previous season's trades—Adrián González, Carl Crawford, Josh Beckett, Hanley Ramírez—and the offseason splurges for Zack Greinke and Hyun-Jin Ryu. Plus, there were millions diverted to Yasiel Puig, who was not yet on the roster.

Kershaw remained the sun around which the Dodgers revolved. With the World Series champion San Francisco Giants visiting Dodger Stadium, Kershaw squared off on Opening Day against Matt Cain, who had replaced Tim Lincecum as San Francisco's No. 1 starter. For six innings, the two pitchers traded scoreless frames. Cain ceded the stage for the seventh inning, but Kershaw remained. Neither team had scored when Kershaw stepped into the batter's box against reliever George Kontos in the eighth. Kershaw took pride in his hitting; he had batted .217 his previous two seasons, the second-best mark among starters. But he had never hit a home run—until Kontos tried to sneak a 92-mph fastball past him. Kershaw crushed the pitch over the center-field pavilion. The dugout went berserk. Kershaw beamed as he rounded the bases, hammered his teammates with high-fives, and accepted a curtain call. Then, after the Dodgers scored three more runs, he attempted to bury his glee—the boyish joy he felt back in Highland Park, when he dominated with both his arm and his bat—and finish the game. "To see him trying not to smile is one of my career highlights," A. J. Ellis recalled. Kershaw needed only nine more pitches to finish the ninth complete game and sixth shutout of his career.

A day after Kershaw displayed his importance in the present, the Dodgers tried to secure his future. During batting practice, Ned

Colletti led Kershaw to a ground-floor suite where several Dodgers officials sat with Kershaw's agents, Casey Close and J. D. Smart. The group was discussing what it would take for him to forgo the privilege of free agency and sign an extension. Close had proposed a six-year contract worth $195 million with an opt-out after five seasons, a pricier sum than the seven-year, $180 million extension Detroit Tigers ace Justin Verlander inked that year. The Dodgers had dreamed up something bolder—with a lesser burden on the team's luxury-tax balance. Walter and Stan Kasten presented Kershaw with a proposal worth $300 million. There was a caveat. The contract lasted fifteen years.

The structure made sense for the Dodgers. The contract would effectively buy out the rest of his career. While Kershaw might not last fifteen seasons, he would almost certainly be worth $300 million before he retired. But the Dodgers misunderstood Kershaw's mindset. He felt financially secure. After missing the postseason for several years, he questioned the franchise's future. And he could not bear the responsibility of owing another decade and a half of fifth days. He knew what that required of him. The prospect unnerved him. During the talks, Kasten tried to assuage Kershaw's fears. "We told him, 'You don't have to play,'" Kasten recalled. If his body broke down, the Dodgers explained, he could still recoup his riches. Kershaw was unmoved. He left $300 million, the largest sum ever offered a player in North American professional sports, on the table.

"I don't ever want to commit to a contract that I don't feel like I can live up to my end of the bargain," Kershaw recalled. "And so fifteen years I just didn't feel was doable for me. It goes back to that anxiety. Having to commit to fifteen years of playing baseball?" He could not consider it. "I just was like, 'I don't know if I'm going to be good. I don't want to do this, if I'm not going to be good.'"

"Could you imagine?" Kershaw said in December of 2022. "I'd have six more years."

* * *

On April 28, Kershaw drove alone to Dodger Stadium to face the Milwaukee Brewers. After he left for the ballpark, Ellen received a call from Chris Kershaw's wife. Chris had died. Ellen wondered how to tell Clayton. She worried that he would hear the news from someone besides her.

A. J. Ellis had the day off, so he watched from the bench as Kershaw struck out twelve in eight scoreless innings. Midway through the game, a staffer grabbed Ellis: Ellen needed to speak with him outside the clubhouse. Ellis rushed from the dugout. Ellen asked Ellis to grab Kershaw's phone. She did not want him to stumble across texts about Chris.

Ellen acted as the buffer between Kershaw and his father's family. Her relationship with Chris was less fraught. "It just was too much for Clayton," Ellen recalled. "There was just part of Clayton, like, I don't know, not knowing what that relationship was supposed to look like, and so kind of wanting to keep it at a distance." She waited in the bowels of Dodger Stadium, in a tunnel leading to the clubhouse, until Kershaw left the game. He descended a flight of stairs and saw her. She told him. They gathered his things and left the ballpark. "For some reason, it's, like, cloudy to me, the whole memory of it all," Kershaw recalled.

Kershaw returned to Dallas for the funeral. He found a Highland Park student to catch his bullpen. He rejoined the team in time to make his next start in San Francisco. He did not want to talk about where he had been. On the rare occasions when Clayton Kershaw spoke about Chris Kershaw to people outside his inner circle, he fixated on the good memories, the years before the divorce. He conjured up images of the father shooting hoops with his son, rather than the broken man in the hospital bed. "We could always just do that," Kershaw recalled. "I remember playing catch a lot, too, until I started throwing too hard. He did all that. Like a dad should. I am thankful for that." Clayton learned about parenting, in a way, from Chris. He knew what sort of father he wanted to be.

*   *   *

After the funeral, Kershaw rejoined a team in strife. He supplied seven innings of one-run ball against the Giants, but the Dodgers still lost, part of a dismal eight-game losing streak. Very little had gone right for the big spenders. Ramírez had torn a thumb ligament while playing in the World Baseball Classic. In his second start, Greinke suffered a fractured left collarbone when San Diego Padres outfielder Carlos Quentin charged the mound after Greinke plunked him. A week later, Chad Billingsley felt pain surge through his right elbow, a precursor for his eventual Tommy John surgery. Matt Kemp, one of the few remaining homegrown stars drafted by Logan White, stumbled as he recovered from offseason shoulder surgery; never again would Kemp contend for the MVP. All the injuries and all the losing prompted potshots. "When the *Titanic* sank," Dylan Hernández wrote that April in the *Times*, "there was a Guggenheim on board."

The man tasked with keeping this ocean liner afloat was Don Mattingly, who was unsure if this was his final season managing the team. Mattingly had been one of the best players of his era, a former MVP who many believed belonged in the Hall of Fame. His reputation was sterling. "He's cloaked in kindness, and he's cloaked in humility," explained Trey Hillman, Mattingly's bench coach from 2011 to 2013. Mattingly stood beside his union brethren during the collusion scandals of the 1980s and stood up to the archaic grooming rules of the Yankees. He experienced the misfortune of playing in the Bronx during a rare fallow period. After he retired in 1995, beset by back problems and eager to raise his children, the Yankees won four championships in five seasons. Mattingly parented his kids, including Kershaw's friend Preston, before returning to the game. For players of a certain age, Mattingly cast a lengthy shadow. "I grew up idolizing Don Mattingly," former infielder Jamey Carroll recalled. Mattingly understood how taxing baseball could be, but he never bragged about his own career. "He just had zero ego," Casey Blake recalled.

Mattingly made people feel comfortable. In the spring of 2012, the team hired a mop-topped fellow named John Pratt as video coordinator. Pratt was only a few years removed from getting his degree in broadcast journalism at Emerson College, in Boston. The clubhouse intimidated him. Mattingly made daily visits to the video room. "He's the nicest man in the world," Pratt said. Mattingly asked about Pratt's family, his childhood. He treated him like one of the guys, busting him for his eccentricities. "I made the mistake one time of telling him that I didn't like the shampoo in the Ritz-Carlton," Pratt recalled. "And it gave him years of fodder."

Mattingly stomached McCourt's final years, when the payroll was trimmed and hope was dimmed, only to find himself out on a limb in 2013. Mattingly lacked a long-term contract and the assurance that the Dodgers wanted him around. The lame-duck status annoyed him. Colletti had hired him, but Mattingly was unsure if Kasten and the new crew trusted him. Mattingly stayed positive as injuries decimated the roster. He maintained his calm when rumors swirled about his job status. And he juggled the egos of his stars all the while. All he sought was the validation of a contract extension.

In June, Kershaw joined the ranks of the grumpy. After he rejected the $300 million deal, talks stalled. Later that summer, Kasten recalled, Close reopened the discussions around the original seven-year framework. The negotiation hit a snag when Ken Rosenthal of Fox Sports reported the two sides were making progress. The story bugged Kershaw. He blamed the Dodgers for violating a mutual agreement not to discuss the deal publicly. The talks continued; money tends to trump chivalry. They were close to a deal worth $210 million when they started haggling over how to insure the contract. There were shouting matches between Kasten and Smart.

The instability of the negotiations, and the uncertainty of his future, did not affect Kershaw's performance. He reached his third consecutive All-Star Game that summer. He lived within the five-day cycle. On the day after his start, he lifted, ran, and played catch. On the second day, he threw his thirty-four-pitch bullpen session. On the third day, he lifted and played long toss. On the fourth day, he climbed the bull-pen mound for the visualization techniques he had cribbed from Derek Lowe. And on the fifth day, he muscled down his turkey sandwich and tossed the baseball against clubhouse walls, then took the field and dominated. The work he did on the first four days allowed him to over-come the nervousness hijacking his brain on the fifth day. He needed the cycle, because if he ignored it "and things didn't go well, there's just that feeling of, like, *You really screwed this one up*," he recalled. "The con-sistency and routine helps the mind."

It also made Kershaw appear, to the uninitiated, unhinged. Michael Young, a seven-time All-Star third baseman for the Texas Rangers, had lifted with Kershaw in the winter. At the end of August in 2013, Colletti acquired Young to help his bench. Young met the team at Coors Field in Colorado on a day Kershaw was starting. Upon entering the clubhouse, Young spotted his offseason workout partner. "Hey, 22, you suck!" Young said. Kershaw managed a half smile and walked away. *Oh shit*, Young thought. Young dropped his gear at his locker and went to the training room. Ellis was there. "First time playing with Kersh, huh?" Ellis said.

By the time Young arrived, the Dodgers had run away with first place in the National League West. The team was in last place on June 3 when Colletti promoted Puig, a twenty-two-year-old signed to a $42 million deal after that brief tryout with Logan White a year earlier. Puig stood six-foot-two, weighed 240 pounds, and straddled the line between bravado and recklessness. He flouted team rules about tardi-ness and received scant punishment; some Dodgers believed Puig was protected by the new ownership group. But the dude could play—and the Dodgers were rolling. "Winning does a lot," Kershaw said after one start that summer. "It puts aside a lot of differences, it puts aside bad blood. Not that we had any of that." González's steadiness, Ramírez's return, and Puig's arrival catalyzed the offense. Puig hit .319 with a .925 OPS that season. His electricity on the bases, the rocket launcher he called a right arm, it all galvanized Dodger Stadium. The team went 69-38 after his promotion, winning the West by eleven games.

The turnaround thrilled Kershaw. He did not want to miss any more Octobers. On the four days he did not play, he occupied the top step of the Dodgers dugout. He was "the biggest cheerleader ever," Skip Schumaker recalled. "He's either eating, in uniform watching the game, or in a pile of his own sweat," Young recalled. On September 19, Kershaw clambered over the railing at Chase Field in Arizona as the team clinched the division. After the players sprayed champagne and domestic beer, Kershaw and the rest detoured to the indoor pool beyond the right-field fence. Kershaw splashed and smiled among his teammates. Then he climbed out and toweled himself off. His schedule called for visualization the next day. He had more starts to make.

*   *   *

On October 3, the 92-win Dodgers returned to the postseason for the first time since 2009, visiting the 96-win Atlanta Braves to begin the National League Division Series. A distance of 1,449 days separated Kershaw from his last postseason start. No longer was he a talented youngster brimming with potential but lacking poise. In a few weeks, he would collect his second Cy Young Award, finishing first on twenty-nine of the thirty ballots, after a season in which he posted the sport's lowest ERA (1.83) while leading the National League with 232 strikeouts. He was, at twenty-five, the best pitcher in baseball—and the most important player on one of the most expensive rosters ever assembled.

Despite some plucky early at-bats by the Braves, Kershaw struck out twelve and limited Atlanta to one run. His teammates built him a nice cushion. The lead grew to five runs in the sixth when Hanley Ramírez hit an RBI double off Jordan Walden, the former D-Bat ace now pitching in Atlanta's bullpen. Kershaw stuck around through seven innings. He logged 124 pitches, his second-highest total of the season. After the

6-1 victory, Kershaw lobbied for more. "He was barking right after the game that he was ready for Game 4," Mattingly revealed a few days later. "We're like, 'No, no, no, no, no.'"

In the early 1970s, the Dodgers pioneered the five-man rotation, which became the accepted standard and created the cycle Kershaw would follow decades later. Starting pitchers grew accustomed to taking the ball after four days of rest. The post-start buildup of lactic acid in the arm took days to drain. "When you pitch, your shoulder and elbow bleeds," longtime manager Buck Showalter explained. "And then you have to flush that out." In times of desperation, usually in October, teams asked their best pitchers to pitch more often. Curt Schilling started three times, twice on short rest, for the Arizona Diamondbacks in the 2001 World Series. CC Sabathia made two starts on short rest during the New York Yankees' 2009 championship run. In 2011, St. Louis Cardinals stalwart Chris Carpenter pitched Game 7 of the World Series on short rest. But those were the success stories: Greg Maddux got smoked in 2001. Kevin Brown recorded only four outs in 2004. Chien-Ming Wang lasted one inning in 2005.

The practice had mostly fallen out of vogue. San Francisco used Matt Cain and Madison Bumgarner on regular rest en route to the World Series in 2010 and 2012. The Phillies didn't use Roy Halladay, Cliff Lee, or Cole Hamels on short rest in 2011. In Detroit, Max Scherzer was willing to slither into postseason games between starts as a reliever, but Justin Verlander maintained his regular schedule. Making his postseason debut as a Milwaukee Brewer in the fall of 2011, Zack Greinke gave up four runs in five innings on short rest, having pitched in the final game of the regular season. He made twenty more postseason starts in the 2010s. None were on short rest.

As Mattingly and Honeycutt plotted the pitching schedule for the Dodgers in 2013, they knew they could line up Greinke behind Kershaw. Greinke had recovered from the fractured collarbone to finish with a 2.63 ERA. Hyun-Jin Ryu, the third starter, had posted a 3.00 ERA. But the fourth starter posed a problem. Ricky Nolasco had given up twenty-two runs in 25.2 September innings. Mattingly told reporters that Nolasco would start Game 4. But privately, in the weeks leading up to the postseason, the Dodgers had been discussing using Kershaw. "You never like it, but we didn't have any choices," Honeycutt recalled. "He was our best pitcher."

After the Dodgers lost Game 2, the team returned to Los Angeles. On the day before Game 3, Kershaw grabbed pizza in West Hollywood with Ellis and Pratt. They downed a few pies and a few drinks before visiting the Comedy Store. Ellis teased Kershaw about how these indulgences might hamper his routine. Kershaw replied that on three days of rest, he wasn't sure what the routine was. He was improvising: He completed fewer sets while lifting on the first day. He shortened his bullpen session on the second day. "I basically just skipped day three," he recalled, doing his fourth-day visualization instead.

After the Dodgers won Game 3, Mattingly called Kershaw into his office. Kershaw listened as Colletti, Mattingly, and Honeycutt told him they did not need false bravado. "I think about this all winter long," Kershaw told them. Everything he did, every day of his five-day cycle, all the reps on the squat rack, all the sprints in the outfield—it all pointed him toward this moment. He did not care that he had not yet signed a long-term deal. He wanted the ball. Kershaw was beaming when he left the office. Hillman told Mattingly that Kershaw looked "like a kid on Halloween that stole the biggest bag of candy you could ever see."

The Braves put up a fight. In the fourth inning, a throwing error by González opened the door for a two-run rally. Kershaw stemmed the tide and lasted six innings, a 91-pitch effort that left the game tied. In the eighth inning, as Braves All-Star closer Craig Kimbrel watched from the bullpen, Puig doubled and infielder Juan Uribe launched a game-winning homer. The Dodgers were moving on, set to face the St. Louis Cardinals in the National League Championship Series. During the raucous celebration, Sandy Koufax, a few months away from turning seventy-eight, wore goggles to deflect champagne spray. Koufax placed his arms on Kershaw's shoulders and expressed his admiration. To Kershaw, Koufax was neither a mentor nor a deity. He was a friend. "He's just a good human being," Koufax explained. They spoke on the phone and grabbed dinner when they could. They shared more than an arsenal. Koufax had sacrificed his left arm in the pursuit of greatness. To him, Kershaw possessed the same spirit. "The one thing that I appreciate about him a lot is, you never really have your best stuff," Koufax recalled. "And when you figure out how to win when you don't have your best stuff, that's special."

* * *

The Cardinals won ninety-seven games in 2013, more than any other team in the National League, which meant the baseball world remained on its axis. The Cardinals had made the postseason ten times in the twenty-first century, winning the National League pennant four times and the World Series twice. The franchise maintained regional hegemony in the Midwest, personified by flagship station KMOX, "The Voice of St. Louis," which broadcast games across forty-four states. The audience marketed itself as "The Best Fans in Baseball." The team had barely skipped a beat since organizational Mahatma Tony La Russa retired and three-time National League MVP Albert Pujols departed after winning the 2011 World Series. "We believed in each other," Cardinals outfielder Jon Jay recalled. "We never quit."

Kershaw returned to his routine. Mattingly slotted him into Game 2 at Busch Stadium. But the series swung before he took the mound— and before even Greinke took the mound in Game 1. As a boy growing up in Corona, California, Cardinals pitcher Joe Kelly got into his share of scraps. At a tryout camp in high school, he decided to impress a collection of scouts by heaving a baseball from the outfield to the third story of a nearby building. Bespectacled and baby-faced, Kelly could generate tremendous velocity. He just didn't know where the baseball was going. On his ninth pitch of the first game, Kelly unleashed a 95-mph two-seam sinker. The pitch veered from its intended target, the glove of catcher Yadier Molina, and connected in a fortuitous location for the Cardinals: the ribcage of Hanley Ramírez.

Ramírez was a few years removed from winning the National League batting title, and injuries limited him to only eighty-six games in 2013. He was brittle but vital. Ramírez finished the game, a 3-2 defeat in thirteen innings, in which the Dodgers managed only one hit in ten chances with runners in scoring position. A day later, as Kershaw prepared to duel with rookie Michael Wacha, the pain prevented Ramírez from swinging a bat, leaving Mattingly to scratch together a lineup without either Ramírez or outfielder Andre Ethier, who had hurried back in September as he recovered from shin splints. In Wacha's mind, the prospect of matching Kershaw loomed larger than the prospect of smothering the Dodgers lineup. "I remember thinking I couldn't give up anything, because he's not going to give up anything," he recalled.

Kershaw lived up to his billing. After six innings, he had struck out five and limited St. Louis to a pair of hits. The Cardinals cobbled together a run in the fifth when leadoff hitter David Freese doubled, took third after Ellis failed to grasp a fastball that skipped behind him for a passed ball, and scored on Jay's sacrifice fly. Kershaw had thrown only seventy-two pitches when his spot in the batting order came up in the seventh. Mattingly did not want to sacrifice one of his seven remaining outs. The hitters kicked themselves for wasting Kershaw's effort in a 1-0 defeat that gave the Cardinals a two-game lead.

Back in Los Angeles, the Dodgers took two of three to extend the series despite a dearth of offense. Ramírez batted .133. Puig struck out in ten of his twenty-two at-bats. Ethier batted .150. Kemp had been shut down in September because he required ankle surgery. For all the money invested by Guggenheim, for all the hype generated around "The Best Team Money Can Buy," for all the turbulence the club survived during the summer, when the series returned to St. Louis for Game 6, everything rode on the left arm of Clayton Kershaw.

Once more, Kershaw was paired against Wacha. "I probably really didn't know what I was doing out there, and the magnitude," Wacha recalled. Kershaw did. He leaned into his October look: he let his beard grow into an ungainly chinstrap and let his hair descend to his shoulders. He had thrown a career-high 236 innings during the regular season and another 19 in the postseason. He had trained all winter, prepared all spring, and toiled all summer to reach this summit. He thought he was ready.

There was a hint of trouble in the second inning, when Kershaw gave up a single and then spiked a pair of curveballs for wild pitches. He did not have good feel for the curve. And the Cardinals were not going to cower before him. The second point was solidified, in dramatic fashion, when second baseman Matt Carpenter stepped to the plate in the third. The Cardinals offered Carpenter a paltry $1,000 bonus after choosing him in the thirteenth round of the 2009 draft. He had no leverage. He had already been in college for five years. That money was well spent. Carpenter reached the majors in his third professional season. He became a regular in 2012. He made his first All-Star team in 2013. Carpenter looked like he was culled from a casting call for La Russa. He eschewed batting gloves. He spoke with a soft, South Texas drawl. He saw more pitches than any player on his team. He personified the Cardinals ethos: spoiling good pitches and smacking bad ones. "If there was ever going to be a team that could combat what Clayton did, I think it would have been us," Carpenter recalled. "We took pride in having those long, grinding at-bats, and making him work, making him earn it."

Kershaw had overrun Carpenter in the first inning with fastballs. For their second encounter, Carpenter altered his approach. His goal was not to strike out. Carpenter kept the bat on his shoulder as Kershaw missed inside with a first-pitch slider. He swung at the next seven pitches. Carpenter fouled off one fastball, then another, then a third. When Kershaw tried a curveball, Carpenter pulled it foul down the first-base line. When Kershaw switched to a slider, Carpenter fought it off down the third-base line. The sixth foul ball enlivened the crowd. A gentle roar greeted the seventh. Carpenter felt like a tennis player fending off a killer serve. As long as he could make contact, he figured, he was still alive. The ninth pitch was a ball inside. It evened the count at 2-2. Carpenter drew more applause when he deflected the tenth pitch, another heater, into the stands. Kershaw gathered himself and fired a slider. Like most of his pitches, the ball aimed for the glove-side half of the plate. Carpenter deposited it into right field for a double. Left-handed hitters like Carpenter had batted .165 against Kershaw during the regular season; when Kershaw picked up two strikes, lefty hitters batted .136. But this was not the regular season.

A deluge followed. Carlos Beltrán singled off the glove of second baseman Mark Ellis. An ill-timed throw by Puig permitted Beltrán to reach second. After Kershaw struck out outfielder Matt Holliday, Molina chopped a single up the middle to score Beltrán. Freese sliced a hit just underneath Kershaw's glove. Kershaw barked at the umpire when a 3-2 fastball to first baseman Matt Adams was called a ball. Kershaw tried to stay composed, but outfielder Shane Robinson chopped a two-run single. In all, the Cardinals stacked together four runs with four groundball singles, a close call on a full-count fastball and Carpenter's refusal to yield. Kershaw stuck around until the fifth, but when the first three Cardinals reached base—two singles, another bad throw by Puig, and a double by Adams—Mattingly intervened.

Kershaw handed over the baseball without protest. He removed his glove and studied his feet as he trudged to the dugout. All around him, Cardinals fans twirled white towels and hooted. The lineup managed only two hits against Wacha in the 9-0 defeat, but no one cared. In the biggest game of his career, Kershaw had combusted. The outcome left the team "shell-shocked," A. J. Ellis said afterward. "I don't have an answer," Kershaw said. "I just wasn't good enough."

In a season of high expectations and clashing egos, Kershaw had been the team's lodestar. So he alone toted the weight of the final defeat. He took no solace in how the Dodgers rebounded from early season troubles or how close the team had come to ending the championship drought.

"What does it really matter?" he said. "Making the playoffs or coming in last place, if you don't win the World Series, it doesn't really matter. If you don't win, what's the point?"

CHAPTER 14

"PLAYOFF CLAYTON"

In a subdivision on the outskirts of Milwaukee, snow blanketed the lawns but the streets were clear. At the end of a cul-de-sac, A. J. Ellis opened his door. He bought the plot in 2015. Ellis, his wife, Cindy, and their three children moved into the house in 2016. By then, his salary had nudged beyond the big-league minimum and into the millions.

"This is the house that Kershaw built," Ellis said.

In a bathroom off the two-car garage, a framed print hinted at piety and mischief: "Wash your hands and say your prayers, because Jesus and germs are everywhere." A reading room overlooked a frozen pond. The hills behind the house were perfect for sledding. A map tacked onto the wall included pincushions where the Ellises had lived: Clarksville, Tennessee, at Austin Peay University; various stops in the minor-league diaspora: Jacksonville, Las Vegas, Albuquerque; and, of course, Los Angeles.

All of those detours led the family to their two-story home in Muskego. During the lonesome summer of 2020, Ellis retreated to his couch and synced up YouTube to the television above his white stone fireplace. Together with his son, Luke, he replayed postseason games from his Dodgers career. It was a way to kill time and relive past glory.

But there was one game he refused to watch, one memory he could not relive. The way 2013 ended was heartrending. What happened the next October was worse.

* * *

In 2014, Clayton Kershaw authored his most decorated individual season. Yet the year served as a bitter signpost. He established himself, without question, as his sport's premier pitcher. And he also fed the growing narrative, one that would follow him for the rest of the decade, that he choked in October—that the things that made him great exposed him to heartbreak when it mattered most. Because the most decorated season of Clayton Kershaw's career ended far sooner than expected. And he was the reason.

During the winter, the front office had solidified its future. In January, Mattingly received a three-year contract. A week later, the Dodgers finalized a longer, more expensive deal. Despite the testy talks the previous summer, Guggenheim kept pursuing Kershaw. "We weren't going to fumble our first big free agent," Stan Kasten recalled. A deal made too much sense. The Dodgers had unlimited resources. Kershaw and Ellen had grown comfortable in Los Angeles. Every summer featured so many guests from Highland Park, Ellen developed a standard tour: the Hollywood sign, Griffith Park Observatory, the Santa Monica Pier. They purchased a home in Studio City; they were hoping to expand their family soon.

That January, Kershaw flew from a private function in Florida to Los Angeles, where he spent hours in an MRI tube as Casey Close hammered out the particulars of the largest contract ever for a pitcher. The seven-year extension cost $215 million, with Kershaw's desired opt-out clause after five seasons. During the talks, Kasten recalled, Ned Colletti asked a question: Would Kershaw really be able to make thirty starts a season for the next seven years? "It was a fair question," Kasten recalled. But Kershaw had not yet turned twenty-six, "and had been so strong, and so dominating," Kasten recalled. Don Mattingly called his son: "Do you think this money will affect Clayton?" Preston was unequivocal: "It won't change him a bit."

The Opening Day payroll escalated to $229 million, the most expensive roster in baseball, but the Dodgers entered 2014 with essentially the same cast as the year before. There were already more full-time outfielders than there were spots in the outfield. To augment the bullpen, the team added Chris Pérez and Brian Wilson, a pair of fading former All-Stars, in addition to Jamey Wright, who worked out with Kershaw in the winter. "He's the easiest guy to catch," Wright recalled. "You don't have to move your glove. You just open your glove and the ball crushes the glove and the glove closes. I was more worried about him catching my bullpens, because now I'm going to throw a sinker and skip one and hit him in the nuts or something like that. I'm scared to death. If I hurt Clayton Kershaw, I'm going to get released."

Wright never hurt Kershaw. A promotional junket did.

For the fourth consecutive season, the Dodgers tabbed Kershaw to start on Opening Day. Except this season, the opener came a week early, on a different continent. The Dodgers were slated to face the Diamondbacks on March 22 in Sydney, Australia.

Consternation about the trip was apparent all spring. "I would say there is absolutely zero excitement for it," Zack Greinke told ESPN, which kicked up a kangaroo's nest down under. A calf issue grounded Greinke. He stayed home with Dan Haren, a two-time All-Star pitcher signed for $10 million, whose arm felt tired. The trip shortened the spring for the pitchers. Rick Honeycutt preferred that starters appear in five exhibitions before the season. Kershaw only pitched in four Cactus League games. Team officials pondered whether Kershaw should make the trip. "I remember there was a debate whether or not to start him," Colletti recalled. "And I'll leave it there." Added Honeycutt, "I don't want to talk about that." Mattingly had not worried about Kershaw's readiness. "But obviously," he recalled, "I should have been."

A few days before the opener, after the fifteen-hour flight, Kershaw spent the afternoon at the Sydney Cricket Grounds searching for his slider. He felt the external pressure from the calendar and internal pressure to meet his own expectations. He did not fly halfway around the world to throw four mediocre innings. His standard remained his standard. And his slider did not meet his standard. The stadium emptied as Kershaw kept throwing. These sessions had acquired a metronomic feel—Kershaw executed the same pitches, in the same sequence, at the same volume, every time. Ellis memorized the progression. He rattled it off to ESPN that spring: "Three fastballs when I'm standing up. I sit, and three fastballs down the middle. Then three fastballs either side. Three changeups away. Fastball inside. Three curveballs to the middle. Fastball inside. Three sliders to the middle. Then he goes to the stretch position. Two fastballs inside, two fastballs away, two changeups, one fastball inside, two curveballs, one fastball inside, two sliders. Back to the windup, and one fastball inside, one fastball away." The session lasted thirty-four pitches. Always. If his fastball wasn't cooperating, or his slider wasn't biting or his curveball kept bouncing, it did not matter. "If it was a bad day, he would leave it there—and maybe just not talk to anybody, just steam off the mound," Honeycutt recalled.

But this time was different. Kershaw searched for the slider long past the thirty-four-pitch mark. He threw about sixty, Ellis recalled. To Ellis, the palpable anger stemmed from stress: Kershaw was not sure if he would be ready, and he couldn't abide taking the mound if he wasn't ready. At the end, he hurled a baseball into the seats with all his might. Ellis and Honeycutt shared a glance. Against Arizona, Kershaw met his standard. He permitted one run and pitched into the seventh inning in a victory. But during the game, Kershaw felt discomfort behind his arm. The pain stuck with him longer than other memories from the visit, like touring the country in a pontoon plane or cuddling a koala. "Australia was super cool," Kershaw recalled. "It was a fun trip. But could have done without the baseball."

On the flight back to Los Angeles, he tossed and turned. Pain flared whenever he lifted his arm. "My triceps," he recalled, "was on fire."

*   *   *

A week after the opener, Kershaw stood in the outfield at Petco Park, trying to prove he was healthy. By his twenty-seventh throw, his arm and his back were bothering him. He argued his case, but the front office still placed him on the disabled list for the first time in his career. He had torn a teres major muscle near his lat, which stabilized his rotator cuff. He risked significant damage in the first year of his new contract. Even armed with insurance, the Dodgers would not allow further risk.

On his first day off the roster, Kershaw ran sprints in the outfield. Teammates wondered what he was doing. "He would get hurt, and you'd think that he was going to be done," Greinke recalled. "And he would keep working hard, and everyone was like, 'Why are you working out so hard? You're just going to hurt yourself more.'" The training staff devised a plan that matched Kershaw's ethos. They built him a five-day cycle. For the first four days, Kershaw lifted and sprinted as if completing his usual routine. On the fifth day, he completed a forty-five-minute circuit of running and torso rotations. "We had to be super creative," strength and conditioning coach Brandon McDaniel recalled. The activity replicated the cardiovascular intensity of a start. He made one hundred rotations, just as he would during a game, only without throwing. Kershaw was too precious to rush, but too headstrong to delay. "It was much more of an art than a science," McDaniel recalled.

By the end of April, Kershaw felt he could return. He emphasized the point by bouncing a ball off the wall outside Mattingly's office. When he came back, on May 6 against the Nationals, he scattered nine hits while allowing zero runs and striking out nine. "You get something taken away from you," he said afterward, "you realize how much you miss it." His five-day cycle expanded to include exercises to protect his back, in addition to the hours he spent keeping his right hip loose, his legs strong, his arm fresh. He was feeling good, back to himself, when he stepped into a doctor's office on June 17. For once, his body was not the subject.

Ellen had been pregnant for two months, but the couple still kept it secret. Inside the office, the doctor showed an ultrasound of a heartbeat. Kershaw felt thrilled and overwhelmed and scared. A year after he said goodbye to his father, he would become one himself. A day later, Kershaw stowed his excitement. Another fifth day was upon him. The Colorado Rockies were visiting Dodger Stadium, and Kershaw intended to grant them his usual inhospitality. The Rockies were not a particularly good team, but they were a familiar opponent, overflowing with respect for Kershaw. "I looked forward to facing him, almost more than anybody, just because I knew that he was going to give everything he had that night," Colorado second baseman DJ LeMahieu recalled.

Kershaw was never better than on the night of June 18, 2014. He completed the first three innings in forty-six pitches without permitting a man on base. By the fifth, Ellen started getting texts from friends. The Dodgers led by eight runs. The only drama was Kershaw's flirtation with history. He had not thrown a no-hitter since that charmed outing against Justin Northwest his senior year. Kershaw possessed exquisite command of his curveball, which Ellis used to complement the usual medicine of fastballs and sliders. A seventh-inning throwing error by Hanley Ramírez cost Kershaw a perfect game, but a nifty scoop by third baseman Miguel Rojas and a deft pick by first baseman Adrián González kept the no-hit bid alive.

The television cameras found Ellen, with Vin Scully narrating her glee. "Amongst the large crowd, the big heart of his wife Ellen beats a little faster," Scully said as Kershaw walked off the mound after the eighth. In the dugout, Ellis and Honeycutt studied the opposing lineup card. Ellis felt a presence behind him.

"What do you guys got?" Kershaw asked. "What are you thinking?"

He was looking for a scouting report on infielder Charlie Culberson, who had entered the game earlier in a double switch but hadn't hit yet. Neither Ellis nor Honeycutt wanted to jinx Kershaw. They stayed quiet.

He did not wait for an answer. "Pitch to strengths?" Kershaw said, shorthand for fastballs and sliders on the inner half. The catcher and the coach stayed silent and nodded. When Culberson came up, he lofted a first-pitch fastball into right field. "If you watch the tape, it's the only two-handed catch of Yasiel Puig's career," Ellis recalled. The last batter, outfielder Corey Dickerson, had as little chance as the rest. Kershaw buried him with a glove-side slider, his fifteenth strikeout of the day, to wrap up the no-hitter.

Kershaw lifted his arms and spread them wide to welcome Ellis. The Dodgers sprayed Kershaw with water as his warmup music, Fun.'s indie-pop hit "We Are Young," thumped over the speakers. Ellen burst into tears and wended her way down to the field. She stood nearby as Matt Kemp and Puig soaked Kershaw with buckets of water and red Powerade.

Ellen ignored the stickiness of her husband's jersey and wrapped her arms around his chest. It would not just be the two of them for much longer. But for now, for this magical night, it still was. Afterward, they strolled through the parking lot together. Kershaw held the game ball. "That's kind of cool, huh?" he said.

*　　*　　*

If the no-hitter represented Kershaw's peak, for the rest of the regular season he never descended. He strung together forty-one consecutive scoreless innings. In seventeen starts, he authored four complete games and finished the eighth inning in nine other outings. He lasted at least seven innings in every game but one. In between outings, he conducted himself with the same studied goofiness, soaking up in-game knowledge from hitting coach Mark McGwire, trading scouting tips with Greinke, or playing catch with Haren, whom Kershaw nicknamed "Thunder Dan," after Dan Majerle of the Phoenix Suns. Then he took the mound and embarrassed hitters. "I could never fathom someone dominating the way he dominated," recalled Haren, who started the 2007 All-Star Game. "To the point where I was jealous. It just seemed so easy." Mattingly structured his relief usage around Kershaw starts. On the day before, Mattingly could empty his bullpen without fear. When Kershaw took the mound, the relievers could have absconded to Tijuana and no one would have noticed. "It got to the point where it made me not believe in jinxes anymore," reliever J. P. Howell recalled.

Kershaw finished with a 21-3 record and a 1.77 ERA, securing his fourth consecutive ERA title. After the season, he became the first pitcher to win the National League MVP award since Hall of Famer Bob Gibson in 1968. A third Cy Young Award arrived, almost as an afterthought. "He was untouchable," McGwire recalled. "I remember saying to Donnie, 'Don't even think about taking him out of the game.' They were not even making contact. Who cares about a pitch count?"

For the 2014 postseason, the Dodgers intended to ride Kershaw as far as he could take them. Despite all the money poured into the team, they still sported a suspect bullpen. A few years earlier, Kenley Jansen, Kershaw's minor-league catcher, had converted into a reliever. Jansen wielded a wicked cutter that opposing hitters could not touch. He became one of the best closers in the sport. But the rest of the relievers were a collection of untested newbies and shot veterans. The bullpen ranked twenty-third in ERA and sixteenth in strikeout rate. Their collective mediocrity was only heightened when Kershaw took the mound. "It was tough to go get him," bench coach Tim Wallach recalled. "Donnie and I would sit and talk, and say, 'It's probably time. But who is better?'"

The Dodgers were not a one-man band. Greinke and Hyun-Jin Ryu were both excellent again in 2014. Puig made his first, and only, All-Star team. González remained a steady run producer. Kemp overcame his irritation about losing his spot in center field to Puig and put together a strong season. Justin Turner, a castoff from the New York Mets, emerged as a useful bench player. Mattingly tried his best to mollify the egos of his stars. Puig, in particular, drove him to distraction. "I'm so tired of your shit!" Mattingly yelled at Puig during one blowup inside his office. Kershaw considered Puig's behavior an occasional detriment, but he did not care so long as Puig unleashed his talent on opponents. "We've had worse people here than Puig," Kershaw recalled.

The National League Division Series offered a rematch between the 94-win Dodgers and the 90-win Cardinals. Animosity lingered between the teams. Joe Kelly was gone, traded to Boston, but the Cardinals still pitched inside with impunity. That July, after St. Louis pitcher Carlos Martínez plunked Ramírez, Kershaw retaliated by drilling Matt Holliday. The storylines wrote themselves. St. Louis had punctured Kershaw's veneer of invincibility. Now he was back, performing at his best, annoyed by the suggestion he sought revenge. The day before Game 1, Kershaw fielded questions about the previous year's ending. "Why doesn't anybody ask me what it feels like after a win in the postseason?" he said.

By the sixth inning of the first game, Ellis was pondering his answers for friendlier questions from the press. The Dodgers led, 6-1, having trounced Cardinals starter Adam Wainwright. With two outs, Kershaw faced Matt Carpenter, his gloveless nemesis. Carpenter lifted a first-pitch fastball over the right-field fence. Carpenter stayed stoic as he rounded the bases. A four-run deficit still felt vast. "When you're facing Clayton Kershaw, you don't think you're ever in it until he walks off the mound," Carpenter recalled. Kershaw completed the frame and returned for the seventh. He had thrown eighty-one pitches, in 96-degree heat. "It was smoking hot," Ellis recalled. "It was so hot that day," Honeycutt recalled. "I remember it being warm," Carpenter recalled.

There was a growing realization in baseball that pitchers fared worse when facing hitters for the third time in a game. It was often better to use a fresh reliever rather than a tired starter. But Kershaw thrived when navigating a third time through the lineup. In 2014, he was actually better on his third turn through the order than his second: Opponents posted a .573 OPS when facing Kershaw a second time and a .568 OPS when facing him a third time. "He used to scoff at the whole third-time-through thing," Kasten recalled. "Well, yeah, if you're Clayton Kershaw, it's not a thing. But it is a thing." During their time together, Kershaw and Mattingly spoke often about how long he should last in games. Kershaw told Mattingly to remove him whenever the manager felt there was a better option in the bullpen, like using Jansen in the ninth. "But don't take me out thinking I'm tired," Kershaw insisted. "I'm not tired. I don't get tired." The coaches struggled to determine when he was bluffing. "He could be completely gassed, and he would never let you know it," Wallach recalled.

As St. Louis's best hitters batted for a third time, in the seventh inning of an unseasonably hot day in Los Angeles, Kershaw remained on the mound. The move felt obvious to the Dodgers coaches, who believed in Kershaw's stamina and distrusted their bullpen. It was the age-old question: who was better? But the Cardinals were a seasoned, resourceful team, capable of adjusting on the fly. They knew Kershaw would continue to pound the inner half of the plate with fastballs and sliders. They prioritized contact over power. A 93-mph fastball broke the bat of Holliday, who still muscled a leadoff single past Kershaw's outstretched glove. It was only the third hit of the day for St. Louis. For the first time all afternoon, Kershaw was pitching out of the stretch.

His approach did not change. Heaters, sliders, inner half. The next batter, Jhonny Peralta, smacked a fastball into center. Yadier Molina lined a first-pitch slider up the middle. All of a sudden, the bases were loaded and the tying run was at the plate. "Every hit they got was just singles right up the middle," Honeycutt recalled. "You just go, 'What the heck's going on here?'" Honeycutt rang the bullpen. But he stayed inside the dugout. In his suite above the diamond, Ned Colletti felt helpless: "I remember standing up there going, 'Please, somebody stop the game.'"

Ellis, like Honeycutt and Mattingly, stayed in his assigned spot, unable to improvise. He stuck with the strategy that Kershaw had mastered in recent years, the strategy that led to all those scoreless innings all during the summer, the strategy that experienced hitters could predict. He called twenty-nine pitches for Kershaw in the seventh. Only one was a curveball. "It was probably the worst inning I ever called in my career behind the plate," Ellis recalled. Ellis kept signaling pitches that worked in May and June and July. But this was not May or June or July. In time, he would believe that played a factor. What made Kershaw great, his commitment to routine that instilled his sense of superiority over opponents, may also have depleted him. "Clayton expends so much emotional energy, even before he takes the mound in the regular season," Ellis recalled. "And amplify that even more for a playoff game. Honestly, I think there was an emotional drain that was tapped out, as well, by the time we got to the seventh inning."

Ellis stuck with the plan. Kershaw did not want to pause. It was like one of his emergencies back in the minors, when he attempted to power past the competition in times of trouble. The strategy backfired. Matt Adams singled on a slider to cut the lead to three. After a strikeout, Kershaw faced Jon Jay. "I just tried to tap the ball and not get too long," Jay recalled. When Kershaw flung a 94-mph fastball, Jay redirected it through the left side of the infield to trim the deficit to 6-4.

With Kershaw at ninety-nine pitches, Mattingly visited the mound. Kershaw assured him he felt fine. There were two left-handed hitters coming up, the sort of hitters Kershaw drubbed. Rather than use lefty reliever J. P. Howell, who was warming up, Mattingly stuck with his ace. Tired? Kershaw did not get tired. Who was better? No one— except, on this day, the opponent. After another strikeout, Kershaw dueled once more with Carpenter, whose eleven-pitch at-bat the previous year began the season-ending nightmare. This encounter lasted only eight pitches, all of them fastballs and sliders. It still ended in heartbreak for Kershaw. The crowd chanted "M-V-P" as Kershaw picked up two strikes, only to groan as Carpenter launched a 95-mph fastball off the wall in right. Upon impact, Kershaw shrunk to a crouch. He hung his head as three runs, enough to put St. Louis ahead for good in an eventual 10-9 defeat, crossed the plate. He retreated to the dugout and held his head in his hands.

It was improbable but not inexplicable. Kershaw had attempted to bully his way, mostly with his fastball, past gimlet-eyed foes who knew what to expect. The Cardinals punished him for his predictability. "A terrible feeling," Kershaw called it. "There are no words you can use right now," Ellis said. After the game, Kershaw slipped into an elevator on the ground floor of Dodger Stadium. He leaned against the wall and stared at the floor. The lift carried him to his car. He would not pitch again in Los Angeles that year.

*   *   *

John Pratt, the video coordinator who had become one of Kershaw's confidants, drove down Sunset Boulevard after Game 1 with his radio silenced and his windows rolled up. His time with the Dodgers included "a lot of really difficult postseason losses," but that game against the Cardinals "still stands alone as the most shocking loss I saw firsthand," he recalled. He could not believe what happened. And he could not explain why.

The next morning, Pratt got a call from Dodgers executive Rick Ragazzo. Pratt needed to scour the footage and discern if Kershaw had given himself away. St. Louis had mauled Kershaw once he started pitching out of the stretch in the seventh. Maybe he was tipping his pitches. On the Fox broadcast, announcer Harold Reynolds fixated on the possibility that the Cardinals were stealing Kershaw's signs from second base and relaying them to hitters. "They were reacting like they knew what was coming," Logan White recalled.

Nearly a decade after the series, former Cardinals scoffed at the idea. "That was always a thing, 'Oh, the Cardinals have something,'" Jay recalled. "We never had anything." They sounded almost insulted. "That was the narrative back then, that we had his pitches," Carpenter recalled. "But that was not the case." In the years to come, the concept of sign stealing would be conflated with cheating after the Houston Astros used illegal cameras to gain an edge. Even when within the confines of the rules, the practice still suggested subterfuge. It suggested that St. Louis hadn't won—Kershaw had lost. The Cardinals rejected that framing. "We weren't relayed anything," Adams recalled. "We didn't see anything that he was doing differently on his fastball compared to his off-speed stuff."

After Game 1, Pratt and Dodgers officials studied the wreckage. "Nobody ever found anything," Pratt recalled. Honeycutt wondered if the Cardinals caught a different bend in Kershaw's elbow and wrist when he raised his arms. "If there was a slight thing—I mean, we looked in every direction," Honeycutt recalled. Pratt still harbored suspicions. "I think they had something on his curveball," Pratt recalled.

McGwire often joked with Kershaw about the pitch. "His curveball, I could see it coming a mile away," McGwire recalled. When Kershaw threw curves, McGwire thought, he lifted his arms and tilted his chest higher than usual. "I used to joke with the coaches in the dugout: 'Can't you see that curveball coming?'" McGwire recalled. He possessed keener eyes than most. "You could get me out with that slider," McGwire liked to tell Kershaw. "But if you ever hung me a breaking ball, it's going a mile."

* * *

Four days after Game 1, Kershaw stood on the mound at Busch Stadium, trying for the second year in a row to avoid elimination in St. Louis. He clung to a 2-0 lead, but the Cardinals were circling. St. Louis started the seventh inning with a pair of singles. At the plate stood the go-ahead run, in the form of Adams. Behind the plate, Ellis refused to repeat his mistake from the first game, when the patterns became so predictable. He called a curveball.

Despite the opening disaster, Kershaw was pitching on short rest again in Game 4. "For some reason," Ellen recalled, "the last game always landed on Clayton." In Game 2, Greinke evened the series with seven scoreless innings. Two days later, St. Louis pushed the Dodgers to the brink. Scott Elbert, a seldom-used reliever, surrendered a game-deciding homer. After blowing Game 1, Kershaw did not stump to start Game 4. But he leapt when offered the chance for redemption. "The easy thing to do," Michael Young recalled, "would be to say, 'I know what's going to happen if I'm on full rest: I'm going to go seven and I'm going to shove. I can sit back, wait for that and continue to do it, every single time. Or I could say: Fuck it.' Well, he wouldn't say that. He would say, 'Screw it. I'm going to take on the challenge.'"

If Kershaw was tipping out of the stretch, in Game 4 the Cardinals could not take advantage when runners reached in the fourth and the fifth. He struck out the side in the sixth. He entered the seventh with nine strikeouts. On a third turn through the lineup, though, Holliday singled off second baseman Dee Gordon's glove and Peralta blooped another hit just past Ramírez. "Those are both outs," Mattingly recalled. "And then we're gonna blame Kersh?" To the plate came Adams, a twenty-third-round draft pick out of Slippery Rock University, the sort of player the Cardinals specialized in finding. The matchup should have been a mismatch. Adams batted only .190 against lefties in 2014, with three home runs. A left-handed batter had never homered off Kershaw's curveball in the majors. Yet when Kershaw followed Ellis's instruction and threw a curve, Adams recognized the shape. "I saw that thing pop up, and knew that pitch was going to be a good one for me to go after," he recalled. Adam hammered the ball. Ellis jumped up in horror. Kershaw assumed the familiar position, hunched at the waist as a season swirled down the drain. After the ball cleared the right-field fence, Adams skipped as he approached first base, his 263-pound frame practically levitating. "It felt like my feet didn't touch the ground, rounding the bases," he recalled. He was hyperventilating so badly he ducked into the tunnel to catch his breath.

It took Kershaw a while to leave his crouch. He cast his eyes around the stadium—the Cardinal red throngs waving white towels and red pom-poms, fireworks bursting in the distance, the opponent rounding the bases. It had happened. Again. Mattingly removed Kershaw, but there was little to be done. The 3-2 loss felt academic.

"I can't really put it into words right now," Kershaw said afterward. "Bad déjà vu, all over again."

Ellis held his head in his hands and wept. In baseball, where the clubhouse opens to the media minutes after season-ending postseason defeats, private misery can become public knowledge. Swarms of reporters hustle to interview the grieving players and coaches. Navigating this scene requires tact and timing. After a while, Ellis dried his tears and looked across the room. He saw Dylan Hernández of the *Times* interviewing Kershaw, who had already spoken with the group.

God dang it, Dylan, Ellis thought. *He just did the scrum. What are you doing?*

The next day, Ellis understood. Hernández wrote a story about Ellis's future with the team. Ellis had hit .191 that season. The Dodgers were considering cutting him. The first quote came from Kershaw, whose voice cracked as he spoke about his friend. "I don't know what I'm going to do," Kershaw said, "if he's not back."

* * *

On November 12, seven of Kershaw's childhood friends piled into the home he had purchased in Highland Park. The votes for the Cy Young Award were being announced that night. Kershaw was a lock to win, just as he would win the National League MVP a night later. His friends came to celebrate him—and check their phones to see if they were being roasted online.

The tradition had started the year before. Six pals—Josh Meredith, the Dickenson twins, Patrick Halpin, Ben Kardell, and Will Skelton— came over for the 2013 Cy Young Award presentation. They were still dressed in the chinos, blazers, and button-downs they wore to work in banking, commercial real estate, and energy investment. "This is how we actually dress," Skelton explained. "As embarrassing as it is." They stood around as Kershaw conducted television interviews. Someone—possibly Ellen, possibly a producer, possibly

Kershaw himself—encouraged them to jump into the shot. So they stood behind their buddy, beaming but awkward, as Kershaw spoke to ESPN and other outlets. The white-collar backdrop incited instantaneous social media dunking.

"For the next year, we were just reading the comments of all the ridiculous things people were saying about us," Skelton recalled. "'The Mayonnaise Crew.' Or 'These guys look like they can really do some taxes.'" The most lasting dig came from Barstool Sports, which called them the "Mean Street Posse," a callback to a pro wrestling stable of rich kids from Greenwich, Connecticut. Robert Shannon joined the group for 2014. The scene repeated itself. Kershaw won his third Cy Young. His buddies got cooked for their attire. "We knew how ridiculous we looked," Skelton recalled. They figured they would spend every November gathering around Kershaw to show off their sweaters and slacks.

*　*　*

The calendar in January 2015 featured a pair of major events for the Kershaw family. On January 25, Clayton was scheduled to receive the Cy Young Award and MVP trophy at the Baseball Writers' Association of America's dinner in New York. On January 30, Ellen was set to give birth. Nature intervened: Ellen went into labor before the ceremony. The Kershaws welcomed their daughter, Cali Ann, into the world on January 23. Tears coated Kershaw's face as he cradled his daughter. "It was hard for him to wrap his head around being a dad, taking care of the little one, until he held her," Ellen recalled.

Clayton figured he would skip New York. Ellen was insistent. She understood the rarity of his achievement. Clayton had written a speech and spent hours practicing it. "You have to go," Ellen told him. "Because this will never happen again." Kershaw sat on the dais of a ballroom at the Hilton in midtown Manhattan, as a tuxedoed audience saluted baseball's best. A good friend introduced him. "He's tried to get better every year," Sandy Koufax had said the year before, when he handed Kershaw the 2013 NL Cy Young Award at this same dinner. "And if he gets better after the year he had this year, I'd like to apply for next year's job of presenting this to him again." And so Koufax did.

In his speech, Kershaw took the audience through his typical day at the ballpark—not the fifth day, but the four that led up to those evenings of anxiety and greatness. He mentioned the clubhouse attendants and training staff, John Pratt and Rick Honeycutt, Don Mattingly, Tim Wallach, and Mark McGwire. He praised his teammates. Near the end, he choked up as he mentioned Ellen. "Sorry, I just had a kid," he said. "Bear with me." From the audience, Jim Melson FaceTimed so Ellen could watch. When she saw her husband stumble over his words, she realized he was ready to be a father. "He was never an emotional person," Ellen explained. "I mean, growing up, I never saw him cry or anything. He becomes this puddle of mush when he talks about our kids."

Kershaw closed with a wink toward his new reputation. He had not forgotten how his season had ended. And he would not soon forget.

"My last thank-you goes to the St. Louis Cardinals," Kershaw said. "Thank you for reminding me that you're never as good as you think you are."

* * *

And maybe it was that simple.

Maybe Kershaw, the best pitcher on the planet, had run into an opponent in possession of his Kryptonite. Maybe the Cardinals knew what was coming, either through intuition or surveillance. Maybe Kershaw did the same thing for too long against a team too experienced.

Or maybe there was something else.

Sitting on his couch, inside the house he credited to his friend, across from the television that never broadcast their greatest collapse, Ellis turned Shakespearean: What made Kershaw great during the regular season might have made him susceptible to failure in the postseason.

"I don't know how much Clayton will like this," Ellis said. "My theory on 'playoff Clayton,' I'm hesitant to even share it."

Ellis considered how Kershaw tortured his body and trained his mind to be mentally, spiritually, physically, emotionally ready for every fifth day, to take the mound with no regrets.

"I've never been around somebody who could get themselves to this maximum level on a Wednesday getaway day in Cincinnati at 12:10 P.M. When there's eighteen hundred people in the stands, we're trying to wake up as a team.

"But he would still max out. And he did it thirty-four times a year."

Ellis raised his right hand above his head.

"He's always here."

Then he raised his left to the same level.

"In the playoffs, everyone gets here. And I think he got the sense of it. And so he would try to go [higher].

"And there was nowhere to go."

CHAPTER 15

THE ROOSTER

In the spring of 2015, the Dodgers brass met with Clayton Kershaw. He saw faces both familiar and new. The meeting took place in Don Mattingly's office at Camelback Ranch, with Rick Honeycutt in attendance. But the discussion was led by two men Kershaw had only known for a few weeks: Andrew Friedman, the team's new president of baseball operations, and Farhan Zaidi, the team's new general manager.

Friedman and Zaidi spoke with every Dodger that spring, in part to get to know the players and in part to introduce themselves. They were members of a newer generation of executive, faithful to the applications of analytics and conversant in the business principle of arbitrage. They did not see a barrier between the front office and the clubhouse. In order for a team to succeed, the two men believed, there needed to be synergy rather than separation. The duo gave each player a list of individual strengths and goals. For Kershaw, the strengths were numerous. He was the reigning MVP. His success was rooted in his dedication and his mastery of his position's fundamentals. He did more or less everything well: He threw strikes. He missed bats. He held runners. He fielded his position. He stayed composed with runners on base. He lasted deep into games and he never shrank from competition.

Friedman and Zaidi extolled his virtues for a while, before they suggested a goal: Kershaw should throw his curveball more often. They were taken aback by his reply.

"That," Kershaw grumbled, "will never happen."

During the previous four seasons, Kershaw had demonstrated the apex of what a pitcher could do. But Friedman and Zaidi wanted to show him where the sport was going. They believed data could help any player, even the best of the best. Which meant they were asking Kershaw to sacrifice the resource he hoarded above all: control.

*　*　*

On the flight home from St. Louis, hours after Matt Adams's homer landed, Ned Colletti wondered if he would be fired. After the game, Colletti had bumped into Bill Plaschke of the *Los Angeles Times*. "I think you're going to be in trouble here," Plaschke told Colletti. A few days later, Colletti and Stan Kasten went to dinner. "I'm going to have to make personnel changes, including you," Kasten explained. There would not be a search for a new executive to run the team. Kasten had already found his man: Friedman, the architect of the thrifty but thriving Tampa Bay Rays.

In 2005, Rays owner Stu Sternberg installed Friedman, only twenty-eight, as his general manager. Three years later, Tampa Bay reached the World Series for the first time in franchise history. From 2008 to 2013, competing with deep-pocketed American League East foes like the New York Yankees and the Boston Red Sox, the Rays averaged ninety-one wins per season and made the postseason four times. The *Moneyball*-era Oakland Athletics captivated the analytically inclined in the 2000s; the Rays inherited that mantle in the 2010s. Sternberg plucked Friedman off Wall Street, where he had worked at Bear Stearns. Sternberg preached to Friedman the value of optionality, a financier's way of saying you should have a lot of options when making decisions. Under Friedman's watch, Tampa Bay pioneered how defenses were aligned, bullpens were constructed, and rosters were managed.

Friedman found value in marginal moves. He evoked the principle of arbitrage, believing small transactional victories piled up. Friedman knew how to stretch a buck better than any other executive in the sport. The final tab for the 2013 Dodgers was about $236.9 million. The team won ninety-two games. So did the Rays, whose roster cost about $64.6 million.

Friedman was unsure if he wanted to leave Tampa Bay. His family was comfortable. He appreciated Sternberg and his staff. After Kasten offered the job, Friedman lined up the pluses and minuses in a spreadsheet. The analysis told him to stay. But the prospect of complacency, of getting stale as he grew older, frightened him. He signed a $35 million contract, uprooted his family for Los Angeles, and set about finding a chief lieutenant.

When Friedman called, Zaidi experienced a similar ambivalence about the Dodgers. He had applied for a job with the Oakland Athletics in December of 2004, with a résumé that included a degree from the Massachusetts Institute of Technology, an economics doctorate from Berkeley, and an affinity for Britpop. Billy Beane was charmed by the Oasis fan in the ill-fitting suit. There were few people in baseball who looked like Zaidi: a Muslim of Pakistani stock, born in the Philippines and raised mostly in Canada, who had never played beyond high school.

At first, Zaidi specialized in quantitative analysis; he built Oakland's in-house projection system, known as "FarGraphs." He soon expanded his horizons. He incorporated scouting into his research, which led to the acquisition of Cuban outfielder Yoenis Céspedes and slugging first baseman Brandon Moss. During the draft, Zaidi became the "Tools Police." Whenever a scout could not identify a legitimate tool on a prospect, Zaidi activated a siren. Beane nicknamed him the "Emotional Stats Guy," a name Zaidi co-opted for his fantasy football team.

Zaidi felt the pull of loyalty to Oakland. The Dodgers were offering him the chance to become a general manager, a significant promotion for a team with significantly more resources. But Zaidi didn't want to leave. He wrote an email to Beane and owner Lew Wolff about his decision to stay. Before he sent it, he went for a run. A couple of miles into his route, Zaidi started hyperventilating. He felt consumed by the fear of missing this chance. He stopped running and walked home. "I have to do this," he told his wife.

Friedman and Zaidi shared an office at Dodger Stadium that fall while revamping baseball's most expensive team. Their primary goals were deepening the forty-man roster, fixing a pricey but ineffective bullpen, and improving clubhouse chemistry. The team relied too much on injury-prone players like Matt Kemp and Hanley Ramírez. The acrimony of the previous two seasons—much of it revolving around Yasiel Puig—made regular headlines. Despite the challenges, Friedman and Zaidi inherited a wealth of talent assembled by Colletti, who stuck around as a consultant, and Logan White, who joined San Diego's front office after the new regime arrived. The farm system featured budding stars like shortstop Corey Seager, left-handed pitcher Julio Urías, and first baseman Cody Bellinger. The big-league roster included anchors like Adrián González, Zack Greinke, Kenley Jansen, Hyun-Jin Ryu, and Justin Turner.

And, of course, there was the franchise cornerstone. When the Dodgers approached Zaidi, he thought about Kershaw. As general manager, he saw himself as "the caretaker of the greatest pitcher of this generation." They needed to build a club worthy of his presence.

"When you have Clayton Kershaw on your team, he gives you such a head start on every other team in baseball," Zaidi said. "Now it's your responsibility to do the rest of it."

*   *   *

Soon after his arrival, Friedman called to gauge Kershaw's assessment of the club. Friedman did not afford the same platform to other players; he did not want to form too many relationships while revamping the team. Kershaw agreed with Friedman's plans. The roster was top heavy and riven with discord. Change felt necessary.

When Kershaw reported to spring training that February, he saw the fruits of the overhaul. For several feverish weeks that winter, the front office cooked up interwoven deals that demonstrated new priorities. Kemp? Traded to San Diego. Ramírez? Departed in free agency to Boston. Chad Billingsley? Gone, his contractual option declined, his time in Los Angeles over. Dan Haren, Dee Gordon, Miguel Rojas— all traded away. The new Dodgers included Los Angeles Angels second baseman Howie Kendrick, San Diego Padres catcher Yasmani Grandal, and a pair of Miami Marlins rookies: catcher Austin Barnes and utility player Kiké Hernández. The team signed Brett Anderson, Kershaw's former Team USA buddy, and Brandon McCarthy, Kershaw's occasional offseason throwing partner. Beneath the surface, Friedman and Zaidi were launching several initiatives that would make the player-development system the envy of the sport. Even on the surface, the alterations were significant.

The changes did not just apply to personnel. Colletti considered the clubhouse a sanctified space for the players. The new guys were around more often. Friedman bantered with players, offered suggestions, heard their complaints. Friedman carried himself like the bantam-sized jock he had been before injuries ended his career at Tulane University. He could talk to ballplayers and billionaires alike. Zaidi did not exactly self-identify as a nerd, but he understood the perception. He possessed enough self-confidence to not take himself too seriously. When Steve Dilbeck of the *Los Angeles Times* wrote that the Dodgers had been overtaken by the Geek Squad, the branded moniker for Best Buy's customer service repair staff, Zaidi offered to use a mini-screwdriver to fix the writer's laptop. Zaidi rode the elliptical in the weight room during games; he even dared to chat with Kershaw while the ace exercised.

Friedman and Zaidi aimed for incremental progress with Kershaw. He did not need to change much. But there was room for growth in the sequence of his pitches, how his defenders aligned behind him, even in who caught him regularly. Kershaw did not immediately accept any

advice. "I want to know their reasons," he recalled. Friedman came prepared with data. It did not always sway Kershaw. "I'd like to think I
don't suggest random stuff to anybody," Friedman recalled. "But Kersh
is certainly batting cleanup on the All Don't Bring Random Stuff to
Someone team." Even small tweaks, like the positioning of outfielders,
sparked debate. The team wanted to play the outfielders deeper to protect against extra base hits. Kershaw objected because "he was like, 'I
just can't take when I give up a little flare and it drops for a hit,'" Zaidi
recalled. The front office refused to relent. "And now I look back," Zaidi
recalled, "and I'm like, 'It's Clayton Kershaw. If he wants to play his
outfield at regular depth, what are we doing picking this fight with
him?'" The arguments lasted years. When a hit dropped in shallow left
field early in 2016, new outfield coach George Lombard saw Kershaw
glaring at him from the mound. Lombard found bench coach Bob
Geren: "Am I going to have to put up with this shit all year?" "No,"
Geren replied. "Just once every five days."

His catcher carried himself with the same stubbornness. "I always
thought of myself as open minded," A. J. Ellis recalled. "Looking back?
So closed-minded." Ellis liked Friedman and Zaidi. They were sharp,
funny, personable. But he found their methods more cute than cutting
edge. "In 2015," Ellis recalled, "I was naive, and thought, 'Hey, that's
nice. Bring in your little small-market models in here and we can talk
about them. We're the Dodgers . . . You're gonna learn the way we do
business here, real fast. Just take notes and learn, Andrew.'" Kershaw's
obvious preference made it tough for Grandal, a switch-hitter with
more offensive potential than Ellis. The prospect of catching Kershaw
was "terrifying," because he feared upsetting the ace, Grandal recalled.

It did not help that Kershaw stumbled through the early weeks of
2015. He was oddly . . . hittable. He did not complete the seventh inning
until his fifth start of the season. Baseball defined a "quality start" as an
outing where a pitcher lasts at least six innings and permits no more
than three earned runs. Kershaw did not agree with the adjective. "Six
innings and three runs is not a good start," he recalled. "Seven innings

and three runs, potentially, is okay." To do that, he felt, was the "bare minimum of what you need to do."

After a rainout in Colorado in early May, Ellis synced up some video of Kershaw to study with Honeycutt and John Pratt. They noticed a problem with the slider. They noticed hitters were adjusting to Kershaw's glove-side favoritism. And then they noticed someone was standing behind them.

"What the frick, you're a pitching coach now, Ellis?" Kershaw said. He huffed for a little longer and then bolted toward the field. Honeycutt turned to Ellis: "You got busted."

Ellis lumbered outside to play catch. Kershaw insisted he would be fine. The next day, he yielded five runs to the Rockies and could not finish the sixth inning. In June, he lost three starts in a row for the first time in his career, including a defeat to the Texas Rangers that Kershaw called "the most frustrating game I've ever pitched." As the summer progressed, Friedman and Zaidi tried something Colletti never dared: they tried to change how Kershaw pitched. Specifically, they asked him to vary his sequences, showing him how hitters were ready when he threw first-pitch fastballs and back-foot sliders to the same locations too often. It took a while for Kershaw to hear them. He carried himself with supreme confidence. "If I get strike one," he once told teammate Jamey Wright, "you should be out." The confidence doubled as a shield. "I don't think I was that outwardly arrogant," Kershaw recalled. "But in [my mind], I was. *No one's going to tell me how to pitch. I'm doing fine. I don't need your help.*"

He was wrong. But he needed time to recognize it. For the first time in many years, Kershaw was not the best pitcher on his own team.

*   *   *

Sizing up Zack Greinke was never simple. In the spring of 2002, Kansas City Royals scouting director Deric Ladnier hung around Apopka High, in the suburbs of Orlando, trying to decide if the kid was worth taking with the sixth pick in the draft. Greinke was an excellent athlete. He could play shortstop or third base. He loved to hit. He had the right size—a six-foot-two frame that could hold muscle. His mechanics were pristine, repeatable, the sort of delivery culled from an instructional video. Greinke toyed with opponents. "He was so uniquely talented at the ability to control the game, the hitters," Ladnier recalled. "He was a unicorn when it came to that type of stuff."

To Ladnier, it seemed like Greinke relied more on his brain than his arm. Greinke could spot his fastball, but the velocity hovered in the upper 80s. He could spin a curveball, with enough movement to confound hitters, but less break than a good big-league bender. His changeup wasn't even necessary; the other kids couldn't touch his fastball, anyway. And he knew his reputation. Before a game that year, he sought out Ladnier.

"I've heard that you don't think I can throw hard," Greinke said.

Ladnier told Greinke that wasn't true.

"Well," Greinke said, "I'm going to throw hard today."

Ladnier pulled out his radar gun behind the plate. For two innings, Greinke pumped only fastballs: 96 mph, 97 mph, 98 mph. Afterward, Greinke found Ladnier.

"I told you I could throw hard," Greinke said.

The game came easy to Greinke. Finding a place for himself in it did not. Like Kershaw, Greinke reached the majors at twenty in his second full professional season. His route to stardom took longer. Like Kershaw, Greinke was an anxious child, prone to catastrophizing. Playing for the Royals exposed him to catastrophes. Greinke got knocked around often. He could handle the stress of pitching, but the days between starts tormented him. He needed daily competition to occupy his mind. One day in 2006, while shagging flies in the outfield, Greinke turned to teammate J. P. Howell. "Man, if they don't let me play shortstop, I'm just gonna go to the PGA Tour," Greinke told Howell. A day later, as Howell remembered it, Greinke told the Royals he was walking away from baseball. Greinke figured there was a 10 percent chance he would ever return.

The Royals granted him time to reset. A doctor diagnosed Greinke with social anxiety disorder and depression. A Zoloft prescription helped. After a couple of months, Greinke returned. The team assigned him to the minors as Atlanta Braves executive Dayton Moore took over the baseball operations department. Moore considered assessing Greinke's well-being a primary objective, but he wanted to give the kid space. Early in Moore's tenure, he heard a knock on his door: Zack Greinke had driven from Wichita to see him. Moore listened as Greinke outlined why he preferred life in the minors. There was less pressure, more purity. He liked it there. He did not want a promotion to the majors.

Near the end of the season, Moore dispatched his lieutenant J. J. Picollo to check on Greinke. They met before a game in Tulsa. Greinke never made eye contact. Picollo tried some small talk. A garbage truck rolled down the street.

"That's what I want to do one day," Greinke said.

"What are you talking about?" Picollo said.

"I want to collect garbage," Greinke said. "I think it's a very noble profession."

Picollo did not know how to respond. He was similarly stumped when Greinke reiterated his disinterest in returning to the majors. The Royals still called him up that September. He joined the starting rotation the next spring. In 2009, aided by the medicine, anchored by his elegant delivery, he won the American League Cy Young Award.

Before he signed with the Dodgers, Greinke bounced around. The Royals traded him to Milwaukee. The Brewers traded him to the Angels. In his first two seasons as a Dodger, Greinke lived up to his contract with a 2.68 ERA and several strong postseason starts. His time as a Dodger only burnished his reputation for bluntness. Everyone who played with Greinke came away with a story. He once asked Mike Sweeney, a media-friendly Royal, "How are you so good at faking it?" When Ellis quizzed Greinke how he might improve the Dodgers, Greinke replied, "I'd trade you." After playing catch with Brett

Anderson, Greinke told him, "Don't ever throw your changeup again." In a team meeting, he once chastised the Dodgers for not washing their hands after defecating.

Greinke meshed well with Kershaw. "They're more alike than people would think," Tim Wallach recalled. They could talk ball for hours. Kershaw appreciated Greinke's capacity for evolution, changing his arsenal to match his physical capability. Greinke marveled at Kershaw's ability "to shut out all the outside noise and be prepared to do the best in that game," Greinke recalled. It amused Greinke to watch Kershaw practice changeups and arm-side fastballs but never throw them in games. Within their daily approach, their differences were apparent. Kershaw wore his cleats in the clubhouse several hours before his starts. Greinke wished he could show up at 6 P.M. for 7 P.M. starts. Kershaw mapped out every minute of his schedule. Greinke flew by the seat of his pants. "I'm like the least routine guy there is," Greinke recalled. "I wake up and however I feel that day decides what I'm going to do that day."

In 2015, Greinke rode that strategy into the best season of his career. He posted a 1.66 ERA, the lowest mark by any qualified starting pitcher since Greg Maddux's 1.61 in 1995, to end Kershaw's streak of consecutive ERA titles at four. Kershaw still finished strong. He altered the grip to his slider and rediscovered its depth. He applied some of the front office's sequencing suggestions. By the end of the season, his ERA had returned to its usual plane, 2.13, with 301 strikeouts, the most by any pitcher since 2002. (In an upset, he finished third in the Cy Young voting, behind Greinke and the winner, Cubs pitcher Jake Arrieta.) Same as it ever was, heading into October—except little things kept changing.

*　　*　　*

When the *SportsNet LA* broadcast returned from commercial on September 24, viewers caught an unusual sight: Clayton Kershaw was barking at Don Mattingly. Dugout debates between Kershaw and Mattingly were common. "He never wanted to come out," Wallach recalled. But these discussions usually happened later in the day. Now Mattingly was telling Kershaw his day was done after five innings and eighty pitches. Hair coated in sweat, face wrenched in disbelief, Kershaw waved his arms and raised his voice. Mattingly shook his head. Honeycutt stood quietly behind the manager. The argument was serious enough that Kershaw refused to discuss it with reporters. It was clear that the Dodgers—under new management but still run on a daily basis by Mattingly—were chipping away at Kershaw's iron grip.

The starting pitcher wields privileges that are unique in major North American sports. On his given day, the pitcher controls the pace of the game and the approach against the opponents. The pitcher has the ball. In those days, before the advent of the pitch clock, the game could not continue until he decided to throw. For Kershaw, the child who loathed the helplessness of waiting for rides home, control mattered more than for most. He demanded the opposing lineup "as early as humanly possible," recalled former Giants visiting clubhouse manager Abe Silvestri. "That used to drive him nuts." The teams exchanged lineups through Silvestri, who usually received a text from Giants coach Ron Wotus. Honeycutt stalked Silvestri, waiting for the message. The chain of anxiety extended from Kershaw to Honeycutt to Silvestri. "To the point where I would be like, 'Rick, you don't think I fucking know?'" Silvestri recalled. Sometimes Silvestri walked to the Giants clubhouse to say, "Guys, you're killing me down there."

On the days he did not pitch, after he completed his tasks—the lifting and stretching and running that prepared him for the fifth day—Kershaw still had energy to burn. Silvestri compared him to a rooster, who would "go where the action is." He bopped around the room, taking its temperature, cataloging things he noticed. He might ask the kitchen staff where they got their fruit. He might chat with Silvestri about his children or ask for restaurant recommendations. He might ask a beat writer if a recent haircut stemmed from a lost wager. He visited John Pratt in the video room and commented on the early games. He gained a reputation for omniscience: just as he memorized license plates, Kershaw "could rattle off statistics for guys at the snap of fin-gers," Pratt recalled.

Kershaw often struggled to self-identify as a leader. He was unsure if a pitcher could heft that responsibility. But he brandished his influence in certain ways. Kershaw ran regular spring-training Ping-Pong tour-naments. (To raise money for his charity, he also began staging Ping Pong 4 Purpose, a celebrity tournament held each summer at Dodger Stadium.) He scouted the competition. "He is such a fanatic about Ping-Pong," former Dodgers pitcher Chase De Jong recalled, "that if he heard that there was a non-roster invite who had a little game or whatever, he would stay until that guy's day was done, and then once that person was ready, he was like, 'Let's go. Let's play.'"

Kershaw oversaw the weight room soundtrack. "My first year," strength and conditioning coach Brandon McDaniel recalled, "ninety percent of my job was to appease his music tastes." Kershaw preferred upbeat electronic music, turning the weight room into an offshoot of Electric Daisy Carnival with squat racks and protein shakes. In later years, teammate Ross Stripling demonstrated the motivational poten-tial of Blink-182, which Kershaw permitted unless it was the day after his start. For the Day One Lift, Kershaw required tunes that quickened his pulse. The room became a more communal place, where teammates fed off Kershaw's energy and the beats from the sound system. "It's got a little bit of a dance party feel to it," McDaniel recalled. (The vibes were not uniformly immaculate. "Him taking over the weight room DJing—so annoying," Ellis recalled.) The camaraderie deepened after Chase Utley, the former Phillies star, was acquired in the summer of 2015. Utley introduced the group to No Shirt Sundays, a practice that requires little further explanation.

The control applied to Kershaw's own outbursts. He disliked swear-ing. So did his wife. On the mound, though, sometimes he slipped. Early in his career, Ellen was watching a game with her family on Amelia Island when the broadcast captured him shouting, "Fuck!" Ellen was horrified. They had just started Kershaw's Challenge. He was a role model. "I just said," Ellen recalled, "like, 'I know that you feel like you are held to an unrealistic, higher standard than anybody else has to be. Sorry about it.'" She suggested he cover his face with his glove. Otherwise, she decreed, every time she caught him swearing he owed her $1,000. "He never paid me," Ellen recalled. "But it was just the threat of it." When she saw his mouth buried in his mitt, she understood he had heard her.

"Time," Kershaw often told Ellen, "is my most valuable commodity." Early in their marriage, Ellen realized their only arguments involved being on time, "like I was still getting ready and he was pacing out the door," she recalled. Time mattered more to him than money, more to him than status, Ellen thought. He obsessed over time because it begat control. He never forgot relying upon others to ferry him to practices and games as a child. "So he started trying to grab control of time," Ellen recalled. That was why he mechanized his schedule. That was why he never took days off. He wondered why teammates lacked his dedication, his desperation. "I couldn't understand why some people wouldn't do certain things," he recalled. "Like, how do you just show up and play? Do you not want to be good at this game?"

Kershaw straddled the line between maintaining control and not lording his authority over others. He might judge them to himself. But he rarely spoke out. He disliked conflict. Pratt and Kershaw once squabbled during an Uber ride to the ballpark. Kershaw had been "crabby" with him, Pratt recalled. At the ballpark, Pratt decided to shun the ace. The treatment lasted a couple of hours. Ellis came into the video room. "Clayton keeps asking if you're mad at him," Ellis said. (Their relationship was important for more reasons than baseball: Kershaw partnered with Pratt in the team's $5,000 buy-in fantasy football league. Pratt could manipulate the roster so long as he kept Kershaw apprised. "He was the one that was paying for the team," Pratt recalled. "So it was the least we could do.")

After a good outing on the road, Kershaw often cracked a beer to unwind. But even then, he maintained his composure. "I've seen him drink and have more than a couple," Ellis recalled. "But it never changes his disposition. He's always hyperaware." Maybe the only place Ellis saw Kershaw cede control was on flights. As a passenger, there was nothing he could do. So he ripped farts, drank beers, and played cards with Ellis, Greinke, and Turner. "He was not beholden to anything," Ellis recalled. "He was at the mercy of travel."

He was, if only for a few hours, free.

*   *   *

Five days after spraying invective at Mattingly, Kershaw sprayed champagne. For the third year in a row, the Dodgers won the National League West, and they did it at AT&T Park, the home of their perennial rivals from San Francisco. And the clincher featured a matchup worth cherishing, as Kershaw dueled with fellow southpaw Madison Bumgarner. "I loved it," former Giants manager Bruce Bochy recalled, "when he and Bumgarner went head to head."

Drafted a year after Kershaw, Bumgarner had accomplished things his peer had not. Bumgarner had never won a Cy Young Award—and he would never finish in the top three—but he owned three World Series rings. In 2014, he carried the Giants across his broad shoulders. Bumgarner posted a 1.03 ERA that October, including a shutout in the Wild Card Game, a shutout in World Series Game 5, and most remarkably, five innings of scoreless relief on two days of rest in Game 7. It was the sort of performance Kershaw had never managed in the postseason, which only furthered discussion about his October fallibility. The contrast between Kershaw and Bumgarner—between the choker and the hero—aggravated Kershaw's teammates. "It's pretty sad, you know?" recalled former Dodgers reliever Brandon League. "That's the burden of being the best. Everyone wants to bring you down."

But Bumgarner was not one of those people. He considered Kershaw the best pitcher ever. An avid rancher, Bumgarner once referred to his finest specimen as "a Clayton Kershaw horse." When Bumgarner bumped into Ellis during batting practice, "he would always want to

talk about Clayton," Ellis recalled. At the plate, Bumgarner punctuated his swings with a grunt. He worried Kershaw would take offense.
"Tell him I'm sorry," Bumgarner told Ellis. "It just comes out." Kershaw and Bumgarner squared off four times in 2015. San Francisco won
the first three. The Dodgers led by two in the fourth matchup when
Kershaw hit in the fifth inning. At the plate, Kershaw prided himself
on annoying other pitchers. He shortened his stroke and focused on
extending at-bats. He prolonged this one against Bumgarner for thirteen pitches, fouling off fastballs and cutters, as the Dodgers dugout
cheered him on. When Kershaw finally grounded out, the Dodgers
could hear Bumgarner's frustration as he ran to back up first base.
"Fuck!" Bumgarner howled. Bumgarner could not finish the sixth
inning. Kershaw completed the twelfth shutout of his career.

The new regime did not immediately improve the club's record.
The 2015 Dodgers won ninety-two games, two fewer than in 2014.
But the team's fortunes improved in one aspect: they avoided St.
Louis in the first round of the postseason. The 100-win Cardinals
loomed on the other side of the bracket, though, as the Dodgers hosted
the 90-win Mets in the National League Division Series. Despite Greinke's remarkable season, the Dodgers still slotted Kershaw into Game
1, because the team trusted him on short rest for Game 4. His counter-
part in the matchup was Jacob deGrom, a right-handed pitcher who
was born three months after Kershaw but was only pitching in his second big-league season. He did not become a full-time pitcher until his
junior season at Stetson University, a small school north of Orlando.
He took a circuitous route to the majors; he was rehabbing from Tommy
John surgery when Kershaw won his first Cy Young Award in 2011.
DeGrom won the National League Rookie of the Year award in 2014
and pitched even better in 2015. He was a freakish athlete and a bit of a
bully, capable of walking across the clubhouse on his hands and willing
to peg the children of teammates with Nerf footballs.

In Game 1, deGrom bullied the Dodgers. His fastball buzzed at 96
mph across seven scoreless innings. The Mets took a 1-0 lead when

second baseman Daniel Murphy pulled a Kershaw fastball beyond the right-field fence. Kershaw kept the Dodgers close, with eleven strikeouts heading into the seventh. But in that frame, he faltered. Kershaw walked two batters and deGrom bunted them into scoring position. Facing left-handed hitter Curtis Granderson with two outs, Kershaw tried to escape. He missed high with a fastball, low with a curveball, *just* outside with a fastball. He looked up, his teeth gritted. He had walked only forty-two batters during the entire regular season. Now he walked three in one inning, the one he could not conquer in October. "The seventh-inning thing," Pratt recalled, "is undeniable."

When Mattingly signaled for reliever Pedro Báez, Kershaw did not protest. In the on-deck circle, Mets captain David Wright felt relief. "You really wanted to get Clayton Kershaw out of the game," Wright recalled. "Because whoever was coming in—it didn't matter who it was—you would have a much better shot than against Clayton Kershaw." Mattingly had learned from the previous seasons. He intervened before Kershaw could melt down. But it still didn't matter. Wright looped a two-run single just past Kendrick at second. Both runs were charged to Kershaw, who took the loss in a 3-1 defeat. The narrative about him now spanned both coasts. "Those postseason demons are hungry," Mets announcer Josh Lewin said on the WFAN broadcast. "Clayton Kershaw just can't get away from them."

* * *

On the field in New York before Game 3, Kershaw found Terry Collins, the Mets manager and former Dodgers farm director. The two clubs were furious with each other. In Game 2, the Dodgers tied the series, in part because of Chase Utley's late and ferocious slide into Mets shortstop Rubén Tejada. Utley broke up a double play, which allowed the Dodgers to take the lead. He also broke Tejada's leg. In the subsequent uproar, Utley sent an apology to Tejada through David Wright. The Mets were not exactly mollified. When Joe Torre, from his perch in the commissioner's office, levied a two-game suspension against Utley, Kershaw suggested his former skipper had been bullied into the punishment. If Kershaw ever had a son, he later said, he would want his boy to play baseball like Utley. Tension was thick that evening at Citi Field, with fans clamoring for Utley's head. One held a sign suggesting Utley supported the Islamic State of Iraq and Syria.

Amid the tumult, Collins chatted with Kershaw.

"You pitching tomorrow?" Collins asked.

He knew the answer. Everyone knew the answer.

"I don't know yet," Kershaw said.

"Please," Collins said. "Don't insult me."

Later that day, Collins received a text: "I'm in there tomorrow." At his press conference, Collins took a question: Did he have a preference on facing Kershaw or a fully rested Alex Wood in Game 4? Collins stifled laughter. "Yeah, I got a preference," he said. He meant no disrespect to Wood, Collins continued, "but I don't want that other monster on the mound." Mattingly spoke in similar terms when he announced Kershaw would return on short rest. "Do you have to explain that one?" Friedman and Zaidi had changed plenty about the Dodgers. One reality remained: the franchise still depended on Kershaw.

Greinke won Game 2, but when Brett Anderson got crushed in Game 3, that meant Kershaw would once again pitch on a compressed schedule with the season on the brink. A crowd assembled in the video room before the game. Pratt sat at his laptop. Ellis, Honeycutt, and Wallach pored over scouting reports. Greinke started a conversation about fantasy football. As the men bantered about waiver-wire strategy and Kansas City Chiefs running back Charcandrick West, Kershaw appeared. The talk stalled when he grabbed a chair and sat down. Kershaw broke the silence: "What are we talking about?" And then something odd happened. Kershaw joined in. "He still had a glazed-over look on his face, but he was talking to us," Pratt recalled. "And I was like, 'So weird.' And you could feel in that moment, like, 'Maybe he's just trying something else.'"

For whatever reason, Kershaw pitched that night as if unperturbed by the challenge of the Mets, the drain of short rest, or even the specter of the seventh inning. Staked to an early lead after crucial hits by González and Turner, Kershaw protected the advantage. Once more, Murphy tagged him for a solo shot early. Otherwise, Kershaw limited the traffic on the bases, with eight strikeouts. A chopper from Granderson ticked off Kershaw's glove to lead off the seventh. Mattingly permitted Kershaw to navigate the frame, which he did without incident. Turner made a slick snag of a hard-hit grounder to preserve Kershaw's gem. The Dodgers won, 3-1, to send the series back to Los Angeles for a fifth and final game.

* * *

The play that decided Game 5 pitted the Dodgers' embrace of data against one veteran Met's gumption. The Dodgers led by a run when Daniel Murphy singled to start the fourth inning. After Greinke secured the first out, the defenders behind him shifted to guard against Lucas Duda, a left-handed-hitting first baseman who tended to pull baseballs toward right field. Second baseman Howie Kendrick moved closer to first base. Shortstop Corey Seager shifted closer to the bag at second. Third baseman Justin Turner took a spot in between first and second. Third base was unoccupied.

This sort of defensive alignment had proliferated across the sport after Friedman popularized it in Tampa Bay. And it loosened a memory in Murphy's mind. He thought back to playing third base for Jacksonville University in a tournament at the University of South Alabama. When Murphy napped after the pitcher issued a walk, the runner on first base capitalized on his inattentiveness and jetted from second to third. Murphy had stolen only two bases in 2015, but he had never forgotten that play. As Greinke faced Duda, Murphy studied the alignment of infielders. "You can't get out trying to put your invisibility cloak on in Game 5," he recalled. He decided the gambit was worth it. Greinke walked Duda with a 3-1 changeup. The pitch was close enough

that Duda paused before trotting to first. Murphy jogged toward second with an oddly upright gait. He was moving faster than he intended,
he recalled, "because I'm hyperventilating on the inside." Murphy
glanced at Greinke, who had shuffled off the mound, head down,
toward Grandal. Greinke's distraction cleared one hurdle. Turner was
walking toward third base. Two down. Kendrick was stationary. That
left Seager, a rookie who had played only twenty-seven major-league
games before the postseason. As Murphy approached second base, he
looked up. Seager's eyes grew wide. "He realized all hell was about to
break loose," Murphy recalled. "And I sprinted like a maniac."

By the time Greinke saw what was happening, Murphy was sliding
safely into third. Those extra ninety feet proved pivotal when Murphy
scored on a sacrifice fly. Two innings later, he took Greinke deep for the
decisive blow in a season-ending 3-2 defeat. The Dodgers could mount
no comeback against deGrom, the budding ace pitching on regular
rest. The homer, Murphy later reflected, was cool. But the stolen base
meant more. The play came, he explained, from "the accumulation of
all these things you've learned over time on the sandlot fields—on the
wounds that you have, on the wounds you've laid on other people."

For once, the responsibility for the final loss hung on someone's
shoulders besides Kershaw. But the song remained the same.

*   *   *

On the flight back to Los Angeles, before the Dodgers lost the series,
Pratt approached Kershaw. Pratt had been thinking about the hours
before Game 4, when Kershaw chatted about fantasy football rather
than stewing in isolation. Kershaw had defied his routine. And it had
not backfired. Maybe, Pratt suggested, he could remember that before
his next postseason outing. Maybe he did not need to raise his game
even higher in October. Maybe just being himself was enough.

"And he thanked me," Pratt recalled. But he never saw Kershaw
attempt to relax before a postseason game again.

CHAPTER 16

BACK PAINS

In one of his first acts as manager of the Los Angeles Dodgers, in the winter after the 2015 season, Dave Roberts traveled to Highland Park. He wanted to meet Clayton and Ellen Kershaw, to establish a bond, to lay out his vision for how the team would function in the coming years.

"I'll do whatever you need," Kershaw told him.

What Roberts needed, above all, was something that did not come easy to Kershaw. Roberts needed his trust. Only later did Roberts recognize how precious that commodity was—and how easily it could evaporate. "I never imagined all that was going to come with this job," Roberts recalled. "And even specific to Clayton."

Roberts needed his trust because he hoped Kershaw could help him unite the clubhouse. On the verge of his forty-fourth birthday, Roberts felt up to the task. An itinerant childhood as the son of a Black marine and a Japanese mother taught him to build relationships. A ten-year big-league career granted him credibility. A moment in the spotlight during the 2004 postseason, stealing a crucial base that helped Boston end the Curse of the Bambino, showed him how to handle fame. A boundless sense of optimism propelled him as he survived a bout with Hodgkin's lymphoma. He was cheery, chatty, bursting with enthusiasm. His friends called him "Doc." He believed the team must coalesce around a shared purpose: ending the championship drought. Kershaw had to be a part of that. "The number one goal is for us to create an unbreakable bond within the group," Roberts told me that February, for one of my first stories after becoming the Dodgers beat writer at the *Los Angeles Times*.

The team was still being reshaped by Andrew Friedman and Farhan Zaidi. Don Mattingly was gone. After 2015, Mattingly sought a long-term extension, which the Dodgers were not prepared to offer. He was not fired and he did not resign, but he did leave to manage the Miami Marlins. The Dodgers initially favored farm director Gabe Kapler as Mattingly's replacement, but Roberts impressed the group during interviews. He understood the language Friedman and Zaidi spoke, even if it was not his lingua franca. He would not object to infield shifts or abbreviated outings for pitchers.

Roberts was not the only new face. Zack Greinke was gone. He opted out of his contract and entered free agency. In early December, Friedman was finalizing a six-year deal with Greinke worth about $160 million, the largest free-agent contract in franchise history. As the Dodgers dealt with the details, an unlikely suitor emerged: the Arizona Diamondbacks, upstarts in the National League West, willing to pay $206.5 million. To replace Greinke in the rotation, the Dodgers brought back Brett Anderson, signed three-time All-Star Scott Kazmir, and landed Japanese star Kenta Maeda.

Yasiel Puig was still around. During the winter, a brief controversy flickered when Andy Van Slyke, the father of Dodgers outfielder Scott Van Slyke, said in a radio interview that Kershaw had told the front office to trade Puig. Kershaw never denied that Puig's antics grated. "I think he, at some points, became a detriment," Kershaw recalled. "But I've never asked them to trade anybody." Roberts intended to dedicate plenty of bandwidth to Puig. He assumed that Kershaw, the meticulous worker, the model citizen, would not cause headaches. He did not yet understand all the effort required to attain Kershaw's trust.

That process, Roberts would soon discover, would be "extremely difficult," he recalled. "I just don't think that he's ever going to let a manager all the way in. We have a really good relationship. But he just doesn't let people get close to him."

* * *

Doug Padilla broke the biggest Dodgers story of the 2016 season, in part, because he was running late.

He also got the scoop for ESPN because he was observant, and because he was wily. But, mostly, on the morning of June 27, Padilla nailed the timing. That was how he learned, before any other reporter, that Clayton Kershaw had injured his back. The injury would demarcate Kershaw's career. There was the time before he hurt his back and then there was every day after.

Up until that point, Kershaw looked like he might win another MVP trophy. His ERA was 1.79 with 145 strikeouts in 121 innings. Kershaw had accumulated 5.3 wins above replacement, according to FanGraphs, the most in the sport, well ahead of Los Angeles Angels star Mike Trout and Houston Astros second baseman José Altuve, who were both worth 4.1 WAR. "Just utter dominance," recalled Corey Seager. He had thrown three shutouts in May alone. "Clayton Kershaw, before his back injury, he was Michael Jordan," Roberts recalled. "When [Jordan] wanted to score sixty points and take over a game, he could do it. When Clayton Kershaw wanted to go a complete game, or eight innings and hand it to Kenley, he could do it." And the team needed every inning he could provide. The rotation was falling apart with Greinke gone. Anderson had injured his own back. Kazmir was struggling. Alex Wood, a funky southpaw acquired the previous summer, hurt his elbow. Hyun-Jin Ryu was recovering from shoulder surgery. Brandon McCarthy was rehabbing after Tommy John surgery. The bullpen was exhausted. After one of Kershaw's gems, several relievers lined up at his locker to hug him, grateful for the rest.

But in June, Kershaw's back started bothering him. The area had often given him trouble; in the morning after starts, he struggled to bend and touch his knees. But now he needed longer to loosen up, and his range of motion felt limited. Kershaw pitched through the discomfort: eight innings of two-run ball on June 10; an eleven-strikeout outing on June 15; seven innings on June 20. He ignored warning signs from his body and refused to reduce his intensity. It wasn't until June 26, against Pittsburgh at PNC Park, that his condition hampered his performance. John Pratt was watching from the video room as Kershaw required eight pitches to put away the opposing pitcher. "I knew it immediately," Pratt recalled. "He is one hundred percent hurt."

But no one in the public knew, until Padilla wrote the story a day later. Padilla was a lovable scamp, a sportswriting lifer whose career had taken him from Southern California to Minneapolis to Chicago and back to Los Angeles, where he covered the Dodgers for ESPN. He enjoyed the camaraderie of the beat as much as the competition. When other reporters jawed with each other, Padilla knew how to defuse things: "You two should take your shirts off and wrestle," he'd say.

The night after Kershaw's clunker against Pittsburgh, the Dodgers stuck around for a Monday matinee. When the clubhouse opened to reporters, Padilla was running a few minutes behind. On one side of the room, the beat writers surrounded first baseman Adrián González. As González held court, Padilla saw Kershaw wearing an electronic stim machine on his lower back. Padilla kicked himself: he figured the other writers had already talked to Kershaw. Rather than irritate Kershaw, Padilla waited for Roberts's pregame media session. Except no one asked Roberts about Kershaw's back. So after the pack dispersed, Padilla pulled Roberts aside. Roberts confirmed that Kershaw was banged up but downplayed the severity. He told Padilla that Kershaw would make his next start.

Padilla hammered out a few paragraphs. As he typed, the ESPN machinery whirred. The website sent out an alert and Padilla went on *SportsCenter* with the news: the best baseball player on the planet was hurt.

After the game, reporters approached Kershaw.

"Who wrote that?" Kershaw said. He bolted into the trainer's room. Then he poked his head into Roberts's office. Then he saw Padilla. The writer stood about a foot shorter than the pitcher. Padilla listened as Kershaw aired the grievances he had aired about his hip in 2012. But Kershaw had bigger problems than journalistic nuance. His back was far more damaged than his manager had revealed.

*   *   *

While in graduate school, strength and conditioning coach Brandon McDaniel was bantering at a bar with one of his professors. McDaniel, the eager student, suggested that "playing sports was a healthy thing." The professor peered over his glass and corrected his pupil: "The same stresses that make you good are the same stresses that break you."

To make himself great, to win all those awards and earn all that money, to work with all his heart, Kershaw subjected his body to hellacious strain. All those miles running in the outfield, all that lifting after his starts, all the kinetic energy reabsorbed with every delivery to the plate—all of that came with a cost. Kershaw flew to Los Angeles to meet with back specialist Dr. Robert Watkins. The examination revealed a herniated L5-S1 disc in his lower spine.

With hindsight, the breakdown looks inevitable. From 2011 to 2015, Kershaw threw 1,128 regular-season innings, more than every pitcher but veteran James Shields, plus another 49 ⅓ innings in the postseason, some of it on short rest. "He was the only guy at the time that was going on three days' rest every year," Pratt recalled. Kershaw had injured the labrum in his hip and the teres major muscle in his back. He pitched through pain in a way that endeared him to others willing to make the same sacrifice. "No matter how he felt, he expected to take the mound," Dan Haren recalled. "I'm not knocking anybody, but some guys will go out for a start, and they feel like crap, and then they don't want to go out there."

But Kershaw later felt his own obstinance undermined him. "He loved to squat—with pretty heavy weight," Rick Honeycutt recalled. On the

first day of the cycle, without fail, Kershaw squatted with the barbell
hoisted across his shoulders. "I never had great form," Kershaw recalled.
"That's one of my biggest regrets in life, that I back-squatted for as long
as I did." The practice imperiled his health. "The gravitational pull was
going right down to that area he injured," McDaniel recalled. Yet he kept
squatting and running and throwing his bullpens with 100 percent effort,
all so that when he took the mound, he felt armored by his readiness. "I
wish I worked out a little bit smarter," Kershaw recalled. "But at the same
time, even if [McDaniel] had told me to, I probably wouldn't have."

Watkins administered an epidural injection on June 29. Kershaw
intended to power past this injury as he had powered past the hip problem and the back problem. But a disc does not heal like a muscle. Seventeen days after the epidural, Kershaw threw a simulated game at
Dodger Stadium. Roberts figured his ace would be back soon. Then he
got a call from Friedman: "We've got some bad news." Kershaw's back
was hurting again. Doctors told Kershaw there was an 80 percent
chance he would need surgery to repair the disc. Kershaw heard there
was a 20 percent chance he could still pitch. "Your body can heal itself,"
he recalled. He knew the surgery would be brutal. Anderson had
undergone a similar procedure. "Back surgery, man, you can't move,"
Kershaw recalled. "It's just the worst."

Kershaw targeted a September return. But he still craved control.
On the day Roberts announced the sim-game setback, he was asked
if season-ending surgery was more likely. Roberts conceded it was.
A flurry of tweets and stories followed. Someone in Los Angeles—
presumably a large left-hander—saw them. Later that day, a Dodgers
media-relations staffer complained to reporters that the headlines were
misleading. The staffer was reminded that Roberts said surgery was
more likely. The staffer returned later to say that the team would issue a
statement from the medical department. A little while later, the staffer
informed the writers that the medical department would not issue a
statement. It was not a fun afternoon to be a member of the Dodgers
media-relations department. Roberts soon stopped offering opinions

on Kershaw's progress. The candor damaged their relationship. "Early on, my first year, there were a lot of surface conversations and getting along really well," Roberts recalled. "But then something would happen, and it just felt like we're back to square one."

Dodgers staffers canvassed physical therapists, biomechanical experts, even military doctors for advice on stabilizing Kershaw's spine. The trainers recommended Kershaw change his routine at the squat rack. "They just proved to him that it was detrimental to him, compressing the disc in his back," Honeycutt recalled. Kershaw ditched the barbell for kettlebells. There was more stretching, more hip stabilization, more everything. "It was insanity, how much time he was putting into this," McDaniel recalled. "I think other athletes would have bailed out. The warmup alone was as long as most people's workouts." Yosuke Nakajima, the massage therapist, believed Kershaw healed faster than other humans. This was why. "He does those things because he loves to compete and be the best he can be," Honeycutt recalled.

The team stayed afloat without Kershaw, surpassing the Giants to gain control of the National League West for the fourth consecutive season. After keeping the club together amid so many injuries, Roberts won National League Manager of the Year. Corey Seager was the Rookie of the Year. Justin Turner continued to flourish. The front office acquired Rich Hill, a thirty-six-year-old lefty vagabond who had reinvented himself as an excellent starter. But the team still needed its ace.

The doctors told Kershaw he faced no further risk if he tried to come back. "It was like, 'Hey, you need to do this for six weeks. And if you do, you might have a chance,'" he recalled. Either his body would heal or it would not. What he could not have predicted was who would be gone when he returned.

* * *

A. J. Ellis was shooting hoops with his son at West Hollywood Park around noon on August 25 when he received a text from Dave Roberts requesting his presence at Dodger Stadium.

The season had not been going well for Ellis. The team platooned him with Yasmani Grandal, but Ellis failed to hit left-handed pitchers. He was batting .194. He had not hit a home run since April. His relationship with his superiors suffered. "I didn't play well enough to earn trust—but I felt like I deserved trust because of my track record," Ellis recalled. Ellis believed Roberts's gregariousness to be phony. "I don't think I had the open-mindedness to Dave Roberts, him coming in, and me, doing my role to help support him as a new manager," Ellis recalled. Roberts saw Ellis as a clubhouse dissident. "I specifically, intentionally tried to target A. J. as an ally," Roberts recalled. "I knew he had a pulse on the clubhouse. And I was trying to gain his trust. And I could never get it. I just felt that there was a point that that dynamic wasn't going to work." The lines of communication frayed. In August, the team acquired reliever Josh Fields in a trade that sent future All-Star Yordan Álvarez to the Houston Astros. The Dodgers thought Fields should throw fastballs up in the zone, an approach popularized in the coming years. Ellis never received the message. When he caught Fields, he called fastballs down. "That was a big tension point between me and Dave and Andrew," Ellis recalled.

The conflict represented an industry-wide battle, as a new fleet of executives incorporated data into decision making. In the days of *Moneyball*, those decisions manifested in how teams were built. By the 2010s, those decisions changed how the game was played. It took time for Ellis, who joined the front office of the San Diego Padres after he retired, to realize "the people wearing the khaki pants impact the game more than the people wearing the costume." And few executives were more influential—in terms of how rosters were constructed, prospects were developed, and players were used—than Friedman and Zaidi. "Those two guys are without a doubt the driving force behind what's happened in the last decade," Ellis recalled.

The data showed Grandal was elite at using his glove to manipulate the umpires and turn balls into strikes, a skill called "framing." The Dodgers viewed Grandal as their best catcher. That meant he should be available to catch their best pitcher. But separating Kershaw from Ellis, who best understood his moods and his approach, proved challenging. On occasion, Kershaw questioned the composition of the lineup when he pitched. The front office could parry protests about second base or left field. But Kershaw was more adamant about Ellis, the partner he trusted above all. (Zaidi chuckled when reminded Ellis caught Kershaw on Opening Day in 2016. "Man, we were such pushovers," Zaidi said.) Ellis received eleven of Kershaw's first sixteen starts in 2016. The front office felt Kershaw performed just as well with Grandal. Kershaw did not agree. The relationship "made it difficult to manage the roster in the most efficient way," Zaidi recalled.

To Ellis, the biggest problem was not that he didn't connect with Roberts, or that he presented himself as a closed book to the front office, or that Kershaw only wanted to throw to him. It was a more eternal baseball problem. "Because I stunk," Ellis recalled. "No, seriously. I was not a good player that year." He figured the team would let him depart in free agency after the season. He thought 2016 was his last, best chance to win a title in Los Angeles.

Then he got the message from Roberts.

Ellis alerted his wife, Cindy, and brought his son home. On the way to the ballpark, he started dialing. His agents did not answer. Kershaw was rehabbing. Ellis couldn't reach another confidant, San Diego Padres manager Andy Green. Ellis pulled into the Dodger Stadium lot just as Roberts was parking.

"What's going on?" Ellis asked. Roberts wanted to wait until they got into his office. The awkwardness continued as they descended a rickety elevator toward the clubhouse.

"How's Cindy doing?" Roberts said.

"Honestly," Ellis said, "she's a nervous wreck right now, Dave."

Roberts asked Ellis to wait in the clubhouse. Ellis brainstormed scenarios that did not include the inevitable. Then Ellis got a text to come to Roberts's office. Friedman, Roberts, and Zaidi were there. "We've made the decision to acquire Carlos Ruiz," Friedman said. Ruiz had been a stalwart behind the plate in Philadelphia. Ellis wondered how the team would use three catchers. Then Friedman delivered the blow: Ellis was part of the trade.

Ellis started to cry. He ignored the subsequent praise from his former bosses. He left the office to call his wife and his agents. Then he texted Kershaw to meet him in the dugout. Kershaw wept when Ellis told him. They sat together for a while. Ellis stared out at the diamond. He had been a Dodger since Logan White took an eighteenth-round flier on him in 2003. He considered Dodger Stadium the best office in America. Now he was just another visitor. The rest of the clubhouse was stunned; the team was nearly no-hit that evening by Giants pitcher Matt Moore. But Kershaw took the departure the hardest. Ellis left his car at the stadium. Kershaw drove him home. He hugged Cindy and helped Ellis pack. For Kershaw, the shock and anger lingered for weeks. He rebuffed Friedman's explanations. "His thing was 'There's nothing to talk about,'" Friedman recalled. "And it took us some time to work through that." The executive and the ace did not clear the air until the next year. "That's just how I deal with stuff, just put everybody at arm's length," Kershaw recalled. "I do that from time to time with everybody. Probably just a coping mechanism. Don't let anybody too close, you know?" Ellis had been one of the few to breach Kershaw's boundaries. And now, if Kershaw was going to make it back from the brink, he would have to do it without his closest ally.

For a long time afterward, A. J. Ellis rooted for Clayton Kershaw. But he did not root for the Los Angeles Dodgers.

* * *

The edges of Kershaw's eyes ran red as he stood at his Dodger Stadium locker after Game 4 of the National League Division Series against the Washington Nationals. He had just made a postseason start on short rest for the fourth year in a row. His back ached. His mind was still foggy. He struggled to formulate sentences. "I'm exhausted, just physically and mentally drained," he said. His pitching line included lumps. But the Dodgers had won.

In October, only survival mattered. Which suited Kershaw just fine. He had not accumulated many style points since he returned from the injured list in September. He permitted four earned runs in five regular-season starts. He struck out twenty-seven batters in twenty-eight innings. But to wizened observers, he did not look the same. The back injury altered his delivery so he drifted, ever so slightly, to his right when he landed, reducing some of the fastball's backspin. During Kershaw's first outing back, on September 9 in Miami, Pratt noticed the slider lacked its usual depth. Instead of diving, the pitch backed up over the plate. "That [had] never happened," Pratt recalled.

The first round of the postseason both demonstrated the front office's interest in managing Kershaw differently than in years past and underscored the franchise's reliance on him. The 91-win Dodgers ceded home-field advantage to the 95-win Nationals, a team powered by stars like Max Scherzer, a member of the 2006 draft class who signed a seven-year, $210 million deal in free agency after winning the Cy Young Award in Detroit; Bryce Harper, the No. 1 pick in 2010; and Daniel Murphy, the man who antagonized Kershaw and Greinke with the Mets in 2015. At the beginning of the series, Kershaw informed team officials that after he pitched Game 1, he wanted Game 4. The front office felt Kershaw transcended the consequences of short rest. "He is an outlier in all of Major League Baseball," Roberts said. Even if he wasn't meeting his usual standard: in a 4-3 Game 1 victory, Roberts pulled Kershaw after five innings of three-run baseball, citing an inability to control the slider. Any thought of holding Kershaw out for Game 5 vanished after the team lost the next two games. Three months after Kershaw stared down back surgery, he took the baseball on three days of rest for Game 4.

Kershaw subdued the Nationals for six innings. Nursing a 5-2 lead, Roberts imitated Mattingly and tried to push Kershaw through the seventh. Four batters later, there were two outs and two men aboard, both courtesy of groundball singles. Up came Harper. With his fastball touching 95 mph, his pitch count past one hundred, Kershaw emptied the tank. Harper maintained his discipline in an eight-pitch walk. Roberts opted for another Mattingly impression: he asked Pedro Báez to clean up Kershaw's mess. Báez hit a batter with his first pitch to drive in a run. Roberts turned to lefty Luis Avilán, who promptly served up a game-tying, two-run single to Murphy.

In the dugout, Kershaw felt the familiar dismay. Another October meltdown. Another brilliant outing marred by a final inning. Another early exit on the horizon. He ran his fingers through his hair. He stared at the ground. He brooded inside his dirt-caked uniform, a product of a double that extended the lead he eventually lost. He was still numb when Chase Utley stroked a go-ahead hit in the eighth which led to a 6-5 victory. Kershaw struggled to explain his emotions afterward. "I felt really, really good about it—until the last four minutes," Kershaw told reporters. "It's a weird feeling, more than anything. But you've got to just swallow your pride, realize we won the game and be excited about it."

*　　*　　*

The next evening, after the Dodgers landed at Dulles International Airport, most of the traveling party took a bus to a hotel in Arlington, Virginia. Kershaw caught a cab to Nationals Park with McDaniel, Nakajima, and trainer Nate Lucero. Kershaw needed to prepare for the 103-win Chicago Cubs in the next round. If the Dodgers could defeat Washington, Kershaw planned to pitch against the Cubs on short rest. So he stayed within the cycle. He lifted. He ran in the outfield. He grabbed a glove and asked McDaniel to play catch as the sun set over the empty ballpark. The lights were off, so Kershaw threw beneath the moonlight. The subject of Game 5 never came up.

Back at the hotel, the front office scanned the roster to diagram a pitching plan against Washington. The conversations continued into the next afternoon. At the ballpark, Roberts met with Friedman,

Zaidi, and director of baseball operations Alex Tamin. Honeycutt, bench coach Bob Geren, and bullpen coach Josh Bard gauged the readiness of the players. The start and finish were covered. Hill volunteered to pitch on short rest. The Dodgers wanted him to face thirteen hitters, a total based on the left-handed batters in Nationals manager Dusty Baker's lineup. Kenley Jansen, a first-time All-Star at closer, could collect the final six outs. But the middle of the game was a mess. Roberts believed in only two relievers, veteran Joe Blanton and rookie Julio Urías. During batting practice, Bard told Blanton to be ready by the fourth inning. Roberts told Jansen to be ready by the fifth. In a perfect world, Roberts wanted to orchestrate a handoff from Hill to Blanton to Urías to Jansen. He did not live in a perfect world.

During Roberts's pregame news conference, Bill Plaschke of the *Times* mentioned the 1988 National League Championship Series, when Orel Hershiser materialized from the bullpen to save a game against the Mets: "Would Kershaw be available for an out?"

"Absolutely not," Roberts said.

Roberts had never considered the possibility. Zaidi wondered if Plaschke had lost his mind.

*   *   *

Nearly forty-four thousand fans packed into Nationals Park, tucked inside DC's Navy Yard on the banks of the Anacostia River, with the US Capitol beaming in the distance beyond the left-field wall. Those in attendance caught a classic, the sort of game that tortured everyone. The Dodgers took a 4-1 lead. The trio of Hill, Blanton, and Urías combined for eighteen outs, an admirable effort that left Roberts in need of a pitcher as the seventh inning began. He wanted to save Jansen for the eighth. But when reliever Grant Dayton allowed a two-run homer, Jansen shouted at Bard.

"Call down," Jansen said. "I want to get in the game."

Before Bard could reach the phone, it rang. Roberts needed Jansen for the seventh.

Panic rippled through the Dodgers executive suite above the diamond. Kershaw and Utley did the math in the dugout. It did not add
up. A nine-out save was too much, even for Jansen.

"We don't have anybody to finish this game," Utley said.

A light bulb flickered.

"Well," Kershaw said, "I could do it."

Utley asked if Kershaw had thrown a bullpen session that day. Kershaw had not. Utley asked if Kershaw was sure he could go. Kershaw
decided he was. Utley told Kershaw to speak with Roberts and Honeycutt. "If there's any chance of you being available to pitch," Utley said,
"you better tell them right now."

Kershaw found Honeycutt.

"Is the plan for Kenley to go three?" Kershaw asked.

"That's the plan," Honeycutt said.

Kershaw volunteered. "Absolutely not," Honeycutt said. Kershaw
kept pressing until Honeycutt grabbed Roberts. "No way," Roberts
said.

Kershaw knew the coaches were distracted, triaging an emergency
in real time. They were reacting on protective impulse. He bargained
with them. He figured once the process started, it would be difficult to
stop. "Just let me go try and get loose," Kershaw said. He promised to
be honest about how he felt. Roberts and Honeycutt let him go.

Kershaw bolted up the twenty-eight-step stairway to the clubhouse.
There was no time for routine. He popped the anti-inflammatory Toradol and jumped into the hot tub. McDaniel was running to the trainer's
room when he spotted Kershaw soaking. McDaniel pumped his fist.
Back at his locker, Kershaw threw on his jersey and cleats. He
descended the stairs, into an alcove beside the dugout, underneath sec-
tions 116 and 117. He threw into the batting cage's netting while monitoring the game. When the eighth inning ended, Kershaw put on his
warmup jacket and climbed a flight of seven steps into the Dodgers
dugout. His presence was spectral but unmistakable, a source of bewil-
derment and giddiness to teammates. "Everybody was legitimately

worried," Wood said. *"Is this the right thing to do?* But Clayton is going to be Clayton."

Roberts told Kershaw to be ready for Murphy, due up fourth in the ninth. Then Kershaw walked onto the field, where he crossed paths with Jansen.

Am I dreaming? Jansen wondered.

* * *

As he strode along the left-field line toward the visitors' bullpen, Kershaw tucked his chin to his chest. The breeze swept his hair. It was twelve minutes past midnight. The Fox broadcast captured his lonely trek. The camera did not catch the freakout in Friedman's suite.

Friedman had been huddling with his lieutenants, sweating and stewing through the evening. He had no idea why Kershaw was on the field.

"What the fuck?" Friedman said.

He figured it must be a ploy to rattle Dusty Baker. As Kershaw loosened up in the bullpen, a phone rang inside Friedman's suite. It was a member of the training staff. "Kersh is going to see if he can get loose," the trainer said. "And there was nothing we could do to stop him."

In the bullpen, the relievers held their fists aloft, a ritual for any pitcher about to enter the game. Kershaw punched his way down the line. He warmed up as Jansen returned for the ninth. After Jansen walked two batters, Roberts left the dugout. Murphy was up. The Dodgers needed two outs to advance. Roberts raised his left hand and pointed his index finger. At third base, Justin Turner wondered what was going on. He turned to see someone trotting in from the bullpen. *Oh shit,* Turner thought. *This is awesome.* In the on-deck circle, Murphy gaped. *Ha!* he thought. *Completely fucking reasonable.*

A cascade of jeers greeted Kershaw. He slowed to a walk in the infield dirt. Jansen waited for him. Roberts took the baseball from Jansen and slipped it into Kershaw's glove. The last time Kershaw saved a game, in the 2006 Gulf Coast League playoffs, Jansen was his catcher.

Back then, Kershaw's unscheduled appearance in relief irritated officials like Logan White. Now any hope of advancing in October
depended on him. "Please," Jansen told Kershaw, "pick me up."

Kershaw turned to Carlos Ruiz, a catcher who had never caught
him, the catcher for whom the Dodgers traded away Ellis. They strate-
gized for a moment. Kershaw intended to challenge Murphy. He could
not afford to lose an off-speed pitch in the dirt and allow the winning
run to advance into scoring position. Kershaw rocked into his delivery
and flung a first-pitch fastball, 95 mph, up and in. Ruiz had set up outside, and he dropped the pitch. Ball one. Kershaw licked his left hand
for grip. In the dugout, Jansen felt overcome by stress. Roberts shifted
on the balls of his feet. Ruiz trotted to the mound again. They settled
on another fastball.

The radar gun registered the pitch at 95 mph. It rode far closer to the
heart of the plate than Kershaw desired. "I was trying to throw it really
hard, down and away," Kershaw said. "I missed, up and in." At the last
moment, the pitch ran an inch or so inside, perilously close to the barrel
of Murphy's bat. Murphy turned his hips and swung. He hung his head
at the harmless pop fly bound for the glove of second baseman Charlie
Culberson. "He fucking got his haymaker inside of me," Murphy
recalled. "And they had to shovel me off the mat."

The denouement featured little drama. Baker had splintered his
lineup when he double-switched a relief pitcher into third baseman
Anthony Rendon's spot in the batting order to begin the eighth. Instead
of Rendon, a dangerous right-handed hitter, Kershaw faced light-
hitting infielder Wilmer Difo. At 12:41 A.M., he spun a two-strike
curveball that buckled as it approached the plate. Difo touched only
the air. The ball bounced off Ruiz's chest. Kershaw raised his arms as
Ruiz threw to first base to secure the victory.

A mob greeted Kershaw. Ruiz leaped into his arms. Kershaw had
done it. Pitching on one day of rest, he saved the Dodgers.

*   *   *

Kershaw never wore goggles during champagne celebrations—he preferred to let his eyes burn. He sloshed through puddles of bubbly and Budweiser in the Nationals Park visitors' clubhouse. At one point, he looked like he might puke into a trash can.

"We've got to win eight more of these?" he said.

There was little time to sleep. Kershaw ate breakfast with McDaniel and video advance scout Danny Lehmann at a diner at 5 A.M. The team flew to Chicago later that morning. At Wrigley Field, Kershaw tried to reorient himself. On the bullpen mound he visualized his next start, going through his delivery without a baseball, just like he learned from Derek Lowe as a rookie. He could barely savor his save. He understood that if the Dodgers did not advance, it would become a footnote.

The Dodgers had gone nearly thirty years without a championship. For the hopelessly hopeful, gleefully inebriated Cubs fans who flocked to Wrigley Field, three decades was nothing. In Chicago, the wait had lasted more than a lifetime, 108 years heading into 2016, a lost century blamed on billy goats, black cats, and a woebegone fellow named Bartman. To end the futility, the Cubs hired Theo Epstein, the former boy-genius executive behind the Red Sox team, featuring Roberts, that won the 2004 World Series and ended an eighty-six-year curse. With the Cubs, Epstein undertook a rebuilding effort known as "tanking," losing big-league games in search of minor-league gains through higher draft picks. Borrowed from basketball, where for decades teams had been sacrificing the present to jockey for better draft positioning, the practice became a scourge across baseball. But for the Cubs, tanking netted a core group of players who were young and versatile and hungry. And they were curious how much Kershaw had left. "The fact that he's been on such a heavy load lately," Cubs manager Joe Maddon said before Game 2, "it's going to be just interesting to see where he's at."

After watching his teammates lose Game 1, Kershaw supplied in Game 2 his usual six innings of scoreless brilliance. And in the seventh, protecting a one-run lead, he ran into his usual trouble. With two outs, a runner at first, and second baseman Javier Báez at the plate, Roberts visited the mound. Kershaw covered his mouth with his glove. "I can get this guy," Kershaw said. Roberts gave him the chance. Báez smashed a fastball into center field. The crowd leaped in anticipation. Kershaw hunched at the waist, mouth open, agony stretched across his face. Outfielder Joc Pederson sprinted toward the ivy . . . and stopped at the warning track. Pederson lifted his glove for the third out. Kershaw stood up and heaved a sigh. He wiped his face and permitted himself a rare indulgence. He smiled. (The grin disappeared, after the 1-0 victory, when a reporter opened Kershaw's press conference by asking if he thought Báez's ball was gone. "That's your first freaking question?" Kershaw said.)

But the Dodgers dropped two of the next three, which meant when the series returned to Wrigley Field for Game 6, Kershaw needed to win to keep the season alive. The Cubs attacked him with insight from a former ally. Mike Borzello, the coach who witnessed the genesis of Kershaw's slider, had joined the Cubs after 2010. In preparing for the series, Borzello informed the staff that Kershaw rarely threw his curveball when behind in the count. That nugget aided the team's adjusted approach for Game 6. They were tired of trying to beat Kershaw to the spot inside. They intended to ignore everything he threw on the inner half, especially sliders, and just look down the middle. "If you look in on him, you're playing right into what he wants," Borzello recalled. The strategy capitalized on Kershaw's new reality as he dealt with back trouble. No longer was his command exquisite. After the injury, the months dedicated to rehab, the workload in the first round, he felt exhausted. "It ends up catching up with you," he recalled.

The Cubs jumped Kershaw for two runs in the first inning, helped when rookie outfielder Andrew Toles lost a ball in the lights. The crowd started braying Kershaw's name, elongating the syllables like playground bullies.

"Kerrrrrrrrrshaw."

"Kerrrrrrrrrshaw."

"Kerrrrrrrrrshaw."

Another run scored in the second. Kershaw served up a homer in the fourth. He was out of answers. In the fifth, he faced Anthony Rizzo, who often joked with Borzello about how much he savored facing the best. "I want Kershaw," Rizzo liked to say. Kershaw lowered his arm angle on a fastball, hoping for some extra velocity to best Rizzo. The ball landed in the right-field seats. Kershaw surrendered five runs in five innings in a 5-0 defeat. For the third time in four years, the final loss rested on his shoulders. The yoke was growing heavier.

Kershaw stumbled through the clubhouse in a daze. "Most guys would not have come back at all from what he suffered," Friedman told reporters. Kershaw did not want to hear it. When he failed in the postseason at twenty-one, he told himself it was the Lord's way of keeping him humble. He was a kid with a long career ahead. Now he was a man with a growing family, more riches than he could ever have imagined, more accolades than one mantle could hold. His faith had been rewarded. He had provided for his mother. He had provided for himself. He had built the sort of life he always wanted. And still he felt agonized by failure, drawn into the five-day cycle, unable to slake the thirst.

All that remained was winning the World Series. Kershaw thought he had a chance in 2016. He had sacrificed so much. He had tried to be a hero. And still he came up empty.

CHAPTER 17

SHATTERED

Patrick Halpin stood in the left-field stands at Minute Maid Park in Houston on October 29, 2017, wondering if his ears were deceiving him.

Halpin, proud member of the Mean Street Posse, had tickets in the Dodgers friends and family section for the franchise's first World Series in twenty-nine years. He was a friend of Clayton Kershaw who felt like family. His pal had finally reached the promised land: The Fall Classic, the grandest stage, the last box left to check on a Hall of Fame résumé. The narrative of October failure was about to end, so Halpin decided to attend every game. He was watching Kershaw cruise through the early innings of Game 5 against the Houston Astros when he turned to his buddy's wife.

"Do you hear that noise?" Halpin asked. (Ellen did not recall this conversation.)

A ballpark fills dead air with different sounds: an organist's keys, artificial hand claps. What Halpin heard sounded like "a loud crack that would reverberate through the stands," he recalled. He thought the timing was strange. The crack seemed to be coming from the speaker system just before Kershaw would throw a pitch.

"It was this loud knock," Halpin recalled. "And we could hear it. And we were like, 'That's so weird.'"

The game would become the fulcrum of Kershaw's legacy. As the night unfolded, Halpin could not place the noise. But it sounded a lot like banging.

* * *

In 2017, the collective vision of Andrew Friedman, Farhan Zaidi, and Dave Roberts came to fruition. They built the best team in the history of the franchise, at least since Dem Bums left Brooklyn. At long last, the front office had assembled a roster worthy of Kershaw. The team lacked flaws and played with heart. The group took Kershaw to heights he had never before experienced. In turn, he was exposed to heartache he never could have envisioned.

In some ways, he had begun to change. His family helped him. On November 18, 2016, Ellen gave birth to a boy. They named him Charley Clayton Kershaw. The children softened their father, ever so slightly, on the fifth day and beyond. On the days he pitched, rather than brood and binge *CSI*, he played with Cali and changed Charley's diapers. He could block out his anxiety until he left for the ballpark. The small adjustment was "a blessing," he explained. "I don't think I could have made it much longer doing it that way." He was beginning to wonder how he could stomach being away from the children when they started school in a few years. His family reminded him what mattered. He found it hard to fixate on his rare bad outings when his kids wanted to play afterward. He adjusted to the disruptions to his schedule, to the lack of sleep, to the fear he felt when Cali started to cry. To Ellen, Clayton "always just had a stiff upper lip. This can-do attitude. And because it was just him and his mom, there weren't a whole lot of emotions growing up." That changed with the children. "He's the biggest sap there is when it comes to any of them," Ellen explained. "He can well up with tears so quickly for them."

Some habits died harder than others. Kershaw had learned some lessons from his back injury, but he still worked out like a maniac. "I would run outside every day," Kershaw recalled. "And I would lift almost every day. And I would throw a bullpen as hard as I could. I think that compounded things. And I still did that, even after I got hurt." His faith in the cycle guided him as he dealt with a new, unexpected weakness: he had suddenly become more prone to home runs. His baseline numbers were strong—he ended the season with a 2.31 ERA, 10.4 strikeouts per nine innings, and a second-place finish in the Cy Young voting—but he surrendered twenty-three homers, seven more than ever before. After one homer-heavy outing in New York, Kershaw assaulted the bench in the Citi Field dugout with his foot. At the urging of Friedman and Zaidi, he increased the usage of his slider. Rick Honeycutt encouraged him to throw his fastball out of the strike zone. Kershaw, the late listener, changed because he was caught in an industry-wide power surge. In 2017, hitters bashed 6,105 home runs, eclipsing the record of 5,693 set during the steroidal bloat of 2000. Some pitchers blamed the composition of the baseballs, which varied in their slickness and hardness. Kershaw and his teammates collected particularly egregious balls as evidence.

On July 23, Kershaw had a more pressing problem than the balls. As he warmed up for the second inning, pain rippled through his back. From behind the plate, catcher Austin Barnes turned to the umpire. "He looks kind of messed up," Barnes said. A slider made Kershaw wince. Roberts and trainer Nate Lucero visited the mound. Kershaw waved them off. His fastball velocity dipped, but he still struck out Matt Adams, his former Cardinals antagonist, for the third out. He would not return. Word of his injury filtered through the dugout. In between innings, John Pratt bumped into Hyun-Jin Ryu in the food room. The pitcher pointed to the broadcast. "Oh shit," Ryu said. The diagnosis was less dire than that of the previous year. Kershaw had strained a muscle in his lower back, but he had not injured the disc. He required rest but not surgery. The Dodgers set a timetable of four to six weeks, a nugget unearthed by Ken Rosenthal of Fox Sports. A familiar tug-of-war over information occurred. "There's no timetable," Kershaw said. The concept irked him. If he returned in three weeks, he reasoned, people would ask why he rushed back. If he returned in seven, people would wonder what took so long. He considered his health to be private, which ignored the reality of his status as the highest-paid, most prominent player on the best team in baseball.

Even when injured, Kershaw sought control. He disdained rehab outings. "He would rather throw those four innings at Dodger Stadium than Rancho Cucamonga," Zaidi recalled. Kershaw loathed providing updates on his progress. He engaged in a playful feud with Ken Gurnick, the veteran beat writer from MLB.com. Whenever Kershaw threw his rehab bullpens, usually before most reporters had arrived at the park, Gurnick found a seat in the stands nearby to watch. "And it would always annoy him," Gurnick recalled. Kershaw glared at Gurnick or pretended to chuck the ball at his head. One time Gurnick sat in the Dodger Stadium press box, unable to get to the bullpen before Kershaw started to throw. After a while, Kershaw stopped the session. Gurnick heard Kershaw yell his name across the empty ballpark; the lefty had mistaken a white-haired member of the cleanup crew for the writer. "That's Clayton," Gurnick recalled. "Sometimes you think he's got tunnel vision, because he's so intense. But he also has the ability to be aware of everything going on around him."

Even with Kershaw on the shelf, the Dodgers kept rolling. Justin Turner made the All-Star team for the first time. When Turner first joined the club, back in 2014, he surveyed the room and saw baseball royalty: Matt Kemp, Hanley Ramírez, Adrián González, so many decorated, well-compensated veterans. "I walk in and I'm like, 'Oh my God. Do I belong here?'" Turner recalled. By 2017, Turner had become a leader and a lineup fixture. He blended the grittiness of a Long Beach upbringing with a willingness to embrace new information, like the swing changes that rescued his career and helped ignite the sport's launch-angle revolution, in which players stopped settling for singles and started swinging for the fences. Turner embodied the 2017 Dodgers: tough as nails and smart as hell.

The rest of the roster was just as fierce. Corey Seager had become one of baseball's best young hitters. The refurbished player-development system was starting to bear fruit. Cody Bellinger evolved into a power-hitting force who supplanted González at first base. The franchise's reliance on the mercurial temper of Yasiel Puig reduced after a little-regarded trade for utility player Chris Taylor. The deal became emblematic of the organization's success. Taylor hit twenty-one homers after revamping his hitting approach, like Turner. After signing an $80 million deal to stay in Los Angeles, Jansen established himself as the game's best reliever in 2017. For once, he had a legitimate set-up man: Brandon Morrow, the electric arm chosen by Seattle two picks ahead of Kershaw in 2006. Morrow could never stay healthy as a starter. As a reliever, though, he could overpower hitters with elevated fastballs.

Morrow debuted with the Dodgers in late May, just as the team surged into first place. He joined a club that opened its arms to new faces, young and old. "It was never like, 'Oh, we don't do that here,' or 'That's not how we do it here,'" Turner recalled. Rookies were not subjected to much hazing. Kershaw sought an environment that differed from the snake pit he entered in 2008. He did not treat the rookies as usurpers siphoning service time. He saw them as teammates trying to help capture a title. When young pitcher Ross Stripling violated the team's dress code with a crummy Under Armour T-shirt, Kershaw pulled out his phone and ordered Stripling three collared shirts from Mizzen+Main. "Don't ever show up like that again," Kershaw counseled. As Greg Maddux once did with him, Kershaw welcomed younger guys to sit beside him in the dugout. His reputation for clairvoyance only grew. "He can tell you, just by watching the rhythm of the game and knowing the hitter's strengths versus the pitcher's strengths, what pitch is coming," Joc Pederson recalled.

When the team acquired Pirates reliever Tony Watson at the trade deadline, one of the first Dodgers to text him was Kershaw. He invited Watson's family to his house. Watson's wife, Cassie, relied on Ellen to acclimate to Los Angeles. "She had all the connections and all the contacts," Watson recalled. At the end of the year, the team called up outfielder Tim Locastro for a last-minute postseason audition. Locastro had spent the weeks after his minor-league season ended painting his parents' basement in Auburn, New York. Soon after Locastro found his locker at Coors Field, Kershaw extended his hand. "You see on TV how he's such a superstar and everything," Locastro recalled. "And then you get to see him in person and he's one of the most down-to-earth dudes you're ever going to meet."

While lifting one day that summer, Kershaw chatted with Stripling, who was caught between roles. Stripling wanted to start. The Dodgers saw him as a reliever. He told Kershaw he was worried he'd be stuck in the bullpen for the rest of his career. Kershaw looked Stripling in the eye. "Strip, I think you're really good, man," he said. "I think you can be a starter." The encouragement meant the world to Stripling. "When he says anything to your face, it feels monumental," Stripling recalled. A year later, Stripling made his first All-Star team—as a starter.

*   *   *

As the July 31 trade deadline approached, the Dodgers conducted internal calculus and external scouting. The team had grown wary of using Kershaw on short rest in October. The team had structured its roster "to avoid putting Kersh in that position," Friedman recalled. A second back injury tipped the scale further. "We just got to the point where we were like, 'It's not worth it for the performance, for the risk,'" Zaidi recalled. To bolster its starting trio of Kershaw, Hill, and Wood, an All-Star in 2017, the team needed a fourth starter. They sought the most talented, most enigmatic player on the market: Yu Darvish.

Darvish had been a superstar in Japan before joining the Texas Rangers in 2012. He inspired hyperbole. A manager referred to him as "J. R. Richard with Greg Maddux feel." On the afternoon of the deadline, Friedman and Zaidi negotiated a deal. In exchange for three prospects, the Dodgers received three months of Darvish: August, September, and October. The final month mattered the most. After the trade was complete, Zaidi texted Roberts, who was flying with the team to New York: "We got Darvish."

"You've got to be fucking kidding me," Roberts replied.

Darvish awed peers in ways that not even Kershaw could. "We got our Ferrari," Jansen said. Those who spent time around Darvish envied his physicality, creativity, and ability. He stood six-foot-five and could do things with a baseball that other humans could not. Yet those gifts manifested on an intermittent basis. He mastered pitches and then he discarded them. He battled himself as often as he battled opponents.

For the Dodgers in the summer of 2017, Darvish was the key to the franchise's postseason hopes. His arrival boosted the rotation. The bullpen benefited from the addition of displaced starter Kenta Maeda. Even after a bizarre late-season 1-17 skid, the Dodgers won 104 games, the franchise's best total since moving to Los Angeles. When Kershaw returned in September, he was still susceptible to homers, still less dominant than he had been before the herniated disc in 2016. The executives decided not to ask Kershaw if he felt comfortable pitching in the postseason on short rest. If they did, he would volunteer for the assignment and the team might not be able to resist. "I mean this in the most complimentary way: I don't think he was wired to be able to say, 'No, I can't do that,'" Zaidi recalled.

The Dodgers swept the Arizona Diamondbacks in the first round. In the National League Championship Series, the Cubs folded in five. Kershaw delivered six innings of one-run baseball in the 11-1 clincher. In the celebratory delirium, he sprayed bottles of Korbel Brut and splashed Budweiser. His teammates chanted his name as he used the Warren C. Giles Trophy as a beer luge. His eyes stung and his voice went hoarse. He thought about his childhood. "When you're a little kid, you want to go play in the World Series," Kershaw said. "That's all you ever dream about. I never thought in a million years I'd get to say that. But I'm going to play in the World Series."

After a while, he snuck outside. He carried Charley in his arms through the weathered undercarriage of Wrigley. Ellen and Cali met them on the field. Jim and Leslie Melson stood nearby. Kershaw held his son while chasing his daughter around the mound. It was, he decided, one of the best nights of his life.

* * *

Five days later, in Game 1 against the Houston Astros at Dodger Stadium, Kershaw authored the best outing of his postseason career. He struck out eleven Astros in a 3-1 victory. The atmosphere did not bother him. Kershaw wore his warmup jacket zipped to his chin despite the 103-degree pregame heat. The opponent did not bother him. Houston could not handle his fastballs and sliders. And his own history did not bother him. Kershaw overcame a leadoff single and a botched double play to survive the seventh inning.

It was a stinging rebuke to the chorus who questioned his October history.

And it was the last time the Dodgers felt good against the Astros.

Houston presented a formidable obstacle, particularly with the four hitters at the top of the lineup: outfielder George Springer, third baseman Alex Bregman, second baseman José Altuve, and shortstop Carlos Correa. The quartet powered a lineup that led the sport in batting average, on-base percentage, and slugging percentage. All four feasted on high fastballs—the signature offering of Jansen and Morrow. Dodgers executives scoured video and studied heat maps, unable to discern an easy path through the foursome. Morrow searched for a reliever with his arsenal who had success against Houston. He came up empty.

Dodgers officials noticed something else in preparing for the series. When the Astros faced the Yankees in the American League Championship Series, Houston's pitchers and catchers used elaborate sign sequences, even without a runner on base. It was common for teams to flash a variety of signals when a runner stood at second, where he might be able to pick the sign and tip off the hitter. But to do so without a Yankee in position to see the opposing catcher seemed odd—as if the Astros were protecting against an unseen threat. Dodgers scouts "during our prep for that series talked about how there was a lot of smoke around the Astros relaying signs in illegal ways," Friedman recalled. Another alarm was triggered as Chase Utley sifted through "more video than you can imagine," he recalled. Something felt off. The Astros took pitches they shouldn't have taken and hit pitches they shouldn't have hit. "Their numbers were just a little better than I thought they should be," Utley recalled.

Utley was convinced: the Astros were doing something to steal signs.

The act of sign stealing, using the eyes to nab signals sent from catcher to pitcher, was as old as the game itself. In the years before Major League Baseball implemented instant replay and permitted teams to establish video review rooms, stealing signs was an art. The usage of technology made it more of a science. And while the Astros were far from the only club to use the video room to steal signs—both the Yankees and Red Sox would be tsk-tsked by commissioner Rob Manfred for the practice in 2017—they demonstrated how far it could go.

At the outset of the 2017 season, according to an MLB investigation that consisted of sixty-eight interviews and the review of 76,000 emails, the Astros used a center-field camera to steal opponents' signs, which were transmitted from the video room via calls to the dugout. This practice was illegal but considered common among many teams. It still required the signs to be relayed to a player on second base, who then had to communicate the signs to the batter. All across the sport, pitchers were wary of any runner at second. "Any good team was good at doing that," Kershaw recalled.

Where the Astros innovated was finding a way to transmit the signs in real time. They devised a system both primitive and devious. Early in the season, at the urging of bench coach Alex Cora and veteran Carlos Beltrán, Houston installed an extra monitor just outside the dugout that displayed the center-field camera feed, the investigation determined. Players tipped off their teammates by banging a trash can or rattling a massage gun against the metal bench. The scheme frustrated manager A. J. Hinch enough that on two occasions he smashed the monitor with a baseball bat. But new monitors replaced the old ones. Hinch never stopped the cheating. Even those who preferred not to use the scheme, like Altuve, understood its power. At Minute Maid Park, Altuve told a teammate, as reported by Evan Drellich of the *Athletic*, "We're going to have the boom-boom-boom."

The Dodgers heard rumors about Houston's skullduggery but lacked the details. "I remember we had home run balls in BP going into their bullpen, and they wouldn't let us in there," Corey Seager recalled. During the series, Andre Ethier later told the writer Jon Weisman, several Astros asked about the prolific Dodgers offense. "They were questioning us, kind of half joking, 'What are you guys doing? You guys are hitting the crap out of the ball.' That should have been the smoke right there. Obviously, they were doing something themselves, and they probably felt we were."

The rumors prompted Rick Honeycutt to gather his pitchers before the series. Honeycutt encouraged the group to protect their grips, monitor the placement of their gloves, and change their signs frequently, as if there was a runner at second base at all times, especially when playing in Houston, where the Astros had not lost all postseason. The message resonated with some more than others. Not every player was as paranoid as Utley, who had helped decipher the Dodgers' signs with Philadelphia in the previous decade. "I was like, 'Why is this a fucking thing?'" Brandon McCarthy recalled. "I thought that was being weird and overly protective." But McCarthy followed the instructions. When he pitched in a Game 2 loss at Dodger Stadium, he used an elaborate sequence with no runners on base. George Springer still launched the game-winning home run off him. Darvish declined to take the same precautions for Game 3 at Minute Maid Park and could not finish the second inning. For Game 4, Wood decided to change signs every ten pitches. "We'd heard whispers of some of the shady stuff they'd been doing," he later said. Out in the visitors' bullpen, tucked beyond the fence in left-center field, Dodgers relievers peered toward the Astros bullpen and attempted to discern a pattern. Several pitchers tracked someone in an Astros uniform whom they believed was relaying signs: The Dodgers thought if the Astro stood up straight, he was signaling an incoming fastball. For an off-speed pitch, the Astro leaned on his elbows. "You could see some shady shit going on in their bullpen," Stripling recalled.

The precautions could feel counterproductive. Tony Watson devised a simple system. If Watson opened his mouth, Barnes used one set of signs. If Watson closed his mouth, Barnes used another. Then Watson took the mound for Game 3, with the towels whipping and the crowd howling underneath an enclosed roof. "It's a close game, and you want to do well, and you're trying to control your breathing already," Watson recalled. "And now I'm out here and I've got my mouth open. I'm like, 'Oh shit, that's so noticeable.'" The safeguard created an additional layer of stress—one that Kershaw refused to add to the load he already carried.

Before Game 4 in Houston, Kershaw sat inside the video room, running through his scouting sheets to prepare for Game 5. Pratt vocalized his concern. "I think something weird's going on," he said. Pratt suggested Kershaw protect his signs more carefully, as Honey-cutt had advised. Kershaw dismissed the idea. He was willing to switch his signs every two pitches with a runner at second base. But to alter his entire approach felt foolish. He thought it would clutter his mind and disrupt his timing. He did not want the distraction, not when the threat felt so remote. "I was trying to wrap my head around how on earth—if I give one sign with a runner on first base and third base—are they going to get the signs?" Kershaw recalled. "How do you do that? The catcher's covering up, so the first-base coach can't see it. And I'm not tipping. Pratt is good, he knew I wasn't tipping. How on earth are they getting these signs? I was just like, 'There's no way I need to do this.'"

Even those he trusted, like Honeycutt and Pratt, could not convince him. "He thought his signs were good enough not to be stolen," Honeycutt recalled. "And he didn't change them."

What doomed Kershaw was less hubris than failure of imagination. He understood that when a runner stood at second base there was extra risk of technologically aided thievery. But the concept of teams using illegal cameras to relay signs in real time felt impossible. "You just don't fathom that that's happening," Honeycutt recalled.

"I think most teams at the time, like, you're in a video room and people are still trying to get signs with a runner on second," McCarthy recalled. "We all thought there were, like, rules of war. Like, we're all playing *Battlefield: Civil War*, and all of a sudden, there was, like, an F-22 that flew over the top of us. We didn't agree to that. Like, what the fuck is this? You didn't know that that was in play."

* * *

A few hours after Kershaw blew off Pratt's suggestion, the Dodgers burst from their dugout to celebrate a victory that evened the series. Switching his signs and avoiding the barrels of the Astros, Wood allowed only one run in a 6-2 Game 4 victory. His gem set the stage for the next night, when Kershaw would get the chance, on regular rest, to put the Dodgers only one victory away from the title. Kershaw bounded from the handshake line and climbed onto the Minute Maid Park mound. In his left hand, he held a baseball. He looked at the plate. He looked at first. He looked at second. For a moment, he envisioned how the next night would go.

He had no idea.

Spotted a 4-0 lead heading into the fourth inning, Kershaw was rolling. Then he walked the leadoff hitter, George Springer, who had struck out four times in Game 1. What happened next happened fast. Altuve, Houston's pint-sized batting champion, spoiled two sliders and then smashed a single. Two pitches later, Correa lined an inside fastball for a run-scoring double. The tying run came to the plate in the form of first baseman Yuli Gurriel. A first-pitch slider caught more plate than Kershaw preferred. Gurriel launched the ball into the left-field

Crawford Boxes and tied the game. Bedlam ensued: fireworks detonated, the ballpark's in-house train whistled, the crowd went bonkers—a cacophony far louder than whatever pre-pitch noise Patrick Halpin thought he heard in the left-field seats.

Kershaw rubbed up a fresh baseball and finished the inning. He wrapped a towel around his arm, slugged Gatorade, and sat alone on the bench as his teammates crowded the railing for the top of the fifth. Unlike in years past, these Dodgers did not fold when Kershaw stumbled. A three-run homer by Bellinger granted Kershaw new life. When Kershaw returned to the mound, the Dodgers led, 7-4. He secured two quick outs. As Springer returned for a third at-bat, Kershaw was one out away from turning over the rest of the game to Roberts's vaunted bullpen.

Except Kershaw could not put away Springer, his patsy only a few days earlier. Springer ignored off-speed pitches that dipped beneath the zone. He spoiled an inside fastball. He fouled off a rare backdoor slider. After eight pitches, Springer walked. Up next was Alex Bregman, Houston's irrepressibly confident third baseman. He wore the No. 2 in part because he was chosen second overall in the 2015 draft— and he was salty he wasn't taken first. He presented enough of a threat that when Kershaw snuck a curveball over the plate for a second strike, Roberts pondered an audacious act. He considered removing Kershaw and replacing him with Maeda in the middle of the at-bat. *I'm going to take him out, right now*, Roberts thought. He saw how fatigued Kershaw was, the combination of physical and emotional exhaustion that A. J. Ellis had seen in those games against St. Louis. Sweat ringed Kershaw's eyes and dirt dusted his cap. When Bregman stepped out of the box, Roberts raced through the variables, the value of a fresh reliever versus a weary starter, the potential calamity awaiting when he went to get the ball, the inevitable postgame circus, the concern about embarrassing the greatest pitcher of a generation. Roberts had spent the past two seasons trying to earn Kershaw's trust, to the point where he hoped his ace understood the manager intervened only when he felt the Dodgers would benefit. But he could not do it. He stayed put. "I didn't want to make it about me," Roberts later said.

So Roberts watched as Kershaw toiled for ten pitches. Bregman took two backdoor sliders for balls. He fouled off fastballs and curveballs. He looked notably comfortable. After dominating Game 1, as *Sports Illustrated*'s Tom Verducci later noted, in Game 5 Kershaw issued more walks (three) than strikeouts (two) for the first time since 2010. He threw thirty-nine sliders and induced one whiff. In strategizing for Game 5, the Astros planned to ignore Kershaw's slider, according to people familiar with their thought process. It remains a mystery if the illegal sign-stealing apparatus aided that strategy; those connected with the Astros have denied using the trash can during the postseason. But they suddenly stopped chasing. "They were spitting on curveballs," Honeycutt recalled. "They were spitting on backdoor sliders. They were spitting on every ball that was [on the edge]." Bregman did not need much aid for the final two pitches. Kershaw sprayed a fastball outside and then lost a slider in the dirt. Bregman trotted to first. Roberts came to the mound. He took the baseball and tapped Kershaw's backside.

With Kershaw gone, the impending nightmares transitioned from pitcher to catcher. At times, Austin Barnes played the part of a punching bag. He was listed at five-foot-ten, which was generous. Andre Ethier called him "Tyrion Lannister," the dwarf sage played by Peter Dinklage in *Game of Thrones*. And that wasn't even Barnes's best nickname. When Barnes was a rookie in 2015, Utley treated him like a gofer. If he needed coffee, Barnes fetched it. If Utley sought tacos in San Francisco, Barnes hit the streets. After a while, Ellis interceded.

"You have no idea what his name is," Ellis said.

"It's Sam," Utley said.

"It's Austin," Ellis said.

"Well, it's Sam now."

Two years later, when MLB permitted players to wear jerseys with nicknames for a weekend, Barnes sported "SAM" across his back. By

October, though, he had displaced Grandal as the starting catcher. He often texted Ellis for advice about catching Kershaw. Ellis schooled the youngster on how to communicate with Kershaw, when to intervene and when to stick to strengths. He wasn't much of a hitter, but pitchers appreciated him. "Barnesy takes such pride in calling those games," Kershaw recalled.

Barnes thought he had dialed up the perfect sequence to fool Altuve for the final out. He called six off-speed pitches in a row from Maeda, sliders away and changeups in. With the count full, with the Dodgers one strike away from preserving the three-run lead, Barnes figured Altuve would not be ready for a fastball. Maeda flung a 93.6-mph heater. Barnes was wrong. Altuve clobbered the baseball beyond the center-field fence to tie the game. The same symphony arose: fireworks, train whistles, bedlam. For years afterward, Barnes pondered that sequence, unable to comprehend how Altuve had cracked his code.

* * *

Alone on the bench, Kershaw rubbed his chin and stared at the ground. He had blown a four-run lead and then made it possible for Maeda to blow a three-run lead. This was not one inning too long. This was not one batter too many. This was a collapse with the world watching. His reputation was in tatters. After a while, he got up and left.

Inside the clubhouse, Kershaw saw the same fate befall the other Dodgers pitchers. To protect an 8-7 lead, Morrow lobbied to pitch the seventh, appearing in his fifth consecutive game. In the opposing dugout, at least one Astro perked up. "The same guy?" Gurriel asked. Houston banged Morrow around: six pitches, four hits, two homers. Morrow stumbled out of the dugout and found Kershaw sitting on the clubhouse floor, half dressed and distraught. Morrow grabbed two water bottles and handed one to his teammate. Morrow slunk down next to Kershaw. They sat in silence as the Dodgers lost in extra innings, 13-12. Kershaw was still stunned when he spoke to reporters. He mumbled about losing his command but offered no explanation. "Everyone's pretty exhausted after that one, emotionally and physically," he said. It hurt him the most. But it hurt the others to see him so shattered.

"When bad things happen to bad people, you don't even care," McCarthy recalled. "It's almost like a good thing. But when bad things happen to good people, it's hard to make sense of it." To McCarthy, Kershaw did everything right, yet the game refused to reward him. "It's just more heartbreaking," McCarthy recalled.

*　*　*

A day later, back in Los Angeles to prepare for Game 6, Honeycutt cued up video and suffered through the horror once more. He watched Kershaw spot sliders and snap curveballs. The Astros did not flinch. *How did they take that pitch?* Honeycutt wondered.

Honeycutt reemphasized the importance of changing signs, but the damage was done. Hill and the bullpen held the Astros to only one run in a Game 6 victory, which set up Darvish for redemption in Game 7. Darvish combusted, giving up five runs while collecting just five outs. Two days after his debacle in Houston, Kershaw provided four innings of scoreless relief. It did not matter in a 5-1 defeat. There were no paeans to his heroism written that evening. After a twenty-nine-year wait, the Dodgers had returned to the World Series. But they did not hoist the trophy. Kershaw hung his arms over the dugout railing and pressed his chin to the padding as the Astros—just like the Cubs did, and the Mets did, and the Cardinals did, and the Phillies did, and even the McKinney North Bulldogs did—formed a dogpile after defeating him.

As Kershaw mourned, the Astros reveled. Beltrán joined the Fox broadcast for a segment that only looked sinister in retrospect. Alex Rodriguez, Beltrán's former Yankees teammate, listened as Beltrán preached the importance of communication. "Was there any sharing information with Darvish?" Rodriguez asked. Beltrán suppressed a smile. "Was he doing anything, perhaps, with his glove that those hitters looked so comfortable?" Rodriguez said. Beltrán's eyes went wide.

"Jesus Christ, man," Beltrán said. The others on the panel cackled. "Whoa!" Keith Hernandez said. "Inside info!" David Ortiz said.

The Dodgers were not laughing. Darvish was despondent. As Roberts addressed the group, Turner slung an arm around Darvish, the hired gun who let them down. To some, like ESPN's Stephen A. Smith, who had insisted after Game 5 that "[if] the Los Angeles Dodgers lose this World Series, it's going to be because of Kershaw," there was only one goat. Kershaw had never played on a team as good as the 2017 Dodgers. He understood he might never play on a team that good again. "Maybe one of these days I won't fail, we won't fail, and we'll win one of these things," Kershaw told *USA Today.* The postseason, he said, felt like it lasted twenty-seven years. He was spent, sore, sorrowful. Ellen agonized for her husband. "That's what really hurt me so much, just knowing what he endured," Ellen recalled. "And this failure that he felt."

The Dodgers packed their bags, wiped their tears, and waved their goodbyes. Utley commiserated with Pratt. They had been skeptical about Houston before the series. The subsequent seven games heightened their suspicion. The uncertainty ate at them. Had the World Series been stolen?

"We'll know in a few years," Utley told Pratt, "when these guys change teams."

CHAPTER 18

THE ABYSS

In the days after the World Series, Clayton Kershaw put on a brave face. The family gathered what they needed from their home in Studio City and returned to Highland Park. He tried to stay busy. He tried not to wallow. He tried to move past the most profound professional failure of his life. None of it came easy.

"I saw how much that World Series, in particular, crushed him," Ellen recalled. "It was so, so hard."

Kershaw did not always vocalize his melancholy. The children brightened him like little else could. But Ellen understood that when her husband went quiet, when he appeared lost in thought, he was trying to process what had happened, to understand why he had come up short yet again. "There's nobody who puts more pressure on himself than him," she recalled. She was not the only one to notice. Patrick Halpin recalled those months as "a very sensitive time at the Kershaws' house." His buddies avoided discussing the Astros. "We didn't really want to talk about it," Halpin recalled. "It was obvious that Clayton didn't want to talk about it."

The 2017 World Series could have been the happy end of Kershaw's postseason narrative. No one could watch Game 1 of that series, when Kershaw iced Houston in the smoking heat, and call this man a choker.

But the roller coaster of Game 5 tilted the scales out of Kershaw's favor. He had lost in a fashion that could not be forgotten, not by the public, and not by him. He had become the rare baseball player to whom ESPN's *First Take* might devote a segment.

His friends and teammates grumbled about his lack of luck, his extended usage, the failure of those around him. "If we had won Game 7," Kenley Jansen recalled, "nobody would talk about it." In October, other Dodgers reasoned, Kershaw shouldered a burden greater than any of his peers—pitching on short rest, in relief, returning from injury. "Shit that no one's ever done, that no one else would even be asked to do," Alex Wood recalled. "Think of any great pitchers going to the Hall right now. You see any of those guys do that?" His buddy Will Skelton once calculated Kershaw's postseason ERA without including runners other relievers permitted to score. "It's a particular sore spot for me," Skelton recalled. Ellen pondered using social media to defend her husband, but she always decided against it. It would only make things worse.

His phone overflowed with messages from friends, rivals, teammates, those who competed against him, those who admired him. After the postseason defeats, former Dodger Josh Lindblom often texted Kershaw. The two men stayed close even after Lindblom's career took him to Philadelphia and Oakland and eventually Korea. "I don't think you can ever tell how much it hurt him, because he would never show it," Lindblom recalled. "But as you get to know him, you just know how much he cares."

Despite the sorrow, Kershaw did not stay idle. On his first day back in Texas, he ran a six-hour camp in West Dallas for four hundred kids. Two weeks after Game 7, he started lifting. A month after Game 7, on his seventh wedding anniversary, he visited Los Angeles to recruit two-way Japanese phenom Shohei Ohtani. "If we get this guy," he told Ellen, "it'll be worth it." (The Dodgers did not get that guy. "Just a gigantic waste of time," he said after Ohtani joined the Los Angeles Angels.) Six weeks after Game 7, Kershaw picked up a baseball again.

As part of the workouts, Kershaw invited a new pitcher. "After the 2017 season, how it shook out, myself and my family, we were disappointed," Yu Darvish recalled. "During that hard time, he reached out and asked me to play catch with him." Being a Dodger had invigorated Darvish; before the trade, he had contemplated retirement. The World Series devastated him. Darvish felt the same sadness Kershaw felt. They were no longer teammates; Darvish had entered free agency. For Kershaw to extend his hand uplifted Darvish. "He's very kind, kind in a way that he can think about other people," Darvish recalled.

Kershaw lobbied Darvish to rejoin the Dodgers. Darvish was wary how fans would receive him. He worried his children would be hounded at school. When Farhan Zaidi flew to Dallas to meet with Darvish, Kershaw tagged along. Over sushi, Zaidi committed "probably one of the worst functional short-circuits of my life," scooping wasabi with his fingers and absent-mindedly rubbing his face. "Rarely in my life have I felt that kind of pain," Zaidi recalled. Both pitchers cackled as Zaidi stumbled into tables en route to the bathroom. The agony was for naught: Darvish signed a six-year, $126 million contract with the Cubs, who offered more money than the Dodgers.

Kershaw received another Dodger in Highland Park that winter. Walker Buehler had debuted that September but watched the World Series from the stands. Team officials believed Buehler would be ready in 2018. They wondered if Kershaw might mentor him. The two made an odd couple. Buehler operated with a self-assurance that could be off-putting. He talked relentless amounts of shit, despite his boyish features, wiry frame, and lack of big-league results. And he swore like the Kentucky horsemen he had grown up around. A significant portion of his sentences included variations of the word "fuck"—it is hard to fathom how much money he would have donated to Ellen's swear jar.

At the behest of Brandon McDaniel, Kershaw opened his door to Buehler. His home featured a gym modeled after the Dodger Stadium weight room. He had replaced his backyard grass with artificial turf so he could push around a weighted sled. Kershaw put his guest through the paces of his offseason routine. They lunched at Kershaw's favorite restaurant, a Tex-Mex joint called Banditos. (Kershaw had met the owner at a Dallas Cowboys game and pocketed his business card, thrilled to reduce the wait for a table.) Kershaw realized he had little to offer Buehler. "I was just like, 'Man, this guy has no reason to be here,'" Kershaw recalled. Buehler was the product of a vastly different baseball upbringing. At Vanderbilt University, Buehler met the motion-capture gurus from Driveline, a pitching laboratory in the Pacific Northwest where players were flocking in search of improvement, the sort of place Kershaw brushed aside. They did not speak the same language. Buehler talked about the separation between the shoulder and the hip, the value of weighted balls, the biomechanics of his surgically repaired right elbow. Kershaw talked about throwing sliders down in the zone. "That was when the whole thought of mentoring Walker was even in the realm of possibilities," Kershaw recalled. "He doesn't want anyone telling him what to do. He didn't need me to do that."

What Kershaw did not recognize until later was that he could learn as much from Buehler as Buehler could learn from him. Kershaw did not yet understand that he could no longer bend the game to his will. After the agony against Houston, Kershaw entered the most trying period of his career, in which his body broke down, his arsenal degraded, and he came to admit that his reputation as a postseason choker might actually be deserved. He was about to peer into the abyss.

*   *   *

One morning that February, Kershaw sat at his Camelback Ranch locker and studied the schedule. Something was amiss. Someone had moved the usual 9:15 A.M. meeting.

"So the meeting is at 9:40 now?" he said. "That's great. I literally plan my whole day around this. Who can I punch in the mouth?"

He pointed at bullpen catcher Steve Cilladi.

"You? Can I punch you?"

Cilladi laughed as he relayed that Kenley Jansen had changed the time.

"Can I punch Kenley in the mouth?" Kershaw asked. He found Jansen and expressed his displeasure. "I wasn't even on the team and I got a phone call that day," recalled A. J. Ellis. "That's how much it drove him nuts." The obsession about time and control remained. When a meeting ran long one morning, Kershaw flopped to the floor to stretch mid-presentation. When a reporter asked if he had moved on from the World Series, Kershaw rejected the premise. "I just kind of absorb it," he said. He shrugged when asked if that was healthy. "I'll let you know if I explode at some point," he said.

Pitching did not alleviate the crankiness. After the longest season of his career, Kershaw suddenly could not generate the usual life on his pitches. "I feel like in 2017, I had the best stuff I've ever had," he recalled. "And in 2018, it diminished. I don't know if it was just the workload or just the [shortened] offseason. I don't know what happened." For the entirety of Kershaw's career, his average fastball clocked between 93 and 94 mph, a reasonable speed enhanced by the pitch's backspin. Now the radar gun was registering velocities at 90, 91, sometimes even 88 or 89. Even more troubling, the shape of the pitch was changing. Rather than disorient the batter by seeming to rise, the pitch cut, ever so slightly, toward his glove side. "He just hated for his fastball to cut," Rick Honeycutt recalled. "He wanted his fastball to be true. And that became a little tougher, after the back injuries." His slider lost some of its depth, staying flat rather than diving. For nearly a decade, Kershaw had dominated because of backspin on his fastball and depth on his slider. Now the pitches looked less distinguishable: The fastball cut too much and the slider didn't drop enough. "It was basically the same pitch," recalled bullpen coach Mark Prior. John Pratt once logged a fastball as a slider. "It's not a slider," Kershaw grumbled. (He grew even grumpier if anyone referred to the pitch as a cutter: "I hate the word 'cutter' with a passion," he explained. "A cutter is just a bad fastball. I throw a slider.")

That spring, Kershaw turned thirty. He had pitched ten seasons in the majors. He understood the actuarial tables. The hourglass only contained so much sand. Yet he worried about the need for drastic change. Part of the reason Kershaw achieved greatness, his teammates felt, was he never lost sight of his strengths. He trusted the five-day cycle—the lifting, the running, the anxiety—because he felt lost without it. He ignored suggestions that might derail him. He changed when necessary but never before. "Why would he change?" Justin Turner recalled. "Why would he do something different? And if he does do something different, is he going to lose some of that edge that was making him great?"

Kershaw often consulted thirty-nine-year-old veteran Chase Utley, the eldest member of the Dodgers, about how to manage his health. In his twenties, Utley had been one of the best players in the game. After he reached his thirties, his body broke down. It was "extremely challenging" to feel betrayed by your health rather than your ability, Utley recalled. He could relate to Kershaw's plight.

"You know, as a player, a few things that get you where you want to go," Utley recalled. "Now the question is: Are those few things also holding you back?"

*   *   *

As the 2018 season unfolded, Kershaw sat with Ellen and talked about leaving Los Angeles. He had two more seasons and $70 million left on his seven-year contract but also an opt-out clause at the end of the year. In recent years, other pitchers had cleared the salary bar he set. David Price signed a seven-year, $217 million contract with the Boston Red Sox. Zack Greinke's six-year, $206.5 million deal with Arizona set a new record for the largest annual average salary for pitchers.

If Kershaw opted out after 2018, he would be entering his age-thirty-one season, a year older than Price when he signed with Boston, a year younger than Greinke when he left the Dodgers. Both Greinke and Price had bounced around the league before their mega-deals. Price had been traded twice. Greinke had been traded twice, and already gone through free agency once. They were willing to do something that Kershaw was unsure he wanted to do. They were willing to pursue greener pastures.

Kershaw and Ellen discussed how to proceed. Kershaw was not interested in scoring a new record payday. But he was curious how other teams valued him. He had simple qualifications for any potential suitor: "Clayton was looking at: What are competitive teams that are in great locations?" Ellen recalled. Over the years, Kershaw had mentioned his curiosity about other Southern California teams. "San Diego would be such a fun place to live," he often told her. She felt the same about Anaheim. They could get a place by the beach, soak up the sun, with a bit less traffic. But neither the Angels nor the Padres were contenders.

The Cubs and the Yankees were a different story. Kershaw and Ellen had heard great things about Chicago, where the Cubs were still the toast of the town after winning it all in 2016. The Yankees had just reached the American League Championship Series with a young core. The Big Apple appealed to Kershaw. "I think it would be super cool to play in New York," Kershaw recalled. Living in Manhattan, wearing the pinstripes, toeing the rubber at Yankee Stadium: Kershaw could see himself doing it.

There was reason to consider the Texas Rangers, too. Marianne had begun to lose her memory. For years, Kershaw had noticed his mother repeated questions and seemed forgetful. She was eventually diagnosed with Alzheimer's. The family moved her into an assisted living memory-care facility. "She kept fighting us, because she wanted to keep driving," Kershaw recalled. "But driving was not an option." Both Jim and Leslie Melson had recently been diagnosed with cancer. The Kershaws wanted to be able to travel back and forth to Dallas when necessary. But any move came with a cost. They worried about the strain on their children, and they expected their family to grow. A new team might come with logistical complications. They had planted roots in Los Angeles. "He's immensely loyal," Jim Melson recalled. "And I think that loyalty carries over to the Dodgers and these decisions he's making nowadays. It's not about the money side of it. It's about family. It's about the loyalty to the team that helped create his successes." They had built relationships across the organization. Kershaw's Challenge felt connected to the community. His charity Ping-Pong tournament at Dodger Stadium had become a summertime staple. And they expected the Dodgers to compete every year. The comforts of the familiar outweighed the allure of the unknown.

"Why mess up a good thing?" Ellen recalled.

*   *   *

On May 31 of that year, Brandon McCarthy gazed at a television inside the Atlanta Braves clubhouse. He had left the Dodgers the previous offseason, as part of a complicated trade that included Adrián González and brought back Matt Kemp. Kershaw appeared on the screen, pitching against the Phillies in his first appearance in nearly a month. A bout with biceps tendonitis sidelined him in May, but he talked his way out of rehab starts, uninterested in wasting bullets in the minors. The rest did not help him against Philadelphia. "He looked fucking awful," McCarthy recalled. Kershaw's fastball velocity dipped into the 80s, slow enough to fool observers. "Just because it says slider on the scoreboard," Yasmani Grandal said afterward, "it doesn't mean we weren't throwing fastballs." Yet McCarthy noticed something as Kershaw slogged through five innings of one-run baseball, with his body clearly compromised: the Phillies still couldn't hit him. Kershaw could still throw strikes. He maintained his delivery. He managed the situation. It reminded McCarthy of those conversations with Greinke about Kershaw's preternatural gift for getting hitters out.

"It just blew me away," McCarthy recalled. "Like, why isn't he giving up runs?"

The subsequent diagnosis was familiar. Kershaw had strained a muscle in his lower back. He sat out another few weeks. He made eighteen more starts in 2018 but never struck out more than nine batters in a game. He threw a hundred pitches only four times. He completed the eighth inning just once. For the first time since 2011, he was not invited to the All-Star Game. The lost life on his fastball stayed gone. "It was like the constant search to get where you once were," Kershaw recalled.

The injuries further strained his relationship with Roberts. Kershaw chafed at restrictions. When most pitchers logged six innings in fewer than a hundred pitches, they exulted in a tidy outing. Kershaw felt he had let the team down. Roberts absorbed the frustration. Kershaw raged to excel—but when his body precluded excellence, he just raged. Roberts wanted Kershaw to believe the manager acted in his ace's best interest, but their interests were not always aligned. "You're dealing with a superstar who was dealing with injuries who didn't want to acknowledge them," Roberts recalled. "Because he doesn't want to lose that edge. So how do I, we as a staff, protect a player who doesn't want to be protected, or feel he needs to be protected?"

A sense of grumpiness pervaded the clubhouse. "Who cares?" Jansen harrumphed when reporters asked about his cutter's diminished velocity. Roberts felt wounded by lingering criticism about bullpen decisions and annoyed by persistent questions about lineup construction. Younger players like Cody Bellinger, Kiké Hernández, and Joc Pederson were irritated about losing at-bats in platoons. The unity from 2017 was gone.

Yet the Dodgers reached the World Series again, on a journey that demonstrated how Kershaw had fallen in the team's pitching hierarchy. To win the National League West, the Dodgers turned to Buehler for Game 163 against the Colorado Rockies. With Hyun-Jin Ryu starting Game 1, the Dodgers defeated Atlanta in the first postseason round. It took seven games to outlast Milwaukee to collect another National League pennant. The trophy came with an invitation to get throttled by the 108-win Boston Red Sox. "We did not expect to go to the World Series," Kershaw recalled. "I think it was just by default. Nobody else was that good." The Red Sox thrashed him. After collecting a save out of the bullpen in Game 7 against Milwaukee, Kershaw started Game 1 at Fenway Park on two days of rest. He gave up five runs in four innings.

The series ended in Game 5, when Kershaw lasted seven innings but yielded four runs. "Obviously, the Red Sox, I had nothing by the World Series," Kershaw recalled. "I was dead."

The defeat opened all facets of the organization to judgment. Roberts heard Dodgers fans braying for his ouster and read a nasty tweet from President Donald Trump about his in-game strategy. The front office had neglected to upgrade the bullpen at the trade deadline. The offense never materialized. There was less chatter about whether Kershaw could win the big one. "This isn't a 'Kershaw in the playoffs' issue," one team official said. "This is just a 'Kershaw in 2018' issue." The indictment now spread across the entire franchise: Why couldn't the Dodgers win the big one?

"It might not be a personnel thing," Kershaw said after Game 5. "It might just be a 'play better' thing."

*   *   *

In the end, Kershaw opted out of his contract but never reached free agency. He accepted a three-year, $93 million extension during the team's exclusive negotiating window after the World Series. The brevity of the deal came as a surprise: Kershaw had become more vocal about the scourge of tanking, a practice that led the Cubs and the Astros to the World Series but plenty of other teams to ruin. He disliked when owners feigned poverty. He still left money on the table, unwilling to test the market, unsure how his body might decline during a longer deal, unsure how his spirit might flag if his ability waned. "I think this year especially—maybe rightfully so—there's been a lot of people saying that I'm in decline or I'm not going to be as good as I once was," Kershaw said after signing the contract. "I'm looking forward to proving a lot of people wrong with that."

The night he inked the deal, Kershaw and Ellen dined in Dallas with the McDaniels. It was one of four trips McDaniel made to Highland Park that winter. McDaniel stressed that Kershaw needed to be amenable to new ideas. Kershaw sounded more willing to deviate from his dogmatic approach to squatting and sprinting all the time. McDaniel fixated on Kershaw's flexibility and pliability, two characteristics compromised by back trouble. McDaniel studied the movement patterns of Kershaw's ankles, hips, knees, and spine. He examined golfers and tennis players, searching for any link to improve Kershaw's rotational force. On the first trip to Texas, McDaniel focused on the stability of Kershaw's core. On the second trip, they strengthened the shoulder. On the third, they discussed ways to generate better velocity. For the final visit, they considered how the elements blended together.

When he reported to Camelback Ranch, Kershaw looked trimmer, invigorated by the offseason. Team officials were cautiously optimistic. The feeling did not last long. Early in camp, his left shoulder felt sore. For the first time since 2010, the Dodgers needed someone besides Kershaw to start Opening Day. Roberts had signed a new contract during the offseason, but the franchise was shifting into a new phase. Farhan Zaidi left to run the San Francisco Giants, although his imprint on the club—like signing Max Muncy, a lightly regarded first baseman who morphed into an All-Star slugger—lasted. The mood in the clubhouse felt brighter. In the winter, the team had finally traded Yasiel Puig, whose behavior outweighed his importance at the turnstiles. Yasmani Grandal departed in free agency. The team reacquired Russell Martin, the starting catcher when Kershaw debuted in 2008. In his final big-league season, Martin mentored the catcher of the future, rookie Will Smith. The clubhouse was overflowing with homegrown talent. Bellinger bashed forty-seven homers that season while playing Gold Glove defense in center field en route to winning the National League MVP. Buehler looked like an ace. There was more talent on the way. Early in the season, Kershaw noticed this group arrived earlier to the ballpark than any team he had played on. "A lot of young guys," he said, "who want lunch."

Andrew Friedman believed it was the best team he had ever assembled. The Dodgers won 106 games, besting the record set in 2017. The lineup was dangerous and the rotation was deep. Buehler established himself as the cocksure tip of the spear. Ryu won the National League ERA title and finished second in the Cy Young voting. Rich Hill posted a 2.45 ERA. The wealth of talent reduced reliance on Kershaw—even if he still wanted to carry the load. To John Pratt, who spent hours in the video room with Kershaw in between starts, the looming strain of the postseason became apparent. As the years passed and the October struggles mounted, when the calendar flipped to September, Pratt noticed Kershaw's answers shortened and his patience thinned. During a game on September 6, Kershaw looked confused when Roberts removed him after ninety-nine pitches midway through the fifth inning. "Why?" Kershaw asked. In the dugout, he kicked a water cooler and screamed. He finished the season with a 3.03 ERA, tenth best among MLB starters, but his worst since his rookie year. The offseason had not proved a panacea. His fastball velocity tumbled from 90.9 mph in 2018 to 90.4 mph in 2019. And he still hung more sliders than he preferred.

Yet while organizing the rotation for the first round against the 93-win Washington Nationals, the Dodgers made a curious decision. Game 1 belonged to Buehler. But the team slotted Kershaw for Game 2, rather than Ryu, the better pitcher in 2019. The reasoning revealed an organization caught between Kershaw's reality and his reputation. If the series reached a fifth game, Roberts explained before Game 1, the Dodgers wanted Kershaw available to pitch in relief.

The stage was set for disaster.

* * *

It never should have gotten that far.

On May 31, Washington was 19-31, ten games back in the National League East, with about a one in five chance of reaching the post-season. The team won nine of its next eleven games, pulling out of the nose dive to make it back to .500 by the end of June and punch a ticket to October with a 46-27 record in the second half—not far from the 46-24 second-half pace of the Dodgers. After downing Milwaukee in the Wild Card game, Washington flew to Los Angeles. A perennial contender, the Nationals papered over holes with stars. Max Scherzer and Stephen Strasburg were two of the best pitchers in baseball. Juan Soto had emerged as the game's preeminent young slugger, a twenty-year-old with an incredible eye and frightening power. Anthony Rendon married excellent defense at third base with surprising pop. In a five-game matchup, the gap in depth between the two clubs only meant so much. The stars would decide the series.

Buehler turned in six scoreless innings in a Game 1 laugher, but Strasburg outpitched Kershaw in Game 2. Kershaw permitted three runs in six innings, a quality start in the scorebook, a disappointment for him. The Nationals were unimpressed by the talent of their hosts and unsurprised by their strategies. "Our guys became too predictable in what we were calling," Honeycutt recalled. A two-game split in Washington brought the series back to Los Angeles for Game 5. The Nationals lined up Strasburg, who had fashioned an admirable career despite never quite living up to the outrageous hype after Washington chose him No. 1 overall out of San Diego State in 2009. Strasburg never won a Cy Young and only made three All-Star teams. But he was excellent in October. Against Buehler, it was an even match. The Dodgers homered twice to build a 3-0 lead. Buehler kept the Nationals quiet before yielding a run in the sixth.

And that was when things got weird.

As Buehler faced his first real trouble of the evening, Kershaw warmed in the bullpen, looking to replicate his relief feats from the previous three Octobers. The mere presence of Kershaw among the relievers was curious. The Dodgers possessed, in Friedman's estimation, "the deepest bullpen we've had in terms of the number of options, the different looks." Rather than rely on that group, the team added Kershaw. A starting pitcher, Friedman later explained, "can be a really attractive bullpen option." And so the Dodgers ignored the foreshadowing. Kershaw had given up a career-high twenty-eight homers that season. He had not thrown a fastball in 2019 that clocked 93 mph, his average velocity in 2017. His first-inning ERA in 2019 was 5.79. During a six-start stretch in August and September, Kershaw surrendered thirteen homers and posted a 5.24 ERA. And his left arm was killing him. "My shoulder hurt so bad," he recalled. Whenever he raised up to throw, it felt "like a knife." He did not believe he required surgery, so he pitched through the pain. "I was like, 'I need to chill out,'" Kershaw recalled. "But during the season, you can't chill out."

Instead of resting, Kershaw embarked on a rescue mission. Buehler had thrown ninety-seven pitches, a sum he surpassed in fewer than half his regular-season starts. As Kershaw had in so many postseasons before, Buehler returned for the seventh inning, an ace asked to do just a little bit more. Buehler hit a batter and walked another, exiting with the go-ahead run at the plate, in the form of left-handed-hitting outfielder Adam Eaton. Roberts patted Buehler on the stomach and took the baseball. Kershaw loped in with his head down, as "We Are Young" blared across Chavez Ravine. Unlike relievers asked to save him in years prior, Kershaw prevented catastrophe from befalling Buehler. After Eaton failed to check his swing on an 0-2 slider, Kershaw pounded his glove and unleashed a roar.

"He emptied the tank against Eaton," Justin Turner recalled. "He had that huge adrenaline rush. The fans went nuts. He went nuts.

"And then . . ."

What happened next remains a subject of dispute.

Kershaw wrapped his left arm in a towel and retreated to the end of the bench. Rendon and Soto, the two best Nationals hitters, would bat in the eighth. The duo presented a logistical challenge for Roberts. Rendon batted from the right side, Soto batted from the left. Behind Soto were a pair of veteran right-handed hitters, Howie Kendrick and Ryan Zimmerman. Roberts needed to decide which of his relievers could navigate that gauntlet. A couple of years earlier, Roberts might have turned to Kenley Jansen for a two-inning save. But Jansen had fallen off since the 2017 World Series; his ERA had risen from 1.32 in 2017 to 3.71 in 2019. The best option to face Soto might have been journeyman southpaw Adam Kolarek. Soto was 0-for-3 against Kolarek during the series. "Kolarek is literally on the postseason roster to face Soto," Ross Stripling recalled. But Roberts could not start the inning with Kolarek facing a right-handed hitter like Rendon. Kenta Maeda, his best righty, had pitched in both Game 3 and Game 4, and Roberts did not want him to face Soto. Julio Urías, the talented lefty, was unavailable after pitching in Games 2, 3, and 4.

So Roberts looked toward the end of the bench, where the greatest pitcher of his generation sat with his aching arm wrapped in a towel. Kershaw was willing to keep pitching but thought he would not return for the eighth. He figured his only assignment was Eaton. "Doc doesn't really say anything unless you're done," Kershaw recalled. "He comes and tells you you're done. So if he doesn't say anything, you just keep going. So I just kept going." Roberts remembered the moment differently. "After he came back out, he goes, 'I want to get Rendon and Soto,'" Roberts recalled. Rick Honeycutt split the difference. "I remember [Kershaw] looking surprised when Doc said that he still had it," Honeycutt recalled. He loosened a chuckle. "Looking back, you wish that wouldn't have happened."

So there was Kershaw, alone on the mound protecting a 3-1 lead, set up to fail. In the batter's box, Rendon eased into his stance, a slouch that belied his talent. There were a lot of people in baseball who thought Rendon didn't really enjoy the sport. There was no one in baseball who thought Rendon wasn't excellent at it. When Rendon matriculated at Rice University, the head coach gathered his assistants: "You want to see Hank Aaron's wrists?" He packed lightning in his hands.

Kershaw had prepared to appear with runners on base, so he decided to continue pitching out of the stretch. Rendon passed on a first-pitch curveball outside the zone. Will Smith called for a slider. Kershaw raised his arms skyward. The pitch dove beneath the strike zone. Rendon did not care. He drove the baseball beyond the left-field fence, a homer that cut the lead to one and left Kershaw shaking his head. "Rendon did a nice piece of hitting," Honeycutt recalled.

Kershaw circled the mound while Rendon circled the bases. Soto stepped to the plate. A few weeks away from his twenty-first birthday, Soto was the youngest man on the field, but he might also have been the best. That season he had become the first player to hit thirty home runs in a season at age twenty since Frank Robinson. "Juan Soto just might be Ted Williams," the decorated baseball scribe Jayson Stark wrote. Soto possessed a regal bearing at the plate, smirking and slithering around the box. He loved nothing more than taking a close pitch, shuffling toward the pitcher and grabbing his junk. Soto reminded viewers that baseball, at its core, centered on one man throwing a sphere and one man holding a club.

Against Kershaw, there was no macho posturing. There was merely one bad pitch, a slider at Soto's belt, a pitch that Dodgers officials later charted as possibly the worst Kershaw threw all season. Soto detonated the baseball. Kershaw crumpled onto the mound. He peeled off his cap. When he gathered the courage to turn around, it was already over. The baseball landed more than a dozen rows deep into the right-center pavilion. 3-3.

All at once, the moment felt breathtaking, unfathomable, utterly predictable: it had happened again. Again. Again. How? After 2013 and 2014 and 2016 and 2017 and 2018—how? How could this have happened again? When Kershaw accepted a new baseball from Smith, his shoulders scrunched, as if crushed beneath the weight of it all. To Randy Wolf, a teammate more than a decade prior, Kershaw looked destroyed. "I've just never seen that look on Clayton's face, when Soto hit that home run," Wolf recalled. "It was such a look of disbelief, of like, 'Are you kidding me?' It was as if the pressures and the comments of postseasons past had just collapsed on him."

Kershaw would not throw another pitch in 2019. He looked as if he never wanted to pitch again.

The TBS camera found Kershaw alone in the dugout. The imagery conveyed bottomless sadness. His forearms rested on his thighs. He gazed at a floor strewn with sunflower seeds and paper cups. For seventy-five minutes, the amount of time required for the Dodgers to lose the game in ten innings, Kershaw remained in that position. On occasion, he looked up at the field. On occasion, he held his head in his hands. Mostly he looked down, overcome with that noxious brew of embarrassment and disappointment. The camera stayed with him for the bitter finale of another lost season, beaming his grief to friends, family, and former teammates.

If previous October collapses invoked the lament that fortune never smiled on Kershaw, this one was different. This one upset his team-mates. "He went out there, did his job, and then had to go do more," Turner recalled. "And it all got put on his back. That's what everyone is pissed off about. Because it added to the stigma, 'Oh, he's not perform-ing in the postseason,' which is bullshit. I mean, the whole thing is crap." Stripling felt "heartbroken" for Kershaw. "You're kind of pissed at whoever made the decision to keep him out there, when we had what we had in the bullpen," Stripling recalled. Jansen was also bothered. "I felt like it shouldn't be him," he recalled. "If that should have happened, it should have happened to me." He added, "I'm not throwing anybody under the bus or anything. I love the coaches. I love Dave Roberts. I love Andrew Friedman. But that shouldn't be Kersh's situation. That should be my situation." (Roberts said he did not regret sending Ker-shaw back out. "No," he recalled. "Because we talked about it. He was on board.")

In the clubhouse afterward, the Dodgers threw their arms around their fallen ace. Will Smith told Kershaw how much he admired him. Rich Hill teared up when discussing Kershaw. Honeycutt, who would retire a week later, told Kershaw that he loved him. The words could not salve the wound. Standing before reporters, Kershaw made no excuses. He had tried. He had failed. He had felt this pain before. But he was not sure it had ever hurt this much. "Everything people say is true right now, about the postseason," Kershaw said. "I understand that. Nothing I can do about that right now. It's a terrible feeling. It really is." When Daniel Hudson, a Dodger in 2018 and a joyous

National in 2019, saw Kershaw's interview, "It was frickin' heartbreaking, to be honest with you," Hudson said. Matt Adams, the former Cardinal who spent 2019 with Washington, experienced similar pity. "As any human being would with a good heart, you don't like to see the same stuff happening to the same guy, especially one of the best pitchers in history," Adams recalled. (Not every National felt sympathy. "There is no crying in baseball," Scherzer told me.)

Watching from his home outside Wisconsin, A. J. Ellis texted Kershaw his support. The game left him furious, a feeling that never dissipated. "I'm still very angry about that," Ellis recalled. But Ellis cared less about the tactical decisions than how his friend recovered.

"Part of me," Ellis recalled, "was like, 'How much can one man take?'"

CHAPTER 19

THE REVOLUTION IN THE
INDUSTRIAL PARK

In the days after the collapse, Clayton Kershaw received more condolences than answers. His phone filled with messages, which buoyed his spirits, ever so slightly, as he mourned another lost season. A text came from Paul Goldschmidt, the perennial All-Star first baseman. Like Daniel Hudson, Goldschmidt was moved by Kershaw's postgame remarks. Goldschmidt thought he understood some of the burden spread across Kershaw's shoulders. He lived underneath his own. "You feel that weight of the disappointment of not performing for your team, for your organization, for fans, for everything, and it weighs on you," Goldschmidt recalled. "But sometimes how you handle failure speaks almost more about you than how you handle success." Goldschmidt decided to tell Kershaw "how much respect I had for him."

The ballplayer fraternity treated Kershaw better than the press and the public. (In a column after Game 5, I ripped the Dodgers for being "hopelessly wedded to the mythology of Clayton Kershaw.") Teammates praised Kershaw for pitching through pain. "He was playing through real injuries, hip, labrum, all kinds of stuff," J. P. Howell recalled. "I don't even know what the details were about the injuries, but it wasn't like a tiny, three-day thing. It was like, 'Hey, you should take six months off.'" They wondered why Max Scherzer and Justin Verlander, Kershaw's only true peers, skirted similar examination. "Those guys haven't had very much success in the postseason, either, and no one says anything about them," Justin Turner recalled. "No one says a word about them. Like, hello?"

Kershaw often reflected on Theodore Roosevelt's monologue about "The Man in the Arena." The first part of the speech—"It is not the critic who counts . . ."—was usually wielded by cantankerous athletes tired of the prying eyes of the press. But Kershaw cared more about the next sentence, in which Roosevelt praised the man "whose face is marred by dust and sweat and blood; who strives valiantly; who errs, who comes short again and again," and who "if he fails, at least fails while daring greatly." That was Kershaw. He could stomach the criticism if he could stay in the arena. "People come up to me and they make excuses," Kershaw recalled. "They say, like, 'Well, you shouldn't have been pitching,' or 'You shouldn't have come out of the bullpen,' or 'It wasn't right what they did. That would never happen now.' That may all very well be true. But at the time, I was pitching and we lost. I failed. It hurt. It didn't feel good. It still doesn't feel good. But at the end of the day, I don't have any regrets about what happened."

He added, "Could Donnie have used me differently? Could Doc have used me differently? Or whatever it may be. They maybe could have protected me. But what player is ever going to stand up here and say, 'Ah, I wish they protected me more'? That is the softest thing to ever say. So you wear it."

A few days after Game 5, Brandon McDaniel visited Kershaw in Los Angeles. "What do I do?" Kershaw asked McDaniel. Kershaw would turn thirty-two in April—he was no longer spry, no longer invincible, but he was far from geriatric. Both men believed Kershaw could regenerate his fastball velocity and rediscover his slider depth. "The frustration was, 'I know there's more in the tank, and I need to unlock it,'" McDaniel recalled.

Maybe, McDaniel suggested, an outside voice might help. He mentioned a pitching laboratory in the suburbs of Seattle that did innovative work. Kershaw had brushed off invitations in the past. He was averse to change, wedded to routine, a traditionalist who still believed a pitcher's record mattered more than his spin rate. He cared about throwing strikes and holding runners, not motion-capture sensors and high-resolution cameras. But a line from the film version of *Moneyball* stuck with him: "Adapt or die." "When you're desperate for answers—or you just want to be back to what you were—you'll do a lot of stuff," Kershaw recalled. He told McDaniel to set up an appointment that would have sounded outrageous only a few years earlier.

Clayton Kershaw wanted to go to Driveline.

*   *   *

In the summer of 2012, as Kershaw was grappling with the hip injury that cost him a Cy Young Award, a twenty-nine-year-old college dropout named Kyle Boddy rode a bus into Seattle to meet executives from the Tampa Bay Rays. For several years, Boddy had tried to foster a revolution in the obscurity of an industrial park near Sea-Tac airport. Boddy thought, as the authors Ben Lindbergh and Travis Sawchik wrote in *The MVP Machine*, that "baseball's entire minor-league and player-development structure needed to be rethought and rebuilt from scratch." He believed that by harnessing data he could enhance a pitcher's fastball and change the shape of his breaking ball. Some of the ideas on his blog, *Driveline Mechanics*, impressed a Rays executive, who invited Boddy to the team's hotel suite after a game against the Mariners.

Boddy met Andrew Friedman, the future leader of the Dodgers. Boddy thought he might land a job. Friedman encouraged him to stick with the revolution. Boddy had a better chance of changing baseball as an outsider. Lindbergh and Sawchik's book chronicled just how influential he became. The game evolved in the 2010s as players tapped into the knowledge of inquisitive interlopers like Boddy—whose work experience included Olive Garden server and PokerStars customer-service rep—rather than chaw-chewing, sun-poisoned lifers. Boddy encouraged players to strengthen their arms with weighted balls. He studied deliveries with high-speed cameras, tracked biomechanical data, and suggested subtle tweaks that produced significant results. "When you go watch the video, you can see the hair on your finger," pitcher Dan Straily explained to the *New York Times* in 2017. The granular discussions were the point: Driveline appealed to pitchers who thirsted for the tiny edges that meant the difference between millions and the minors.

Boddy butted into the industry by questioning its shibboleths. He stuck around because his methods netted results. "You get some of these guys who were undrafted or late-round picks who are like test-tube babies—all of a sudden, they go into the pitching lab and they come out like Frankenstein, throwing like 100 mph," former Texas Rangers general manager Jon Daniels said. As pitchers flocked to Driveline, the gospel spread. Boddy outlined his ideas in a book called *Hacking the Kinetic Chain*. He proselytized to nonbelievers both young and old. When Boddy spoke at Vanderbilt in 2015, a scrawny junior interrupted him. "I've read half of your book," Walker Buehler said, "and there's no fucking way anyone could do this." Boddy and Buehler debated concepts for an hour. (To explain vertical rise, the paradox of the fastball that doesn't seem to descend, Boddy cited Kershaw.) Buehler was further converted that summer, after the Dodgers selected him in the first round, as he recovered from Tommy John surgery. To chart Buehler's strength program, the Dodgers assigned Dr. James Buffi, whose résumé included a PhD in biomechanics and a Driveline internship. Through conversation with Buffi, Buehler emerged carrying more muscle and using a regimen that clashed with Kershaw's.

"Walker's taught me a lot, honestly," Kershaw recalled. "Just about life. As far as there are different ways to do things. The way that he works and the way that I work could not be more different." When Buehler first joined the rotation in 2018, the dichotomy confounded Kershaw. "He works for, like, ten minutes a day," Kershaw recalled.

"He's a strong guy, lifts a lot of weight. Super quick-twitch, super skinny. Moves really fast. I'm this big, old, chunky dude, who moves slow, who's in there forever." In time, Kershaw recognized that he should consider aping Buehler, rather than the contrary.

The Dodgers offered their players outlets for adaptation. The front office outfitted its facilities with high-tech Rapsodo and Edgertronic cameras to analyze pitchers. They bought Blast Motion sensors to measure swings. The team even installed a three-dimensional virtual reality lab at Dodger Stadium. And they excelled at identifying underperforming players, linking them up with iconoclastic outsiders like Boddy and reaping the benefits.

A chorus of Driveline acolytes was growing in Kershaw's ear. For a while, he dismissed the outré methodology and zealotry. "Earlier in my career, there's no way in hell I would have gone up there to do that," he recalled. Then his friend Chris Young visited the facility after 2017. While playing catch with Kershaw that winter, Young answered his pal's questions about the process. Brandon McCarthy made a similar pilgrimage that offseason. Alex Wood vouched for young Driveline staffer Rob Hill. Kershaw pocketed the insight. "As you get hurt, you get more of an open mind," Kershaw recalled. "Or when your velo starts going down. You become more open when it's not going as good."

His peers praised the weighted-ball program and pontificated about fastball "vert" and shoulder-hip separation. At times, the language sounded foreign. "He wants answers, and he doesn't want the long-winded version of that," McDaniel recalled. It was not easy for Kershaw to discuss his delivery. "Clayton never liked talking mechanics," Rick Honeycutt recalled. "He didn't want to hear me say 'mechanics.'" He preferred feel to verbiage. "If I'm missing up, I aim down," he once told teammate Stephen Fife. "If I'm missing right, I aim left." Kershaw threw every pitch as hard as he could. "I've got to be on top of the baseball, and you've got to be able to rip it down," he explained. He used the most basic cues. "He always told me," Tony Watson recalled, "'The only thing I think about on my slider is *down*.'"

His devotion to the five-day cycle permitted this simplicity. "I've never played with any pitcher who executed the way he executed," Wood recalled. Kershaw's routine sharpened his delivery. Mike Bolsinger, the pitcher from the McKinney North High team that eliminated Highland Park from the 2006 playoffs, later reached the majors and spent two seasons in Los Angeles. Bolsinger studied Kershaw's bullpens. At the end of the session, Bolsinger noticed the mound looked pristine. Kershaw's right foot landed in the same spot after every throw. "And then I'd see a rookie throwing, and just making a mess of the mound," Bolsinger recalled. Years later, Dodgers reliever Caleb Ferguson noticed the same thing. "His repetition with everything that he does is so perfect," Ferguson recalled.

But the five-day cycle had led Kershaw to disaster in 2019. His velocity had not regenerated. His final two sliders of the season had landed in the seats. "He got to a point where clearly something was not clicking," Mark Prior recalled. "So he needed to shock the system." Prior was part of the changing cast that would greet Kershaw in 2020. Rich Hill and Hyun-Jin Ryu departed in free agency. John Pratt left the video room for the scouting department. Prior, a 2000s phenom whose career was upended by injuries, replaced Honeycutt as the pitching coach. Prior blended hard-earned wisdom with technical fluency. "We're not afraid to outsource things," Prior recalled. "If the message can be impactful coming from a different voice, so be it."

Before he flew to Seattle, Kershaw texted with A. J. Ellis. The trip surprised Ellis. To travel to Driveline, Ellis felt, demonstrated how far Kershaw had fallen—and how much he had grown.

"That," Ellis recalled, "was a massive moment of vulnerability for him—and openness."

* * *

Eight days after Soto's homer landed in the Dodger Stadium pavilion, Kershaw and McDaniel pulled into the industrial park outside of Sea-Tac. The Driveline facility was empty save for a quartet of staffers. The group had been scrambling to prepare. Rob Hill was twenty-four, a couple of years removed from a playing career that topped out in the NAIA. Now he was trying to extend the career of a first-ballot Hall of Famer. "It was one of those sorts of things that you can really only, like, dream about," Hill recalled.

Kershaw felt closer to a fugue state. His body and spirits were in shambles. His shoulder would require a pain-killing injection that winter. He disrobed as Hill attached motion-capture devices to his frame. A staffer asked what music would pump him up. Standing in his underwear, a little more than a week after abject failure, Kershaw sounded exhausted. "They were like, 'Let's go! Let's throw your hardest!'" Kershaw recalled. "I was like, 'You know what, guys? Whatever. I don't need all this.'" Kershaw reared back and fired as the cameras clicked and the computers registered his data. He could barely crack 84 mph. "It was just painful to try to throw that hard," he recalled.

The assessment, in Hill's words, sounded like gobbledygook. "The biggest pieces that came up were some of the stuff with his separation," Hill recalled. "So, like, the timing of when his upper and his lower body started to create distance and create torque. And those two, in conjunction with their timing around foot plants, like when the foot comes down. And the impact of that on where the arm was, as well. He had essentially gotten a little more open with his torso over the years. And then the arm went in some different places, as well." In simpler terms: after Kershaw hurt his back, his delivery changed, in ways that mostly evaded the naked eye. "As you get older, you don't move as well," Prior recalled. "You don't move as well as you did when you were twenty-five. So it's like, can you get them back into the positions, in a different manner, to be able to do what they used to do?" While Kershaw still landed in the same spot with every throw, the process to get to that spot was flawed. "The chain itself was firing in the right order," Hill recalled. "But the pieces weren't in the right place at the right times."

The analysis permitted Kershaw to correct these imperfections. The Driveline crew also sold him on the benefits of weighted balls, which could strengthen his arm to recoup velocity. At McDaniel's behest, Kershaw added arm-care activities to his five-day cycle. Before he fixated on preparation. Now he emphasized recovery. Kershaw knew his fastball would never sit in the mid-90s again. He could live at 91–92 mph, so long as the heater looked different from the slider. His visit to the industrial park at Sea-Tac, the locus for a movement he had once dismissed as silly, proved significant. He did not overhaul his approach or turn his back on the five-day cycle. But he incorporated some suggestions into his routine. The difference would be stark. "Going up to Driveline lengthened his dominance," John Pratt recalled. "It led to this renaissance in the latter part of his career." Kershaw was less bombastic.

"Gave it a shot," he recalled. "Didn't hate it. I still do some of it."

*   *   *

Twenty-six days after the Driveline folks attached sensors to Kershaw's bare chest, a website called the *Athletic* published a story that furthered the damage beneath it. Ellen Kershaw was in her front yard when a neighbor approached.

"Did you hear?" he asked.

"Hear what?" she said.

"About the Astros."

CHAPTER 20

SHUT DOWN

In the end, Chase Utley was right.

He was right about what the Houston Astros had been doing during the 2017 World Series. And he was right about why the truth emerged. The team did not stay together. Some left Houston unhappy about the experience. One pitcher bounced around the American League, warning his new teammates about his old club's scheme. His name was Mike Fiers. In November of 2019, he received a phone call from Ken Rosenthal, the venerated baseball writer from the *Athletic*.

"We are writing about sign-stealing in 2017," Rosenthal said.

Rosenthal was the more presentable half of a reporting duo chasing the story of a lifetime. He had been tipped off by his partner, Evan Drellich, who had covered the Astros at the *Houston Chronicle* before eventually joining Rosenthal at the digital startup. They made an amusing pair. As he approached his sixtieth birthday, Rosenthal carried himself with the same energy and enthusiasm he had covering Cal Ripken's Orioles for the *Baltimore Sun* in the 1980s. Rosenthal sported bow ties for charity while broadcasting games on Fox Sports. He broke more news than any other baseball writer. "His cachet in the industry is unmatched," Drellich wrote. Not yet thirty-five, Drellich wore discounted Brooks Brothers threads beneath a semi-permanent cloud of cigarette smoke. He covered the industry with relentless cynicism. He had been a thorn in the side of Astros general manager Jeff Luhnow. It was nothing personal. If you told Drellich the sky was blue, he'd ask to see it in writing.

Drellich first learned about the extent of Houston's cheating during the 2018 postseason. Astros staffers outlined to Drellich how the team installed a center-field camera that zoomed in on the opposing catcher, watched the feed on a monitor inside the dugout, and relayed the signs through banging a trash can with a bat. During that same postseason, before the Astros lost to the Red Sox in the American League Championship Series, Jeff Passan of *Yahoo Sports* cited anonymous players who had seen the Astros use the trash can. Major League Baseball claimed to have investigated the matter but been unable to corroborate it. The story caused a brief tempest, then faded after the Astros were eliminated. Drellich decided not to let it go. (Not every reporter was as dogged. When Dodgers officials complained to me in 2018 about the Astros stealing signs, I dismissed them as sore losers.)

When Rosenthal called Fiers, Drellich had been reporting the story for more than a year. Rosenthal asked if the rumors were true. Fiers confirmed how the scheme worked. Then he did something extraordinary. He agreed to go on the record. "They were advanced and willing to go above and beyond to win," Fiers said. The admission by Fiers added significant heft to the story when it published on November 12. It was hard to dismiss allegations when they were confirmed directly by a player willing to put his name on it. Another unlikely source bolstered the story's staying power. Jimmy O'Brien, a Yankees fan and YouTube impresario known as Jomboy, highlighted the banging from footage of a game mentioned in the story. The video erased any doubt for Dodgers players. It was one thing to read about a scandal. It was quite another to hear the evidence clear as day. "The Jomboy video sticks out," Alex Wood recalled, "where you're like, 'Holy shit. They're banging on trash cans.'"

After Ellen Kershaw read the story, she found Clayton alternating between checking his phone and taking calls. "Do you really think it's true?" Ellen asked. He did. The story suggested what Utley and others had felt all along: the Dodgers had been cheated out of a championship. The night that forever ruined Kershaw's postseason legacy, Game 5 at Minute Maid Park, was tainted. For Kershaw, the knowledge pressed upon the two-year-old bruise. "I had already felt so bad after the World Series," Kershaw recalled. "It's not like I could feel any worse." Outrage faded into acceptance. Ellen felt her husband handled it better than she did. "I went zero to a hundred," Ellen recalled. "I was, like, ready to kill. And he was so much more levelheaded. And that was astounding to me. And maybe it's because all the rest of us were fired up for him. But he just remained calm about it. And I just was so annoyed, and he was so levelheaded about it. Part of that is his faith. And him just thinking like, 'Well, if we were supposed to win, we would have won.'"

Kershaw reminded himself that his existence encompassed more than baseball. "The life that he has built is so far different from the life he grew up having," Ellen recalled. When they were twenty-two, the Kershaws wrote a book titled *Arise* with Ellen's sister, Ann. In one passage, Clayton outlined his shared hope for marriage. "Sunday night dinners are always important, and our home will feature a revolving door of people coming and going," he wrote. "Dogs are to be treated like humans, and card games are to be taken very seriously. We'll play pranks and watch *The Office* before going to sleep. The last activity of the day will be praying together." A decade later, almost all of that had come true. Their home in Highland Park served as a waystation for members of the Melson family and the Mean Street Posse alike; when Preston Mattingly, retired from baseball and trying his hand at college basketball, could not make it home for his family's Christmas, the Melsons invited him over and dressed him as Santa Claus. The Kershaws filled their home with laughter and light. Sometimes they swapped out *The Office* for sitcoms like *New Girl*, a show Kershaw liked so much he made a cameo in 2014. There were no dogs, because the kids were allergic, but Kershaw did not mind. He loved helping Cali draw, watching

Charley romp around the house. Being apart from them wore on him. That January, the family grew once more: Ellen gave birth to a second boy, Cooper Ellis Kershaw.

Kershaw's family and friends tried to distract him from the scandal swirling around the sport that winter. Some days were easier than others. When the house quieted down and Kershaw found himself alone with his thoughts, he drifted back toward that night in Houston, when the train whistled and the fans howled and the Astros swung and never missed.

"You can't help but go back," Kershaw recalled, "and be like, 'Man, what if? What if we won that game? What if I just pitched mediocre and we won? What if we won that World Series? How would things be different?'"

*   *   *

Rob Manfred, the commissioner of Major League Baseball, launched an investigation into the Astros after Drellich and Rosenthal published their story. The findings led to sprawling changes across the sport. After two months of interviewing witnesses, scanning video, and following the electronic paper trail, MLB announced yearlong suspensions for Astros general manager Jeff Luhnow and manager A. J. Hinch. "While it is impossible to determine whether the conduct actually impacted the results on the field, the perception of some that it did causes significant harm to the game," Manfred wrote. Both were fired within hours of the report's publication. A day later, the Red Sox fired manager Alex Cora, the Houston bench coach in 2017 and the skipper who led the Sox to a title over the Dodgers a year later. The report had identified Cora, along with veteran Carlos Beltrán, as the masterminds of the banging scheme. Before the week was over, the Mets fired Beltrán, who had just been hired to manage the team. (A separate investigation, also sparked by a story from Drellich and Rosenthal, into allegations against the 2018 Red Sox led to the suspension of the team's video replay operator.)

The scandal rolled in waves. New events kept provoking Kershaw and the other Dodgers who had suffered at the Astros' hand. First there was the story. Then there were the videos, first from Jomboy and then others from Tony Adams, an Astros fan who charted usage of the trash can. Then there was the report from Manfred. And then, at the outset of spring training that February, there were the apologies. "I think I was pretty pissed for a while," Kershaw recalled. "And then you start seeing how some of those guys handle it, and it makes you even more mad."

Hinch, the manager who smashed the monitor but never stopped the cheating, expressed remorse. Luhnow insisted he never knew about the scheme. "I am not a cheater," he wrote in a statement after Astros owner Jim Crane fired him. Luhnow blamed Cora and other lower-level staffers. At spring training, Altuve and Bregman offered sheepish press-conference apologies. Crane hijacked the event with contradictions. At one point, he said that sign-stealing "didn't impact the game." Then he insisted he had never said such a thing. He sounded confused about accepting any blame for the scandal, which Manfred deemed an extension of a toxic culture fostered by Luhnow and authorized by Crane. "No," Crane said, "I don't think I should be held accountable."

"I remember watching their press conference from spring training, and how they butchered that so bad," Kershaw recalled. "I remember their owner being an idiot. I remember their GM being an arrogant prick. I remember Altuve—I remember him being remorseful. I remember that. I remember it affecting Bregman. I remember it affecting Springer. I, at least, knew that they felt the weight of it."

The punishments stopped at the suspensions for the executives. The Astros did not have to vacate the World Series. The players escaped unscathed, save for public scorn. None were suspended. None were fined. That was by Manfred's design. At the outset of the investigation, Manfred offered immunity in exchange for testimony through a deal with the Major League Baseball Players Association. Manfred felt he could not uncover the truth otherwise. Other players questioned the necessity of Manfred's bargain. "I don't agree with the punishments, the players not getting anything," Angels star Mike Trout said. Kershaw wondered why the union protected players who cheated the game. It reminded him of the union standing by those who knowingly violated the performance-enhancing drug policy. "It makes you mad at our union," Kershaw recalled. "Like, we need to change the rules. If a guy takes steroids, if a guy like A-Rod, or whatever . . . you don't have to protect him. If Ryan Braun wants to lie all the time, you don't have to protect him. If you cheat the game, maybe there should be a clause that you get out of the union, or something."

When the Astros defended themselves, they grumbled that they weren't the only team using technology to steal signs. The Red Sox and Yankees were both quietly disciplined by MLB for the practice in 2017. In their initial story, Drellich and Rosenthal focused on the Astros but took pains to contextualize the proliferation of sign-stealing as an industry-wide issue. Accusations had been flying for years—many of them at the Dodgers.

During the 2018 National League Championship Series, MLB inspected Dodger Stadium camera wells in search of hidden high-speed cameras, the writer Andy Martino later reported. After a frustrating game at Dodger Stadium in 2019, Mets ace Jacob deGrom prowled for a hidden camera with general manager Brodie Van Wagenen. "They found nothing," Martino wrote. In a book about the Astros scandal, Drellich reported that MLB investigated the Dodgers after Joc Pederson burst into the video room during the 2018 World Series and asked Chase Utley, "Hey, did you get the signs yet?" Pederson later said he was never contacted by the league about the incident. He thought it was clear that he was joking. He asked the question directly in view of an MLB security official monitoring the room to make sure teams were not using it to steal signs. "It was just, like, talking shit to the guy, like messing around," Pederson recalled.

That spring, for at least the first few days, the job of baseball writers became simple. Go up to a player, turn on your tape recorder, and mention Houston. At Dodgers camp, Justin Turner and I argued about an old story I had written. I was about to walk away when Turner shrugged. "Aren't you going to ask me about the Astros?" He proceeded to blast Manfred, who had referred to the Commissioner's Trophy as a "piece of metal" when making a rhetorical point about the futility of vacating the title. "The only thing devaluing it right now is the fact that it says 'Commissioner' on it," Turner said. For a little while, baseball felt like pro wrestling: everyone was cutting promos. Mike Fiers hung a whistle inside his locker at Athletics camp. Cody Bellinger accused Altuve of stealing the 2017 American League MVP award from Yankees slugger Aaron Judge. Carlos Correa defended Altuve, who preferred not to use the trash can. "If you don't know the facts, then you've got to shut the fuck up," Correa said.

Kershaw stayed above the fray. When pressed by *Sports Illustrated*'s Tom Verducci, he admitted he had not changed his signs. He did not want to linger on the topic. "I'm not going there," Kershaw said. He had suffered enough, he decided. That was part of the reason he refused to rage publicly about it, or dissect conspiracy theories, like a rumor the Astros eventually signaled pitches through buzzers attached to their bodies. "I almost don't want to believe it," Kershaw told Verducci. "And you know what? Not that they deserve the benefit of the doubt, but unless something comes to light, I'm just not going to believe it."

The chatter about the Astros and the stealing of signs—a constant discussion of the past—hummed throughout Camelback Ranch in those early days of spring. There was a far more sinister peril encroaching, a mysterious virus already declared a public health emergency in the United States. It would take weeks before that breached the baseball bubble. In the interim, as the sun shone upon the Arizona desert and a 162-game season stretched out in front of the Dodgers, the newest member of the club wondered why his teammates lacked focus. And so, on the eve of the first full-squad workout, Dave Roberts received a request from his new right fielder: Mookie Betts wanted to address the team.

*   *   *

Markus Lynn Betts might not have been the best player in baseball, but he came close. He had made his first All-Star team in his second season with the Red Sox and won the American League MVP award in his fourth. In an era when players accentuated their strengths rather than correcting their flaws, Betts excelled because his strength was his lack of flaws. He stood only five-foot-nine but leveraged all the power possible from his 180-pound frame. He walked nearly twice as much as he struck out. When he wasn't hitting, he could aid a team with his arm, his legs, or his glove.

Andrew Friedman had coveted Betts for years. He had come close to acquiring Betts in the summer of 2019, only for Boston to go on a winning streak and take the player off the market. A few months later, when Chaim Bloom, Friedman's former assistant in Tampa Bay, interviewed to take over the Red Sox baseball operations department, Friedman suggested if Bloom was hired, they might be able to make a blockbuster trade. After Bloom got the job, negotiations with Friedman sprawled for months. Why the Red Sox, a veritable financial behemoth, would want to trade Betts, a homegrown superstar, would for years agonize folks in Bangor and Burlington and Brockton. But the Dodgers benefited from Boston owner John Henry's zeal to slip beneath the sport's luxury-tax threshold. Friedman had been waiting nearly three years for an opportunity like this.

In the winter after the 2017 season, Friedman and Farhan Zaidi made a trade with the Braves that Friedman described as "a little more subtle than most." After years of paying the luxury tax, which discouraged spending for the big-market teams, Dodgers owner Mark Walter wanted to reset. Friedman dealt first baseman Adrián González and three others to Atlanta. The deal brought back Matt Kemp and opened up a slot on the team's payroll. At some point in the future, the Dodgers could add another star making about $30 million a year. The team spent years trying to fill the spot. The team could not swing a trade for 2017 National League MVP Giancarlo Stanton or Cleveland shortstop Francisco Lindor. The winter after he crushed Kershaw's spirit in Game 5, Anthony Rendon rebuffed the Dodgers in free agency. That same winter, the Dodgers offered ace Gerrit Cole a $300 million contract. Cole opted for a $324 million deal with the Yankees.

The whiffs set up Friedman for a windfall when Henry tasked Bloom with reducing Boston's payroll. Acquiring Betts was such a coup that Friedman had to pretend he had not swindled his protégé. Betts's arrival left the Dodgers feeling giddy. But he also altered the alchemy within the clubhouse. For years, the room had revolved around leadership from Kershaw and Justin Turner. The core had shared the same triumphs and scars. Betts offered fresh eyes. And he did not like what he saw at Camelback Ranch. Granted the floor by Roberts, Betts aired some grievances.

"I know I'm new here," Betts began, a modest opening before throwing down a gauntlet. When the Red Sox won in 2018, Betts explained, the team carried itself with a daily urgency. A year later, the Red Sox lost that shared purpose, lost their way, and lost a chance at a repeat. Betts did not want his new team to follow that path. They could not take days off. They could not take *plays* off. He suggested the Dodgers fine themselves $20 for every mistake. His message was not subtle. "To come in the first day and get in front of the team and challenge everybody, I think kind of surprised a lot of guys," Turner said that spring.

To some in the organization, the rhetoric preached by Betts matched the ethic of another player in the room. It sounded like Betts was telling the Dodgers to be more like Clayton Kershaw. When Stephanie Apstein of *Sports Illustrated* told Kershaw about the comparison, Kershaw laughed. "I don't know how to compliment him without it sounding like I'm complimenting myself," he said. He was leaning into humility that spring. He incorporated into his training regimen suggestions from Driveline and advice from younger teammates like Buehler. He was chucking weighted balls in hopes of a revival. "There's ways to work out that can help your pitching," Kershaw recalled. "And not just lifting to get strong and sore, and then start again the next day."

Between the clamor of the scandal and the arrival of Betts, less attention was paid to Kershaw that spring. On February 28, Kershaw pitched for the first time since Rendon and Soto went deep. The radar gun at American Family Fields of Phoenix, the spring home of the Milwaukee Brewers, registered a shock. Kershaw peeked over his shoulder to check the numbers. They represented a beacon from the past: 91 mph, 92 mph, even 93 mph. The shape of the pitch had improved, too. Instead of cutting, the fastball stayed true and deceived the batter by appearing to rise. "It's got that life at the end," he said. For the first time since 2017, he thought he could enter a season without his arsenal diminished or his body compromised.

Thirteen days later, the world shut down.

*   *   *

Kershaw dealt with a few diversions to his usual schedule on March 12. One was planned: on his 6:30 A.M. drive to Camelback Ranch, he picked up a writer, Wright Thompson of ESPN, who would trail him that day. When Thompson brought up the 2017 World Series on their drive, Kershaw talked about the traffic.

Another diversion was silly. Kershaw confronted Pedro Moura, a writer from the *Athletic*, who had first written about his Driveline trip several weeks earlier. All spring, scouts had been raving about Kershaw's revival. A rumor had spread about him visiting the Sea-Tac industrial park. Moura, an observant and inquisitive reporter, asked Friedman, who confirmed Kershaw's visit. When Moura approached Kershaw, the pitcher asked who had told Moura. Informed it was Friedman, Kershaw replied, "I'm gonna have to yell at him." Kershaw praised Driveline but declined to provide specifics. Moura wrote his story and went back to Los Angeles. When Kershaw saw Moura again on March 12, he expressed his frustration. "There was a better way to handle that," he told Moura. Kershaw did not want people to know he had gone to Driveline, even if he could not articulate why. He thirsted for control, even in inconsequential moments.

The last diversion presented a total break with control. The night before, the NBA had suspended its season after Utah Jazz center Rudy Gobert tested positive for Covid-19. Major League Baseball floated forward like a ghost ship for one more morning. The clubhouses had been closed to reporters. Kershaw sat glued to the Dodgers clubhouse television. Major League Soccer shut down. College basketball tournaments were cancelled. At last, Manfred suspended spring training and delayed Opening Day by at least two weeks, an early hint of the lack of understanding about the totality of the encroaching pandemic. Kershaw drove Thompson back to the writer's hotel. Sandy Koufax called to wish Kershaw "good luck and good health" if the season ever started.

Clayton and Ellen hunkered down in Highland Park as the pandemic paralyzed the country. The Kershaws formed what Ellen called a "quaran-team" with her family. Their bubble included the family of her sister, Ann, who lived two doors down, and their parents, who lived a few blocks away. Jim Melson had recovered from lung cancer, but Leslie was still fighting pancreatic cancer. The family prioritized time together. "So we just couldn't risk, at all, exposing her to anything," Ellen recalled. They watched the news and consulted the Centers for Disease Control and Prevention. They contacted the charitable arm of the Dodgers to raise money for those in need. They savored the time with their children. Clayton helped Cali with her art, ate pancakes with Charley, tracked Cooper's baby monitor. They swam in the backyard. Charley was just learning how to swing at Wiffle balls. "When I look back on it, I think back on what a blessing it was for us, in so many ways," Ellen recalled. "Yes, I mean, part of it was awful. But our kids were the right age. It was okay that we got to stay home. That's all they needed, at that point, was just some good family time."

Kershaw waited for an announcement about when the sport would return. The negotiations were fraught between the owners and the Major League Baseball Players Association. The two sides needed to agree upon health and safety protocols for the uniformed personnel. A harebrained scheme of playing the season in Phoenix and its surrounding suburbs was briefly discussed and then discarded. Teams could not open ballparks to the public, which cost the owners money and reduced their interest in a lengthy regular season, which was when players actually received paychecks. The players demanded prorated salaries. The owners responded with proposals for seasons far shorter than the players preferred—when the players asked for a 114-game season, the owners responded with a 76-game offer. Both sides declined to bend. Such is the nature of labor negotiations in America. Kershaw sat out the labor battle, disinterested in the rhetoric from both sides. "I don't think that was my calling," Kershaw recalled. "I don't think I'm great at that stuff. All the business side. I'm not great at fighting for every single dollar."

*   *   *

As the Kershaws huddled in Highland Park, unrest unfolded across the country. On May 25, a Black man in Minneapolis named George Floyd was arrested after a store clerk accused him of using a counterfeit $20 bill. The police handcuffed him and placed him facedown in the street. For nine minutes and twenty-nine seconds, as a woman with a cellphone camera recorded the brutality, white police officer Derek Chauvin knelt on Floyd's neck. "I can't breathe," Floyd said repeatedly. He died underneath the weight of Chauvin's knee.

The killing sparked the largest protest movement in American history and prompted discussion of a racial reckoning. Floyd was merely the latest unarmed Black man to die a high-profile death at the hands of law enforcement: Eric Garner in Staten Island, Tamir Rice in Cleveland, Michael Brown in Ferguson, Missouri, countless others. Earlier that year, police officers in Louisville shot and killed twenty-six-year-old Breonna Taylor in her own home. Floyd's murder resonated with people who felt trapped inside during the pandemic, unable to distract themselves from the footage of a police officer kneeling on a man's neck, ignoring his pleas for mercy. Kershaw was one of those who could not look away. When he watched the video, he felt stunned. "I had never really watched—I just never really had seen something like that," he said.

As protests swept the country, ushering many out of their homes for the first time in weeks, Kershaw wanted to talk to his teammates. He felt it could not wait until the squabbling between the owners and the union ended. In June, along with Ross Stripling, Kershaw convened a Zoom call with Dodgers players and coaches. Before the call, Kershaw contacted Nichol Whiteman, the executive director of the Dodgers Foundation and the daughter of Jamaican immigrants. They had worked together often. The Kershaws helped the Dodgers build and repair baseball facilities across Los Angeles. When the pandemic arrived, the Dodgers partnered with Kershaw's Challenge to raise money. Kershaw cared about charity work. His foundation aimed to help with housing and education for kids in Dallas and Los Angeles. There was the orphanage in Zambia. In the winter before the 2019 season, Kershaw visited the Dominican Republic and listened to children tell their stories about being ensnared in sex trafficking. He wanted to do something in the wake of Floyd's death. "What should we be talking about?" he asked Whiteman.

She suggested Kershaw open the floor to his Black peers. On the call, Kershaw listened as Betts, Dave Roberts, first-base coach George Lombard, pitcher David Price, and strength coach Travis Smith talked about being Black men in America. Lombard told the players about his mother, Posy, a white woman who marched with Martin Luther King Jr. Stripling later told Lombard he was embarrassed that he had spent so much time around the coach without knowing his history. The stories surprised Kershaw, too. He listened as his teammates detailed being profiled in stores or fearing for their lives when interacting with police. "It was sobering for me to understand that still goes on," Kershaw said. He lived within a cocoon of whiteness in Highland Park. He did not recall learning in school about Juneteenth or the Tulsa race massacre. He knew little about redlining. When Colin Kaepernick protested police brutality in 2016, Kershaw did not understand why. He said nothing when backup catcher Bruce Maxwell did the same in 2017 and was subsequently shunned by baseball. As he talked to his Black teammates and considered their experience, Kershaw was told that silence represented complicity.

On Juneteenth that summer, Kershaw posted on his Twitter account for the first time since the previous September. He disdained the hollow rhetoric of social media, but felt he still should say something. "Silence won't cut it," he wrote. "We have to start by saying something and STANDING UP for our Black brothers and sisters. I want to listen, I want to learn, I want to do better and be different. I want my kids to be different. Black lives matter and I am committed to taking a stand and affecting change—starting with myself." A few weeks later, Kershaw led a collection of mostly white players in a video announcing an initiative to raise money for local organizations in Los Angeles. He opened and closed the video. "We must unapologetically say that Black lives matter," he said. He did not want to stop with a few posts. "How do I support the Black community on the ground in LA?" he asked Whiteman. She connected him with community leaders and groups that worked on criminal-justice reform, improving education, and increasing employment opportunities. Those efforts matched his own charity work: he wanted to help children. "I want us to focus on trying to make sure that Black kids have the same opportunities as our kids," he said.

The protests continued as the baseball season began. Unable to strike an agreement with the union, Manfred used unilateral power to schedule a sixty-game season with an expanded postseason featuring sixteen entrants. The stadiums would be empty. The travel would be regional. The players reported for "summer camp," the cynically cheery name for the abbreviated version of spring training, on July 1. The season began on July 23. Slated to start Opening Day, Kershaw was scratched after hurting his back in the weight room. When he debuted on August 2, though, his fastball sat at 92 mph and his slider generated eleven whiffs. He looked, if not exactly like his old self, then close. But the eeriness of these games, with their piped-in crowd noise and masked-up dugouts, made them hard to enjoy. And the world outside of baseball kept roiling.

On August 23, a police officer in Kenosha, Wisconsin, shot a Black man named Jacob Blake, stirring another round of protests. In the NBA bubble in Florida, teams walked off the floor. In San Francisco, where the Dodgers were supposed to play, Betts informed the team he would not take the field. Roberts also did not intend to manage the game. Kershaw and the others discussed how to proceed. "Once Mookie said he wasn't going to play, that really started our conversation as a team," Kershaw said. "We felt the best thing to do to support him was to not play, with him."

Early in that pandemic-distorted season, as protests raged across the country and the virus's death toll ticked upward, Kershaw and the Dodgers were remembered more for what they said and did away from the field than anything that happened on it. That would change once the postseason arrived.

* * *

On October 1, Kershaw took the mound as a postseason starter for the twenty-sixth time. He had never pitched an October game like this. The atmosphere at Dodger Stadium was unsettling. The bleachers were empty. Cardboard cutouts filled the seats behind the plate. The canned buzz of artificial crowd noise, which sounded something like ambient dread, filled the stadium. It had been a weird year.

Kershaw had held his fastball velocity during his ten-start season. He posted a 2.18 ERA with sixty-two strikeouts in 58.1 innings. But the success was still difficult to savor. His children could not attend games.

The family felt more isolated in Los Angeles than in Dallas, where they could walk down the street to see friends. They lacked a similar community in California. "Everybody has hedges and gates," Ellen recalled, a far cry from the interlocking lawns of Highland Park. Every decision felt freighted. "There was so much weighing on our shoulders of 'We have to stay healthy and isolated because we cannot risk the chance of getting Covid, giving it to Clayton, Clayton giving it to the Dodgers, and the whole organization going down,'" Ellen recalled.

The Dodgers avoided infection. They entered the postseason as the No. 1 overall seed and hosted the Brewers for a three-game Wild Card round. Buehler spun a gem in Game 1. A day later, Kershaw turned back the clock: eight scoreless innings, three hits, thirteen strikeouts. The Brewers were hapless, a team that lost more games than it won in 2020, but Kershaw still enjoyed his evening. It felt like the beginning of a fortuitous run.

After the sweep, the Dodgers packed their bags and prepared for a lengthy trip. To cut back on travel and protect against the virus, MLB designated four neutral sites for the later postseason rounds. The American League drew Los Angeles and San Diego. The National League drew Houston and Arlington, Texas, not far from Highland Park. The Texas Rangers had just opened Globe Life Field, which would host the National League Championship Series and the World Series. That was where the Dodgers were headed. Destiny—or whatever cosmic force came into play that awful year—was bringing Clayton Kershaw back home.

CHAPTER 21

THE PINNACLE
OF THE DREAM

The Las Colinas Resort advertises itself as "The Essence of Texas Escapism." In October of 2020, Clayton Kershaw and the rest of the Dodgers arrived at the property, located in the heart of the Dallas-Fort Worth metroplex, with bags packed for a twenty-six-day stay. The resort functioned as Major League Baseball's answer to the National Basketball Association's Covid-mandated bubble. All the players, coaches, staffers, and their family members were given rooms. If the team kept winning, it would not need to travel. The road to the World Series went through Texas.

For the Kershaws, the location was fortuitous. The Melsons dropped off supplies for the children at the valet stand. The protocols prevented anyone inside the bubble from interacting with the outside world. But the proximity to Highland Park meant friends and family could attend postseason games, which were open to the public at partial capacity after being closed during the regular season. Leslie Melson might not have been able to see the team otherwise. As October rolled around, Ellen recalled, the woman who treated Kershaw as her fifth child was "in her weakest state." "We basically had to carry her in," Jim Melson recalled. She was determined to see the Dodgers chase a champion-ship. "This, truly, was as much her dream as it was Clayton's, for him to win a World Series," Ellen recalled.

After settling into the bubble, the Dodgers swept the San Diego Padres in the first round of action at Globe Life Field. Kershaw logged six innings of three-run baseball in Game 2. Cody Bellinger climbed the center-field wall to steal a home run from Padres star Fernando Tatis Jr. The final game was a 12-3 Dodgers romp that earned the club four more days of downtime before the next round.

By then, the Dodgers had grown used to the drawbacks and benefits of living in Las Colinas. The luscious golf course that abutted their rooms was deemed off limits, but they were free to splash around the pool or play cornhole or mash video-game controllers together. The hotel provided all their meals. "We ate an enormous amount of chicken wings from room service," Bellinger recalled. "They were so good. And all you could eat was room service. I wonder what the end bill was for MLB." For players who had attended college, the bubble approximated their on-campus experience, a time of intense bonding with no inter-ference from the outside world. "I loved the bubble, itself," Walker Buehler recalled. "Besides the fact that we were essentially imprisoned there, it was actually great fun."

For many players, perspective on the experience depended a great deal on whether or not they had children. Gavin Lux, a twenty-two-year-old bachelor, was "fucking bored out of my mind," he recalled. For the parents, there was far more joy. The children scampered the halls and tossed footballs on the grass outside. There were playdates for the first time in months. On Halloween, the kids trick-or-treated from room to room. The cabin fever Ellen felt in Los Angeles lifted. "We got to go to baseball games again," she recalled. "We got to see each other. There just didn't feel like there was that huge risk."

*   *   *

After the Dodgers dispatched San Diego, the Atlanta Braves checked into the property at Las Colinas, slated for a seven-game National League Championship Series without days off. On paper, the Braves presented a formidable challenge but remained the underdogs. The Dodgers had marauded through the sixty-game regular season. The team won forty-three games, a pace similar to that of the 116-win 2001 Seattle Mariners. Mookie Betts, who had signed a twelve-year, $365 million extension during the shutdown, looked like a bargain. Corey Seager and Justin Turner were still excellent. Will Smith displayed calm behind the plate that belied his relative inexperience. A rival analyst described the group as "one of the very best baseball teams ever assembled," in part because of Kershaw. His fastball looked lively and his slider looked nasty. And the Dodgers were managing him with greater care. Friedman and Roberts had learned from the previous seasons. They did not need to push Kershaw beyond the sixth inning. The team's high-octane bullpen could handle the final third of the game. All Kershaw had to do was stay healthy.

On October 10, two days before the series opener, Kershaw was throwing a bullpen session when a muscle in the lumbar region of his back "kind of, like, gave out," he recalled. He stopped throwing as discomfort radiated through his body. The diagnosis was less severe than previous injuries. Kershaw was suffering from back spasms, which could heal with a few weeks of rest. He did not have that time to spare. The team scratched him from Game 2. Kershaw listened as the medical staff plotted out options. His best hope was a series of injections, three in a row: Marcaine, cortisone, and Toradol, to numb the area, fight the inflammation, and reduce the pain. "I'd never gone to those lengths before," he recalled. "And I hope I don't have to again."

The staff administered the trio of shots to test its effect on Kershaw's system. He played catch and threw a bullpen. "It was like, all right, it's okay," Kershaw recalled. The Dodgers lined him up for Game 4. By then the ferocious Braves lineup had slugged the team to a 2-1 series lead. If Kershaw could pitch like himself, if he could avoid the demons that had plagued him so often in October, the series would be even. On the day of the game, Kershaw received the three-shot cocktail again. This time, the mixture upended him. "When you have all that stuff, like, you just feel like a wet noodle out there, with no control of your body," Kershaw recalled. His velocity fell. He could not finish his slider. Everything just felt *off.* "You know at a car sale, the thing that's, like, blowing in the wind?" Kershaw recalled. "That's kind of what I felt like."

Kershaw's shoulder-length hair flapped as the wind whipped through Globe Life Field's open roof. Dirt swirled and stung the players. The setting looked eerie. For Kershaw, the site staged a familiar horror. Through five innings, his lone blemish was a misplaced slider that Braves designated hitter Marcell Ozuna smashed for a solo homer. In the sixth, with the score tied at 1, everything crumbled. Kershaw faced the top of Atlanta's lineup a third time. An infield hit by outfielder Ronald Acuña Jr. sent Kershaw sprawling. First baseman Freddie Freeman doubled home Acuña on an inside fastball. Responsibility for the loss now hung on Kershaw's shoulders. With Ozuna up, Roberts stuck with his wounded ace. When Kershaw hung a full-count curveball, Ozuna smashed an RBI double. Kershaw looked more resigned than shocked. He had played this role, the postseason patsy, the gunslinger outgunned at the end, for so many years. He watched from the bench as the game fell apart, a 10-2 loss.

After the game, Kershaw took his medicine over Zoom. The session lacked the sorrow of Game 5 against Washington. There was little to say; this man's lot in life, it appeared, was to suffer through these moments. Kershaw slumped into a chair. He ran his fingers through his hair. He stared at the microphone. He looked forlorn. He clipped his answers.

"With Ozuna there," asked Jorge Castillo of the *Los Angeles Times*, "what were you trying to do with that pitch, on that double?"

"Get him out," Kershaw said.

He picked at the sleeve of his Dodgers hoodie. He said nothing about the injections, the limited control of his body, the weight on his shoulders after so much October trauma. He distilled his evening into its essence: Once more he had tried. Once more he had failed. His team was one defeat away from elimination. Kershaw took the bus back to the Las Colinas bubble. He was not scheduled to pitch again against Atlanta.

All he could do, he felt, was pray for his teammates to come through.

* * *

Then he thought of something else.

Rather than swallow the bitterness alone, Kershaw grabbed his phone. He ignored his self-consciousness about leadership and thumbed out a message to his teammates on their GroupMe thread. He reminded the players how good they were. He exhorted them to remember the series was not over. "Yeah," he recalled, "it's probably a little cheesy, sappy." But something about the note ignited the chat. Messages pinged through the night—from Turner, from Bellinger and Hernandez, from Joc Pederson and Brusdar Graterol. Joe Kelly, the former Cardinal now relieving for the Dodgers, deputized his son, Knox, to cut an iPhone promo about wanting to see fireworks the next night. Even Seager, a player so insular that Dodgers officials used to lecture him on the importance of cheering his teammates, got into it. "We just rallied around it, to come ready to play," Seager recalled.

For so much of his career, when Kershaw faltered in October, the other Dodgers faltered alongside him. The offense batted .211 against St. Louis in 2013. A year later, after Matt Adams took Kershaw deep, the lineup did not answer. In 2015, defenders napped when Daniel Murphy stole third base. The entire club collapsed against the 2016 Cubs before Kershaw did. Kenley Jansen blew Game 2 of the 2017 World Series; the Astros mauled Yu Darvish in Game 3 and Game 7. In 2018, pretty much no one showed up. The Dodgers should have never faced an elimination game against the Nationals in 2019. At times, Ellen wanted to howl when she read stories that only blamed her husband. But she knew it was futile and unproductive to spread responsibility for the losses. Kershaw had earned this burden. He had to carry it.

Those Dodgers teams lacked a crucial ingredient. None of them employed Mookie Betts. In Game 5, a day after Kershaw's letdown, Betts saved the season. The Dodgers already trailed by two in the third inning with a pair of runners in scoring position. Braves shortstop Dansby Swanson hit a line drive into right field. Betts snagged the ball at his shoe-tops. In the process, Ozuna neglected to tag up properly at third base, leading to a momentum-swinging double play, one of several stumbles made by Atlanta on the precipice of the pennant. Two innings later, Will Smith blasted a go-ahead home run off a Braves reliever named, uncannily, Will Smith. The 7-3 Dodgers victory forced Game 6, where Buehler suppressed Atlanta in a 3-1 victory. On the final night of the seven-day street fight, Turner short-circuited a Braves rally by diving to tag Swanson and whirling to complete a double play at third base. Bellinger supplied the go-ahead homer in the seventh. After he crossed the plate, Bellinger dislocated his shoulder when he leapt to bump forearms with Kiké Hernández. The only thing that could hurt these Dodgers, who punched a ticket to the World Series with a 4-3 victory, was themselves.

*　*　*

For the third time in four years, the Dodgers assigned Game 1 of the Fall Classic to Clayton Kershaw. His opponent lacked the wrecking-ball force and name recognition of the 2017 Astros and the 2018 Red Sox. The Tampa Bay Rays played modernist baseball, with form following function, in relative anonymity. Only one of their position players, veteran outfielder Kevin Kiermaier, commanded an eight-figure salary. Only one of their regular hitters, first baseman Yandy Díaz, hit above .300. No Ray had thrown a complete game since 2016. Tampa Bay distilled baseball to its essence: how to create runs, how to suppress runs, and the mathematical clockwork therein. They positioned their defenders expertly. They layered their lineups deftly. They deployed their pitchers efficiently. The Rays played baseball like the Dodgers did—which made sense, given Andrew Friedman's imprint on both organizations. The difference was Friedman's new team paid for stars like Kershaw and Betts. In an 8-3 Game 1 victory, the Dodgers did not need much more than that. With his back loosened up, Kershaw spun six innings of one-run baseball. Betts catalyzed a rally with a walk and a stolen base in one inning and bashed a home run in the next.

A slew of Kershaw's friends and family joined the thousands of fans inside Globe Life Field. Major League Baseball capped the attendance at 11,500, leaving nearly three-quarters of the building empty. The undersized crowd still provided a respite from the artificial buzzing of the summer. Jim and Leslie Melson put on masks and waded into the throngs. Barred from leaving the family section, Ellen could at least wave at her parents. "And that was as close as we got to them for that month we were in the bubble," she recalled. She kept up with her husband's friends on a special text chain; every year in October the group shifted to a separate chat where Ellen replaced Clayton. Most of the Mean Street Posse still lived in Texas. They marveled at the fluke of the postseason's location. "It was the only way we could have seen him, it being there at that time," Josh Meredith recalled.

For Game 5, when Kershaw returned to the mound, Ellen found the gang seven tickets high above the first-base line: Meredith, Ben Kardell, Patrick Halpin, Robert Shannon, Carter English, and the Dickenson twins all jittered with nerves that night. They usually did when Kershaw pitched. They had traveled far and wide to watch him over the years. In the postseason, they had only known despair. And the 2020 World Series was drifting that way, tied at two games apiece. The Dodgers had lost Game 4 in agonizing fashion, with the bullpen faltering in three separate innings. Up a run in the ninth with Rays at first and second, Kenley Jansen gave up a single to journeyman outfielder Brett Phillips. One run scored when center fielder Chris Taylor fumbled the baseball. Jetting from first base, rookie sensation Randy Arozarena ignored a stop sign at third. He would have been out, except Will Smith lost the baseball and Jansen neglected to back the play up. Arozarena dove home and pounded the plate with his palm. In the dugout, Roberts screamed, spat, and nearly chucked his cap. "It was like that unperfect storm," he said afterward. Ever the optimist, Roberts looked ahead. "Now it's a three-game series," he said. "And we have Clayton going tomorrow."

For a stabilizing force, Kershaw sported an unkempt look. His beard was mangy. Dirt stained his cap and sweat streaked the hair that peeked beneath. The offense spotted him a three-run lead by the second inning. Tampa Bay scratched together two runs in the third. An inning later, another unraveling appeared imminent. Kershaw walked speedy outfielder Manuel Margot. On the next pitch, Margot broke for second and beat the throw from catcher Austin Barnes. The baseball bounced off Taylor's glove. Margot scooted to third, ninety feet away from tying the game with none out.

At his core, Kershaw understood not all outs were created equally. He contoured his attack to the needs of his team. If the Dodgers needed a strikeout, a double play, a quick inning—he could not always articulate how, but he could do it. Brandon McCarthy and Zack Greinke used to call it magic. "I think natural run suppression is some sort of an innate gift, at some level," McCarthy recalled. Or, as Ross Stripling put it: "He just out-competes you, man." With Margot at third, the Dodgers' needs were clear. Kershaw could not let him score. He walked the next batter, outfielder Hunter Renfroe, before infielder Joey Wendle stepped to the plate. Kershaw jammed Wendle with an inside fastball for one out. Margot stayed put. Kershaw struck out shortstop Willy Adames with a curveball. Margot started to get antsy. With Kiermaier up, Dodgers first baseman Max Muncy noticed Margot feinting toward home plate, as if trying to time Kershaw's delivery.

As a left-handed pitcher, Kershaw turned his back to third base. He peeked over his right shoulder to check Margot, but then he lifted his arms toward the sky, exhaled, and gathered himself before throwing. Part of Muncy's job was guarding Kershaw's blind side. Kiermaier fouled off the first pitch. Barnes returned the baseball. Kershaw rubbed it in his hands and glanced at Margot. When Kershaw raised his arms, Margot took off. He was trying to steal home, in the World Series, a move of stunning bravado. Muncy charged forward, pointed to the plate, and yelled across the diamond. "Home! Home! Home!" A play like this did not come up often during advance meetings. The players did not practice it during the season. For a split second, as Margot rushed toward the plate and Kershaw registered the sneak attack, the fate of the Dodgers came down to a duel between one man's moxie and another man's hardwired instincts.

One thing Greg Maddux admired about Kershaw, even as a rookie, was his dedication to all the phases of the sport. Kershaw did not just care about pitching. He cared about winning baseball games. He cared about his at-bats. He cared about fielding his position. And he cared about controlling the running game. As soon as Muncy pointed, Kershaw reacted with exquisite control, dropping his left foot behind the mound to avoid a balk, which would have granted Margot the run. "He's so aware of everything," Muncy recalled. "He knew exactly what he was supposed to do." Straddling the rubber, Kershaw relayed the ball home. Barnes stepped forward to secure the baseball and tag Margot inches away from tying the game. The umpire punched his fist. Kershaw pumped his own. In the dugout, he found his first baseman. "Hey," Kershaw told Muncy, "nice job."

Kershaw did not permit another batter to reach base in a 4-2 victory. He had more trouble corralling Cali and Charley as they clambered all around him while he conducted his postgame Zoom. "You guys are maniacs," he said. He was smiling. In the longest, strangest postseason of his career, he made five starts, with a 2.93 ERA. The Dodgers won four of those games. And now he was one victory away from salvation.

* * *

Matt Gangl walked across the loading dock outside Globe Life Field on October 27, opened the door to a production truck, and settled into his chair before a bank of monitors. As the lead director of Fox's MLB coverage, Gangl had occupied that seat sixteen times in the past twenty-two days, existing otherwise in quarantine. When he checked into his Dallas hotel four weeks earlier, he requested a room with a microwave and a fridge. He subsisted on provisions from a nearby Whole Foods Market and catered meals at the ballpark. "It was a little surreal, when you're doing the same thing, every day, driving the same path," he recalled.

His preparation for that day was a bit different. For Game 6, Gangl formulated ideas with his crew for covering a Dodgers clinching celebration. The franchise had not won the World Series since 1988. Fox trusted Gangl to nail the moment. He schemed out nearly two dozen options to isolate specific cameras. He assigned a camera on Dave Roberts in the dugout. He assigned a camera on Magic Johnson, the most recognizable member of the Guggenheim group, in the stands. And he assigned a camera to follow the player who had become the symbol of this team's agonizing quest for a title.

"One of the key ones," Gangl recalled, "was going to be having something on Mr. Kershaw."

* * *

Kershaw was not lined up to start either Game 6 or 7, so he volunteered to pitch out of the bullpen. The night before Game 6, he informed Ellen, "If they need me, I'll be there." She spent the next evening worrying if her husband would appear in relief. Sitting along the first-base line, behind the Dodgers dugout, she toggled between the action on the field and the relievers milling around the bullpen. Higher up in the stands, Kershaw's pals felt "an incredible amount of stress," Halpin recalled. He added, "There was also this sense of 'How is this going to fall apart again?'"

Game 6 was a minor-key classic. Arozarena hit a solo homer in the first inning. Roberts turned to his bullpen in the second. He pressed button after button, trusting unheralded relievers like Dylan Floro and converted starters like Alex Wood and maligned veterans like Pedro Báez. Rays starter Blake Snell was pitching the game of his life. Through five innings, he had struck out nine and permitted only a single. Snell, a twenty-seven-year-old lefty, exemplified the modern age of pitching, the generation from whom Kershaw stood apart while siphoning knowledge. Snell had won the 2018 American League Cy Young Award despite not completing the eighth inning all season. He excelled at missing bats, not finishing games. His performance deteriorated as he faced hitters for a third time. In sixteen outings in 2020 prior to Game 6, he never completed the sixth inning. On Snell's seventy-third pitch of the game, with one out in the sixth, Barnes singled up the middle. Rays manager Kevin Cash did not hesitate. He removed Snell from the game.

The decision became a flashpoint in the long-standing debate about baseball's changing landscape, a maneuver that subjected the public to roundtable debates and lectures from Bob Costas about the game's fading heartbeat. The Rays used analytical horsepower to make decisions. Cash believed, based on reams of data, that one of his relievers would fare better against the next batter than Snell. He believed he was making the right call. He believed it, months later, even as he still agonized about the decision. In the end, it may not have mattered which pitcher Cash selected to face the next batter. Because the next batter was Mookie Betts.

Betts did not waste time. He cracked a double off reliever Nick Anderson. Barnes scored when Anderson uncorked a wild pitch. When Seager grounded out, Betts sprinted home for the go-ahead run. Roberts asked twenty-four-year-old lefty Julio Urías to collect the final seven outs. Roberts stayed cool as confusion reigned in the dugout. Before the top of the eighth, an MLB official grabbed Justin Turner: he had tested positive for Covid. Turner scrambled into a room behind the dugout as his teammates wondered about his disappearance. Betts capped his remarkable first season as a Dodger by swatting a homer in the bottom of the eighth. In the bullpen, Kershaw paced. For once, at last, he had little reason to worry. Urías zipped through the ninth. The final pitch of the 2020 season was a 97-mph fastball that caught the inner half of the plate for a called third strike. Urías reared back and roared. Barnes pocketed the baseball, chucked his glove and mask, and started a mosh pit. The players vaulted the dugout railing, sprinted in from the outfield, and barreled out of the bullpen. For a few seconds, as the broadcast beamed the images across the country, one man was missing.

*   *   *

Ross Stripling was no longer a Dodger. The team had traded him that summer to Toronto. As he watched at his in-laws' Houston home, he asked the question percolating for so many.

"Where's Clayton?" Stripling shouted at the television. "Show Clayton!"

In the production truck in the loading dock outside Globe Life Field, Gangl obliged. He cut to the shot coordinated earlier in the day, with a hard camera focused on Kershaw as he stood in the bullpen. The camera caught Kershaw as he stared, stone-faced, while Urías pumped the final strike. When it was over, Kershaw closed his eyes, if only for a second, and raised his arms. It took him a long time to reconcile how he felt in that moment. All at once, he recognized the burden that he had carried, the burden that he had tried to ignore, the burden of his greatness. And then he felt it lift. "I've never had a bigger feeling of relief, a sigh of relief, in my life than that," he recalled. He did not need to ponder what went wrong. He did not need to ponder why. He did not need to ponder how. He only needed to savor the victory he had chased for so long. "I didn't know I needed it that bad," he recalled. "But I did."

*   *   *

As Kershaw celebrated, Skip Johnson felt memories rush back. He was watching at his home in Oklahoma, surrounded by his coaching staff and all variety of taxidermied deer.

A year after Kershaw learned the 1-2-3 drill at Cade Griffis's D-Bat facility in Addison, Johnson became the pitching coach at the University of Texas. In the early winters of his career, Kershaw visited Austin to hang with friends and throw bullpens with Johnson. Johnson tried to catch every Kershaw start, even after Oklahoma hired him as head coach. "I wanted Clayton to win so bad," Johnson recalled. "I knew how much heart and soul he's put into the game."

In his mind's eye, Johnson could still see the skinny teenager who couldn't afford lessons. He could see Kershaw spinning curveballs with a hockey puck and altering the trajectory of his senior year. When Johnson thought about Kershaw, he remembered why he had become a coach.

"It's rewarding for me, because I know I've done something to change a young man's life," Johnson recalled. "More than anything in the world, I've done something to change his life."

* * *

Gangl kept the camera on Kershaw as the other relievers trickled out of the bullpen. He beamed as he jogged across the outfield. He gazed upward and lifted his palms, thanking God for the release. He scanned the stands until he found Ellen. He pointed toward her. She burst into tears. "When Clayton is making that run from the bullpen and his arms were lifted up to the sky, I think that was him just tossing the gorilla off, and just being so thankful," Ellen recalled. "I mean, it was a dream! He has wanted to do this since he was probably a six-year-old boy playing baseball. This is the pinnacle of the dream. And it had come true."

* * *

The 2020 postseason tasted bittersweet for Logan White. The bitterness stemmed from the early rounds, when the Dodgers eliminated San Diego, which employed White as an executive. The sweetness arose as Kershaw checked the final box on his Hall of Fame résumé. "It was off-the-charts awesome," White recalled. (White was far from the only former Dodgers official to suffuse with emotion. Ned Colletti, commentating for the team's television network, felt tears in his eyes.) It was easy for White to get emotional when he talked about Kershaw, when he reminisced about catching that preseason scrimmage with his old teammate Calvin Jones, when he thought about failing to sign Luke Hochevar the year before the 2006 draft. He considered himself a mere instrument in a divine sequence. "I'm not sure I did much, if you really want to know the truth," he recalled. "It was all destined. It was all planned out."

Over the years, Mark Lummus, the Mariners scout who first saw Jones's handiwork with Kershaw, ran into White at games. The proud Texan burned with envy. "I've just had to stare at him like, 'Goddamn. You signed the greatest pitcher to ever come out of my state,'" Lummus recalled.

When he mentored inexperienced scouts, Lummus used Kershaw as an example: "He's in the textbooks: 'This is what we're trying to find, boys.'" The scouts needed to discover, as best they could, what motivated these players. Did they aspire to greatness? Did they understand what greatness required? It was less about delivery and spin rate and body type. It was about the brain and the spine and the heart. Did the heart beat for this?

"He showed those traits back then," Lummus recalled. "Logan White saw them. And the rest of us probably didn't see them like Logan saw them."

*　*　*

The clip Gangl directed of Kershaw became the lasting image of the 2020 World Series. "To me, those moments are some of the best we can do in baseball," Gangl recalled. "It really shows players to their base level of the love of the sport, and all those things that really humanize them. It brings you back to what it was like to play that game as a kid."

The footage played on loop at Dodger Stadium for years to come. Seager, the World Series MVP, understood why.

"Honestly, watching Kersh throw his hands up was pretty cool," Seager recalled. "He symbolizes that team. He's been the face of that franchise forever, and the quote, unquote leader. Not quote, unquote leader—the actual leader. Just to watch him relish it the way he did, it was pretty special."

*   *   *

Dave Preziosi was watching from his home in Dover, Massachusetts, thrilled for the kid he once knew.

Preziosi harbored little resentment about his abbreviated baseball career. He got a master's degree. He became a sales rep for a tech company. "It's a good role, good gig," Preziosi said. "I wish I were playing professional baseball. But my time came and went." He got married on the same day, December 4, 2010, as his old teammate. "I just know that because every now and then I would google 'Clayton Kershaw' and see what the news was," he explained. A decade after his release, while living in Washington, DC, Preziosi waved and called Kershaw's name before a game. "For all these years, I've always wondered if he would have remembered me," Preziosi said.

(When I mentioned Preziosi to Kershaw, he squinted at the ground as if sifting through a Rolodex. "How did you find *that* guy?" Kershaw said. "He went to Boston College, right? That guy was nuts. He used to kick his glove every time he threw.")

Over the years, Preziosi fumed when friends goaded him about Kershaw's postseason follies. "I would feel *so* terrible when he didn't do well in the playoffs," Preziosi recalled. After the homer by Matt Adams, "I didn't want to talk to anybody for a couple days." Watching Kershaw celebrate a title, watching him rewrite the narrative, relieved Preziosi.

He hoped Kershaw understood how much their brief time together meant to him.

"Tell him I say hi," Preziosi said. "And I look forward to seeing him at his Hall induction."

*   *   *

Clad in gray commemorative caps and T-shirts, wearing light-blue surgical masks, the Dodgers milled around as Rob Manfred stood on a raised platform by second base, preparing to hand over the Commissioner's Trophy, the proverbial "piece of metal" the team felt the Astros had stolen in 2017. As owner Mark Walter made a speech, Ellen made it down to the field. For years, she had dreamed about hugging her husband after they won the World Series. Now she could.

The scene felt more dystopian than dreamlike, between the masks and the taped-off seats and the daily Covid tests. There would be no champagne celebration—just another round of nasal swabs back at Las Colinas. Many players found the testing overbearing and futile. No one complained when Turner returned to the field to take pictures. "We're all testing positive for 'Champs,' baby!" Joe Kelly yelled.

On the stage, Roberts took the microphone. He could relate to the sudden lightness Kershaw felt. All the postseason defeats had hardened Roberts. Fans at Dodger Stadium jeered him. Members of his family noted social media vitriol. Roberts tried to ignore the noise. He did not always succeed. He was more guarded, less bubbly than he used to be. "It was a huge weight," Roberts recalled. "I guess there was a little validation. I felt the burden." When Roberts began to speak, he thought about the player whose trust he always strived to earn, the player who kept him at arm's length, the player who still deserved his ultimate respect. When Roberts described the team's cohesion and resilience, the first player he mentioned was Kershaw.

"I couldn't be happier for you, Kersh," Roberts said. "You want to talk about a narrative? How about being a champion? He's a champion forever."

*   *   *

The players passed around the trophy that had not belonged to the Dodgers since 1988. When Kershaw clutched the prize, he was beaming "like he's holding his firstborn," Rick Honeycutt said. Honeycutt stood in a suite beside Tommy Lasorda. In retirement, Honeycutt consulted for the Dodgers, but he could not broach the bubble. He hollered and whistled at his former pupils. He saw the glee on the faces of Kenley Jansen and Alex Wood and, of course, Kershaw.

Kershaw felt "like a son to me," Honeycutt explained. He had guided Kershaw out of his teenage years and into stardom and through heartbreak. "Getting someone at such a young age, you almost felt like he was part of you," Honeycutt recalled. Kershaw felt a similar affinity. He felt uncomfortable calling anyone a father figure. But he was grateful for Honeycutt. "He's a guy who is always in your corner," Kershaw recalled. "I'm really thankful I got to have him."

"If I had a daughter, before he got married, I would have been pushing my daughter his way," Honeycutt recalled. "Because he's the type of person that you could trust. I just loved every facet of his being."

*   *   *

A few players hung around for Zoom interviews. Betts, a two-time champion, spoke as if this were just another day at the office. "I was traded to help get us over the hump," he said. "I used that as my fuel." Kershaw looked positively giddy. "I've been saying 'World Series champs' over and over in my head, just to see if it will sink in," he said. He batted aside a question about his postseason legacy, unable to admit the relief he was still processing.

"Those are all bad questions, man—I don't care about any of that," Kershaw said. "We won the World Series. I don't care about legacy. I don't care about what happened last year. I don't care about what people think. I don't care at all, man. We won the World Series. The 2020 Dodgers won the World Series. Like, who cares about all that other stuff? To be a part of that team—all that other stuff is just pointless. It doesn't matter. We won."

* * *

At his home in Wisconsin, inside The House That Kershaw Built, A. J. Ellis witnessed a triumph greater than the ones he had spent his pandemic summer reliving.

"I'll never forget just sitting on the couch, just smiling, watching him run in," Ellis recalled. "Looking to the heavens. The smile on his face. As cliché as it sounds, you can see it all just falling off his back, as he ran. It was just so special for my friend."

The two men texted that night. Ellis called a day later and told his old partner how happy he was, how proud he was—for both Clayton and Ellen. "She's walked hand-in-hand with him throughout his entire career," Ellis recalled, "and through all the traumatic October experiences." The championship belonged not just to Kershaw. It belonged to his entire family.

* * *

In January, as the end neared, the Melsons gathered around Leslie. At one point, she reached for the hand of the boy she had treated like her own son. Clayton Kershaw had arrived at her door nearly twenty years earlier as a chubby kid with the number 52 shaved into the side of his head, an only child whose own home was often empty. Leslie had fed him and she had clothed him and she had invited him on vacations, opening his eyes and his heart to the warmth of a family. She had packed him up before he left home for Dodgertown and the world of professional baseball. She had watched him grow into a man, the husband to her youngest daughter, the father to her grandchildren. She had seen him fail at his craft and she had seen him rise again, year after year.

She had suffered alongside him. She wanted him to know that.

"We did it," Leslie said.

Kershaw was confused. Leslie gripped his hand and repeated herself.

"We did it," she said. "We won a World Series."

CHAPTER 22

THE THREE-PRONGED
CROSSROADS

Clayton Kershaw pulled up a chair across from me inside the Dodgers spring-training complex at Camelback Ranch. It was March of 2023, two years after he buried his mother-in-law and two months before he buried his own. In a week, he would turn thirty-five. So much would happen in the year ahead, in part because he had chosen to return to baseball. He was discussing the choice he had not made, the puzzle he could not yet solve, the timeline that people kept asking him about.

"I have no idea how you make that decision, about when to stop playing," Kershaw said.

He kept a checklist of four boxes. The first was family. "But I know Ellen," he said. "She'll never say, 'This is too much.'" The next was ability. "I'm not going to stick around and be average," he said. "If I'm still good, that's another box." The next was health. His body had been betraying him for years, but at the start of each season he felt revitalized and capable. The last was the possibility of winning. On the Dodgers, a title always felt within reach.

He could not make a decision because he could still check all the boxes.

"If one of those doesn't match up, then that's easy," he said. "But if all those match up, I don't know how you make that decision."

Kershaw had not yet reached the point where the anxiety and the pain and the burden of the fifth day outweighed the joy and the community and the purpose that all those fifth days provided. His heart still beat for the game. Some days the beat felt fainter. But each day he still offered up his body and his mind and his spirit to the demands of the cycle. It was an addiction melded with affection.

"I guess you still have to love doing it," he said.

As far back as his first contract extension, Kershaw had been thinking about when he would walk away. He turned down the fifteen-year, $300 million offer in 2013 because the deal felt endless. After the Dodgers reached the World Series in 2017, Kershaw hinted about a tidy send-off. "If we win, I might retire," Kershaw said. "I might just call it a career." Sandy Koufax left baseball at thirty. Kershaw was thirty-two when the Dodgers won in 2020. He decided to publicize his exit strategy.

After the 2021 season, Kershaw would be a free agent. He told Jorge Castillo of the *Los Angeles Times* he intended to pursue a one-year contract. He presented an annual three-pronged crossroads for himself: He would either sign with the Dodgers; sign with the Rangers, his hometown team; or retire. The transparency was refreshing, especially from Kershaw, who acted as if updates about his health required a security clearance. At times, Kershaw later regretted being open about his plans. It gave people license to ask him about retirement. And he did not intend to act as if his presence on the diamond should be considered a gift.

"I feel like I might be guilty of this sometimes, talking pretty cavalierly about retiring," Kershaw told me at Camelback Ranch. "I feel like that disrespects people who are really grinding to stay around just to play in the big leagues. I don't want to ever seem like I'm ungrateful. I love playing baseball, still. And that's ultimately why you're still here. I love the game. It is a good feeling to know that you have pretty good control over when you're going to call it a career."

He had fought to maintain that control as he entered his mid-thirties. The nature of his quest changed after the championship. And so did his place within the hierarchy of the Dodgers.

* * *

In the spring of 2021, I called Kershaw to ask a specific question I had been thinking about since he won the World Series. Some within baseball downplayed a championship from a sixty-game season. "Somewhere deep down inside, I was a little bit happy" when Kershaw won, Madison Bumgarner recalled. "And was also happy that it came in 2020—so I can say, 'It might not count.'" For Kershaw, it counted. For weeks after collecting the crown, Kershaw blasted Queen's "We Are the Champions," loud enough that neighbors could hear it when they strolled by, often enough that his kids grew sick of the song.

The Dodgers never experienced the traditional post-title rituals. The country remained paralyzed by the pandemic. There was no parade. When the players received their championship rings that April, a crowd of 15,036, the maximum permitted inside Dodger Stadium, greeted them. It was up to each individual to contextualize the achievement. Not all were joyous. Justin Turner felt scapegoated for taking pictures with the team after testing positive. Kenley Jansen felt embittered that he had not been trusted to record the final outs. Walker Buehler felt like he could not wait to win again in a packed stadium and indulge in all the trappings of victory.

So I was curious how Kershaw would respond when I called.

"Do you feel happier now?" I asked.

Silence filled the air for a moment.

"I don't think that's a fair question," he said.

He had a life beyond fastballs and sliders, beyond the rigors of the first four days and the strain of the fifth day. Later that year, at their home in Los Angeles, Ellen tossed Clayton a baseball. She had inked the number 4 between the seams. "And he was playing with it, like he always does, when he looked at it and he was like, 'What?'" Ellen recalled. Their fourth child, a boy named Chance James Kershaw, was born that December. The pull of home felt stronger than ever; Cali and Charley had begun school, while Cooper required monitoring at home. No longer was Kershaw a young man without responsibilities besides fidelity to his wife and dedication to his craft. At times, baseball consumed him. To most, it defined him. But he could not characterize his existence as solely a quest for a title.

"If I said yes to that," Kershaw said, "that'd be like . . . losing in the playoffs is my only reason for living. And that's not true. I think my personal life, family life, has all been great. I've had an absolute blast with my kiddos and family, regardless of what happens in baseball."

He had never seen himself as Sisyphus. But it did feel nice to leave that boulder atop the hill. He was overwhelmed by the outpouring of messages he received after the World Series. He had never asked for his friends or teammates to pity him. It was only after he won that he recognized they "really felt that pain I was going through," he said. He had thought only Ellen shared the burden. The championship crested over him in waves. First there was the relief. Then there was the joy. And then there was the realization of how much his triumph had meant to others. "Just to see how many people were happy for me, man, I was like, 'Man, that's awesome,'" Kershaw said. "I *was* happy. So that was great."

He was entering a valedictory phase of his career. During the spring, Dave Roberts tabbed Kershaw as the team's Opening Day starter, an honor injuries had prevented Kershaw from experiencing in 2019 and 2020. The Dodgers did not consider Kershaw their No. 1 pitcher. Walker Buehler was ahead of him. The team hoped Julio Urías might also supplant him atop the rotation. And there was a new member of the team, a player with a lucrative contract and a contested reputation.

Trevor Bauer, a right-hander who grew up in a suburb of Los Angeles, was one of the most influential baseball players in the first two decades of the twenty-first century. He became synonymous with Driveline, using the pitch-design laboratory to remodel his arsenal, spreading the gospel to all those willing to listen. He also found a venue for spreading other ideas to those who didn't always want to listen. He was a budding content creator and an irritant on social media. He engaged in a variety of ill-advised online acts, from transphobic humor to birtherism to misrepresentation of the views of indigenous people. The most troubling was his harassment of people on social media, especially women. He often met those charges, which were documented in his own tweets, with outrage that his character was being assailed.

The early years of Bauer's career included some mishaps. After the Arizona Diamondbacks traded him in 2012, less than two years after choosing him with the third pick in the draft, catcher Miguel Montero insisted Bauer "never wanted to listen" to instruction. His performance in the 2016 postseason with Cleveland was marred by a drone accident that left him with an injured finger. After a shaky outing in 2019, Bauer spun around and chucked the baseball over the center-field fence as manager Terry Francona came to remove him. Bauer's performance peaked when he won the 2020 National League Cy Young Award with Cincinnati. His timing was ideal, as he entered free agency that winter. Andrew Friedman had been texting members of his front office: "Let's be pigs." He did not want the franchise to rest on its laurels after one championship. And so Friedman engaged in an act of unsavory gluttony. He authorized the signing of Bauer to a three-year, $102 million contract in February of 2021. At a press conference that month, Friedman vouched for the team's vetting of Bauer. He insisted that the new pitcher "is going to be a tremendous add, not just on the field, but in the clubhouse, in the community."

Less than five months later, on June 29, a woman filed a request for a temporary domestic violence restraining order against Bauer in Los Angeles County Superior Court. The woman alleged that Bauer strangled and punched her during sex without her consent. Bauer denied the claim and later filed a defamation lawsuit against the woman. The woman's restraining order request was denied, and Los Angeles prosecutors declined to press charges against Bauer. But after the Dodgers placed Bauer on administrative leave on July 2, during which he continued to be paid, other accusers emerged with similar stories. Major League Baseball levied a two-year suspension that was later reduced by an arbitrator to 194 games. Bauer never pitched for the Dodgers again. After Bauer served his suspension, the Dodgers released him in the spring of 2023. Bauer spent the season pitching in Japan.

The Bauer case cast a pall over the Dodgers in the summer of 2021. Team officials dodged questions about him. The players were stumped about what to say. Kershaw insisted he did not know Bauer particularly well. He appreciated Bauer's insight into pitching. But their schedules did not interact, he explained. "Within the confines of a clubhouse, he was fine," Kershaw recalled. "He was on his own a lot, did stuff at different times than everybody else, worked out at different times." Kershaw objected to Bauer's content-creation apparatus. "He filmed stuff in the clubhouse, which I never really loved," Kershaw recalled. "But, like, overall, I didn't have a bad experience with him." Even in the winter of 2023, as Bauer and the first accuser continued a yearslong flurry of charges and countercharges, Kershaw was unsure what to say about his former teammate.

"I always think it's a good idea to have the legal process [MLB's process] run its course before jumping to any conclusions about what you read about," Kershaw said. "At the same time, I do see how it was a pretty big distraction to everybody. And the way that Trevor was going to handle it, pretty unapologetically, probably made it a little bit harder. That was a little bit of a challenge. But we still dealt with it."

*   *   *

On July 3, a day after the Dodgers visited President Joe Biden at the White House, a deluge interrupted Kershaw's outing at Nationals Park. Kershaw sat in the dugout with a towel covering his left arm. He rubbed the sweat from his brow and attempted to ignore the discomfort.

"That whole season, my elbow hurt," Kershaw recalled. "Probably starting in, like, May. And then it finally crapped out in July."

The Dodgers placed him on the injured list four days later. The public diagnosis was forearm irritation, but the injury was more serious than that. Kershaw had torn a portion of the flexor tendon connecting his arm to his elbow. It was not his ulnar collateral ligament, the part that requires repair with Tommy John surgery. But it was still his first major elbow injury. The medical staff felt he could avoid surgery if he rested. Kershaw sat out July, August, and the first two weeks of September. To compensate for the uncertainty around Kershaw and the absence of Bauer, Friedman made a splash at the deadline, acquiring Washington Nationals ace Max Scherzer, plus former All-Star shortstop Trea Turner.

Kershaw pushed to return for the postseason. He came back firing 89-mph fastballs on September 13 in a victory against Arizona. "There's not a lot of better feelings in the world than getting to pitch here and getting a win," Kershaw said. The feeling would not last long. On October 1, with only three games left in the regular season, he was trying to finish the second inning against Milwaukee at Dodger Stadium when he felt another portion of his elbow give way. Roberts and a member of the training staff left the dugout. After a brief conversation, Roberts placed his hand on the small of Kershaw's back and steered the pitcher off the mound. The stunned crowd managed an ovation. Kershaw held the baseball in his left hand as he walked off the field—a symbol for anyone looking for one after he had raised the possibility of retirement at the beginning of the season.

"Just an accident," Kershaw recalled. "I knew I didn't blow out."

But his season was over. He watched from the dugout as the 106-win Dodgers won a stirring National League Division Series against the 107-win San Francisco Giants before running out of gas against the 88-win Atlanta Braves in the next round. The Braves avenged the previous year's collapse by trouncing the Dodgers en route to the World Series. The Dodgers had tabbed Scherzer to start Game 6 against

Atlanta. After pitching four times in twelve days, including a relief appearance against San Francisco, Scherzer described his arm as "overcooked." The Dodgers scratched him. Buehler pitched Game 6 in Scherzer's place on short rest for the second time in two weeks and got walloped.

A month later, Scherzer signed a three-year, $130 million contract with the New York Mets. In 2022, Buehler underwent Tommy John surgery for the second time.

"I'll always respect Walker for pitching that game," Kershaw recalled. "We lost, he gave up a homer, whatever. He took the ball."

* * *

That winter, Kershaw approached the three-pronged crossroads for the first time: Dodgers, Rangers, or retirement. The Dodgers gave him space and declined to make a one-year, $18.4 million qualifying offer, which serves as a prelude to free agency for most big-ticket players. That meant the team would receive no draft-pick compensation if he signed elsewhere. But the qualifying offer would have had to be accepted or rejected within a two-week window, and Friedman did not want to rush Kershaw.

Kershaw needed the time. His elbow remained compromised. It pained him to wash his hair or write his signature. By December, even if he wanted to sign a contract, he could not. On December 1, Major League Baseball's thirty owners locked out the players as the two sides bickered over a new collective bargaining agreement. The standoff lasted ninety-nine days, a time period in which players and teams could not communicate. Kershaw tested his arm at Highland Park High's indoor facility. His elbow still hurt, but the discomfort eventually dissipated. "If I picked up a ball in January, [and] it was like, 'I need surgery,' and had to miss the next year, I don't know what that would have looked like," he recalled.

At least one Rangers official spent the lockout wondering about Kershaw's health. The previous year, Texas had hired Chris Young—

former All-Star pitcher and fellow Highland Park resident—as general manager. Young wanted the chance to sign his former offseason throwing partner. The Rangers demonstrated the seriousness of their rebuilding efforts by forking over $500 million to land two infielders, Marcus Semien and Corey Seager, the 2020 World Series MVP. Texas lured Seager from Los Angeles with a ten-year, $325 million contract. The team was willing to offer Kershaw a multiyear deal, if he desired it. "There was the sense that it had a real possibility," one person familiar with the talks said.

Kershaw dashed the Rangers' hopes after the new CBA was formalized on March 10. "As soon as the lockout ended, I received a phone call that broke my heart," Young recalled. "But understood it, completely." Kershaw accepted a one-year, $17 million contract with Los Angeles for 2022. He announced the move on Instagram: "We back!"

* * *

The reason he returned became apparent in his first outing of 2022, against the Minnesota Twins on a 38-degree day at Target Field. Kershaw overwhelmed his inexperienced foes. He struck out thirteen. He permitted no hits. He issued no walks. He hit no batters. He kept the bases pristine for seven perfect innings and eighty pitches, more than he had thrown in any of his outings in a spring training shortened by the lockout. After the seventh, he exited the game to the relief of Roberts and pitching coach Mark Prior. He left his bid for the twenty-fifth perfect game in baseball history unfinished. "Blame it on the lockout," Kershaw said that afternoon. "Blame it on me not picking up a baseball until January."

He was thinking about the greater good of the Dodgers, rather than his own individual achievements. Not all of his friends agreed with him. A. J. Ellis called to yell at him the next day. "We would have known the answer in fourteen pitches or less," Ellis told Kershaw.

"I probably regret it now," Kershaw recalled. "I think throwing a perfect game would have been cool." He added, "Doc, he wanted to take me out. Mark wanted to take me out so bad. I could really do what I usually do and make it super hard for them, and stress them out. Or just take it. So I just took this one. Looking back on it, I regret it. I should have at least tried."

He was entering a kinder, gentler phase of his career. There was a sense of ease that was lacking before the Dodgers won the title. Before a Kershaw start in 2021, he crossed paths with Seager, who observed the protocols and kept quiet. Seager was bewildered when Kershaw looked at him and said, "Hey." "I was like, 'Oh my God. What is going on?'" Seager recalled. Kershaw mellowed in pre-start meetings. "You still might get bit on the hand a little bit," Austin Barnes explained. "But that's okay." He offered guidance on parenting to his younger teammates through word and deed. One of Cody Bellinger's most cherished memories in Los Angeles was watching Kershaw hold Bellinger's daughter during a game of cards. "He makes everyone look bad—he's just Super Dad," Joc Pederson explained. In 2022, Kershaw became close with new teammate Tyler Anderson, who had been chastised by Kershaw years earlier for delaying a game because Anderson, while pitching for the Colorado Rockies, finished his pre-start bullpen session late. "I would call him 'the Oracle' or 'the North Star,'" Anderson recalled. "Whatever he would do, I would follow him. He makes the right decision every time."

Kershaw used a light but firm touch to shake the newest Dodger out of a funk that June. Freddie Freeman had made five All-Star teams and won an MVP award as the Braves first baseman. After Atlanta won the World Series, Freeman expected to re-sign and finish his career there. So he felt blindsided after the lockout when general manager Alex Anthopoulos, who had worked for two seasons with Friedman in Los Angeles, opted to trade for Matt Olson, a younger and less expensive replacement. Freeman pivoted to a six-year, $162 million contract with the Dodgers—hardly a consolation prize. But his shock took months to wear off. He was distant from his new teammates. When he returned to Atlanta for the first time, he wept at a press conference and wept again during a standing ovation from Truist Park. His persistent water-works was a topic of clubhouse conversation. In a story in the *Atlanta Journal-Constitution* about the Dodgers-Braves rivalry, Kershaw noted the reception Freeman received and his subsequent emotion. "I hope we're not second fiddle," Kershaw said. "It's a pretty special team over here, too. I think whenever he gets comfortable over here, he'll really enjoy it." The quote caught fire on social media. Freeman got the message. After the series, he sent the Dodgers a group text thanking them for bearing with him. He began to open up with teammates. His relationship with Kershaw improved. Kershaw respected Freeman's dependability. "Just the fact that he goes and plays every single day, and doesn't want to come out, you can use that to the benefit of the team," Kershaw recalled. "That changed my opinion on him a little bit."

Also that June, the Dodgers finally convinced Sandy Koufax to permit the organization to unveil a statue of him outside Dodger Stadium. He had not thrown a pitch since 1966 but his influence still permeated the franchise, in part through the southpaw the Dodgers asked to speak at the ceremony. Kershaw described the genesis of his friendship with Koufax en route to Joe Torre's charity event in 2010. He tried to convey the enormity of knowing a man like Koufax cared about him. When legendary broadcaster Vin Scully retired, Kershaw told the crowd, Koufax said that "the thing I treasure most is he allows me to call him friend." Kershaw stammered through his next words: "That's the same for me. I'm grateful for that, Sandy, and I know you don't believe it, but there's no one more deserving than you of this honor."

A month later, Dodger Stadium hosted the All-Star Game for the first time since 1980. As part of the festivities, Kershaw was selected as the National League's starting pitcher for the first time. Before he took the assignment, he thought about the pitcher considered the best in the National League that season, Sandy Alcántara of the Miami Marlins, a lithesome, six-foot-five right-hander. Like Kershaw in his youth, Alcántara believed he should finish games. Alcántara was the rare pitcher still granted that opportunity. He logged six complete games in

2022, matching Kershaw's career-best mark from the MVP season of 2014. Kershaw asked Marlins manager Don Mattingly, his former skipper, for Alcántara's number. When Kershaw called, he was apologetic. He told Alcántara he was considering retirement and might never get another chance to start the Midsummer Classic. Alcántara assured Kershaw he would not protest. "He called me because he knew I deserved it," Alcántara recalled. "I respect him a lot."

On the day of the game, Kershaw alternated between enjoyment and his usual pre-start lather. When he entered the training room, Pederson, now an All-Star with the Giants, occupied his table. "What are you doing?" Kershaw said. Pederson peeled out of the room, laughing. Kershaw spotted Giants traveling secretary Abe Silvestri, the former visiting clubhouse manager. "He gave me the sweatiest, nastiest hug," Silvestri recalled. Before his first pitch, Kershaw stepped off the mound and looked up, taking in the sea of adulation backdropped by Elysian Park. Kershaw struck out Yankees slugger Aaron Judge and picked off Angels phenom Shohei Ohtani in a scoreless inning. And he did something else, rare for him on a baseball field: he enjoyed himself.

The reverie was short-lived. Sixteen days later, Kershaw's back locked up. He missed nearly a month. He made only twenty-two starts in 2022. He had not made thirty starts since 2015. He had surpassed 175 innings just once during those years. In his first seven full seasons, he logged 1,503.1 innings; in his next seven, he totaled 970. The rigors of the cycle and the violence of the fifth day had reduced him to an exceedingly effective part-timer. He could no longer do the things he once did.

Then again, no one else could, either.

In 2010, when Kershaw threw 204.1 innings with a 2.91 ERA at the age of twenty-two, he was one of forty-five pitchers to reach 200 innings, the modern measure of a pitcher's durability. In 2021, only four pitchers reached 200. The total expanded to eight in 2022 before shrinking to five in 2023. The expectations for pitchers had changed. The industry had learned the perils of facing an opposing lineup for a third time—a reality absorbed by any observer watching Kershaw in October. Relievers began entering games earlier and earlier. Instead of developing pitchers to last deep into games, teams trained them to max out across 4 or 5 or 6 innings. The approach brought the pitchers to the major leagues faster, at a time when clubs still lacked the ability to prevent arm injuries.

The case of Shane McClanahan was emblematic of the perils of the era. He started for the American League opposite Kershaw at the All-Star Game. He had undergone Tommy John surgery while attending the University of South Florida. Tampa Bay chose him in the first round of the 2018 draft. His fastball averaged nearly 97 mph, but he threw off-speed pitches a majority of the time. In four professional seasons, he never tallied more than 166.1 innings in a year. In seventy-four professional starts, he surpassed one hundred pitches precisely twice. The Rays managed him with utmost care, cautious of overexposure, aware of his value.

And in 2023, McClanahan met the same fate as Sandy Alcántara. Both men required Tommy John surgery to reconstruct their elbows.

* * *

After the Dodgers crashed out of the 2022 postseason against San Diego, Kershaw did not dawdle. By September, he and Ellen had decided they wanted to stay in Los Angeles for another season. When he reached free agency, Kershaw handled his own contract talks with Andrew Friedman.

Their relationship had improved over the years. After Ellis was traded in 2016, Kershaw kept his distance from Friedman for months. On a trip to Colorado early in 2017, Friedman asked Kershaw if they could walk together after a game. Friedman laid out his rationale for trading away Kershaw's close friend. It would have been easier, Friedman told Kershaw, to not make the trade, but the marginal upgrade was worth the risk. "I said that, seeing how competitive he is, I hoped one point that resonated with him was that we are incredibly focused on doing anything and everything we can to win," Friedman recalled.

Friedman appreciated Kershaw's intensity, his commitment, and his insight into players. He often consulted Kershaw before making acquisitions at the trade deadline. And he appreciated the ease with which Kershaw conducted free-agent negotiations. "It's been great," Friedman explained. "Just direct, honest. Exactly how you would hope it would go." Friedman benefited from Kershaw's crossroads. It is much simpler haggling with a man who has limited his options. "Like, I'm not going to go play for the Phillies," Kershaw explained. "I'm not going to do that." He added, "It's never going to be like, 'Oh, yeah, let's go see what the Yankees have to offer.'" Kershaw did not want a protracted, messy holdout, like Derek Jeter experienced with the Yankees after the 2010 season. Once again, the Dodgers declined to force his hand with the qualifying offer. On November 11, six days after the World Series concluded, Kershaw agreed to a one-year, $20 million contract for 2023.

Kershaw had given the 68-win Rangers cursory consideration. He called Young to tell him he was returning to Los Angeles before Texas could make a serious pitch. (According to people with knowledge of the situation, the Rangers were considering asking President George W. Bush, who owned the team when Nolan Ryan pitched there, to lobby Kershaw.) Ellen left "the most heartfelt voicemail" for Young's wife, Liz, Young recalled. Kershaw asked Young to keep him in mind in the future. Young assured Kershaw that baseball would not affect their relationship. "I value his friendship, the person he is, and our kids growing up in the same community, all of that, much more than I do anything on the baseball field," Young told me in June of 2023.

"I love the Rangers," Jim Melson told me in December of 2022. "I'd love to think of him being here as a Ranger. But it's hard for me to picture."

*   *   *

Jim Melson kept an office at the Kershaw's Challenge headquarters, less than a mile from the neighborhood the family still called home, where he managed his son-in-law's affairs. On the day after Santa Claus visited Highland Park in the winter of 2022, Kershaw sat on a couch outside Melson's office, gazing at MLB Network on a kitchenette television. The Winter Meetings had been the week before. The Dodgers idled as a series of stars—Trea Turner, Carlos Correa, Xander Bogaerts—signed elsewhere. They were avoiding major acquisitions in order to make a full-pocketed pursuit of Shohei Ohtani the next winter, but Kershaw was still confounded by his team's inactivity. Friedman had assured him that Gavin Lux, the team's homegrown shortstop, would flourish if given an opportunity and render moot the need for a costly addition. Kershaw tended to side with Friedman, but understood the executive was not infallible. They disagreed over the reasoning behind the team's most recent early October exit—a 111-win Goliath toppled by the 89-win Padres in a four-game stunner.

"There are some times when you're like, 'I don't know how the playoffs are going to go,'" Kershaw said. "But with this one, we were like, 'We're built to win.' This one stung a little bit. It just was like, 'Oh my gosh, we just got punched in the mouth.'"

To Kershaw, the blows caught the Dodgers flat-footed because the team leaned upon strategies used to go 14-5 against the Padres during the regular season. San Diego changed its approach for October; in his outing, a 5-3 Game 2 defeat, Kershaw noticed Padres stars Manny Machado and Juan Soto positioned themselves differently in the batter's box. "The more I think about it, I don't think the thought process of 'Well, this is what I've always done' is good enough, at that point, in the playoffs," Kershaw said. "I don't think you can say that. I don't care what you've always done. But you haven't done it this way, in this situation."

Kershaw referenced an ongoing debate he and Barnes conducted with Prior and bench coach Danny Lehmann. The coaches urged pitchers to attack a hitter's weakness. Barnes and Kershaw suggested that approach might not be foolproof. "And they're like, 'No. What they can't hit is what they can't hit. And you've got to keep throwing it and you've got to keep executing it,'" Kershaw said. "But your room for error becomes so low. And they're just assuming the robotic factor of 'Just throw your good slider.' Yeah, but if you do it ten times, you're not going to throw a good one ten times."

After the upset, Friedman attributed it to a lack of timely hitting. Dave Roberts suggested the Padres played with greater urgency and intensity. Kershaw sided with his manager. "I just felt that maybe Doc has a point," Kershaw said. "I don't know if we were, like, cohesively flipping that switch to the playoff mode, like you have to."

For Kershaw, the pain increased when he consulted his own hourglass. He was running out of time.

"In 2013, 2014, or any year before that, it was like, 'All right, we'll just get them next year,'" Kershaw said. "It hurt. And you felt it. Especially when I was the one on the mound for it. You always felt like, 'Oh yeah, we're going to have another chance at it next year. At least we're going to give it another go.' And then recently, the last few years, it's been, like, just more weight."

*   *   *

A day later, Kershaw climbed into his Denali and visited a stage from his past. He was headed to Riders Field in Frisco, the double-A affiliate of the Rangers. Back in 2006, when Kershaw pitched his final high school game there against McKinney North, the stadium was called Dr Pepper Ballpark. It was a minor-league stadium inside a shopping center, tucked in between an Ikea, a Perry's Steakhouse, and an Embassy Suites—a perfect setting for Kershaw to shoot a Skechers commercial.

Outside the entryway to the stadium, tables held platters of fruit and pastries. Inside the lobby, a pair of staffers in hoodies and flannels were taping up elements of the commercial's storyboard. Kershaw's call time was 9 A.M. He pulled into a parking spot outside the stadium at 8:54. The day before, he had sported a full beard. Now he was clean shaven.

"I thought about leaving a mustache to see if I could get out of this," Kershaw said. "You can't take a picture of a guy with a creepy mustache. But Ellen wouldn't let me."

Kershaw had signed with Skechers after Under Armour stopped making his cleats in 2018. He was aware that the brand was not considered hip—if he ever forgot, Buehler was sure to remind him. Skechers offered to build a shoe to Kershaw's specific modifications and partner with his charity. "It's just a great spike," he explained. "Comfortable. And they're super generous with Kershaw's Challenge." That was how he became the face of septuagenarian footwear.

The commercial consumed Kershaw's morning and early afternoon. That was not easy to secure. "Six hours," explained Ann Higginbottom, Ellen's sister and the executive director of Kershaw's Challenge, "is a big deal to him." He agreed on the condition he could leave to pick up the kids from school. It was up to Higginbottom to remind her brother-in-law of his commitment. She often created a paper trail on email or text, she explained, "Because he regularly will say, 'I didn't say that. I didn't do that.'" The proof did not always sway him. "In some ways, he's just a curmudgeon about certain things," Higginbottom explained. "And I know that it's coming. Like baseball card contracts. He agreed to it. He knows he's got to sign cards. But when the box shows up, he's mad about it. And it's like, 'No.' So the way I spin it is like, 'I'm coming over with a box of cards. You tell me what time.' It's almost like helping a toddler get dressed."

On the set, Kershaw betrayed little sign of grumpiness. He gabbed with the director, the grips, the wardrobe people. He ran through his scenes. He performed dozens of takes. He changed costumes several times. He practiced until the phrase "Stretch Fit Skechers Slip-Ins" stopped tripping his tongue. There was one line of dialogue—"The stretching is my favorite part"—that struck him as preposterous, but he declined to object. That would only lengthen his stay on the set. After several takes pretending to stretch an SUV into a limousine, the director pronounced himself pleased with the day's work: "That's a wrap on Clayton Kershaw!"

The crew gave him a round of applause in the parking lot outside the ballpark. It was 2:33 P.M. He raced to gather his things. He scribbled his signature on a few baseballs. On his way out of the stadium, a RoughRiders staffer stopped him.

"Do you have time for a staff photo?" Kershaw managed a smile that looked like a grimace. "I have to pick up my kids in twenty-one minutes," he said. "So I've got one minute." He posed in the center of the shot. He signed another baseball. He stopped with another staffer for a selfie. He hustled to his car. School would let out in eighteen minutes. He hated to be late.

CHAPTER 23

THE SIXTH DAY

Ten months later, Clayton Kershaw opened his front door in Highland Park and invited me back inside. Cali and Charley were at school across the street. Cooper powered Chance on a push car through the living room. Later that night, the Texas Rangers would host the Arizona Diamondbacks in Game 1 of the 2023 World Series in nearby Arlington. Kershaw did not plan to attend. "Absolutely not," he said. "No, I think that would be weird."

There were more pressing concerns for the household. The carpets needed to be cleaned. Kershaw needed to choose a Halloween costume; one year he had dressed as the Incredible Hulk, in another he had been Will Ferrell's Jackie Moon, in several others he had eschewed trick-or-treating to pitch in the World Series. He needed to finalize the schedule for the first surgery of his life, an operation to repair his left shoulder. And he needed to overcome his tendency toward stoicism and express his feelings. His faith, he felt, depended on it.

"I'll get a little honest with you," he told me. "Faith-wise, the last year has been harder for me." He found his connection to God had grown tenuous. "You're supposed to feel the presence of the Holy Spirit when you pray," he said. "And my prayer life sucks. I can't pray well. I have a tough time voicing how I feel."

His internal compass could carry him for only so long. The 2023 season had weakened his body, damaged his reputation, and wounded his pride. At times he felt lonely, cloudy, unsure of his purpose within baseball. As Kershaw approached the three-pronged crossroads yet again, he felt unsure how to proceed. He could not clarify his desires, in part because the answers had once felt so obvious. Those close to him, like Ellen, like A. J. Ellis, challenged him to dig beneath the surface. It did not come easy.

"I don't think I've ever made a big decision in my life," he told me. "Think about it. Knew I was going to get drafted, knew I wasn't going to go to college . . . Knew I was going to marry Ellen, because I dated her all the way through. That was easy. Played for the Dodgers my whole life. No real decisions there.

"And this offseason, it was like four or five big decisions, that I actually have to choose, at once. And it just hit me like a ton of bricks. And it was hard. You're coming at a good time, because I feel a lot more clarity than I did the last ten days."

He had made one decision when he opted to undergo surgery rather than retire. A more shocking choice might follow the operation. His voice grew quiet when he told me how he hoped the offseason would play out. He had not thrown his last pitch. But he might have thrown his last pitch for the Los Angeles Dodgers.

"Gun to my head, I think I want to play here," Kershaw said. "I think I want to leave LA."

* * *

Playing for another team felt improbable back in March, as we sat outside the Dodgers clubhouse at Camelback Ranch.

"I'll tell you what," Kershaw told me. "If I was to win another World Series, I think I can't imagine ending it any better than that."

What happened? How did Kershaw go from envisioning a farewell parade in Los Angeles to plotting his departure?

There was no singular moment of irreparable break between Kershaw and the only professional franchise he had ever known. The fraying of their bond was gradual. His discontent with the Dodgers was apparent that spring, after a passive offseason in which Andrew Friedman had not spent to solve problems with the roster. Kershaw had not intended to be there for most of spring training. He had planned to pitch for Team USA in the World Baseball Classic, a boon for the American team, which had struggled to secure the participation of its most famous players for the exhibition. His participation hit a snag when the exhibition's insurance company reviewed his injury history and declined to cover him. The policies existed to assuage the concerns of teams about players appearing in intense competition just days before the regular season. Without insurance, the Dodgers would be on the hook for Kershaw's $20 million if he got hurt during the tournament.

The Dodgers declined to waive the requirement. Kershaw looked into purchasing his own insurance policy, but balked at the price. The experience galled him. He had fielded calls all winter from Team USA officials lobbying him to play. He agreed to participate, unlike top American pitchers Max Scherzer, Justin Verlander, Gerrit Cole, Corbin Burnes, and many others. And then he was denied permission and found himself stuck in the grind of spring training. His two closest Dodgers friends were playing in the tournament, with Austin Barnes catching for Team Mexico and Trayce Thompson manning the outfield for Great Britain. For most of the spring, Kershaw felt his nearest confidant was massage therapist Possum Nakajima.

The turnover of the roster left him bereft of pals. A. J. Ellis had been gone for years. Same with Brett Anderson and Brandon McCarthy, Zack Greinke and Rich Hill, Jamey Wright and Josh Lindblom. Joc Pederson, who often carpooled with Kershaw to Dodger Stadium when it wasn't the fifth day, departed after 2020. Mookie Betts and Freddie Freeman supplanted Justin Turner and Corey Seager at the heart of the Dodgers lineup. Rick Honeycutt retired. John Pratt took a job with the Los Angeles Angels. Tyler Anderson signed a multiyear deal with the Angels. Even Kenley Jansen—the closer who caught Kershaw in the Gulf Coast League, the goofy trash-talker whom Kershaw schooled in backyard basketball in Midland, Michigan, the only reliever the Dodgers ever trusted to replace Kershaw late in games— was pitching elsewhere. "I miss him," Jansen told me. "It's a part of me that I feel like is gone."

Kershaw tried to be friendly with all the new faces. The younger pitchers idolized him but could not relate to him. Kershaw appreciated Betts's talent and Freeman's reliability, but they were not close. His relationship with Roberts remained cordial but distant. On several occasions while reporting this book, Kershaw asked me if I intended to interview Roberts. He was always wary of what his manager might say about him. "I have a closer relationship with a lot of other players," Roberts told me. "Because that's just not how he's wired. But our relationship works. As far as time, it's taken a long time. It's almost like, with him, you feel like you have to continue to earn that trust." When I suggested that dynamic sounded challenging, Roberts agreed. "It is very challenging," he said. "But he's worth it."

Roberts and Kershaw were united by a common goal. "There's only one reason to keep doing this," Kershaw said. "And that's to win." As he looked around his clubhouse, he wondered if that goal was possible in 2023. Those hopes were dealt a blow early in camp when young shortstop Gavin Lux suffered a season-ending knee injury. "This is the worst team I've been here with," Kershaw said. "Which is hard to say out loud. But I think it's true." I asked if he meant in terms of the personalities. "Just talent," he said.

He was wrong about that. The Dodgers won a hundred games and captured the National League West for the tenth time in eleven seasons. For Kershaw, though, the journey was far from enjoyable.

*   *   *

On the evening of March 28, two days before the season began and four days before his first start, Kershaw flew to Dallas. He spent the next morning making pancakes with his children before ferrying Cali and Charley to school. He played with the kids all afternoon. The next morning, he took a private jet back to California. "And the flight was delayed," Ellen recalled. Her phone flooded with texts from Kershaw, his anxiety rising as he waited on the tarmac while refueling in Phoenix, unable to exert control. "I was like, 'He is having kittens on this plane right now,'" Ellen recalled.

Kershaw made it to Dodger Stadium on time. He dissected the Diamondbacks for six innings on April 1. After the game, a crowd waited by Kershaw's locker. Before he could reach it, a new teammate stopped him. J. D. Martinez was a five-time All-Star but a first-time Dodger. Earlier that afternoon in the clubhouse, he had tried to start a conversation with Kershaw. He apologized after the game: He didn't know about the fifth day. Kershaw waved Martinez off.

"I'm not as crazy as people say I am," he said.

Ellen and the children came to Los Angeles for the game. To celebrate their arrival, Kershaw ordered five batches of balloons. "I think I overdid it," he told Ellen. When the children walked into the house in Studio City, balloons scraped the ceiling of the foyer. The display remained ascendent the next morning, when Kershaw invited me over. The dining room table overflowed with baby gifts. Ellen was planning a group baby shower for seven expectant Dodgers spouses. Kershaw played catch with Charley for a few minutes outside before he had to leave for Dodger Stadium. Cooper, the three-year-old, wandered over as I spoke with Ellen.

"What's something you could tell him about your dad?" Ellen said.

Cooper pondered the possibilities.

"Is your dad small?" Ellen asked.

"Big!" Cooper said.

"Is your dad serious, or is he funny?" Ellen said.

"Funny," Cooper said.

Before he left for work, Kershaw gazed into his backyard. Charley tossed a baseball into the sky and gave it a whack.

"Oh ho!" Kershaw said. "I saw that!"

Charley raced inside.

"Hey, when did you learn how to do that?" Kershaw said.

"I don't know, I just hit it into the pool," Charley said.

"You did?" Ellen said. "Way to go, Charley!"

"Hey, FYI, every ball that goes into the pool is ruined," Kershaw said. "But! That was a great hit."

* * *

The next two months brought Kershaw accomplishment, loneliness, and loss. On April 18, he logged seven scoreless innings against the New York Mets, roaring with uncharacteristic gusto after recording a strikeout with an exquisite backdoor slider to protect a lead and secure the two hundredth victory of his career. Tyler Anderson texted the next morning to congratulate him on the achievement. Kershaw took a little while to respond. He had been in the weight room, lifting, locked in the cycle, which pointed him toward another fifth day.

On the surface, he was charting the same course. His results were excellent. His intensity never flagged. His affable grumpiness remained. During one game that season, starter Dustin May opened an at-bat with a slider, a boon to pitching coach Mark Prior, who had been lobbying Kershaw to try more first-pitch curveballs. "Hey man, we've got every starter to throw first-pitch offspeed," Prior crowed. "Not going to happen," Kershaw replied.

Beneath the surface, though, he was roiling. He worried the front office would not rectify deficiencies in the roster at the trade deadline. "We need so much help," Kershaw told me. "I don't think we're going to do it." His left shoulder had begun to ache, which infected him with dread. The Dodgers afforded him an extra day of rest between outings; the fifth day became the sixth day. It became hard to trust the cycle when his body rejected its requirements. He tried to maintain his schedule while flying between Los Angeles and Highland Park, where his mother's health was rapidly declining. Before the season began, Kershaw had visited Marianne to say goodbye, as he did with his father in 2013. But he kept coming back when he could during the season. "She was pretty much asleep," he explained. "It was time. It was time. Alzheimer's, man, it's no joke." Marianne died on May 13. Ellen memorialized her that afternoon in Inglewood, at a ceremony unveiling a baseball diamond sponsored by Kershaw's charity. Marianne, she told the crowd of kids and parents, "moved mountains" to facilitate her son's career. "She experienced no greater joy than watching her son grow into the man, the philanthropist, the father, and the ballplayer that he is today," Ellen told the crowd.

Less than a week later, the Dodgers announced a programming change for their LGBTQ+ Pride Night on June 16. The team was disinviting a group called the Sisters of Perpetual Indulgence, a group of queer and trans people who satirized sexual intolerance by dressing as nuns. The initial invitation of the San Francisco–based group had triggered protest from conservative Catholic organizations, including Florida senator Marco Rubio lobbying MLB commissioner Rob Manfred. When the Dodgers bowed to the pressure, LGBTQ+ groups across the country condemned the decision. Five days later, the team reversed course and reinvited the Sisters to Pride Night.

Kershaw was unhappy with the situation. He felt the Sisters mocked his faith. Amid the tumult, he pushed the organization to relaunch its Christian Faith and Family Day, which had been sidelined since the pandemic. Kershaw announced the event's return on Twitter. He called a players-only meeting to inform his teammates he intended to speak out against the Sisters, which he did in an interview with the *Los Angeles Times*. While insisting his frustration "has nothing to do with the LGBTQ community or pride or anything like that," he objected to the group's tactics. "I don't agree with making fun of other people's religions," he told the *Times*. "It has nothing to do with anything other than that. I just don't think that, no matter what religion you are, you should make fun of somebody else's religion."

"I put a lot of thought into it, and talked to a lot of different people," he told me that June. "I just came to the conclusion that the Dodgers really put us in a horrible position. It's not an LGBT issue. It's just, like, that group is pretty rough. And I'm all for funny, and satire, but that goes way beyond it. So I did feel like I needed to say something."

In objecting to the Sisters, Kershaw was condemned as homophobic and intolerant. He believed there was more nuance to his position. "I'm a sinful person, just like everyone else," he said. "It's not for me to condemn or judge other people. But there's no way to say that without people just cancelling you. So you treat everybody the same, and do the best I can to love other people as well as I can."

His interpretation of his faith compelled him to speak out. Yet it was not until months later that he could vocalize the turmoil that gripped him throughout the spring and summer of 2023. He felt unsure about the depth of his convictions. His dialogue with God had become fainter. "Sometimes I feel like an imposter when it comes to my faith," he told me in October. "Because baseball has given a huge platform, right? Talk about whatever you want. And Jesus, ultimately, is what I choose to talk about. And I think that is what God wants me to do with my life, is use that platform. But sometimes when you don't feel the Holy Spirit, or I don't feel that, you feel like you're just putting yourself out there without the conviction of doing it."

His plight was not uncommon among adults questioning the metaphysical and the spiritual while entering middle age. But he was also isolated early in the season, with Ellen and the children in Texas while he confronted the pain of his shoulder and the jumble of his psyche. A home stand in early June, after Marianne died and before his family came to Los Angeles for the summer, was particularly deflating. "Too many hours alone with my thoughts," he told me. "It was just sad. I mean, I'm fine. But it's like, at night: 'What am I doing? Why am I here? I could be home with my kids. I'm *choosing* to be away from them right now?'"

What he missed was the life he had spent his entire adulthood building. His partner. His kids. His family. "I think when it's your choice to be away from something that you really love, it's harder," he said.

* * *

Two weeks later, I chatted at Yankee Stadium with Chris Young. On his ride to the Bronx, Young remembered how he felt entering the ballpark as a player: the adrenaline, the anxiety, the rush of competition. "Never to have that again—it's hard," he said. He had retired from pitching in 2018. He had just turned forty-four. His second career had been prosperous; the Rangers had emerged as a contender in 2023. But nothing compared to his old gig.

"I would one hundred percent love to be taking that mound tonight, versus doing this job," Young said. "And I love what I do. I love it! But I've lived my dream job. And for Clayton, that's the thing. When it's over, it's over."

Precious few write their own endings. For the overwhelming majority, either your body breaks down or the game breaks you. Kershaw was one of those few. "My advice for him is to do it as long as he can," Young said. "You can never get it back."

Young, of course, was biased. He still harbored dreams about signing Kershaw. But other former players echoed the sentiment. Dan Haren thought he would enjoy the freedom after retiring in 2015. "It's not easy," Haren told me. "Because everyone thinks, 'Oh, I can golf. I can do whatever I want.' I cannot be sitting at home, watching TV, at eleven o'clock in the morning every day. I'll freaking want to shoot myself." After a year, he took a job in Arizona's front office. Even then, he explained, "There's been times, I drop my kids at school, go work out, eat lunch, pick them up . . . It's like, 'Shit, what the hell did I even do today?'" In the end, Haren acknowledged, Kershaw would have to grapple with the death of his athletic existence. It came for them all.

"Nothing compares to the life I had from when I was twenty to thirty-five," Haren said. "It's just a matter of trying to move on, a second phase of life, I guess."

Even Kershaw's oldest friends, who understood the inner turmoil baseball sometimes wrought within him, agreed. "I can absolutely, totally understand that every fifth day, more than half of a year, you've got this massive anxiety of going through that," Will Skelton said. "I could imagine wanting to be done with it. But I could imagine you never, ever have that feeling again. There's no way to replicate it any sort of commercial way."

At times, Kershaw insisted he could live without that feeling. "I have been telling people this for years, and nobody believes it," Kershaw told me in December 2022. "But I don't think I'm competitive unless I'm playing baseball—or Ping-Pong." I started to laugh. "No, that's it!" Kershaw said. "I don't think I'm that competitive. I don't have to win my board games. I don't have to win playing cards. I think I can turn it off." As an example, he referenced the links. "If I hit a ball in the water playing golf, I'm like, 'Eh,'" Kershaw said. "I don't care."

On one count, Kershaw was correct. His friends did not believe he was not competitive.

"No! What? That's a lie," Skelton said.

"Yeah, that's a bunch of trash," Josh Meredith said.

"That's funny," Shawn Tolleson said. "I would completely dismiss him saying that."

Take golf. Kershaw said he only played four times in the winter after the 2022 season. He made it sound like a minor pursuit, a venue to crack a beer and share some laughs. Several years earlier, though, Tolleson's wife got him golf lessons as an anniversary gift. When Kershaw heard about this, he hired the instructor. For six weeks, the two followed the same schedule. They played catch and lifted in the morning, fueled up at lunch, then went to the course. "It's not the instructor's fault, but it was the biggest waste of money that we ever did, because we got so much worse in those six weeks at golf," Tolleson recalled. The tips corroded their natural athleticism. "It got to where we couldn't even hit the ball," Tolleson said.

His former teammates were unsure if Kershaw was wired for civilian life. "He never skipped a single thing in the nine years that I was there," Justin Turner said. "It's not normal. It's not human." And even away from the diamond, his zeal for control extended into amusing areas. In his twenties, when he had already married and many of his friends were still single, Kershaw would pilfer their phones to investigate their dating lives. Eventually, his pals found protection in iPhone passcodes; Kershaw still cracked a few of them. He also kept tabs through Find My Friends. Meredith was on a business trip when I called him in early 2023. "I'm sure he'll ask me later this week, 'What were you doing in El Paso?'" Meredith said.

*   *   *

For Kershaw, the final months of 2023 were grim with a ruinous ending. On June 27, Kershaw left a start in Colorado after six scoreless innings and only seventy-nine pitches. His shoulder was barking. He received a cortisone shot to dispel the soreness. The injection could only do so much. Before the All-Star Game in Seattle, where Kershaw represented the Dodgers for the tenth time, an MRI revealed he had torn the capsule in his shoulder joint. A damaged capsule usually required surgery. The rehab could take a year. It was the sort of injury that forced pitchers to consider applying for a real estate license.

Kershaw held his head in his hands after he heard the prognosis, Ellen recalled. "Clayton probably felt defeated for ten minutes," Ellen said. "And then he flipped his mindset around. And he was just like, 'Okay, well, maybe I'll beat the odds on this.'" The sunset of his career had never felt closer to the horizon. Yet Kershaw felt he still owed his franchise, his teammates, and himself nothing short of everything. When he met with team officials to decide how to proceed, Kershaw was "incredibly adamant about pitching," Friedman told me.

The team never announced the extent of the damage. Neither did Kershaw. His shoulder felt "completely fine," he said after the All-Star

Game. But he did not return until August 10. At first, he looked like himself, albeit an abridged, five-inning version. To compensate for his compromised shoulder, he altered his delivery, which led to a pinched nerve in his neck that merited an epidural. By September, his fastball was hovering around 88 mph with his slider near 85 mph. The reduced life on the slider made the pitch suddenly hittable.

He was not enjoying himself. Some pitchers reveled in tutoring underlings, and the Dodgers did not lack for them. He was part of a staff featuring rookies like Bobby Miller, Ryan Pepiot, and Emmet Sheehan. Kershaw did not pretend to be an extra instructor for them. "This might be, like, harsh, but I really don't have any interest in helping people get better," he said. "This is probably selfish, but if it benefits me to help Pep and Bobby, then yeah. But I don't, like, care." Some pitchers appreciated transitioning from stuff to smarts. Kershaw was not one of them. "It's way more fun just to dominate every time," he said. He posted a 2.33 ERA in September, but only pitched once a week. The sixth day had become the seventh day. He was procuring outs with his reputation more than his arsenal. He felt nervous as the postseason approached, unsure if he could meet his standards, even in a reduced capacity. The Dodgers needed him. A slew of injuries had decimated the starting rotation. Julio Urías was on administrative leave after being arrested on suspicion of felony domestic violence. As Kershaw feared, the team failed to make a splash at the trade deadline.

In the season's final month, Kershaw spoke with Roberts, who had been open with reporters about Kershaw's physical shortcomings. The transparency irked Kershaw, rekindling familiar frustrations with Roberts. The manager insisted, as he always did, he had Kershaw's best interests at heart. "I was trying to take care of him," Roberts said. "And he was like, 'Just tell them I stink.'" Kershaw did not want to admit frailty. "He didn't want that feeling of being a lame doe, where they could smell blood," Roberts said. The opponents needed to believe that they were facing Clayton Kershaw, the ten-time All-Star, the best of

his generation, the last of his kind—and not a thirty-five-year-old man
with an injured shoulder and an 88-mph fastball.

Late in the season, Kershaw spoke with a few of his younger teammates about the pressure of October baseball. He confirmed what so
many around the Dodgers had thought about Kershaw as he confronted
his postseason demons: he was driven by a fear of failure. "Now," he
explained before Game 1 of the National League Division Series
against Arizona, "it's just a lot more positive." His perspective could
not offset his physical limitations. If the Diamondbacks harbored any
illusions about Kershaw heading into the series, their own bats shattered them. On the second pitch of the game, second baseman Ketel
Marte scorched a curveball into center field. The baseball traveled 115.7
mph, an absolute missile, hard enough to clank off the glove of rookie
center fielder James Outman. After Outman dropped the ball and
Marte scooted into second base, Arizona overran Kershaw. The Diamondbacks took vicious, confident hacks, unfazed by the broken pitcher's résumé. Kershaw could not stop them. He could neither produce
velocity with his fastball nor deceive with his slider. He faced eight
batters. Seven reached base. Arizona scored six runs against him, a
flurry punctuated by a towering homer by rookie catcher Gabriel
Moreno. As Moreno's blast crested the left-field fence, Kershaw hung
his head and hunched at the waist, assuming the position one more
time. Roberts removed him with one out in the first inning and the
game already over. Kershaw sulked in the dugout as the 11-2 defeat
unfolded. The outing bloated his postseason ERA to 4.49, a full two
runs more than his record-setting regular season ERA.

After the game, Kershaw approached Ellen. "I'm done," he told her.
He could not fathom pitching again. "He was in the height of emotions," Ellen said. "And, I mean, this is exactly what insanity is: you
keep doing it expecting different results, and, 'How am I back here?'"
Kershaw felt overwhelmed by the futility of all the hours he spent and
the pain he endured trying to be available for October. "You battle all
year, you grind," he said. "Miserable all year to try and be a part of it.

And then that happens. And it's like, 'That was dumb. Why did I do
that?'"

*   *   *

A day after Kershaw decided to quit, he showed up to work. "I felt sorry
for myself for the rest of the game," he said. "But you can't do that. So
you get over it." He never got another chance to pitch. Arizona eliminated the Dodgers in a three-game sweep on their way to an unexpected appearance in the World Series. The defeat stunned Kershaw,
sending him home still embarrassed. On the flight to Los Angeles,
Andrew Friedman approached him. They talked about pitchers the
team could recruit from Japan, like incoming ace Yoshinobu Yamamoto. The Dodgers were preparing to offer two-way star Shohei Ohtani
hundreds of millions. Near the end of the conversation, Kershaw raised
his own situation. "I told him, 'If you don't want me back, just be honest with me. I get it: it's a weird, sticky situation. We can make it look
as good as we possibly can on both sides,'" Kershaw said. "And he didn't
say, 'No, I want you.' He just said, 'Thank you. I'll be honest with you.'"
Friedman had assumed Kershaw would return. Their conversations
revealed Kershaw's restlessness. "Shortly thereafter," Friedman told
me, "I thought Texas was much more of a real possibility."

Before he returned to Highland Park, Kershaw underwent another
MRI. He still thought he wouldn't need surgery. He expected to rehab
for a few months, resume throwing in January, and sign with either the
Dodgers or the Rangers. "But that was not the order of events," he said.
The examination revealed extensive damage to the shoulder capsule
and surrounding area. Kershaw consulted a handful of doctors, including Dodgers team physician Neal ElAttrache, Rangers team physician
Keith Meister, and Mets medical director David Altchek. "I asked Dr.
Meister, 'If this was Joe Schmo and you saw this MRI, what would you
tell the team?'" Kershaw said. "And he was like, 'I would not sign this
guy.' ElAttrache said the same thing, basically." Altchek hit the same

note: "He was like, 'Yeah, you need to fix it.'" At best, the doctors told him, his shoulder could last a few more months before it fell apart.

Kershaw considered asking Chris Young for advice. Young had undergone capsule surgery in 2011. But Kershaw worried it would be inappropriate to contact his friend so close to free agency. While the Rangers were still alive in the postseason, Kershaw drafted a text to Michael Young, a former teammate and Rangers advisor, in hopes of getting a message to Chris Young, but deleted the message before sending it. A. J. Ellis suggested Kershaw undertake something resembling a darkness retreat—or at least extended time away from his phone. "He told me I should go away for forty-eight hours and just sit there," Kershaw said. For once, he did not take his old catcher's advice.

The three-pronged crossroads had become a thornier proposition. Kershaw needed to consider the depth of his reasons and motivations. His children were not clamoring for him to stop playing. "I think that they would be devastated if he decided to retire," Ellen said. He acknowledged the stress, the preparation, and the pain of the fifth day, but felt it had not become too much to bear. If anything, the misery of 2023 crystallized his commitment. He could not have endured a season like that otherwise. He was not ready to buy the RV and tour the country. He was not ready to become an elementary school crossing guard. He told ElAttrache he would undergo shoulder surgery, the first procedure of his life, in order to pitch again. "This is what I know, man," he told me. "This is it. I do love pitching. I do love baseball. And it is hard at times, but I don't think I'd want it to be any other way. I don't want it to be easy."

"Do we still want to do this?" Ellen asked at one point. "Are we still in it?"

"I still love it," Kershaw told her.

He was trying to express himself more, trying to lose his stiff upper lip. Kershaw and Ellen attended a seminar at their church. The speaker was talking about how to raise well-adjusted children. The two most vital qualities for parents, Kershaw heard, was how they treated each other as spouses and how they spoke about their feelings. Kershaw considered his relationship with Ellen to be strong. The second component tripped him up. "I have feelings," Kershaw said. "But I don't know how to talk about them."

Ellen asked him to be vulnerable. So he tried. He told her about struggling to pray, about feeling like an imposter in his faith. Ellen replied that she sometimes felt the same way. "Everyone who says that they follow Jesus can feel like an imposter because you're not always going to get it right," Ellen said. She counseled him to keep praying, even if his prayers felt insignificant. "What I have challenged Clayton with is that God has the capacity for all of the prayer requests," she said. It was okay if he was praying for his shoulder to heal. She wanted him to feel "more comfortable with approaching God for even the small things," she said. "It kind of goes to a bigger part of who Clayton is. He doesn't ever ask for things. He can't even ask a teammate for a ride to the field without feeling like he owes something in return." The feeling stemmed back to his upbringing, when his mother borrowed money from the parents of his friends. He believed debts needed to be repaid. Ellen reminded him not everything needed to feel like a debt.

While plotting the path beyond surgery, Ellen asked Kershaw what he wanted. Not what he thought was right, not what he felt was best for the family—what *he* wanted. As Kershaw pondered, he recognized his isolation on the Dodgers in 2023. "I thought I didn't have a lot of fun because my shoulder hurt every day," Kershaw said. "I didn't look forward to playing catch. I didn't look forward to working out. I didn't look forward to all the stuff I used to look forward to. And that's true, and obviously a huge weight. But I didn't love the group. They were all great, and I had fun with them. But if you're like, 'Hey, who do you want to go to dinner with?' I had Barnesy, and then . . . Possum. That was it." Ellen's sister, Ann, reminded them that they would miss Los Angeles whenever they left, whether it was now or when Kershaw retired. The novelty of a new team held more appeal than ever. "There's a fine line between routine and boredom," Ellen said. He needed fifty-six strikeouts to surpass three thousand, something only nineteen other pitchers had accomplished. That milestone meant less to him than the chance to redeem himself in October. "I don't care about three thousand strikeouts," Kershaw said. "It would be cool, I guess, but I don't really care. I need to pitch in the postseason better, to end it. I need to do that better, for my sanity. Just to help the team win. Because I've done it. I can do it. But I was so bad this year, that I need to do it again."

As he itemized his desires, the Rangers made more and more sense. He could wake up at home and ready the children for school. He could bring Cali and Charley lunch. In the afternoon, Charley could join batting practice at Globe Life Field. "That," he said, "sounds pretty awesome." He would be home often enough to debrief with the kids before bed. He could shrink the gap between his family and his profession. "I keep waking up and thinking, 'Am I going to have a change of heart?'" Kershaw told me in October 2023. "But it feels like the right thing to do."

On October 31, Kershaw stuffed himself into a Captain America costume as the kids scampered through Highland Park for Halloween. Cali chose to be a sparkle witch. Charley wore a wig as George Washington and acquired so much candy he required a bucket rather than a bag. Cooper was a shark and Chance was a cow. Two days later, the family flew to Los Angeles. ElAttrache operated on Kershaw's shoulder on November 3. Kershaw slept at ElAttrache's home the night after the procedure. He didn't last long in a sling. When Charley asked to play catch, Kershaw used his right arm. By November, he was telling friends he could raise his left arm level with his chest. By December, he felt a return in the summer of 2024 was possible.

Yet as January arrived, Kershaw remained unsigned. After winning the World Series against Arizona, the Rangers were less aggressive in pursuing him than in the past. Texas officials harbored concerns about the health of his shoulder, while dealing with a budget crunch related to their imploding television contract. As usual, Friedman granted

Kershaw space. He sensed that Kershaw's desire for a new beginning—which I also had heard Kershaw express in those unvarnished moments before the World Series, when the pain and frustration of 2023 was still so fresh—was fading. Around Christmas, I traded messages with a Dodgers staffer who admired Kershaw. "Hopefully," the staffer said, "the big guy comes home." The Dodgers were patient with Kershaw but aggressive elsewhere. The team reeled in Ohtani with a history-making ten-year, $700 million contract that reset the franchise's financial outlook. As part of their pitch, Ohtani revealed at his introductory press conference, Dodgers officials had admitted they viewed the first ten years of Guggenheim's ownership—a period in which Kershaw led the club to three World Series and a championship in 2020—as a failure. That appealed to Ohtani's sensibilities. In an unprecedented move, Ohtani offered to defer $680 million of the money until decades later, which effectively served as a loan the team used to land Yamamoto with a twelve-year, $325 million deal. As a bonus, the team traded for Tampa Bay pitcher Tyler Glasnow and signed him to a four-year, $110 million extension. Glasnow, a talented but fragile pitcher, threw a career-high 120 innings in 2023, fewer than Kershaw logged with his wrecked shoulder.

All of a sudden, the Dodgers looked like a superteam again. Only one person was missing. When the Rangers got cold feet, the Dodgers pounced. "The recruiting pitch was just trusting me and letting me figure it out on my own," Kershaw told me. In January, Friedman approached Kershaw with a contract customized for the pitcher's desires. It was a one-year deal that guaranteed $10 million, which included a player option for 2025 and a variety of incentives: Kershaw would not have to report to spring training until March; he could split his time between Highland Park and Los Angeles while he rehabbed; and if he regained his health before summer's end, he could do what he had been doing for the previous sixteen years in Los Angeles. So in late January, shortly after agreeing to the new deal, he picked up a baseball with his surgically repaired left arm and started throwing. It did not feel great. He would not have it any other way. The possibility of another championship beckoned. And so the cycle loomed.

For more than twenty years, from his boyhood to the grandest stage in baseball, Clayton Kershaw gave nothing short of everything to his franchise, his teammates, and his craft. He lived within a cycle that sustained him and tormented him and provided him unimaginable riches. What mattered most to him was the life he had built, the life he was living before Game 1 of the 2023 World Series, a week before his surgery. "I do nothing. I do everything," he said. "Every day is not planned. But then I look at this schedule thing that Ellen has . . ." He opened his iPhone and checked his daily tasks. He was the designated "ringleader," he explained, for procuring artificial turf for the elementary school, "so when it rains, we don't have games cancelled." Cali had volleyball games. Charley's basketball season was starting up soon, and Kershaw was coaching the team again. His immediate future included lunch with Tolleson, his friend for more than twenty years.

"You look at him, and you look at his career, at face value, here you have a guy who literally has everything," friend and former teammate Josh Lindblom said. "Everything you could ever want in a career. But the most important stuff to him is the little stuff that you would never think about. Having the same friends from high school. Being able to be there for your kid's first day of school. Those are the things that mean the most to him. It's not the Cy Youngs. It's not the MVP. As important as that World Series is to him, it's not that. It's all of the other little stuff that you might gloss over.

"On the outside looking in, where you're like, 'Why would he care about that?' Well, he cares about it because he's Clayton. That's why."

*   *   *

On the night before Santa Claus visited Highland Park, back in the winter of 2022, before Clayton Kershaw wrecked his arm and considered leaving Los Angeles, I drove by his home. The schoolyard was dark. The streets were empty. As I rolled past his lawn, I saw a pair of pint-sized kids bouncing on a trampoline. Outside the protective netting, illuminated by the Christmas lights, stood their dad.

Someday Clayton Kershaw's career will end. His life will not. He will continue on, as a husband, as a father, as a man. He will have to work at it with all his heart.

ACKNOWLEDGMENTS

The sun was descending beyond the left-field wall at Dodger Stadium as Clayton Kershaw walked alone out of the bullpen on the third day of June in 2022. I was waiting for Kershaw as he approached the dugout. Earlier in the week, I sent him a message that I was coming to Los Angeles from New York. I wanted to tell him about this project, which I hoped would serve as the definitive work about his time as a Dodger. It would explain his outsized importance to those around him. It would chart his rituals of October heartbreak and the relief of his first World Series championship in 2020. And the book would, I continued, be much better if he decided to participate.

Kershaw did not require much persuasion. He agreed to sit down with me after the season ended. The offer came with a caveat.

"You know I'm not great at talking about myself, or in general," he said. "It's going to be up to you to make me talk."

"I'm going to ask great questions," I said.

Kershaw fulfilled his end of the bargain; readers can decide if I fulfilled mine. Both Kershaw and his wife, Ellen, were generous with their time during the course of reporting this book. My first round of thanks goes to them—and members of the extended Kershaw/Melson family, like Jim Melson and Ann Higginbottom—for their cooperation with the project. The book is much richer because of it. A. J. Ellis also invited me to his home in Wisconsin, which provided another vital addition to the work. I spoke with 215 people for this book, many of them on more than one occasion. This book exists because of their answers.

But it also exists because of the work that came before it. Molly Knight's *The Best Team Money Can Buy* is the definitive account of the early years of Guggenheim's tenure running the Dodgers. Pedro Moura's *How to Beat a Broken Game* is the definitive account of Andrew Friedman's time at the helm in Los Angeles. Both provided invaluable insight into Kershaw. Rereading those books for this project was a pleasure. To chart the early years of Kershaw's career, I relied upon the stories of Tim MacMahon, Ken Gurnick, Tony Jackson, Diamond Leung, and Dylan Hernández. The research of Joshua Benton was essential for understanding Highland Park.

My thanks to the Dodgers media-relations department, specifically the duo of Juan Dorado and Joe Jareck. Lon Rosen and Cary Osborne assisted me in procuring photos for this book. Steve Brener got me a sit-down with Sandy Koufax, who does not exactly do regular media availabilities. John Blundell did yeoman's work setting up an interview with Joe Torre. Mark Bowman provided so many phone numbers that he referred to himself as "Your Goddamn Rolodex." Dan Greene connected me with the manager for my favorite band, The Wonder Years, who were gracious enough to let me use their lyrics for the epigraph.

My employers at the *Athletic* encouraged me to take on this project, for which I am so appreciative. So thank you to Paul Fichtenbaum, Sarah Goldstein, Chris Strauss, Dan Barbarisi, and, incredibly, Marc Carig. And thank you to my cat, Harry the Cat, for waking me up every day at 4 A.M., which allowed me to write this book without it affecting my day job.

I have so many friends to thank, but two deserve special mention. Howard Bryant is an inspiration; I'm pretty sure the first sentence I ever spoke to him was something like, "Hi, I've read all your books." I remain amazed he picks up the phone when I call. He provided a crucial piece of advice as I entered the weeds of this project: "Is this your first book? Oh, then don't worry about it. It's not going to be very good. Just write it." I did my best. Tim Brown is my equivalent of Rick Honeycutt. Not to get too mushy about it, but I am eternally grateful he is in my corner. He shepherded me through this process. When I first mentioned I was interested in writing a book, he didn't hesitate. "You need to talk to David Black," Tim said.

I am still not really sure why David took me on as a client, but I am quite lucky he did. He schooled me on the intricacies of turning a book idea into a book proposal, then served as a tireless, relentless advocate for me while trying to turn it into a book. David directed this project into the guidance of Brant Rumble and the team of Hachette. Working with Brant has been an honor; he edited some of the books that tricked me into becoming a writer. He fielded countless phone calls from me and never lost his preternatural calm; he's the only person I know who can casually reference attending a Matador Records release party and espouse the need for the Atlanta Braves to acquire Dylan Cease.

I wouldn't have written this book if I never covered the Dodgers. When the *Los Angeles Times* approached me in the fall of 2015, Dylan Hernández gave me a call. "Please take this job," he said. "I can't do this anymore." It was daunting to follow him after eight years on the Dodgers beat. He stood beside me then as he stood beside me during this process, as he stood beside me as a groomsman at my wedding last year—by needling the everliving shit out of me and reminding me to always stay humble. Covering the Dodgers for the *Times* represents the highlight of my career. I am forever indebted to Angel Rodriguez and Mike Hiserman for the opportunity. It was an honor to appear in the same pages as Bill Plaschke, Bill Shaikin, Mike DiGiovanna, Pedro Moura, Jorge Castillo, and, when he managed to hit deadline, Dylan.

During my time in Los Angeles, I benefited from the competition and camaraderie of Ken Gurnick, Bill Plunkett, Eric Stephen, Pedro Moura, Doug Padilla, Alanna Rizzo, J. P. Hoornstra, and, of course, David Vassegh. Vassegh, to me, represents the thumping heart of the Dodgers beat. His friendship—not to mention all his contacts throughout several decades of Dodgers baseball—has been invaluable. The beat remains strong. Throughout this process I leaned on stories from Plunk, Eric, Fabian Ardaya, Jack Harris, and Juan Toribio. Plunk was kind enough to decline comment for this book, other than to say, "Go with that."

My thanks to the friends who took the time to read the book as I was writing it: Joel Sherman, Tim Brown, Marc Carig, Lindsey Adler, Adam Kilgore, and Nick Piecoro. Joel turned his wizened eye to these pages and made them better. The Piecoro family—Nick, Zaida, Frankie, Squash, Ruby, Sideeye, and even Little Miss Business—were kind enough to let me stay with them in Phoenix while doing some reporting. My friends Jorge Arangure, Marc Carig, Joe Lemire, Nick Piecoro, and James Wagner provided endless support and occasional ball-busting. The Chain is a 1, for me. The trio of J. T. Horowitz, Matt Weasen, and Phil Yanofsky tolerated my gradual descent into Becoming a Dave Matthews Guy at thirty-six.

My thanks to all the friends for their encouragement, patience, and advice: Rustin Dodd, Pedro Moura, Andy Martino, Jake Mintz, Tania Ganguli, Chris de Laubenfels, Anthony DiComo, Dave Lennon, Ken Rosenthal, Evan Drellich, Jorge Castillo, Chelsea Janes, Dr. Caroline Matas, LeAire Wilson, Dave Sheinin, Barry Svrluga, Jesse Sanchez, Jim Sanders, Michael Rosenberg, Erin Rosenberg, Alden González, Jeff Passan, Ben Nieto, Brett Teal, Sam McDowell, Sam Mellinger, Brendan Kuty, Tyler Kepner, Ian O'Connor, John Clayton, Jaimie Clayton, Rob Gilbert, Mary Marolla, Jeff Peters, Theresa Hubbard, Matt Higgins, Leah Higgins, Kyle Kwiatkowski, Kate Kwiatkowski, Meghan Overdeep, Will Edwards, Alec Saslow, and Isa Saslow.

If I listed all of my family members, Hachette might run out of ink, so thank you to the McCulloughs and the Desches. My mom, Maryann McCullough Nikander, has tolerated my bullshit for my entire life; her capacity for generosity and kindness is unparalleled. Thank you to Tim Nikander, Tom McCullough, Alex McCullough, Lizzie Kerchner, Brian Kerchner, Michele Foust, Andrew Foust, David Nikander, Jasmine Bedoya, and Laura Nikander. And thank you to Michael Apstein, Dee McMeekan, Marissa Apstein, and Gus Christensen.

I dedicated this book to my Ganny, Elizabeth McCullough, who fostered my love of reading at a young age. She died in December of 2023. The most rewarding part of this process was getting to present her with a copy of the manuscript a few months before that. Ganny and my grandfather, Bob McCullough, were the first people to read this book.

My wife, Stephanie Apstein, wrote the best story I've ever read about Clayton Kershaw. The story ran in *Sports Illustrated* in 2018, before we were dating, so I was mostly just mad about it. Revisiting it while writing this book was incredibly helpful. Her aid with this book—and, really, in my life—goes far beyond any single story. Steph devoted countless hours to reading these chapters, and even more hours listening to me kvetch about the process. She is a preposterously kind person and an ideal partner. This work could not exist without her. Then again, neither could I.

NOTES ON SOURCES

I interviewed 215 people for this book, several of them on multiple occasions. I also leaned on my coverage of Clayton Kershaw and the Dodgers dating back to 2016, for both the *Los Angeles Times* and the *Athletic*. Those stories are cited here, in addition to other sources referenced in the text.

CHAPTER 1. THE FIFTH DAY

One day when he was a boy: Alan Matthews, "Kershaw could cash in on strong senior year," *Baseball America*, May 22–June 4, 2006.

CHAPTER 2. HOME LIFE

One night in 1985, the story goes: Russ Pate, "Sittin' in," *Adweek Southwest*, October 14, 1985.

His father, George Clayton Kershaw, met his mother, Alice Irene Evans: "George Kershaw obituary," *Dallas Morning News*, November 2, 2006.

The 1967 yearbook described him: Marksmen Yearbook, 1967, 69.

His term running the school's closed-circuit radio-TV station: Marksmen Yearbook, 1967, 218.

He wrote spots for Coors: Lisa Paikowski, "Southwest MVPs: Zimmersmith duo Zimmers, Kershaw," *Adweek*, February 1, 1988.

He composed an anti-littering song: "Texan makes anti-litter notes," *Abilene Reporter-News,* February 9, 1986.

and another for the Texas Tourist Development Agency: Gary Gerdemann, "On the set," *Adweek Southwest,* September 9, 1985.

An exhibition at Texas Christian University: "TCU to present graphic designers' works," *Fort Worth Star-Telegram,* November 14, 1983.

congratulated them on their nuptials: "Wedded bliss," *Adweek Southwest,* October 5, 1987.

They celebrated victories by head-banging: Clayton Kershaw, Ellen Kershaw, *Arise* (Ventura, CA: Regal, 2011), 30.

he wrote a book report about Sandy Koufax: Hugh Bernreuter, "Loons' Kershaw fits the mold," *Saginaw News,* April 17, 2007.

He helped the fourth-graders at Bradfield Elementary: Al Carter, "Bradfield Elementary: track champions," *Dallas Morning News,* June 1, 1998.

CHAPTER 3. THE BOY IN THE BUBBLE

Texas Monthly outlined the architectural grandeur: Dana Rubin, "What I learned in the Bubble," *Texas Monthly,* January 1994.

a place known for "street after street of Gatsbyesque mansions": Lawrence Wright, "The astonishing transformation of Austin," *New Yorker,* February 6, 2023.

A Dallas Independent School District official used different language: Eric Celeste, "The single biggest problem in Dallas," *D Magazine,* March 28, 2018.

The district benefited from wealth accumulation: Dana Rubin, "What I learned in the Bubble."

The town also used the slogan: James M. Loewen, *Sundown Towns* (New York: New Press, 2018), 120.

Highland Park partnered with University Park: Loewen, *Sundown Towns,* 113.

The district restricted nonresidents: Loewen, *Sundown Towns,* 256.

Only small pockets on the outskirts: Richard M. Kahlenburg, "Zoned out in Texas: How one mother overcame Dallas's discriminatory housing laws," Century Foundation, January 12, 2022.

After the Brown decision: Loewen, *Sundown Towns,* 171.

A Black student did not attend: Chris Sadeghi, "Black History: Meet the man who broke Highland Park IDS's color barrier," WFAA.com, February 5, 2021.

In 2003, the community newspaper . . . caused a national stir: Mark Miller, "American postcard: At last," *Newsweek,* June 3, 2003.

It was shocking, admitted Hearn: Levi Weaver, "'It'll take everybody': What MLB Players' Alliance is accomplishing, what's next," *Athletic,* January 9, 2021.

When Oprah Winfrey visited Africa: Kershaw, Kershaw, *Arise,* 25.

The extended family once rented a bus: Kershaw, Kershaw, *Arise,* 96.

a wunderkind who had been flinging seventy-yard spirals: Gary Klein, "Matthew Stafford's hometown buddies realized new Rams QB was 'the bomb' in sixth grade," *Los Angeles Times,* March 17, 2021.

It was not a choice made lightly at a school like Highland Park: Gary Klein, "'I was short and chunky': Clayton Kershaw's one year as Matthew Stafford's snapper," *Los Angeles Times,* March 17, 2021.

The first inklings of his faith stemmed from curiosity: Kershaw, Kershaw, *Arise,* 42.

He viewed God as a great but distant king: Kershaw, Kershaw, *Arise,* 43.

Ellen found her faith had deepened: Kershaw, Kershaw, *Arise,* 49.

CHAPTER 4. TEAM USA

When he surfaced at a Texas Christian University showcase: Brandon George, "Sizzling summer: Mansfield pitcher's prospects skyrocket after 99 mph toss," *Dallas Morning News,* February 16, 2006.

Dawson was one of the more decorated high school coaches in America: Richard Obert, "The heart of Firebird baseball: Field named for Dawson," *Arizona Republic,* April 7, 2003.

CHAPTER 5. 1-2-3

In December, Baseball America *published a list:* Will Kimmey and Alan Matthews, "Head of the class," *Baseball America,* December 5–18, 2005.

CHAPTER 6. SENIOR YEAR

A preseason story in the Dallas Morning News*:* Tim MacMahon, "Highland Park: Left-hander could set team record for wins," *Dallas Morning News*, February 16, 2006.

He once told a reporter he started working in the fourth grade: Bryce Miller, "Painful childhood helped shape critical Padres cog Logan White," *San Diego Union-Tribune*, March 24, 2019.

White gambled that negotiations could bridge the divide: Steve Henson, "Dodgers report: Rights may be lost to first draft pick," *Los Angeles Times*, August 24, 2005.

After months without progress, Hochevar fired Boras: Tim Brown, "Dodgers No. 1 pick throws a changeup," *Los Angeles Times*, September 9, 2005.

"Do I feel the talent is worth the asking price?": Bill Shaikin, "Dodgers report: Team is a policy dispute," *Los Angeles Times*, May 23, 2006.

To soothe himself, he repeated a passage: Kershaw, Kershaw, *Arise*, 84.

He was at a friend's house: Jim Callis, "Draft dish: Hard-throwing Kershaw leaps to front of lackluster high school draft class," *Baseball America*, May 8–21, 2006.

Twenty-five scouts attended his first scrimmage: David Hinojosa, "Sitting on a pitch: Tolleson won't make decision about career path until after draft," *Dallas Morning News*, February 16, 2006.

He blasted the ball beyond the 364-foot sign: Tim MacMahon, "Kershaw, HP good enough," *Dallas Morning News*, May 26, 2006.

Kershaw felt humbled: Kershaw, Kershaw, *Arise*, 68.

CHAPTER 7. THE DRAFT

When Kershaw heard the news: Tim MacMahon, "HP's Kershaw goes to Dodgers as No. 7 pick," *Dallas Morning News*, June 7, 2006.

"There among palms, palmettos, scrub pines, and swamp": Roger Kahn, *The Boys of Summer* (New York: HarperCollins, 1971), 94.

Rachel Robinson, Jackie's wife, told Kahn: Kahn, *The Boys of Summer*, 403.

Kahn once asked pitcher Joe Black: Kahn, *The Boys of Summer*, 112.

He wanted to reach the majors by his twenty-first birthday: Ramona Shelburne, "Settling in: Kershaw has gone from hot prospect to mainstay of the Dodgers' rotation," *Daily News of Los Angeles*, January 27, 2009.

CHAPTER 8. THE BRIDGE

Like White, he damaged his arm: Ken Sickenger, "Baseball life for them: Topes pitching coach Dishman and wife love their 'diamond' style," *Albuquerque Journal,* July 4, 2012.

When pitcher Steve Johnson's mother visited: Andy McCullough, "A portrait of Clayton Kershaw, in 22 frames," *Athletic,* October 13, 2020.

Teammates called them Chappie and Gus: Tyler Kepner, "Dodgers catcher A.J. Ellis's long climb to success," *New York Times,* March 16, 2013.

The Dodgers hosted the defending World Series champion: Tony Jackson, "Dodgers notebook: Kershaw is impressive; Dodgers 4, Boston 0," *Daily News of Los Angeles,* March 10, 2008.

Torre sauntered over: Tony Jackson, "Dodgers notebook: Billingsley now efficient artist," *Daily News of Los Angeles,* February 28, 2008.

He knew how to celebrate his achievement: Tony Jackson, "Dodgers notebook: Kershaw is impressive; Dodgers 4, Boston 0."

CHAPTER 9.
THE SHADOW OF SANFORD

"Have you ever seen Sandy's hands wrapped around a baseball?": Andy McCullough, "Kershaw on Koufax, Buehler on Pedro, more: Ross Stripling's new podcast gets 'current guys to talk about the best ever,'" *Athletic,* April 12, 2021.

"You're praying he's Koufax": Diamond Leung, "Opposite numbers," *Press-Enterprise,* February 27, 2008.

"Good luck," Koufax told him: Hugh Bernreuter, "Loons' Kershaw fits the mold."

the Dodgers did not want him to exceed 170 in 2008: Dylan Hernández, "Kershaw's labors aren't fruitful," *Los Angeles Times,* June 5, 2008.

When the Suns auctioned the players' pink jerseys: Jeff Elliott, "Southern League Notebook; Dodgers call up Suns ace Kershaw," *Florida Times-Union,* May 25, 2008.

Jazzed about his opportunity: Kershaw, Kershaw, *Arise,* 128.

After a while, he called Ellen: Kershaw, Kershaw, *Arise,* 132.

He said a few words, which he would repeat: Kershaw, Kershaw, *Arise,* 133.

"Can I have the ball back?": Kershaw, Kershaw, *Arise,* 134.

"This is a dream come true": Kevin Pearson, "Dodgers rookie shines as LA pulls it out in 10," *Press-Enterprise,* May 26, 2008.

Sweeney told Kershaw how much the number meant to him: Tony Jackson, "Dodgers notebook: Torre recalls other N.Y. job," *Daily News of Los Angeles.* May 30, 2008.

rookie reliever Cory Wade had to haul a bag of candy: Tony Jackson, "Prospect Wading in the wings," *Daily News of Los Angeles,* June 10, 2008.

A learning experience, he called it: Diamond Leung, "Dodgers discover answer in Park," *Press-Enterprise,* May 31, 2008.

Kershaw told reporters he never set foot in the casinos: Matt Calkins, "Kershaw, LA get well at home," *Press-Enterprise,* September 3, 2008.

"Just one of those things": Bill Shakin, "Dodgers can't get right, er left, matchup needed," *Los Angeles Times,* October 14, 2008.

If he fell behind a batter: Jane Leavy, *Sandy Koufax: A Lefty's Legacy* (New York, HarperCollins, 2002), 86.

CHAPTER 10. HOOKING THE SEAM

the famed catapult that delivered his fastball: Leavy, *Sandy Koufax: A Lefty's Legacy,* 5.

He purchased a Ping-Pong table: Ramona Shelburne, "Settling in: Kershaw has gone from hot prospect to mainstay of the Dodgers' rotation."

Searching for a haircut that summer: T. J. Simers, "Dodgers' Kershaw might be left-hander but is right on," *Los Angeles Times,* July 19, 2009.

Borzello was driving a truck: Dave Desmond, "From the bushes to Yankee bullpen," *Los Angeles Times,* August 21, 1997.

He spoke his mind: Patrick Mooney, "The secret weapon behind the rise of the Cubs," *NBC Sports Chicago,* March 13, 2017.

CHAPTER 11. THE PROPER BALANCE FOR EVERYTHING

After the Dodgers were eliminated in 2008: Bill Plaschke, "Dodgers chased into off-season amid chorus of boos from fans," *Los Angeles Times,* October 16, 2008.

Around 1 a.m. on May 7: Ned Colletti, *The Big Chair* (New York, Putnam, 2017), 210.

Ramírez blamed medication: Dylan Hernández, "Manny Ramirez suspended 50 games for positive drug test," *Los Angeles Times,* May 8, 2009.

"It's a dark day for baseball, and certainly for this organization": "Sources: Ramirez used fertility drug," ESPN.com, May 7, 2009.

He was too young to take the blame for the loss: Bill Plaschke, "Torre should have stepped up a lot sooner," *Los Angeles Times,* October 16, 2009.

"I'm trying to see all these bumps": Kershaw, Kershaw, *Arise,* 152.

"Those experiences . . . keep my competitive heart humble": Kershaw, Kershaw, *Arise,* 153.

an "engineering marvel": Tom Verducci, "How Tiny Tim became a pitching Giant," *Sports Illustrated,* July 7, 2008.

The bride wore a strapless gown of silk taffeta: "Ellen Melson & Clayton Kershaw: Wedding," *Park Cities People,* March 11, 2011.

He stuffed a padded mat onto the plane: Karen Crouse, "In Africa, lessons on passion and perspective for Kershaw," *New York Times,* February 26, 2011.

Some gawked at Kershaw: Kershaw, Kershaw, *Arise,* 62.

He felt moved as he listened: Kershaw, Kershaw, *Arise,* 183.

his plight offered a "sobering reminder": Ian Lovett, "Dodger Stadium beating highlights fans' unease," *New York Times,* April 9, 2011.

McCourt needed a $30 million loan: Bill Shaikin, "Frank McCourt gets $30-million loan to meet Dodgers payroll," *Los Angeles Times,* April 16, 2011.

"deep concerns regarding the finances and operations of the Dodgers": Bill Shaikin, David Wharton, "Major League Baseball seizes control of Dodgers," *Los Angeles Times,* April 21, 2011.

The snub looked worse: Mark Fainaru-Wada, T. J. Quinn, "Ryan Braun tests positive for P.E.D.," ESPN.com, December 10, 2011.

At the Dodger Stadium ceremony: Dylan Hernández, "Kershaw joins the elite group of Dodgers to win the Cy Young, easily outdistancing Phillies' Halladay and Lee," *Los Angeles Times,* November 18, 2011.

CHAPTER 12. DEUS EX GUGGENHEIM

christened him "penniless Frank McCourt": T. J. Simers, "McCourt needs a GM with the write stuff," *Los Angeles Times,* January 28, 2004.

"No matter what I said": Colletti, *The Big Chair,* 188.

An examination of Jamie's divorce petition: Bill Shaikin, "Dodgers' owner-ship at stake in McCourt fight," *Los Angeles Times,* October 28, 2009.

They accumulated real estate: Vanessa Grigoriadis, "A Major-League Divorce," *Vanity Fair,* June 13, 2011.

His presence on the payroll was hidden: Bill Shaikin, "Dodgers tap into 'V energy,'" *Los Angeles Times,* June 10, 2010.

The fallout featured a memorable exchange: Dylan Hernández, "Dodgers noncommittal about role of Vladimir Shpunt," *Los Angeles Times,* June 13, 2010.

At one point, McCourt called Selig: Tony Jackson, "Frank McCourt blasts Bud Selig, MLB," ESPN.com, April 27, 2011.

MLB later accused McCourt: Bill Shaikin, "MLB accuses Frank McCourt of 'looting' $189 million from Dodgers," *Los Angeles Times,* October 25, 2011.

Colletti loathed sitting down in McCourt's office: Colletti, *The Big Chair,* 126.

McCourt scotched a potential trade in 2008: Colletti, *The Big Chair,* 182.

Walter met McCourt in a Manhattan hotel conference room: Molly Knight, *The Best Team Money Can Buy* (New York: Simon & Schuster, 2015), 32.

When Kasten took over, he encouraged Colletti: Colletti, *The Big Chair,* 259.

Hernández had written a story: Dylan Hernández, "Dodgers' Clayton Kershaw reportedly may miss start of next season," *Los Angeles Times,* September 17, 2012.

When he saw a group of reporters: Dylan Hernández, "Kershaw sees surgeon but details are sparse," *Los Angeles Times,* September 19, 2012.

CHAPTER 13. THE FIRST SUMMIT

A 7 a.m. alarm jolted: Knight, *The Best Team Money Can Buy,* 61.

During batting practice, Ned Colletti led: Knight, *The Best Team Money Can Buy,* 79.

all the losing prompted potshots: Dylan Hernández, "Two more in wave of Dodgers losses," *Los Angeles Times,* April 21, 2013.

The lame-duck status annoyed him: Knight, *The Best Team Money Can Buy,* 235.

The story bugged Kershaw: Dylan Hernández, "Clayton Kershaw upset about report on contract talks with Dodgers," *Los Angeles Times,* June 16, 2013.

He flouted team rules about tardiness: Andy McCullough, "Yasiel Puig left behind a complicated Dodgers legacy," *Los Angeles Times,* April 14, 2019.
"Winning does a lot": Knight, *The Best Team Money Can Buy,* 178.
Kershaw splashed and smiled: Bill Shaikin, "Sen. John McCain throws a damper on Dodgers' pool party," *Los Angeles Times,* September 20, 2013.
In the early 1970s: Rany Jazayerli, "Doctoring the numbers: The five-man rotation," *Baseball Prospectus,* August 13, 2002.
During the raucous celebration: Beth Harris, "Dodgers move on in playoffs," Associated Press, October 8, 2013.
The franchise maintained regional hegemony: David Waldstein, "Trying to outrun the Cardinals' long reach," *New York Times,* October 29, 2013.
As a boy growing up in Corona: Pedro Moura, "The triumph of Joe Kelly and the childhood pain he overcame," *Athletic,* February 27, 2019.
The outcome left the team "shell-shocked": Bill Plaschke, "Numb kind of ending for Dodgers," *Los Angeles Times,* October 19, 2013.

CHAPTER 14. "PLAYOFF CLAYTON"

That January, Kershaw flew from a private function: Knight, *The Best Team Money Can Buy,* 7.
Consternation about the trip was apparent: Mark Saxon, "Officials upset at Zack Greinke," ESPN.com, February 23, 2014.
He rattled it off to ESPN: Buster Olney, "Creative Control," ESPN.com, March 20, 2014.
By his twenty-seventh throw: Knight, *The Best Team Money Can Buy,* 246.
He emphasized the point by bouncing a ball off the wall: Kevin Baxter, "Kershaw is back, Dodgers benefit," *Los Angeles Times,* May 7, 2014.
Inside the office, the doctor showed an ultrasound: Wright Thompson, "As Clayton Kershaw waits for baseball to return, a look at his family, legacy and future," ESPN.com, April 15, 2020.
Kershaw held the game ball: SportsNet LA, "Ellen Kershaw's no-hitter memories," https://www.youtube.com/watch?v=t54GfLcPo5U, July 6, 2019.
Puig, in particular, drove him to distraction: Colletti, *The Big Chair,* 194.
The day before Game 1, Kershaw fielded questions: Barry M. Bloom, "Kershaw not dwelling on last October start vs. Cardinals," MLB.com, October 2, 2014.
"A terrible feeling": Knight, *The Best Team Money Can Buy,* 262.

He leaned against the wall: Barry Svrluga, "As Clayton Kershaw tries to pitch his way to October glory, you just can't look away," *Washington Post,* October 21, 2020.

A left-handed batter had never homered: August Fagerstrom, "Clayton Kershaw's big miss, Matt Adams' big hit," FanGraphs.com, October 8, 2014.

"I can't really put it into words right now": Dylan Hernández, "Kershaw, Dodgers again unable to find the answers against Cardinals," *Los Angeles Times,* October 8, 2014.

Hernández wrote a story about Ellis's future: Dylan Hernández, "Kershaw lobbies for Ellis' return," *Los Angeles Times,* October 9, 2014.

CHAPTER 15. THE ROOSTER

On the flight home from St. Louis: Colletti, *The Big Chair,* 377.

A few days later, Colletti and Stan Kasten: Colletti, *The Big Chair,* 379.

When Friedman called, Zaidi experienced a similar ambivalence: Andy McCullough, "How Farhan Zaidi became one of the most coveted minds in baseball," *Los Angeles Times,* March 30, 2017.

As general manager, he saw himself: Andy McCullough, "Applaud Angels for extending Mike Trout. Now comes the hard part," *Los Angeles Times,* March 19, 2019.

Soon after his arrival, Friedman called to gauge: Knight, *The Best Team Money Can Buy,* 270.

He possessed enough self-confidence: Aaron Gleeman, "Dodgers' new GM Farhan Zaidi has a good sense of humor," NBCSports.com, November 7, 2014.

In June, he lost three starts in a row: Mark Saxon, "Clayton Kershaw says he's never been more frustrated," ESPN.com, June 18, 2015.

Like Kershaw, Greinke was an anxious child: Knight, *The Best Team Money Can Buy,* 106.

Greinke figured there was a 10 percent chance: Michael Hunt, "Greinke man of few words but speaks his mind," *Milwaukee Journal–Sentinel,* February 22, 2011.

He once asked Mike Sweeney: Jeff Passan, "Greinke's redemption and pursuit of perfection," *Yahoo Sports,* April 29, 2009.

In a team meeting, he once chastised the Dodgers: Knight, *The Best Team Money Can Buy,* 201.

The argument was serious enough: Bill Plaschke, "An enraged Kershaw balked, but team made right move to pull him," *Los Angeles Times,* September 25, 2015.

An avid rancher, Bumgarner once referred: Tom Verducci, "2014 Sportsman of the Year: Madison Bumgarner," *Sports Illustrated,* December 9, 2014.

He was a freakish athlete and a bit of a bully: Stephanie Apstein, "Will Mets ace Jacob deGrom get the last laugh?," *Sports Illustrated,* July 29, 2022.

Kershaw suggested his former skipper: William C. Rhoden, "Mets fans had their say. Now, lets play ball," *New York Times,* October 13, 2015.

One held a sign suggesting: Fred Kerber, "'Chase Utley (loves) ISIS': Ruthless Mets fans get creative in hate," *New York Post,* October 12, 2015.

Collins stifled laughter: Mark Saxon, "Clayton Kershaw starting Game 4 for Dodgers on short rest," ESPN.com, October 12, 2015.

CHAPTER 16. BACK PAINS

In one of his first acts as manager: Andy McCullough, "As first spring training approaches, new Dodgers manager Dave Roberts focuses on building unity," *Los Angeles Times,* February 16, 2016.

In early December, Friedman was finalizing: Andy McCullough, "Four years later, do the Dodgers regret letting Zack Greinke leave?," *Athletic,* December 4, 2019.

After one of Kershaw's gems: Andy McCullough, "Clayton Kershaw brilliant once again in 1-0 Dodgers win," *Los Angeles Times,* May 23, 2016.

Then he got a call from Friedman: Andy McCullough, "Dodgers cross fingers, dream about October as Clayton Kershaw returns this weekend," *Los Angeles Times,* September 8, 2016.

Roberts conceded it was: Andy McCullough, "Dodgers ace Clayton Kershaw's return date 'uncertain' after setback," *Los Angeles Times,* July 19, 2016.

Yosuke Nakajima, the massage therapist, believed Kershaw: Andy McCullough, "A portrait of Clayton Kershaw, in 22 frames."

He considered Dodger Stadium the best office in America: Dylan Hernández, "A.J. Ellis and Clayton Kershaw get emotional after catcher is dealt to Phillies," *Los Angeles Times,* August 25, 2016.

The edges of Kershaw's eyes ran red: Andy McCullough, "Reconstructing the Dodgers' 2016 Game 5 NLDS win over Washington," *Los Angeles Times,* October 5, 2017.

The front office felt Kershaw transcended: A. J. Cassavell, "Dodgers going with Kershaw for must-win Game 4," MLB.com, October 10, 2016.

Kershaw struggled to explain his emotions: Andy McCullough, "Dodgers edge Nationals, 6-5, in drama-filled game to force NLDS finale in Washington," *Los Angeles Times,* October 11, 2016.

The next evening, after the Dodgers landed: Andy McCullough, "Reconstructing the Dodgers' 2016 Game 5 NLDS win over Washington."

But when reliever Grant Dayton: Andy McCullough, "Reconstructing the Dodgers' 2016 Game 5 NLDS win over Washington."

As he strode along the left-field line: Andy McCullough, "Reconstructing the Dodgers' 2016 Game 5 NLDS win over Washington."

He sloshed through puddles of bubbly and Budweiser: Andy McCullough, "Reconstructing the Dodgers' 2016 Game 5 NLDS win over Washington."

Kershaw covered his mouth: Andy McCullough, "'We've got this guy.' Dodgers' Clayton Kershaw defies his playoff history in a 1-0 win over the Cubs," *Los Angeles Times,* October 16, 2016.

The crowd started braying Kershaw's name: Andy McCullough, "Clayton Kershaw can't save the Dodgers this time," *Los Angeles Times,* October 22, 2016.

CHAPTER 17. SHATTERED

At the urging of Friedman and Zaidi: Andy McCullough, "Dodgers ace Clayton Kershaw tweaks strategy on the mound," *Los Angeles Times,* July 17, 2017.

As he warmed up for the second inning: Andy McCullough, "Dodgers win, but Clayton Kershaw headed to DL after leaving game," *Los Angeles Times,* July 23, 2017.

A familiar tug-of-war: Andy McCullough, "Clayton Kershaw, at last, can call himself a World Series champion," *Athletic,* October 27, 2020.

When Ross Stripling violated the team's dress code: Andy McCullough, "A portrait of Clayton Kershaw, in 22 frames."

He inspired hyperbole: Andy McCullough, "Getting the best of Yu: Can Padres' Darvish find what he's searching for?," *Athletic,* June 9, 2021.

After the trade was complete: Andy McCullough, "'We got Darvish': How the Dodgers' dramatic trade played out," *Los Angeles Times,* August 1, 2017.

Those who spent time around Darvish: Andy McCullough, "Getting the best of Yu: Can Padres' Darvish find what he's searching for?"

In the celebratory delirium: Andy McCullough, "Dodgers crush Cubs in Game 5 to advance to World Series for first time since 1988," *Los Angeles Times,* October 19, 2017.

Kershaw wore his warmup jacket: Andy McCullough, "Clayton Kershaw's dominance leads Dodgers to 3-1 victory over Astros in Game 1," *Los Angeles Times,* October 24, 2017.

Morrow searched for a reliever with his arsenal: Andy McCullough, "World Series Game 5: An inside look at how a championship slipped away from the Dodgers," *Los Angeles Times,* October 3, 2018.

At Minute Maid Park, Altuve told a teammate: Evan Drellich, *Winning Fixes Everything* (New York: Harper, 2023), 230.

several Astros asked about the prolific Dodgers offense: Jon Weisman, "Andre Ethier had the most to lose from the Astros' scandal, but he is far from bitter," DodgerThoughts.com, February 19, 2020.

For Game 4, Wood decided to change: Andy McCullough, "'We'd heard some whispers of the shady stuff': Alex Wood opens up about pitching in Minute Maid Park in 2017," *Athletic,* December 20, 2019.

He wore the No. 2 in part: Nick Piecoro, "Alex Bregman happy with Astros but 'pissed' Diamondbacks didn't take him No. 1," *Arizona Republic,* September 15, 2018.

Roberts pondered an audacious act: Andy McCullough, "World Series Game 5: An inside look at how a championship slipped away from the Dodgers."

After dominating Game 1: Tom Verducci, "Astros' cheating scandal haunts Clayton Kershaw's memory of 2017 World Series," *Sports Illustrated,* February 20, 2020.

And that wasn't even Barnes's best nickname: Ken Rosenthal, "Forget his old nickname, just call Austin Barnes a World Series star," *Athletic,* October 24, 2020.

In the opposing dugout, at least one Astro: Andy McCullough, "World Series Game 5: An inside look at how a championship slipped away from the Dodgers."

Morrow stumbled out of the dugout: Andy McCullough, "A portrait of Clayton Kershaw, in 22 frames."

Kershaw was still stunned: Andy McCullough, "Astros are one win from World Series title after outslugging Dodgers 13-12 in Game 5," *Los Angeles Times,* October 29, 2017.

Beltrán joined the Fox broadcast: Rustin Dodd, Andy McCullough, "Sign language: The week that shook baseball," *Athletic,* January 17, 2020.

Darvish was despondent: Andy McCullough, "Getting the best of Yu: Can Padres' Darvish find what he's searching for?"

"Maybe one of these days I won't fail": Josh Peter, "Dodgers' Clayton Kershaw vows to press on," *USA Today,* November 2, 2017.

CHAPTER 18. THE ABYSS

On his first day back in Texas: Stephanie Apstein, "The Control Pitcher: As free agency looms, will Clayton Kershaw win it all in L.A.?," *Sports Illustrated,* May 30, 2018.

Two weeks after Game 7: Andy McCullough, "Clayton Kershaw faces a year unlike any other in his Dodgers career," *Los Angeles Times,* March 26, 2018.

The Dodgers did not get that guy: Andy McCullough, "Inside the Dodgers' frustrating, failed bid for two-way sensation Shohei Ohtani," *Los Angeles Times,* March 7, 2018.

Being a Dodger had invigorated Darvish: Dylan Hernández, "Yu Darvish returns to Dodger Stadium with a lot of baggage," *Los Angeles Times,* June 27, 2018.

He worried his children would be hounded: Dylan Hernández, "Yu Darvish returns to Dodger Stadium with a lot of baggage."

Kershaw had met the owner: Andy McCullough, "Clayton Kershaw faces a year unlike any other in his Dodgers career."

One morning that February: Andy McCullough, "Clayton Kershaw faces a year unlike any other in his Dodgers career."

When a reporter asked if he had moved on: Pedro Moura, "Clayton Kershaw looking ahead while absorbing Dodgers' World Series setback," *Athletic,* February 20, 2018.

Kershaw's fastball velocity dipped into the 80s: Mike DiGiovanna, "Dodgers' Clayton Kershaw will have MRI after back tightens in return from arm injury," *Los Angeles Times,* May 31, 2018.

"Who cares?" Jansen harrumphed: Andy McCullough, "Should the Dodgers be concerned about Kenley Jansen's velocity?," *Los Angeles Times,* March 31, 2018.

There was less chatter about whether Kershaw: Andy McCullough, "The Dodgers need to stop living in the past with Clayton Kershaw," *Athletic,* October 15, 2019.

"It might not be a personnel thing": Andy McCullough, "Red Sox silence the Dodgers' offense to claim the World Series championship," *Los Angeles Times,* October 28, 2018.

"I'm looking forward to proving a lot of people wrong": Andy McCullough, "Clayton Kershaw heads into Dodgers' season 'trying to regain some stuff I lost,'" *Los Angeles Times,* February 12, 2019.

It was one of four trips McDaniel made to Highland Park: Andy McCullough, "Clayton Kershaw heads into Dodgers' season 'trying to regain some stuff I lost.'"

The Dodgers possessed, in Friedman's estimation": Andy McCullough, "The Dodgers need to stop living in the past with Clayton Kershaw."

When Rendon matriculated at Rice University: Adam Kilgore, "Nationals top draft pick Anthony Rendon stands wrists and shoulders above his peers," *Washington Post,* July 25, 2011.

"Juan Soto just might be Ted Williams": Jayson Stark, "Yes, Juan Soto at 22 just might be Ted Williams," *Athletic,* March 8, 2021.

Honeycutt . . . told Kershaw that he loved him: Stephanie Apstein, "Clayton Kershaw carries playoff failures into another offseason of broken dreams," *Sports Illustrated,* October 10, 2019.

But he was not sure it had ever hurt this much: Stephanie Apstein, "Clayton Kershaw carries playoff failures into another offseason of broken dreams."

When Daniel Hudson . . . saw Kershaw's interview: Andy McCullough, "A portrait of Clayton Kershaw, in 22 frames."

CHAPTER 19. THE REVOLUTION
IN THE INDUSTRIAL PARK

In a column after Game 5, I ripped the Dodgers: Andy McCullough, "The Dodgers need to stop living in the past with Clayton Kershaw."

In the summer of 2012 . . . a twenty-nine-year-old college dropout: Ben Lindbergh, Travis Sawchik, *The MVP Machine* (New York: Basic Books, 2019), 63.

"When you go watch the video, you can see the hair on your finger": Tyler Kepner, "Velocity school: Where pitchers pay to throw harder," *New York Times,* September 4, 2017.

"You get some of these guys who were undrafted or late-round picks": Andy McCullough, "The 100-pitch metronome: Lance Lynn wants to keep going deep for Rangers," *Athletic,* August 19, 2020.

When Boddy spoke at Vanderbilt in 2015: Pedro Moura, "'He's just a ridiculous human': Walker Buehler is a burgeoning star—and an iconoclast," *Athletic,* May 8, 2018.

To chart Buehler's strength program: Pedro Moura, *How to Beat a Broken Game* (New York: PublicAffairs, 2022), 83.

"If I'm missing up, I aim down": Andy McCullough, "A portrait of Clayton Kershaw, in 22 frames."

The Driveline facility was empty: Moura, *How to Beat a Broken Game,* 35.

CHAPTER 20. SHUT DOWN

In November of 2019, he received a phone call: Drellich, *Winning Fixes Everything,* 279.

"His cachet in the industry": Drellich, *Winning Fixes Everything,* 279.

During that same postseason, before the Astros lost: Jeff Passan, "Sources: Red Sox were warned by Indians about Astros attempting to steal signs and information," *Yahoo Sports,* October 16, 2018.

He agreed to go on the record: Evan Drellich, Ken Rosenthal, "The Astros stole signs electronically in 2017—part of a much broader issue in Major League Baseball," *Athletic,* November 12, 2019.

In one passage, Clayton outlined his shared hope: Kershaw, Kershaw, *Arise,* 75.

MLB announced yearlong suspensions: James Wagner, "Astros manager and G.M. fired over cheating scandal," *New York Times,* January 13, 2020.

A separate investigation . . . into allegations against the 2018 Red Sox: Evan Drellich, Ken Rosenthal, "MLB's sign-stealing controversy broadens: Sources say the Red Sox used video replay room illegally in 2018," *Athletic,* January 7, 2020.

Luhnow insisted he never knew: Ben Pickman, "Former Astros' GM Jeff Luhnow: 'I am not a cheater,'" *Sports Illustrated,* January 13, 2020.

Crane hijacked the event with contradictions: Mike Axisa, "Astros owner Jim Crane says sign-stealing scandal 'didn't impact the game' as team issues public apology," CBSSports.com, February 13, 2020.

"I don't agree with the punishments": Jenna West, "Mike Trout says Astros players should be punished for sign-stealing scandal," *Sports Illustrated,* February 17, 2020.

MLB inspected Dodger Stadium camera wells: Andy Martino, *Cheated* (New York: Doubleday, 2021), 194.

After a frustrating game at Dodger Stadium: Martino, *Cheated,* 201.

MLB investigated the Dodgers after Joc Pederson: Drellich, *Winning Fixes Everything,* 258.

He proceeded to blast Manfred: Andy McCullough, "'Is he that out of touch with our game?' Justin Turner blasts Rob Manfred as sign-stealing anger grows," *Athletic,* February 17, 2020.

Mike Fiers hung a whistle inside his locker: Andy McCullough, "After an offseason of MLB upheaval, the A's have the AL West in sight," *Athletic,* February 21, 2020.

Cody Bellinger accused Altuve of stealing: Molly Knight, "The refreshing honesty of Cody Bellinger's rant about the Astros and MLB," *Athletic,* February 14, 2020.

Carlos Correa defended Altuve: Ken Rosenthal, "Carlos Correa rips Bellinger, passionately defends Altuve and says the Astros deserve their 2017 title," *Athletic,* February 15, 2020.

he admitted he had not changed his signs: Tom Verducci, "Astros' cheating scandal haunts Clayton Kershaw's memory of 2017 World Series."

Andrew Friedman had coveted Betts for years: Andy McCullough, "Andrew Friedman's Dodgers are facing the ultimate test of 'process over results,'" *Athletic,* May 22, 2020.

Friedman and Zaidi made a trade with the Braves: Andy McCullough, "Dodgers' epic quest for a superstar ends with Mookie Betts," *Athletic,* July 22, 2020.

Betts aired some grievances: Stephanie Apstein, "Mookie Betts locks in Dodgers' championship expectations," *Sports Illustrated,* March 6, 2020.

His message was not subtle: Matthew Moreno, "Justin Turner: Dodgers 'love' Mookie Betts issuing challenge in team address," DodgerBlue.com, March 6, 2020.

"I don't know how to compliment him": Stephanie Apstein, "Mookie Betts locks in Dodgers' championship expectations."

"It's got that life at the end": Ken Gurnick, "Spring debut buoys Kershaw: 'It was awesome,'" MLB.com, February 28, 2020.

On his 6:30 a.m. drive to Camelback Ranch: Wright Thompson, "As Clayton Kershaw waits for baseball to return, a look at his family, legacy and future."

Kershaw confronted Pedro Moura: Moura, *How to Beat a Broken Game*, 43.

Kershaw sat glued to the Dodgers clubhouse television: Wright Thompson, "As Clayton Kershaw waits for baseball to return, a look at his family, legacy and future."

Sandy Koufax called: Wright Thompson, "As Clayton Kershaw waits for baseball to return, a look at his family, legacy and future."

When he watched the video, he felt stunned: Andy McCullough, "'We should get together': How Clayton Kershaw, Dodgers decided to speak out," *Athletic,* July 20, 2020.

She suggested Kershaw open the floor: Andy McCullough, "'We should get together': How Clayton Kershaw, Dodgers decided to speak out."

Those efforts matched his own charity work: Andy McCullough, "'We should get together': How Clayton Kershaw, Dodgers decided to speak out."

Kershaw and the others discussed how to proceed: Eric Stephen, "The Dodgers follow Mookie Betts' lead," TrueBlueLA.com, August 27, 2020.

It felt like the beginning of a fortuitous run: Jorge Castillo, "Clayton Kershaw, Dodgers sweep Brewers to advance to NLDS," *Los Angeles Times,* October 1, 2020.

CHAPTER 21. THE PINNACLE OF THE DREAM

She kept up with her husband's friends: Alden Gonzalez, "World Series 2020: Inside the night Clayton Kershaw finally became a world champion—in his hometown," ESPN.com, October 28, 2020.

Ellen found the gang seven tickets high above the first-base line: Alden González, "World Series 2020: Inside the night Clayton Kershaw finally became a world champion—in his hometown."

In the dugout, Roberts screamed: Jorge Castillo, "Dodgers suffer stunning 8-7 walk-off loss to Rays in Game 4 of World Series," *Los Angeles Times,* October 24, 2020.

"You guys are maniacs": Andy McCullough, "Clayton Kershaw, at last, can call himself a World Series champion."

He believed he was making the right call: Andy McCullough, "Fellow skippers reflect on Kevin Cash's Blake Snell decision in the World Series," *Athletic,* December 17, 2020.

"We're all testing positive": Fox Sports, "Dodgers win the World Series: Go behind the scenes of L.A.'s historic celebration," https://www.youtube.com/watch?v=WlBX15TFQQ8, October 28, 2020.

"I couldn't be happier for you, Kersh": Matt Martell, "Redemption and vindication: Dodgers win World Series title for first time in 32 years," *Sports Illustrated,* October 28, 2020.

When Kershaw clutched the prize, he was beaming: Andy McCullough, "Clayton Kershaw finally got his World Series ring. The Dodgers ace explains what motivates him now," *Athletic,* March 19, 2021.

He batted aside a question about his postseason legacy: Andy McCullough, "Clayton Kershaw finally got his World Series ring. The Dodgers ace explains what motivates him now."

CHAPTER 22. THE THREE-PRONGED CROSSROADS

Kershaw hinted about a tidy sendoff: Andy McCullough, "Clayton Kershaw, at last, can call himself a World Series champion."

he intended to pursue a one-year contract: Jorge Castillo, "A burden lifted, Clayton Kershaw talks fatherhood—and his uncertain Dodgers future," *Los Angeles Times,* February 10, 2021.

In the spring of 2021, I called Kershaw: Andy McCullough, "Clayton Kershaw finally got his World Series ring. The Dodgers ace explains what motivates him now."

"If I said 'yes' to that": Andy McCullough, "Clayton Kershaw finally got his World Series ring. The Dodgers ace explains what motivates him now."

He engaged in a variety of ill-advised online acts: Pedro Moura, "Introduced as a Dodger, Trevor Bauer declines to address his online behavior," *Athletic,* February 12, 2021.

catcher Miguel Montero revealed Bauer: Adam Green, "Montero on Trevor Bauer: 'He never wanted to listen,'" ArizonaSports.com, February 11, 2013.

Andrew Friedman had been texting: Moura, *How to Beat a Broken Game,* 213.

Friedman vouched for the team's vetting of Bauer: Pedro Moura, "Introduced as a Dodger, Trevor Bauer declines to address his online behavior."

The woman alleged that Bauer: Gus Garcia-Roberts, "Trevor Bauer and accuser settle lawsuits over sexual assault claims," *Washington Post,* October 2, 2023.

He came back firing 89-mph fastballs: Jorge Castillo, "Clayton Kershaw's return an important step for October-focused Dodgers," *Los Angeles Times,* September 13, 2021.

After pitching four times in twelve days: Jorge Castillo, "Max Scherzer says he didn't snub Dodgers because of 'overcooked' arm," *Los Angeles Times,* December 31, 2021.

"Blame it on the lockout": Andy McCullough, "After seven perfect innings, it is clear why Clayton Kershaw came back this season," *Athletic,* April 13, 2022.

Kershaw noted the reception Freeman received: Gabriel Burns, "Braves vs. Dodgers keeps getting spicier. Will we get NLCS round 3?," *Atlanta Journal-Constitution,* June 25, 2022.

After the series, he sent the Dodgers a group text: Fabian Ardaya, "Inside Freddie Freeman's rollercoaster season in L.A.: 'Got my closure. I'm a Dodger,'" *Athletic,* October 10, 2022.

Kershaw described the genesis of his friendship with Koufax: Fabian Ardaya, "Clayton Kershaw finds the words to honor Sandy Koufax: 'No one more deserving than you,'" *Athletic,* June 18, 2022.

CHAPTER 23. THE SIXTH DAY

While insisting his frustration: Jack Harris, "Clayton Kershaw disagreed with Sisters' award, sought return of Dodgers' Christian day," *Los Angeles Times,* May 29, 2023.

His shoulder felt "completely fine": Fabian Ardaya, "Dodgers' Clayton Kershaw to miss more time than expected, eyeing early August return from IL," *Athletic,* July 14, 2023.

INDEX